RASETSU
VOL. 3
Shojo Beat Manga Edition

STORY AND ART BY
CHIKA SHIOMI

Translation & Adaptation/Kinami Watabe
Touch-up Art & Lettering/Freeman Wong
Design/Hidemi Dunn
Editor/Amy Yu

VP, Production/Alvin Lu
VP, Publishing Licensing/Rika Inouye
VP, Sales & Product Marketing/Gonzalo Ferreyra
VP, Creative/Linda Espinosa
Publisher/Hyoe Narita

Rasetsu No Hana by Chika Shiomi
© Chika Shiomi 2007
All rights reserved.
First published in Japan in 2007 by HAKUSENSHA, Inc., Tokyo.
English language translation rights arranged with HAKUSENSHA, Inc., Tokyo.

The stories, characters and incidents mentioned in this publication are entirely fictional.

Printed in the U.S.A.

Published by VIZ Media, LLC
P.O. Box 77010
San Francisco, CA 94107

10 9 8 7 6 5 4 3 2 1
First printing, December 2009

www.viz.com

PARENTAL ADVISORY
RASETSU is rated T+ for Older Teen and
is recommended for ages 16 and up.
This volume contains brief nudity and
fantasy violence.
ratings.viz.com

www.shojobeat.com

Chika Shiomi lives in Aichi Prefecture, Japan. She
debuted with the manga *Todokeru Toki o Sugitemo*
(Even if the Time for Deliverance Passes), and her
previous works include the supernatural series
Yurara. She loves reading manga, traveling and
listening to music. Her favorite artists include
Michelangelo, Hokusai, Bernini and Gustav Klimt.

Shojo Beat

Rasetsu

Vol. 3

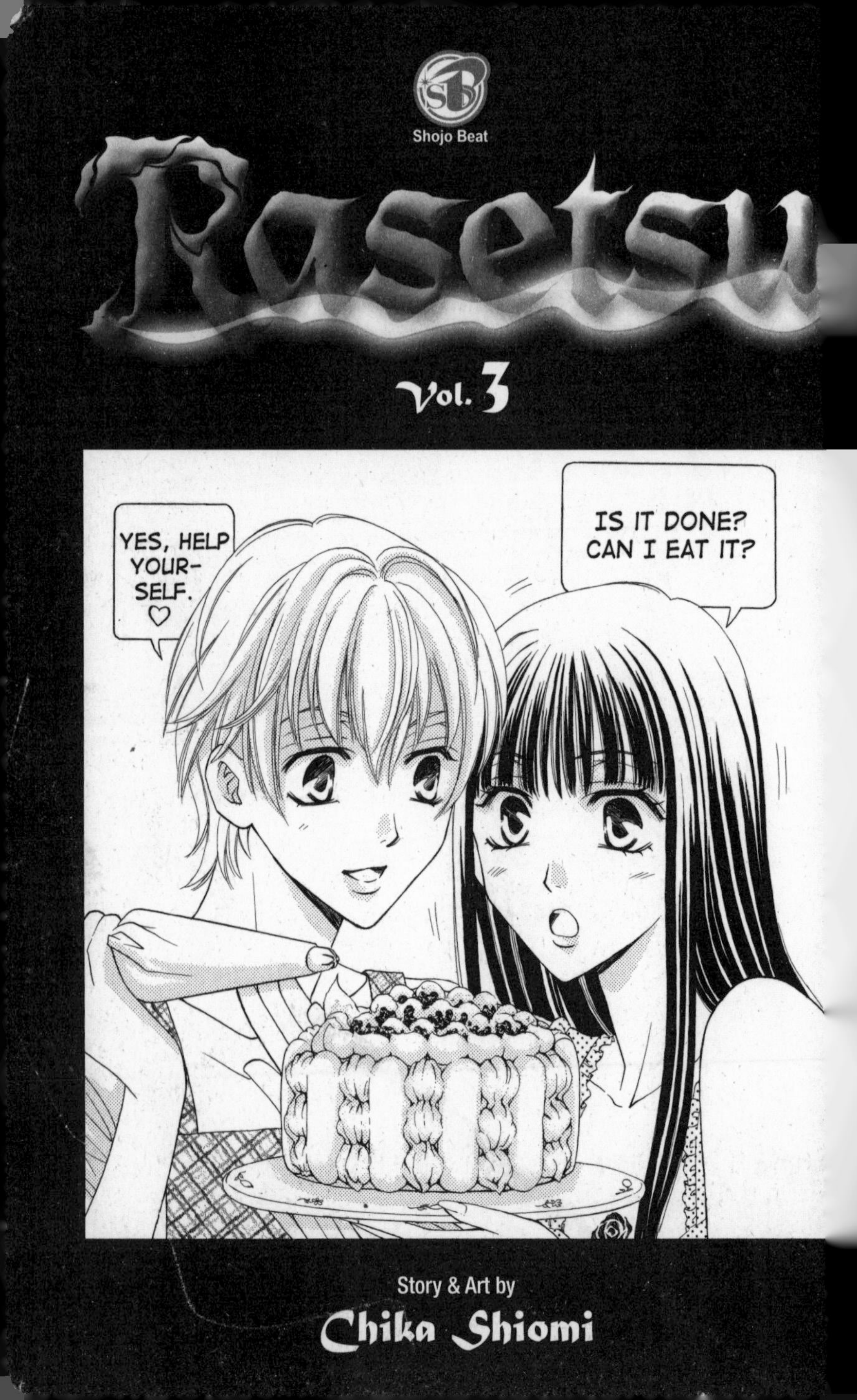
IS IT DONE? CAN I EAT IT?
YES, HELP YOUR-SELF. ♡

Story & Art by

Chika Shiomi

Characters

Rasetsu Hyuga

A powerful 18-year-old exorcist, Rasetsu has a flowerlike mark on her chest—a memento left by a demon. Rasetsu eats lots of sweets to recharge her psychic powers. She's currently looking for a boyfriend.

Yako Hoshino

An ace psychic who controls water, Yako was headhunted by Rasetsu. He still has feelings for the spirit he was in love with in high school...

Hiichiro Amakawa

The chief of the agency where Rasetsu and Yako work. A very powerful psychic.

Kuryu Iwatsuki

A psychic who uses *kotodama* (spiritual power manifested through words). His power works on humans and animals alike.

Aoi Kugi

Does administrative work for the agency. Ever since Yako came to the office, however, he's been left with nothing to do.

Story

The Hiichiro Amakawa Agency deals with exorcisms, and Rasetsu and Kuryu are psychics who work there. One day, Yako visits their office because he needs help with a possessed book. Rasetsu recognizes Yako's supernatural powers and tries to recruit him. He eventually joins the agency and learns that Rasetsu is actually cursed by a malevolent spirit. However, Yako doesn't know that the only way for Rasetsu to break her curse is to find true love—so he derides her for seeming hell-bent on finding a boyfriend… Later during an exorcism, Rasetsu sees a beautiful ghost while helping Yako…!

Rasetsu

Volume 3
Contents

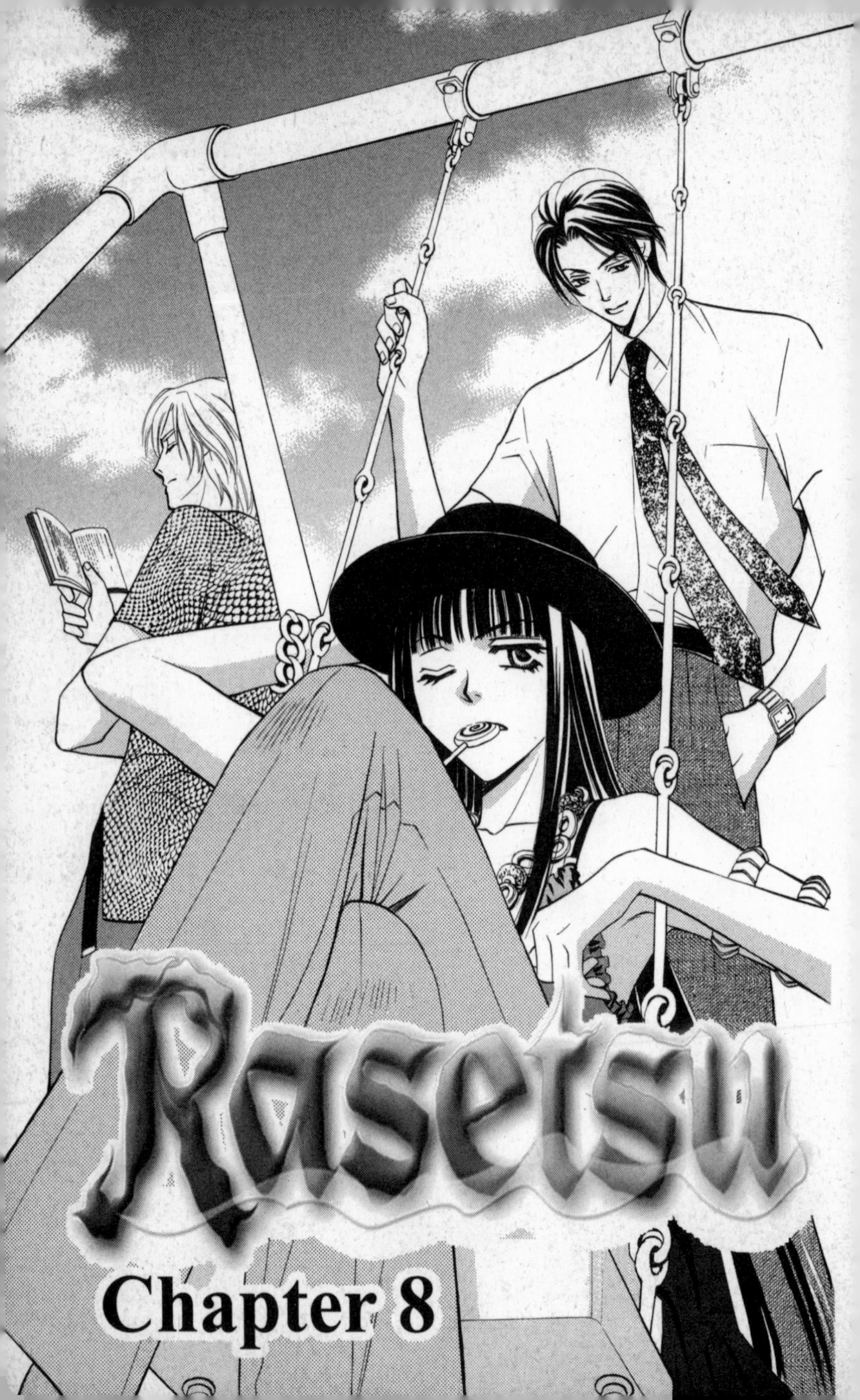
Rasetsu
Chapter 8

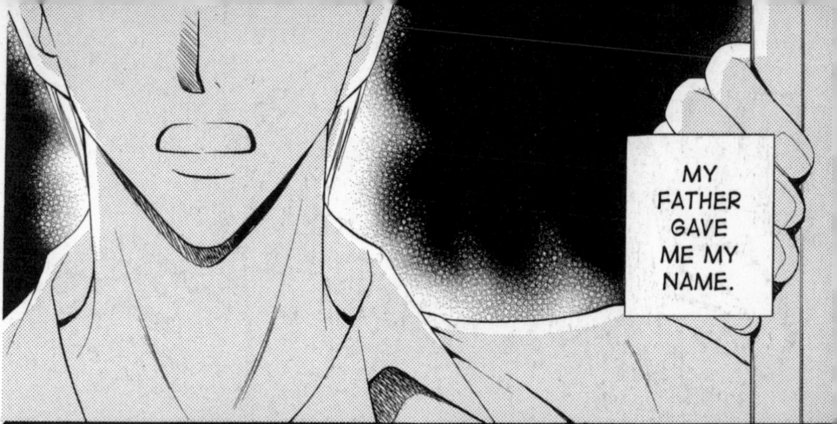
MY FATHER GAVE ME MY NAME.

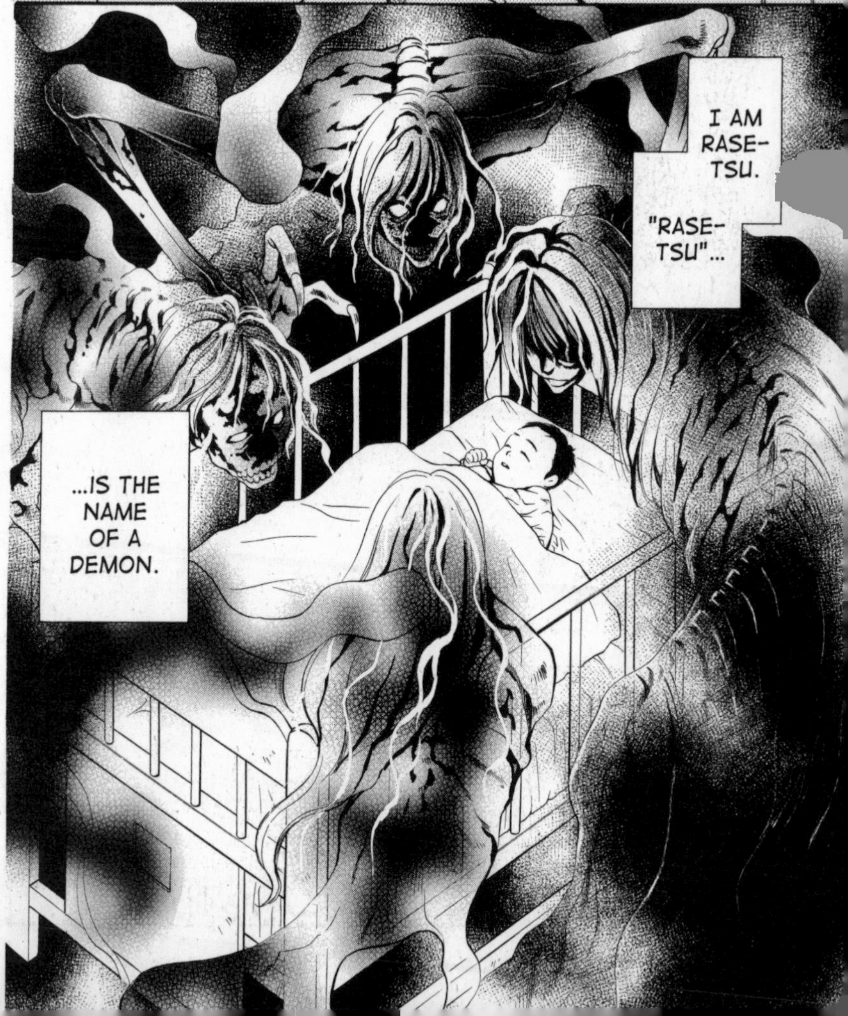
I AM RASE-TSU.
"RASE-TSU"...
...IS THE NAME OF A DEMON.

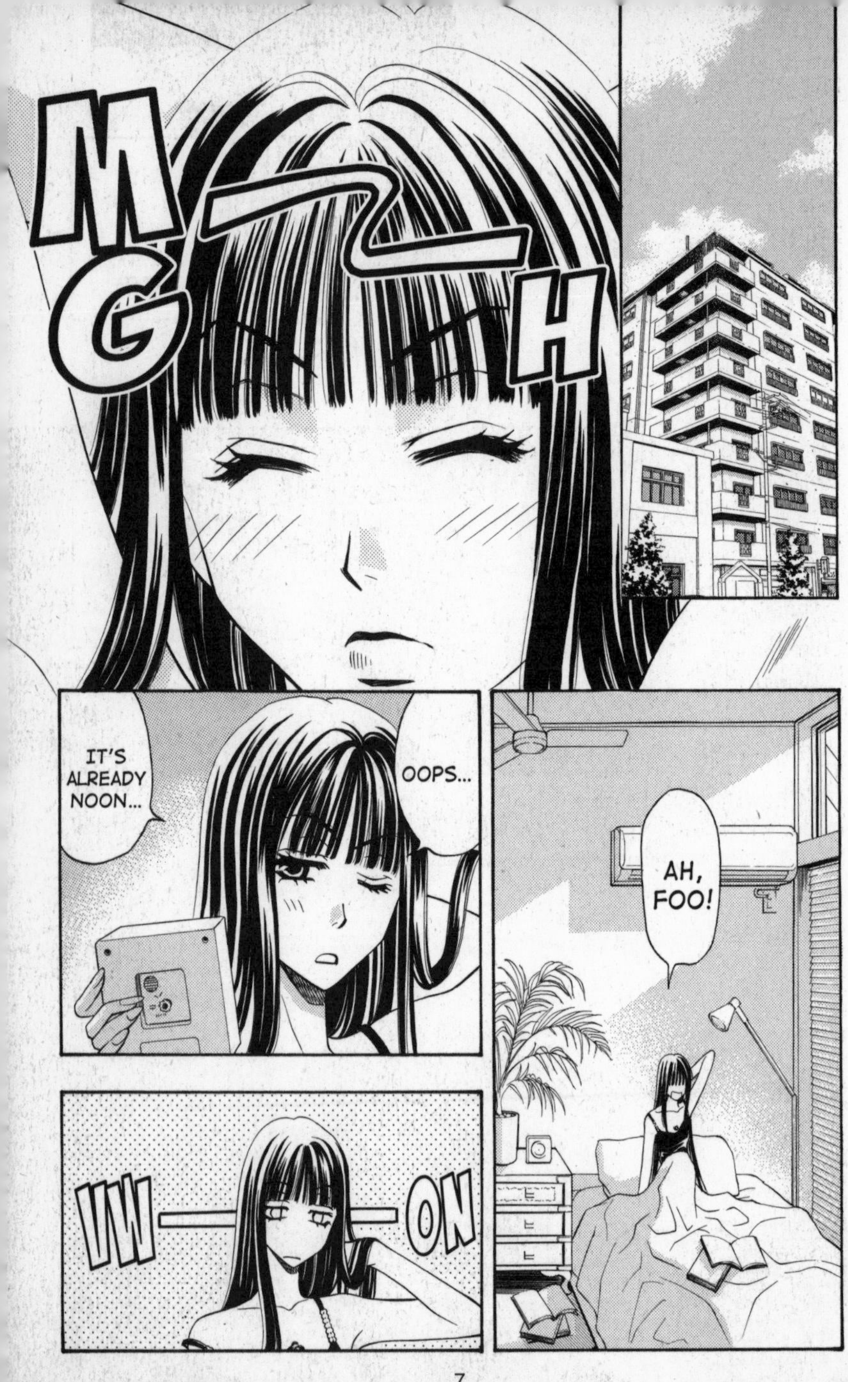
MGH
AH, FOO!
OOPS...
IT'S ALREADY NOON...
VW—ON

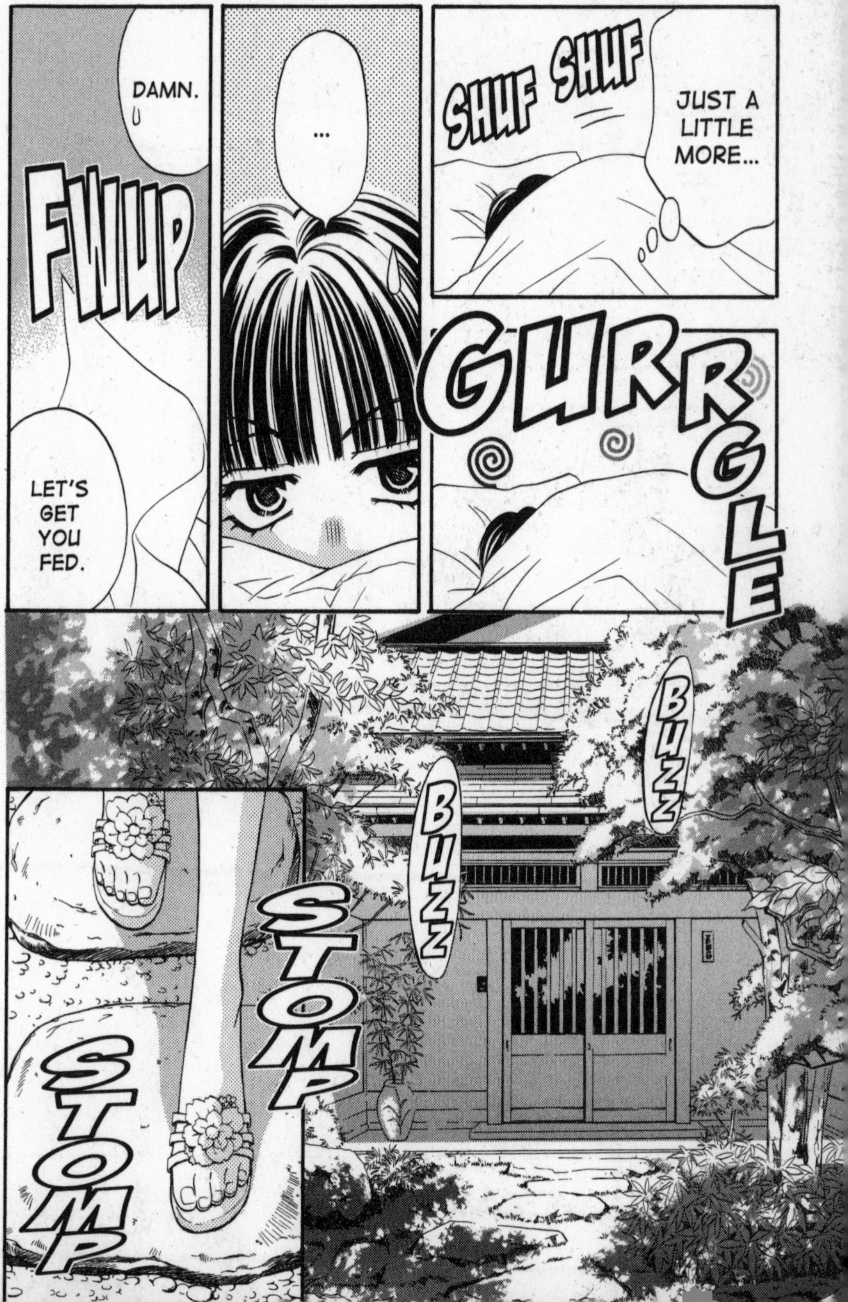
SHUF SHUF
JUST A LITTLE MORE...
GURRGLE
...
DAMN.
FWUP
LET'S GET YOU FED.
BUZZ
BUZZ
STOMP
STOMP

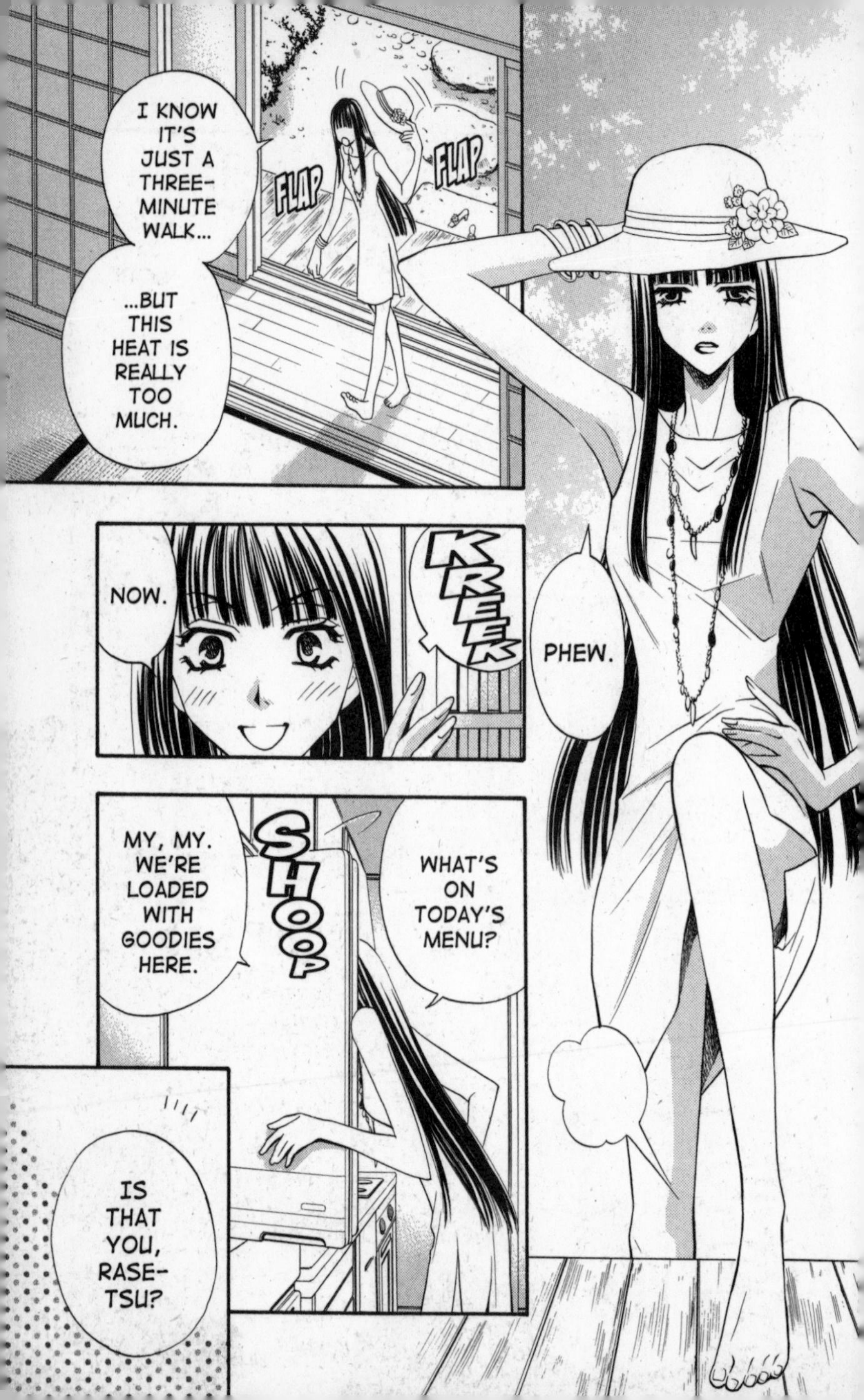
PHEW.
I KNOW IT'S JUST A THREE-MINUTE WALK...
...BUT THIS HEAT IS REALLY TOO MUCH.
FLAP
FLAP
KREEK
NOW.
WHAT'S ON TODAY'S MENU?
SHOOP
MY, MY. WE'RE LOADED WITH GOODIES HERE.
IS THAT YOU, RASETSU?

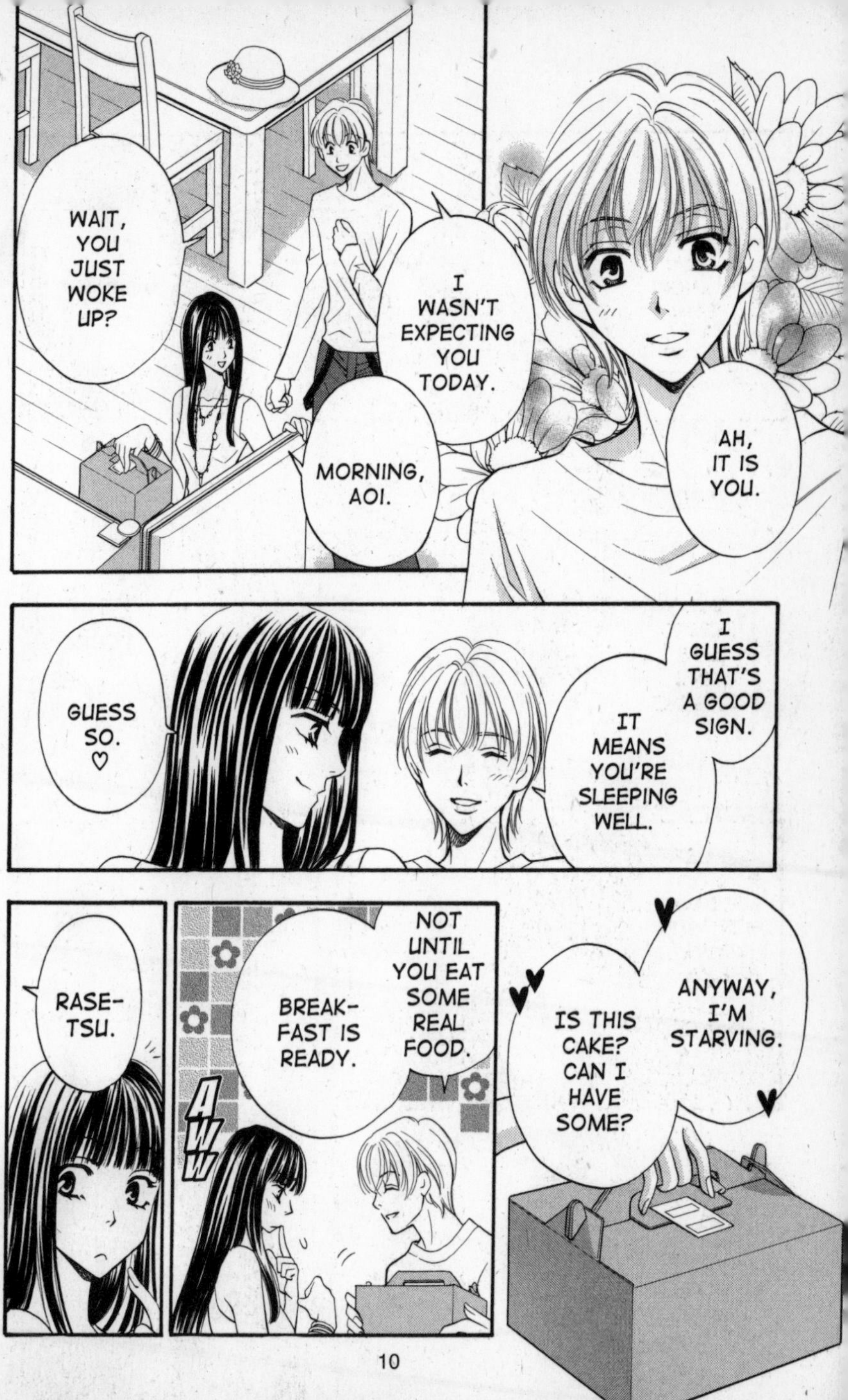
AH, IT IS YOU.
I WASN'T EXPECTING YOU TODAY.
MORNING, AOI.
WAIT, YOU JUST WOKE UP?
I GUESS THAT'S A GOOD SIGN.
IT MEANS YOU'RE SLEEPING WELL.
GUESS SO. ♡
ANYWAY, I'M STARVING.
IS THIS CAKE? CAN I HAVE SOME?
NOT UNTIL YOU EAT SOME REAL FOOD.
BREAK-FAST IS READY.
AWW
RASE-TSU.

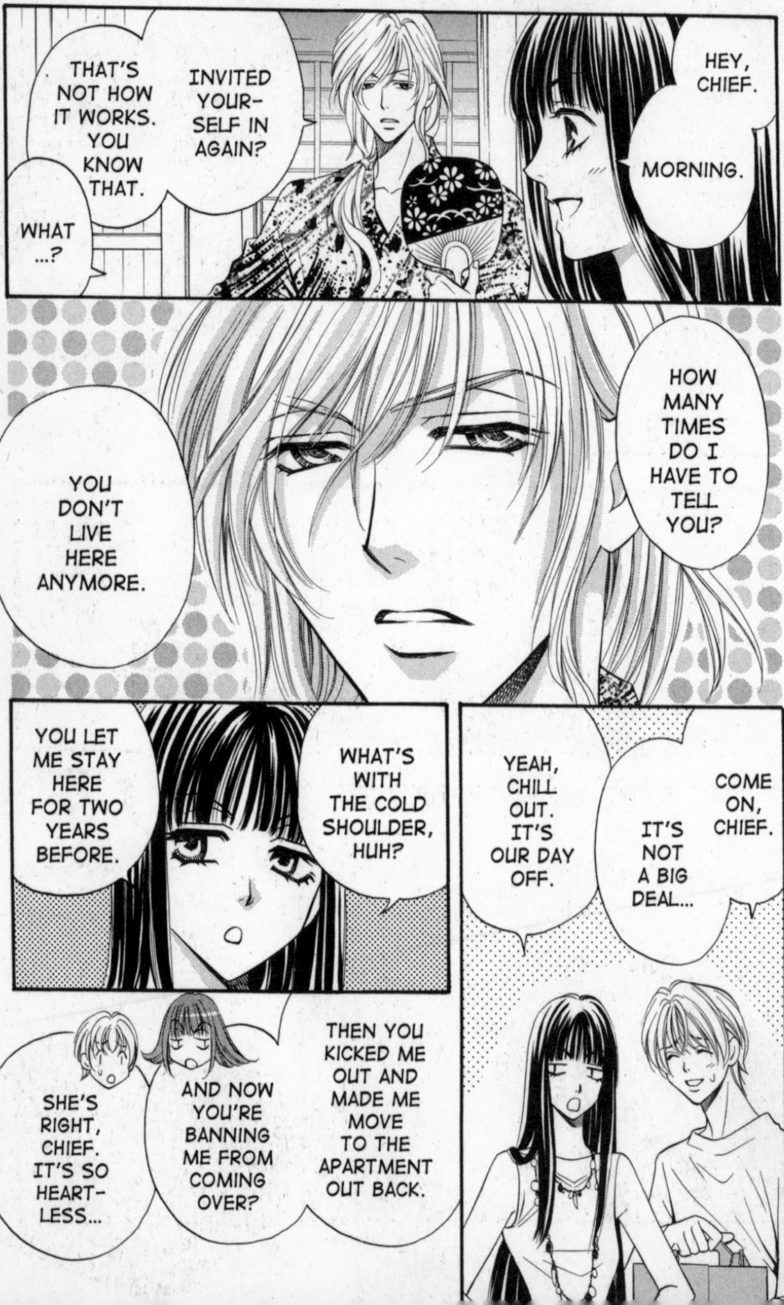
HEY, CHIEF.
MORNING.
INVITED YOUR-SELF IN AGAIN?
WHAT ...?
THAT'S NOT HOW IT WORKS. YOU KNOW THAT.
HOW MANY TIMES DO I HAVE TO TELL YOU?
YOU DON'T LIVE HERE ANYMORE.
COME ON, CHIEF.
IT'S NOT A BIG DEAL...
YEAH, CHILL OUT. IT'S OUR DAY OFF.
WHAT'S WITH THE COLD SHOULDER, HUH?
YOU LET ME STAY HERE FOR TWO YEARS BEFORE.
THEN YOU KICKED ME OUT AND MADE ME MOVE TO THE APARTMENT OUT BACK.
AND NOW YOU'RE BANNING ME FROM COMING OVER?
SHE'S RIGHT, CHIEF. IT'S SO HEART-LESS...

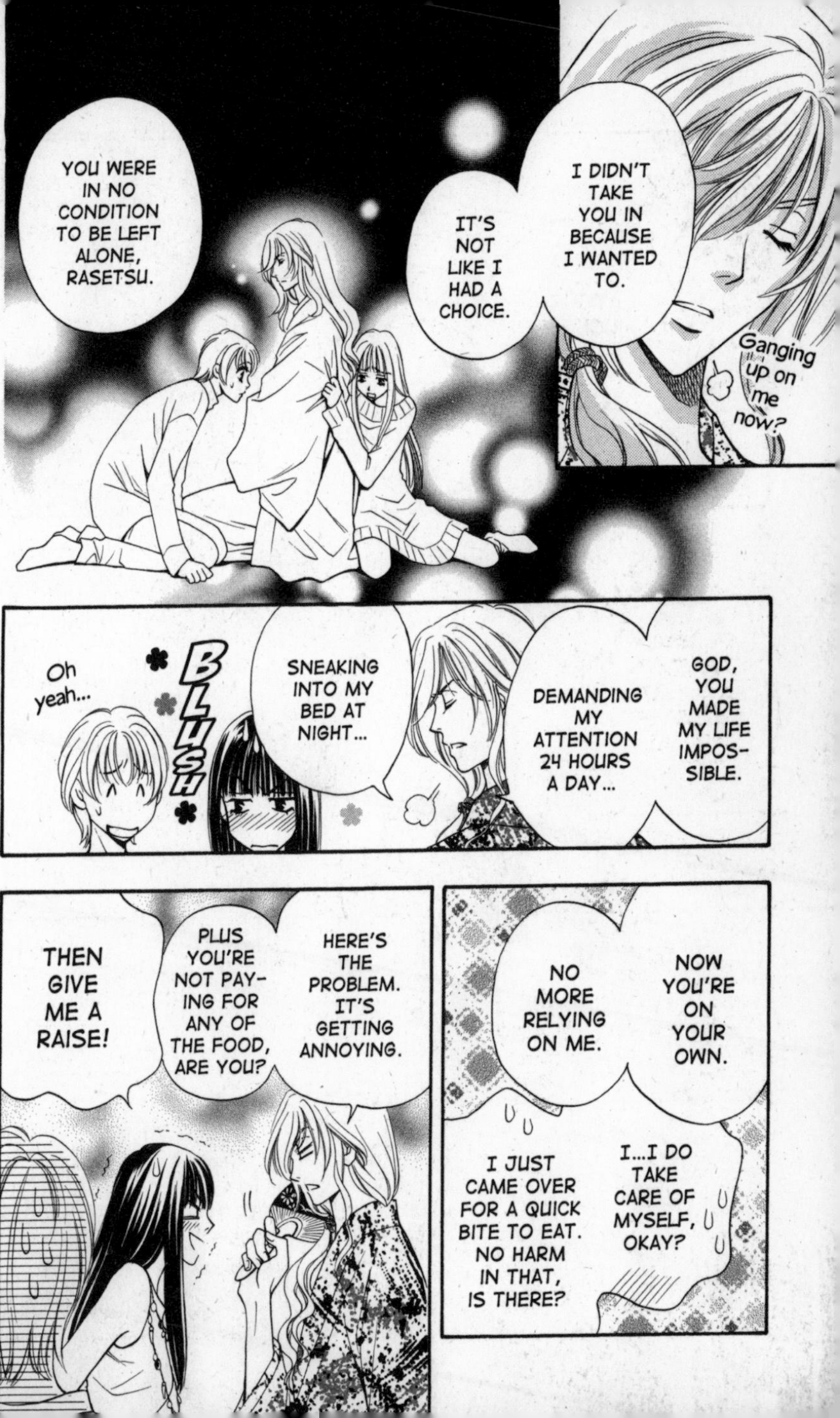
I DIDN'T TAKE YOU IN BECAUSE I WANTED TO.
IT'S NOT LIKE I HAD A CHOICE.
Ganging up on me now?
YOU WERE IN NO CONDITION TO BE LEFT ALONE, RASETSU.
GOD, YOU MADE MY LIFE IMPOSSIBLE.
DEMANDING MY ATTENTION 24 HOURS A DAY...
SNEAKING INTO MY BED AT NIGHT...
BLUSH
Oh yeah...
NOW YOU'RE ON YOUR OWN.
NO MORE RELYING ON ME.
I...I DO TAKE CARE OF MYSELF, OKAY?
I JUST CAME OVER FOR A QUICK BITE TO EAT. NO HARM IN THAT, IS THERE?
HERE'S THE PROBLEM. IT'S GETTING ANNOYING.
PLUS YOU'RE NOT PAYING FOR ANY OF THE FOOD, ARE YOU?
THEN GIVE ME A RAISE!

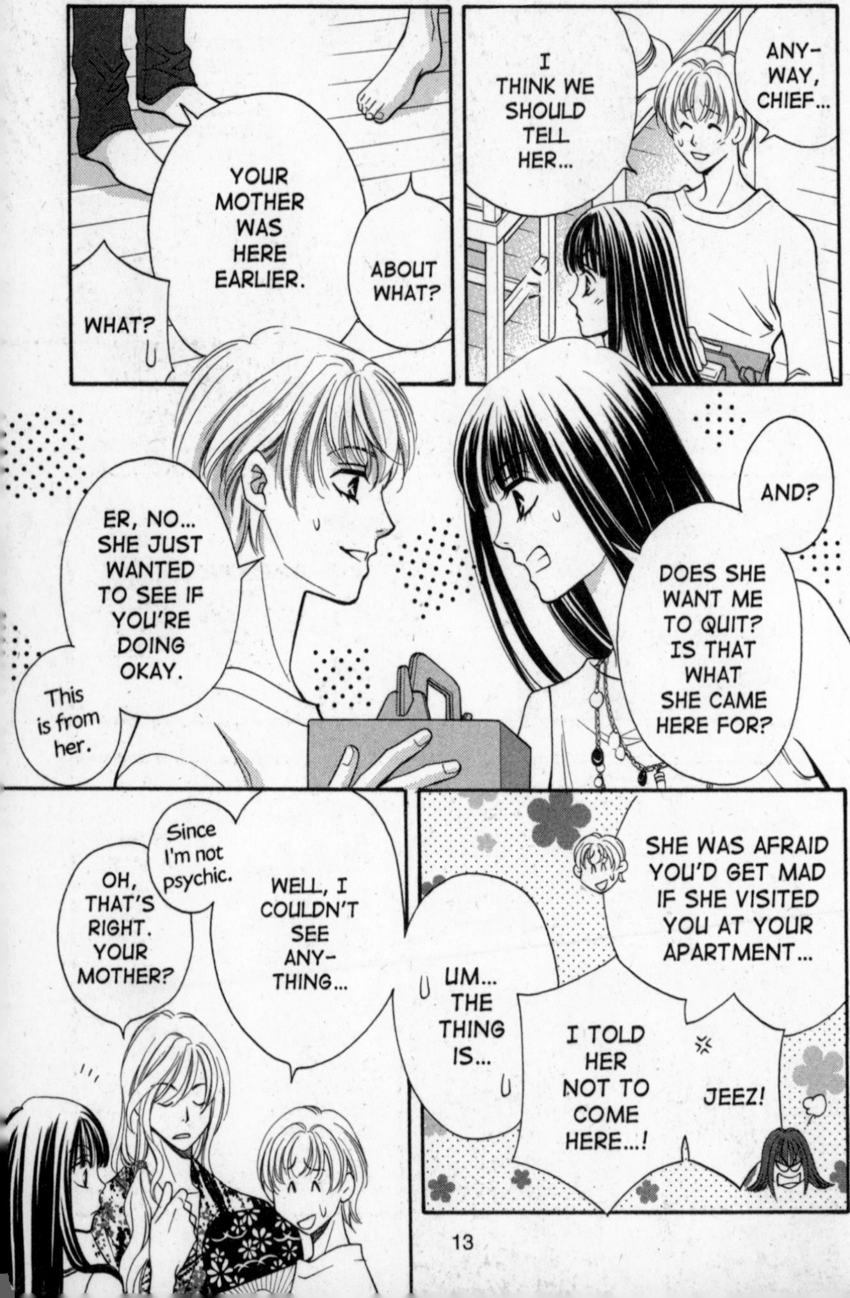
ANY-WAY, CHIEF...
I THINK WE SHOULD TELL HER...
ABOUT WHAT?
YOUR MOTHER WAS HERE EARLIER.
WHAT?
AND?
DOES SHE WANT ME TO QUIT? IS THAT WHAT SHE CAME HERE FOR?
ER, NO... SHE JUST WANTED TO SEE IF YOU'RE DOING OKAY.
This is from her.
SHE WAS AFRAID YOU'D GET MAD IF SHE VISITED YOU AT YOUR APARTMENT...
JEEZ!
I TOLD HER NOT TO COME HERE...!
UM... THE THING IS...
WELL, I COULDN'T SEE ANY-THING...
Since I'm not psychic.
OH, THAT'S RIGHT. YOUR MOTHER?

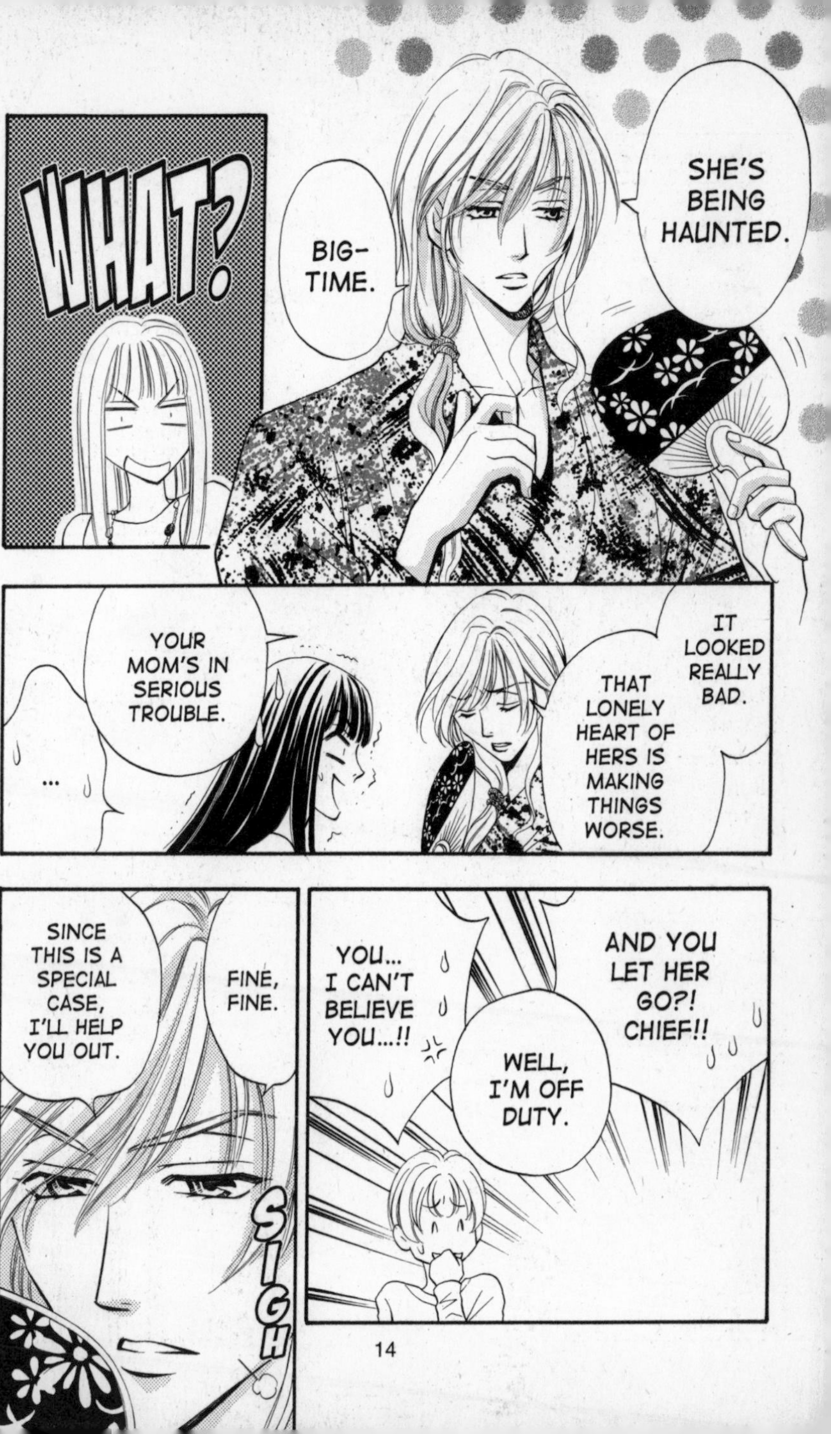
SHE'S BEING HAUNTED.
BIG-TIME.
WHAT?!
IT LOOKED REALLY BAD.
THAT LONELY HEART OF HERS IS MAKING THINGS WORSE.
YOUR MOM'S IN SERIOUS TROUBLE.
...
AND YOU LET HER GO?! CHIEF!!
YOU... I CAN'T BELIEVE YOU...!!
WELL, I'M OFF DUTY.
FINE, FINE.
SINCE THIS IS A SPECIAL CASE, I'LL HELP YOU OUT.
SIGH

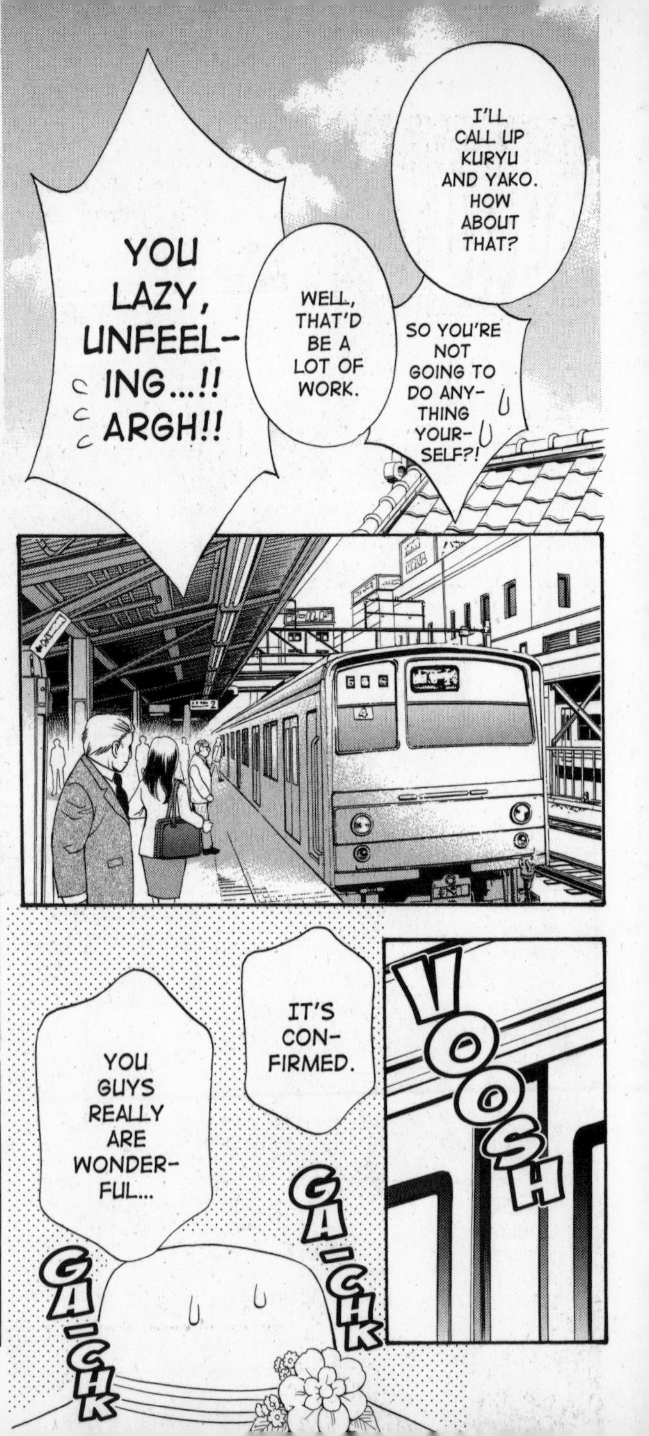
I'LL CALL UP KURYU AND YAKO. HOW ABOUT THAT?
SO YOU'RE NOT GOING TO DO ANYTHING YOURSELF?!
WELL, THAT'D BE A LOT OF WORK.
YOU LAZY, UNFEELING...!! ARGH!!
VOOSH
IT'S CONFIRMED.
YOU GUYS REALLY ARE WONDERFUL...
GA-CHK
GA-CHK

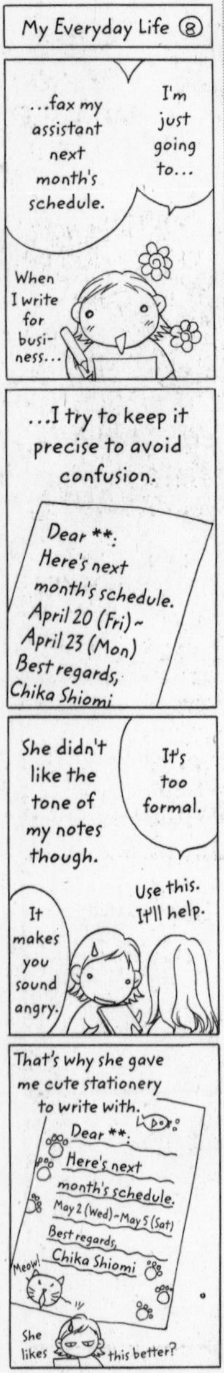
My Everyday Life ⑧
I'm just going to...
...fax my assistant next month's schedule.
When I write for business...
...I try to keep it precise to avoid confusion.
Dear **:
Here's next month's schedule.
April 20 (Fri)~April 23 (Mon)
Best regards,
Chika Shiomi
She didn't like the tone of my notes though.
It's too formal.
Use this. It'll help.
It makes you sound angry.
That's why she gave me cute stationery to write with.
Dear **:
Here's next month's schedule.
May 2 (Wed)~May 5 (Sat)
Best regards,
Chika Shiomi
Meow!
She likes this better?

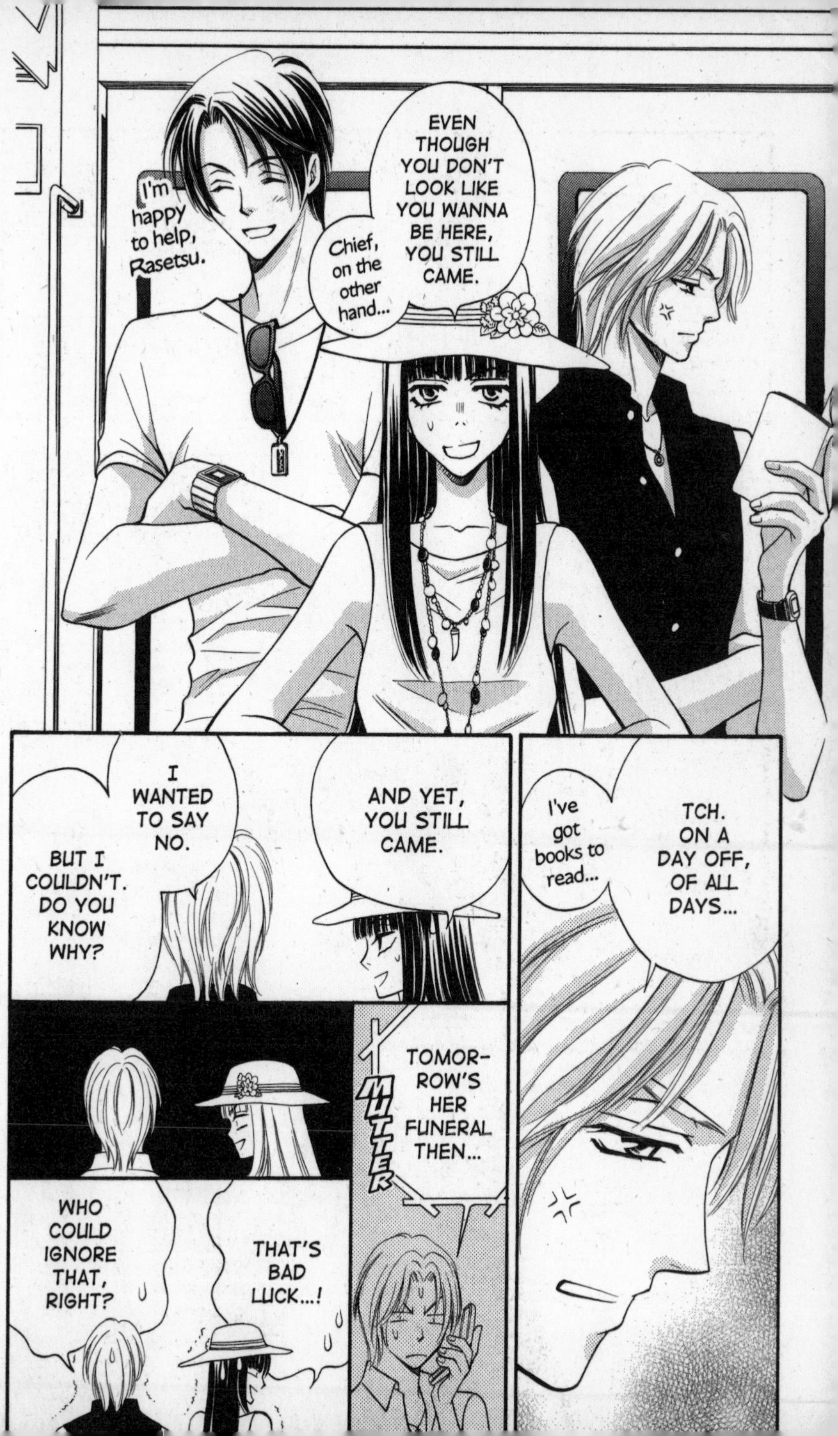
I'm happy to help, Rasetsu.
Chief, on the other hand...
EVEN THOUGH YOU DON'T LOOK LIKE YOU WANNA BE HERE, YOU STILL CAME.
TCH. ON A DAY OFF, OF ALL DAYS...
I've got books to read...
AND YET, YOU STILL CAME.
I WANTED TO SAY NO.
BUT I COULDN'T. DO YOU KNOW WHY?
MUTTER
TOMOR-ROW'S HER FUNERAL THEN...
WHO COULD IGNORE THAT, RIGHT?
THAT'S BAD LUCK...!

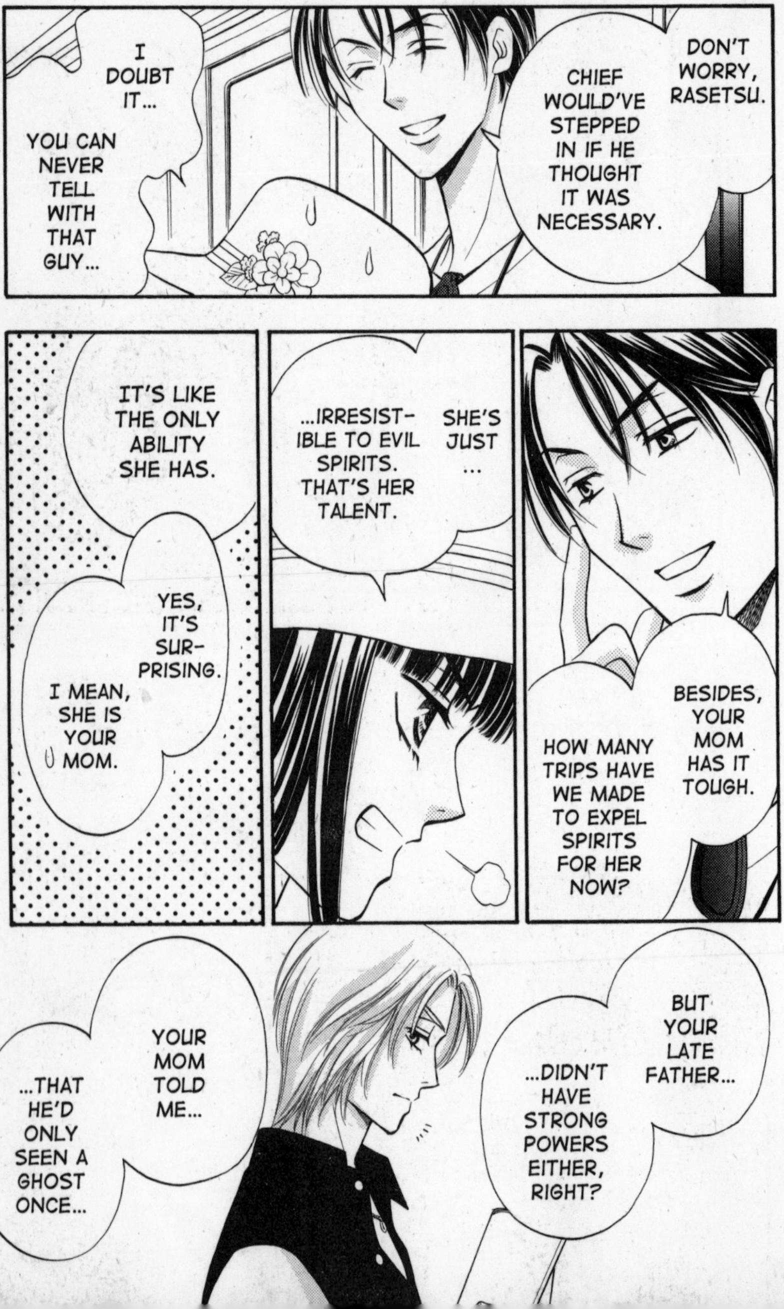
DON'T WORRY, RASETSU.
CHIEF WOULD'VE STEPPED IN IF HE THOUGHT IT WAS NECESSARY.
I DOUBT IT...
YOU CAN NEVER TELL WITH THAT GUY...
BESIDES, YOUR MOM HAS IT TOUGH.
HOW MANY TRIPS HAVE WE MADE TO EXPEL SPIRITS FOR HER NOW?
SHE'S JUST ...
...IRRESIST-IBLE TO EVIL SPIRITS. THAT'S HER TALENT.
IT'S LIKE THE ONLY ABILITY SHE HAS.
YES, IT'S SUR-PRISING.
I MEAN, SHE IS YOUR MOM.
BUT YOUR LATE FATHER...
...DIDN'T HAVE STRONG POWERS EITHER, RIGHT?
YOUR MOM TOLD ME...
...THAT HE'D ONLY SEEN A GHOST ONCE...

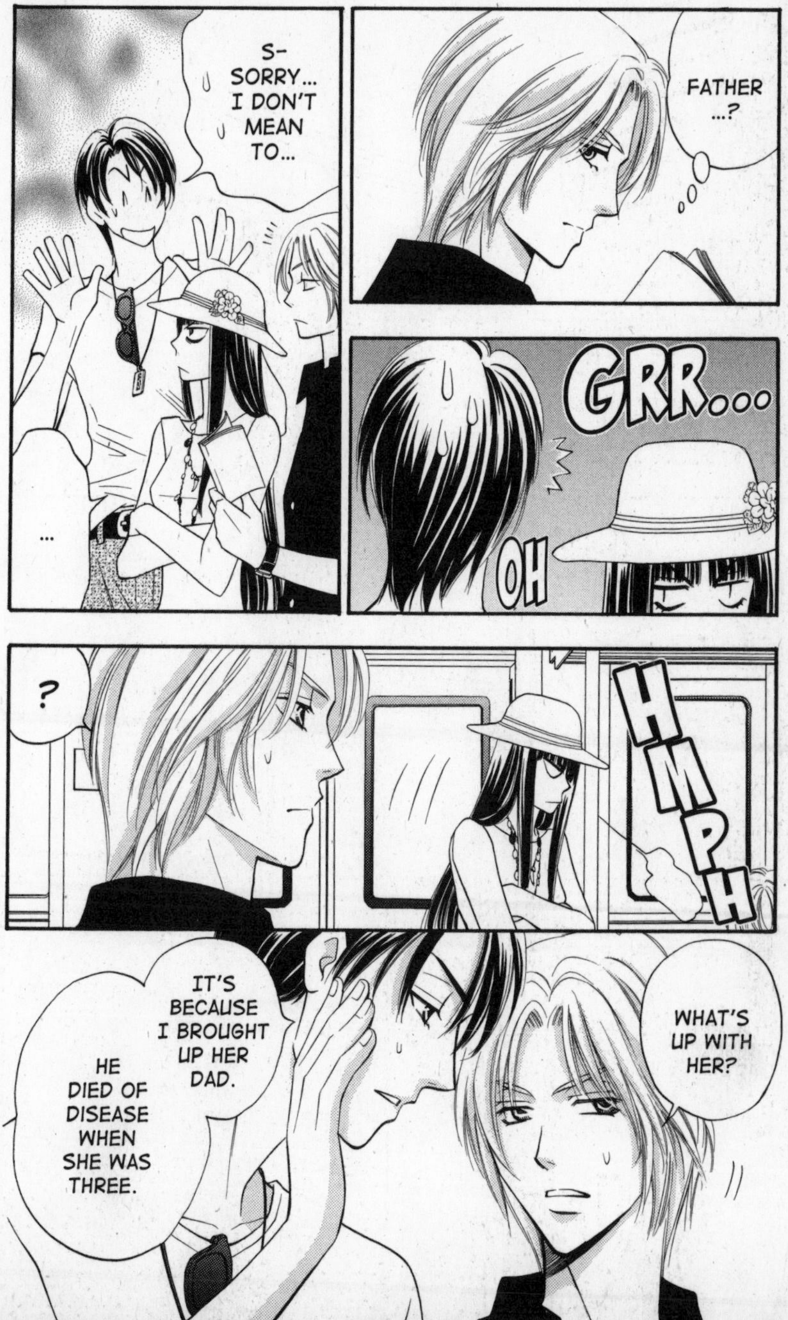
FATHER ...?
GRR...
OH
S- SORRY... I DON'T MEAN TO...
...
HMPH
?
WHAT'S UP WITH HER?
IT'S BECAUSE I BROUGHT UP HER DAD.
HE DIED OF DISEASE WHEN SHE WAS THREE.

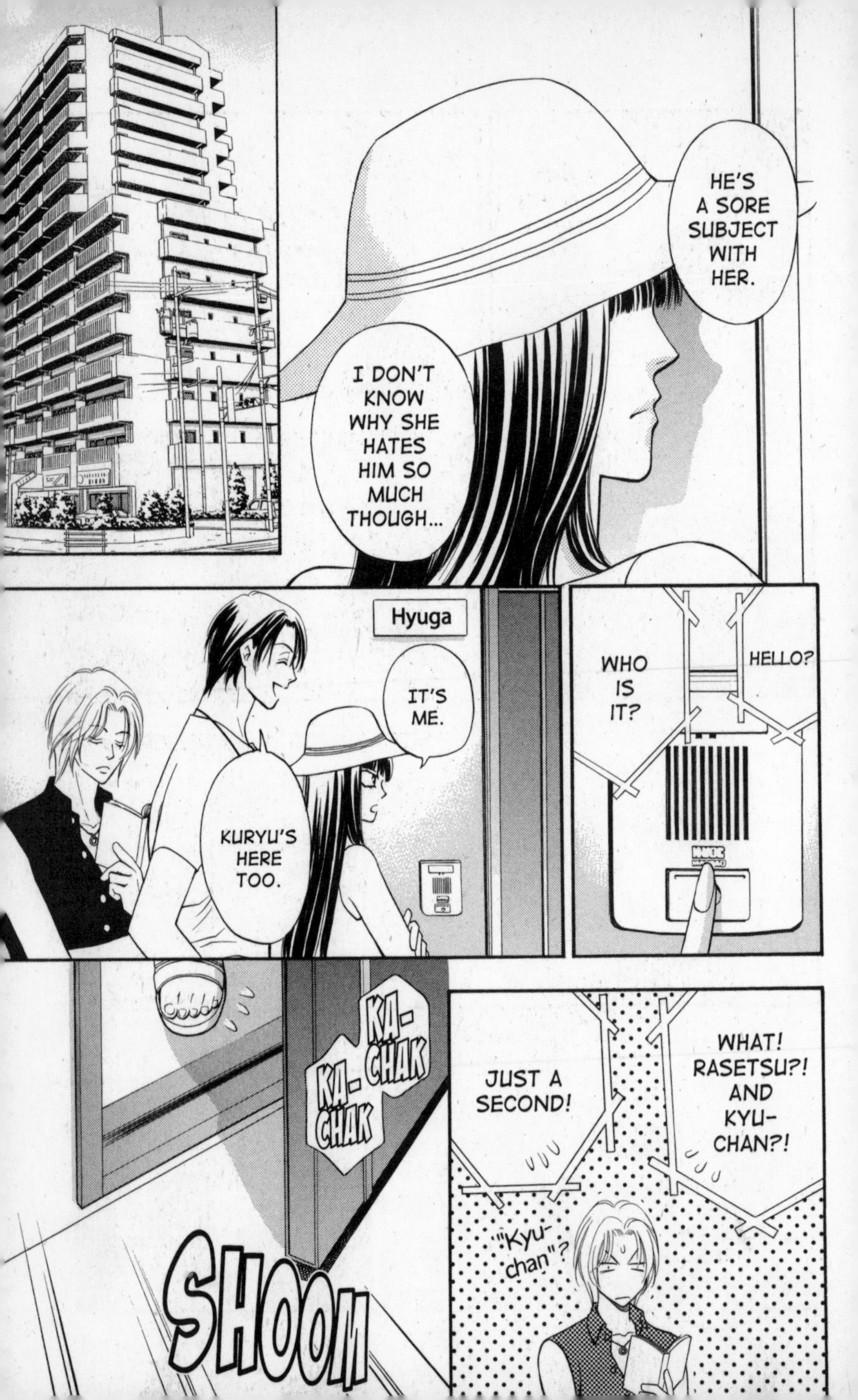
HE'S A SORE SUBJECT WITH HER.
I DON'T KNOW WHY SHE HATES HIM SO MUCH THOUGH...
HELLO?
WHO IS IT?
Hyuga
IT'S ME.
KURYU'S HERE TOO.
WHAT! RASETSU?! AND KYU-CHAN?!
JUST A SECOND!
"Kyu-chan"?
KA-CHAK
KA-CHAK
SHOOM

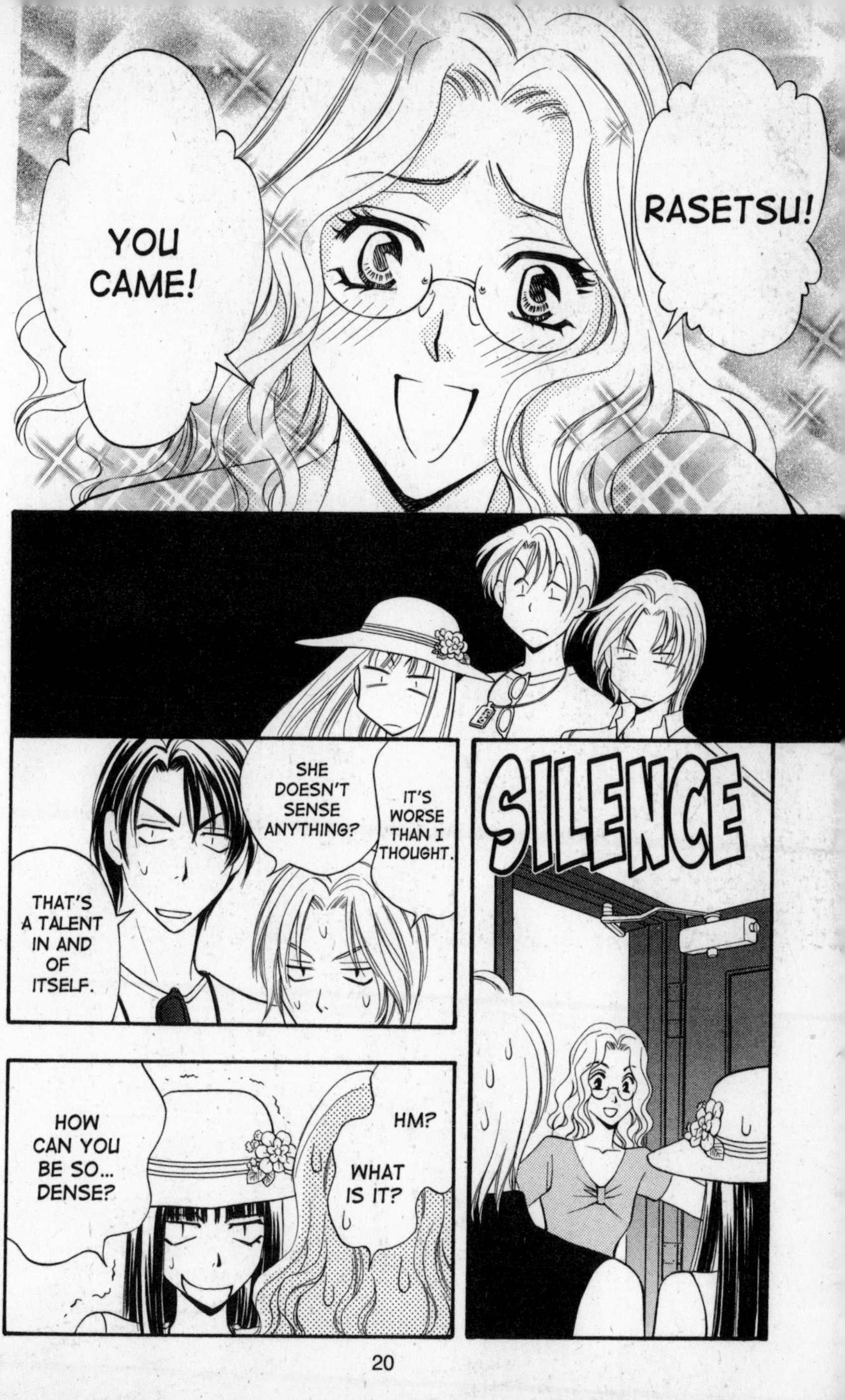
RASETSU!
YOU CAME!
SILENCE
SHE DOESN'T SENSE ANYTHING?
IT'S WORSE THAN I THOUGHT.
THAT'S A TALENT IN AND OF ITSELF.
HM?
WHAT IS IT?
HOW CAN YOU BE SO... DENSE?

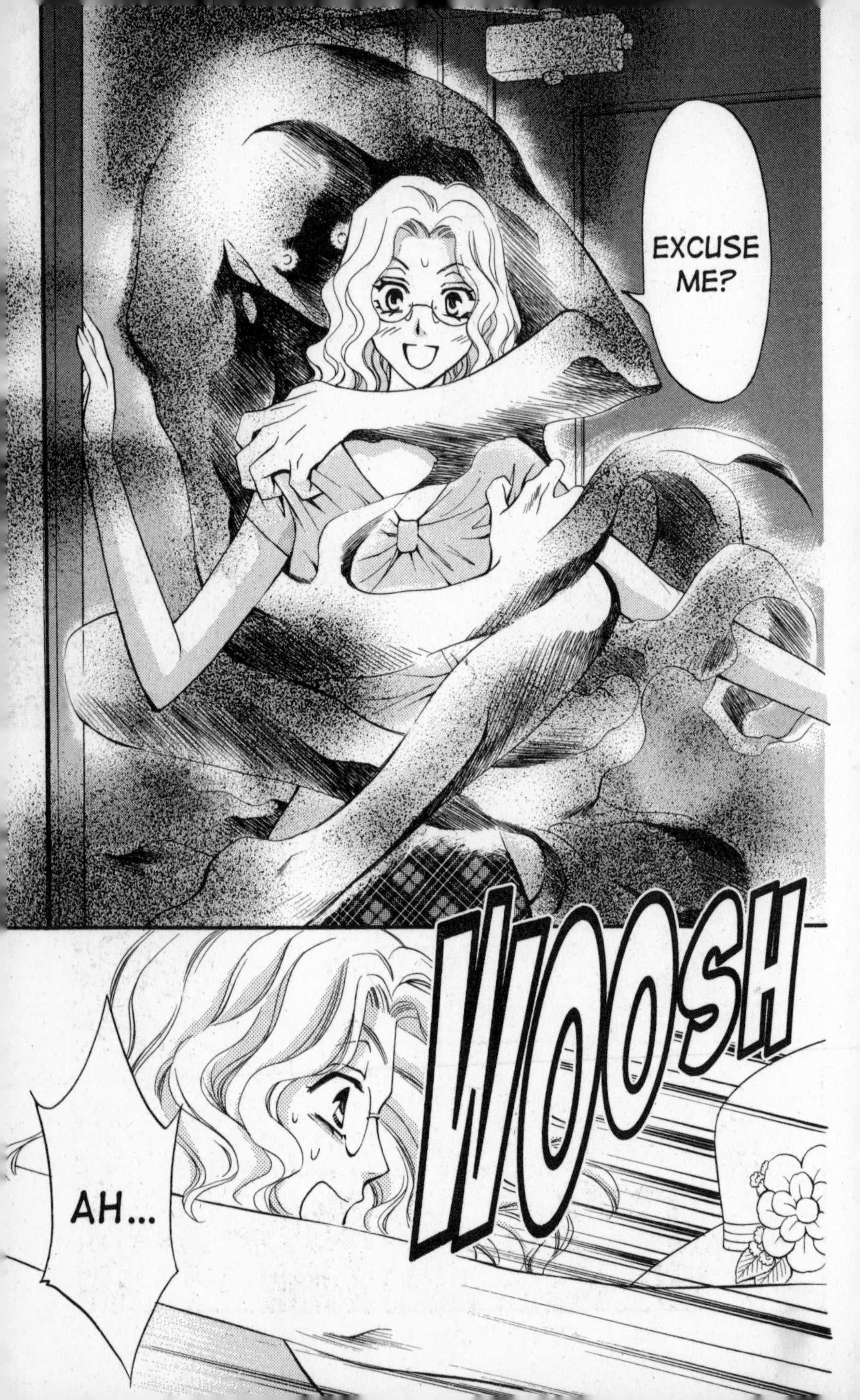
EXCUSE ME?
WOOSH
AH...

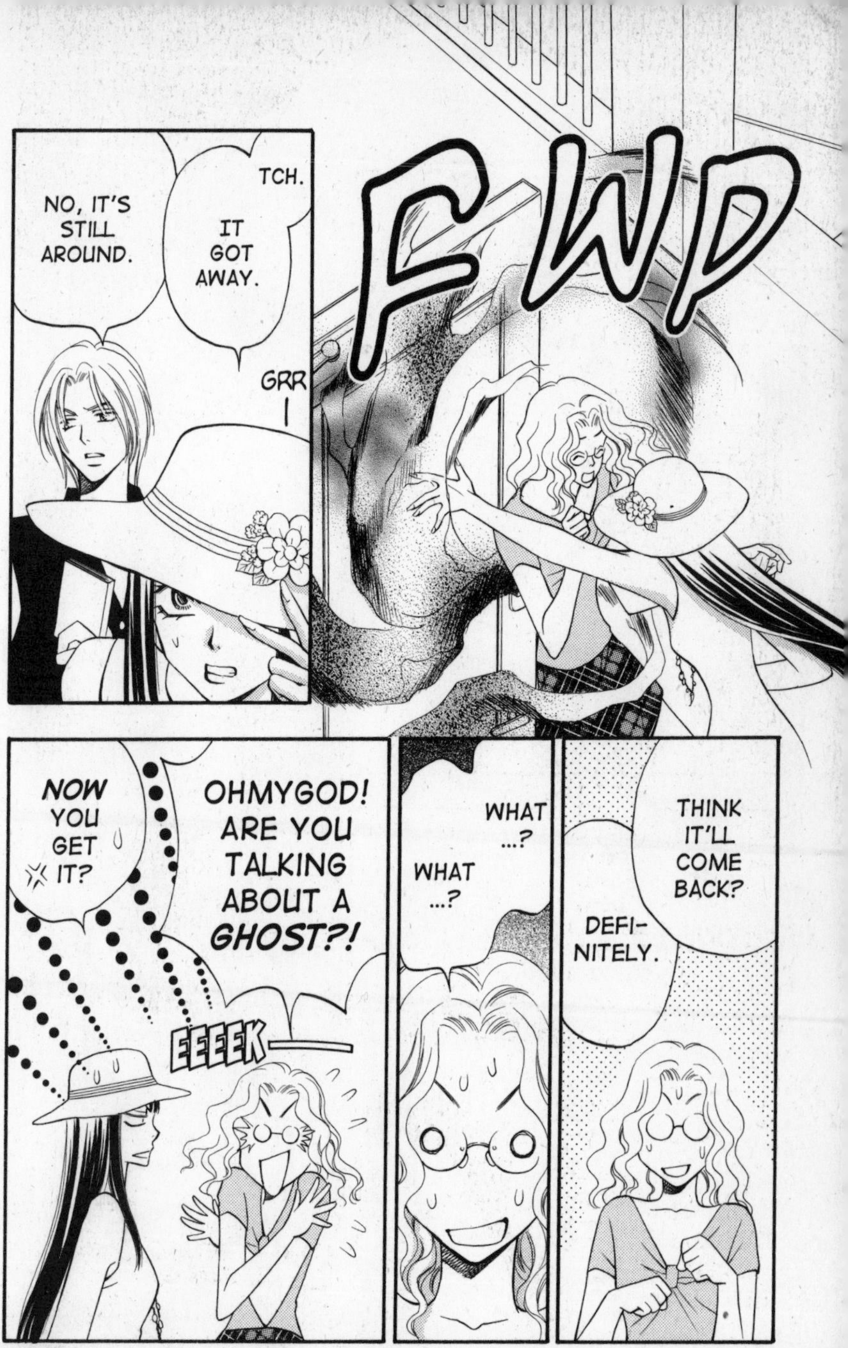
FWP
TCH.
IT GOT AWAY.
GRR
NO, IT'S STILL AROUND.
THINK IT'LL COME BACK?
DEFI-NITELY.
WHAT ...?
WHAT ...?
OHMYGOD! ARE YOU TALKING ABOUT A *GHOST*?!
NOW YOU GET IT?
EEEEK—

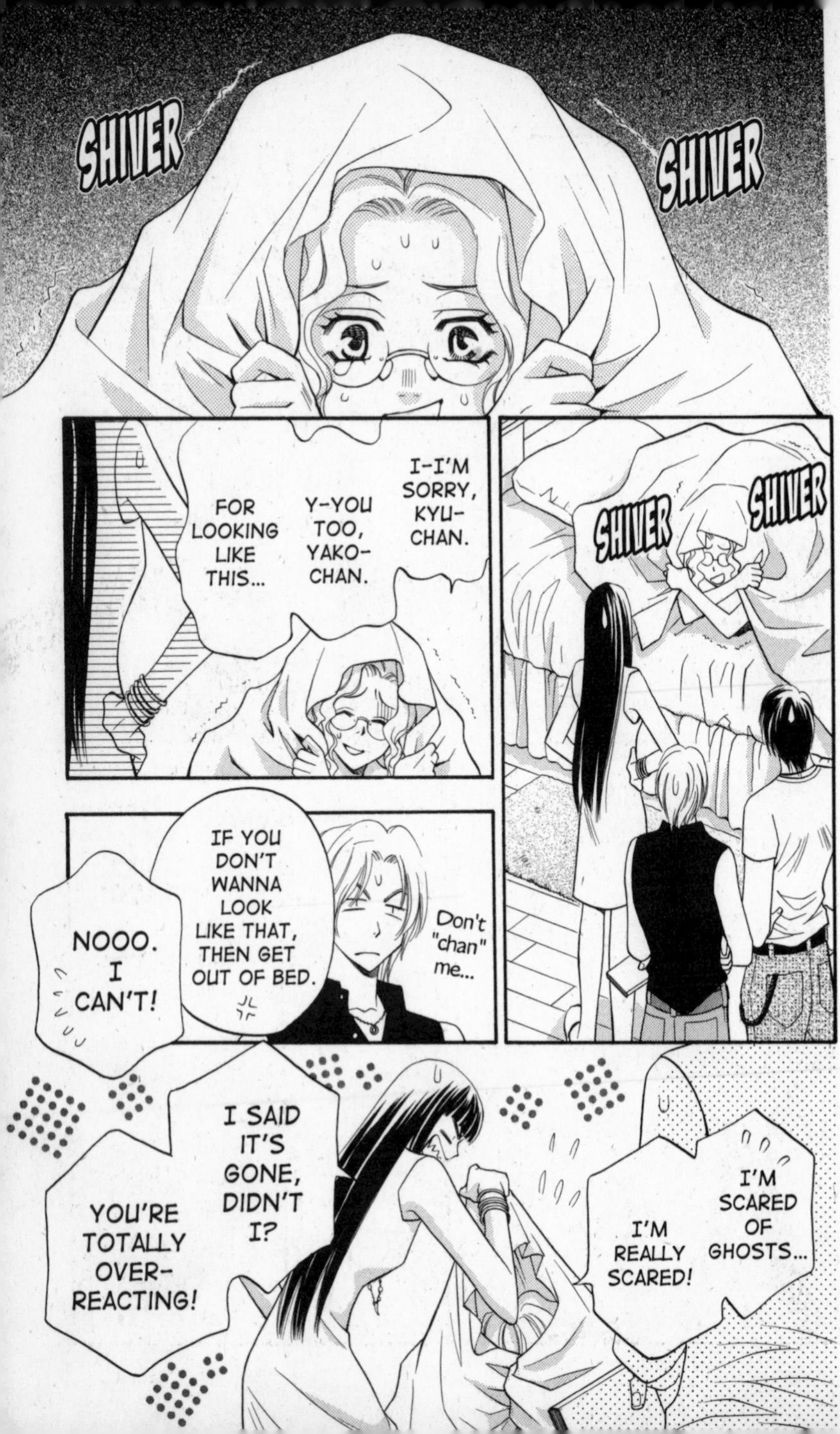
SHIVER
SHIVER
SHIVER
SHIVER
I-I'M SORRY, KYU-CHAN.
Y-YOU TOO, YAKO-CHAN.
FOR LOOKING LIKE THIS...
Don't "chan" me...
IF YOU DON'T WANNA LOOK LIKE THAT, THEN GET OUT OF BED.
NOOO. I CAN'T!
I'M SCARED OF GHOSTS...
I'M REALLY SCARED!
I SAID IT'S GONE, DIDN'T I?
YOU'RE TOTALLY OVER-REACTING!

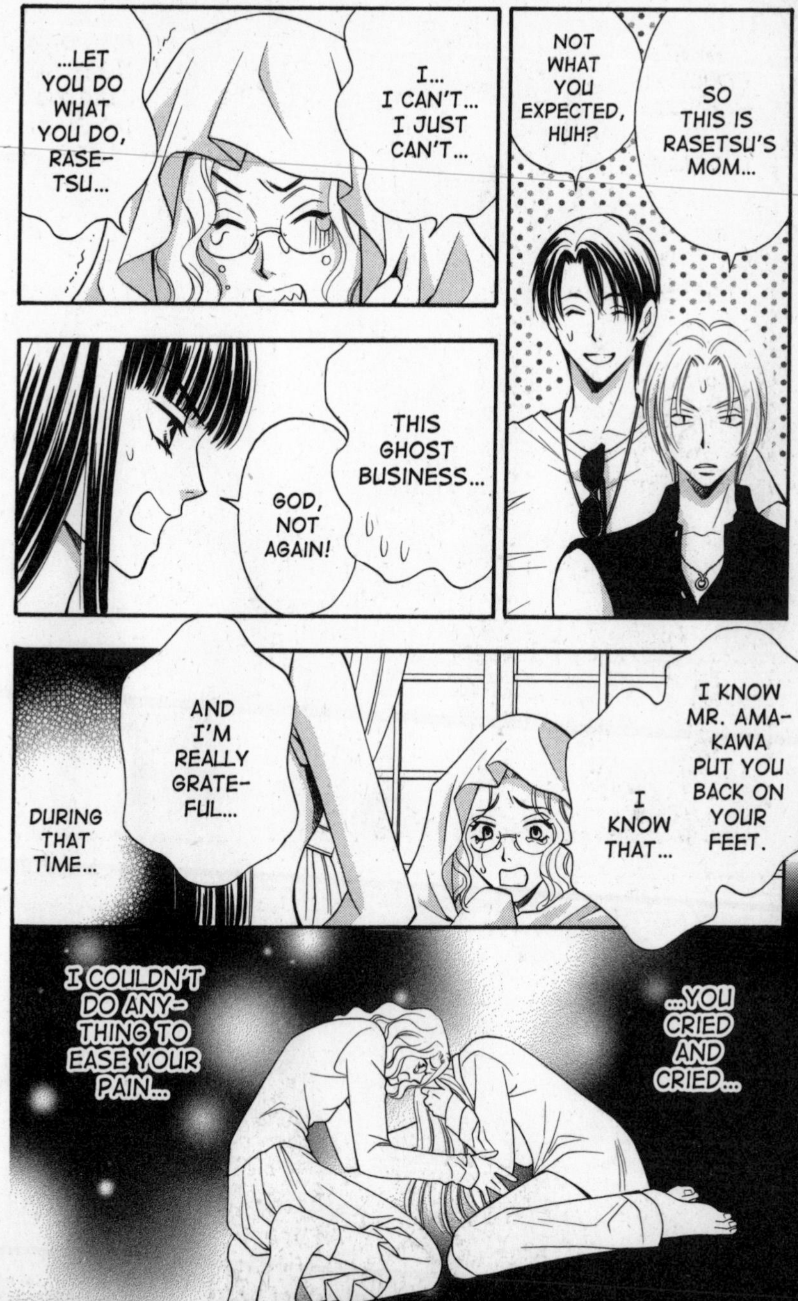
SO THIS IS RASETSU'S MOM...
NOT WHAT YOU EXPECTED, HUH?
I... I CAN'T... I JUST CAN'T...
...LET YOU DO WHAT YOU DO, RASE-TSU...
THIS GHOST BUSINESS...
GOD, NOT AGAIN!
I KNOW MR. AMA-KAWA PUT YOU BACK ON YOUR FEET.
I KNOW THAT...
AND I'M REALLY GRATE-FUL...
DURING THAT TIME...
...YOU CRIED AND CRIED...
I COULDN'T DO ANY-THING TO EASE YOUR PAIN...

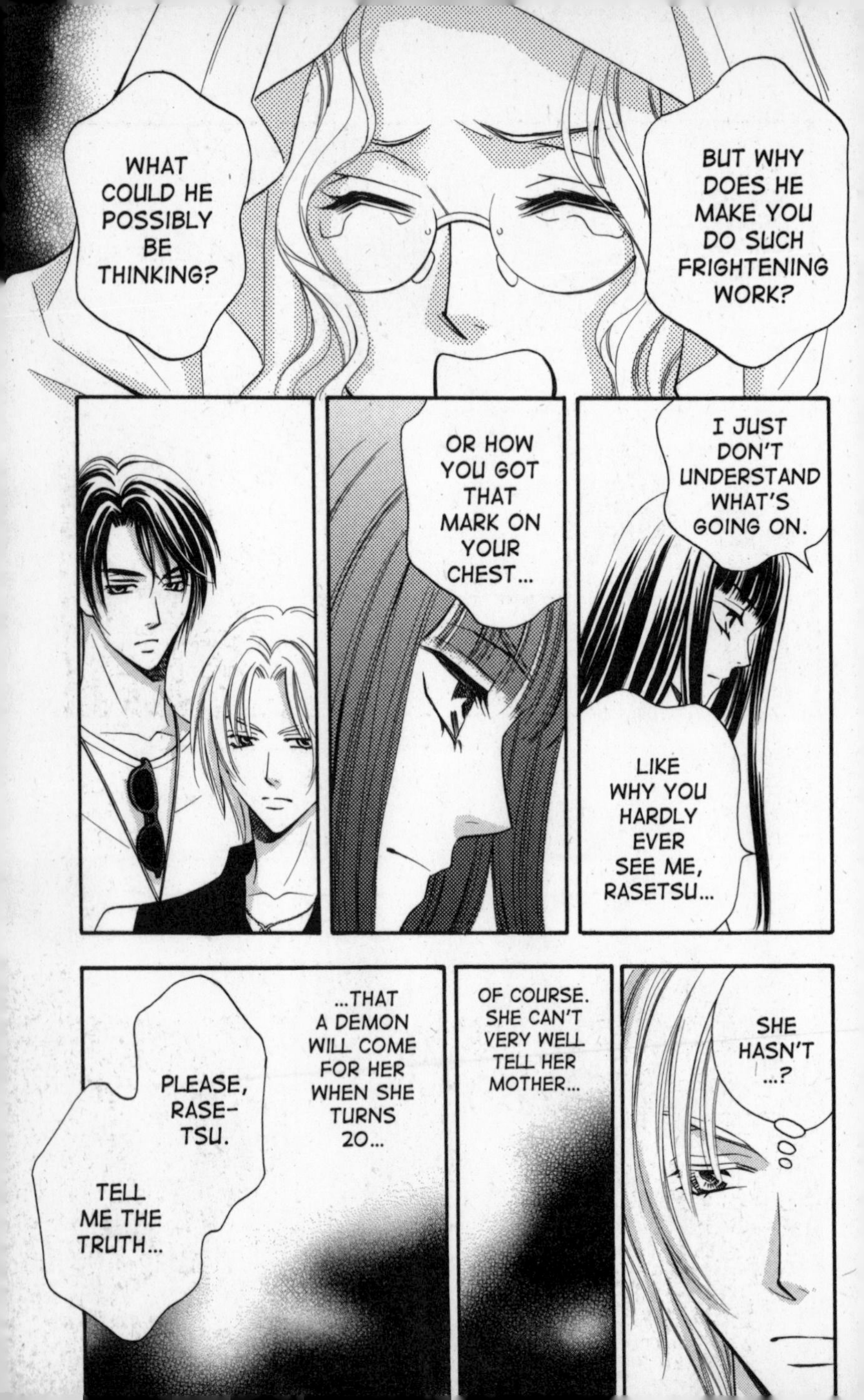
BUT WHY DOES HE MAKE YOU DO SUCH FRIGHTENING WORK?
WHAT COULD HE POSSIBLY BE THINKING?
I JUST DON'T UNDERSTAND WHAT'S GOING ON.
LIKE WHY YOU HARDLY EVER SEE ME, RASETSU...
OR HOW YOU GOT THAT MARK ON YOUR CHEST...
SHE HASN'T ...?
OF COURSE. SHE CAN'T VERY WELL TELL HER MOTHER...
...THAT A DEMON WILL COME FOR HER WHEN SHE TURNS 20...
PLEASE, RASE-TSU.
TELL ME THE TRUTH...

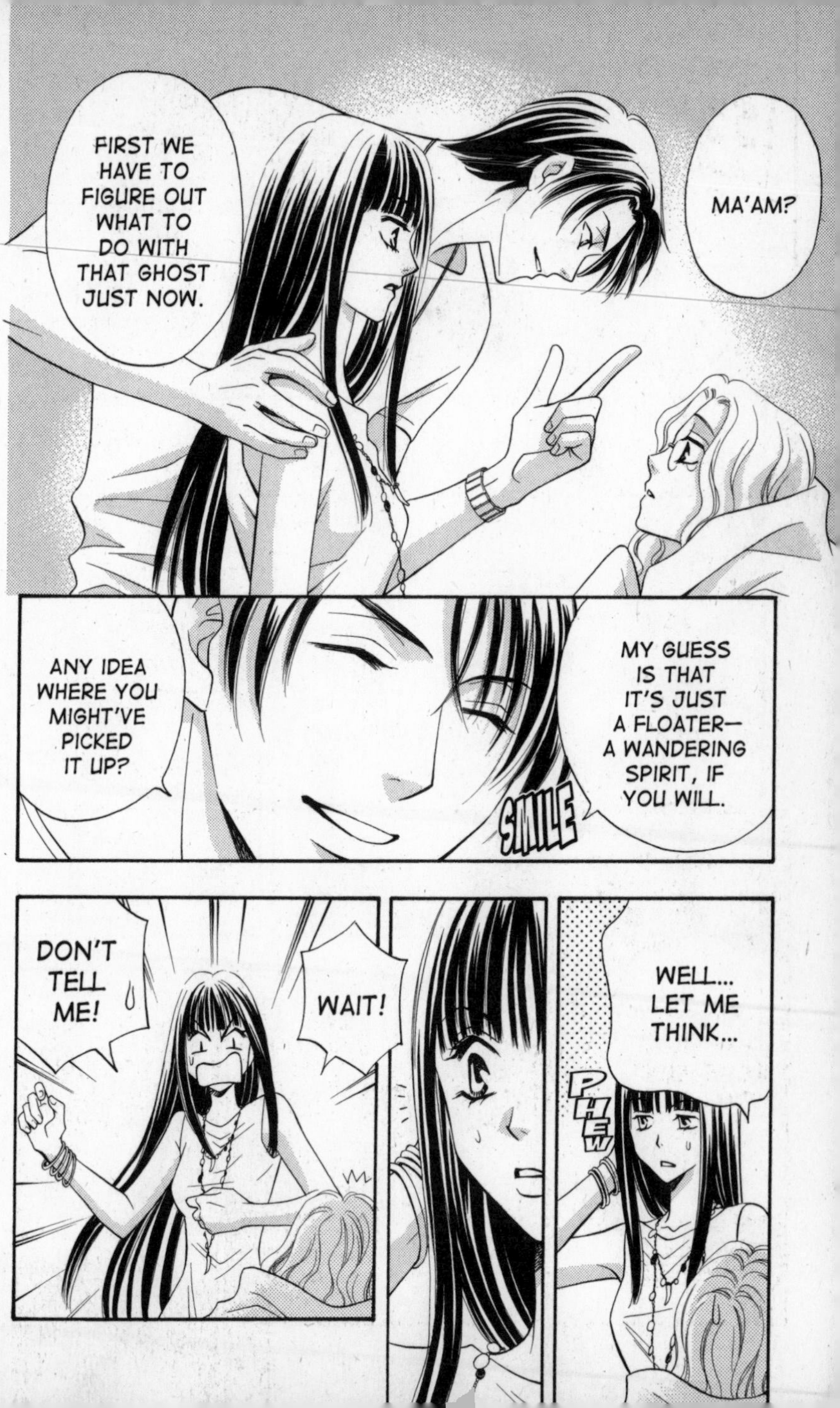
MA'AM?
FIRST WE HAVE TO FIGURE OUT WHAT TO DO WITH THAT GHOST JUST NOW.
MY GUESS IS THAT IT'S JUST A FLOATER— A WANDERING SPIRIT, IF YOU WILL.
SMILE
ANY IDEA WHERE YOU MIGHT'VE PICKED IT UP?
WELL... LET ME THINK...
PHEW
WAIT!
DON'T TELL ME!

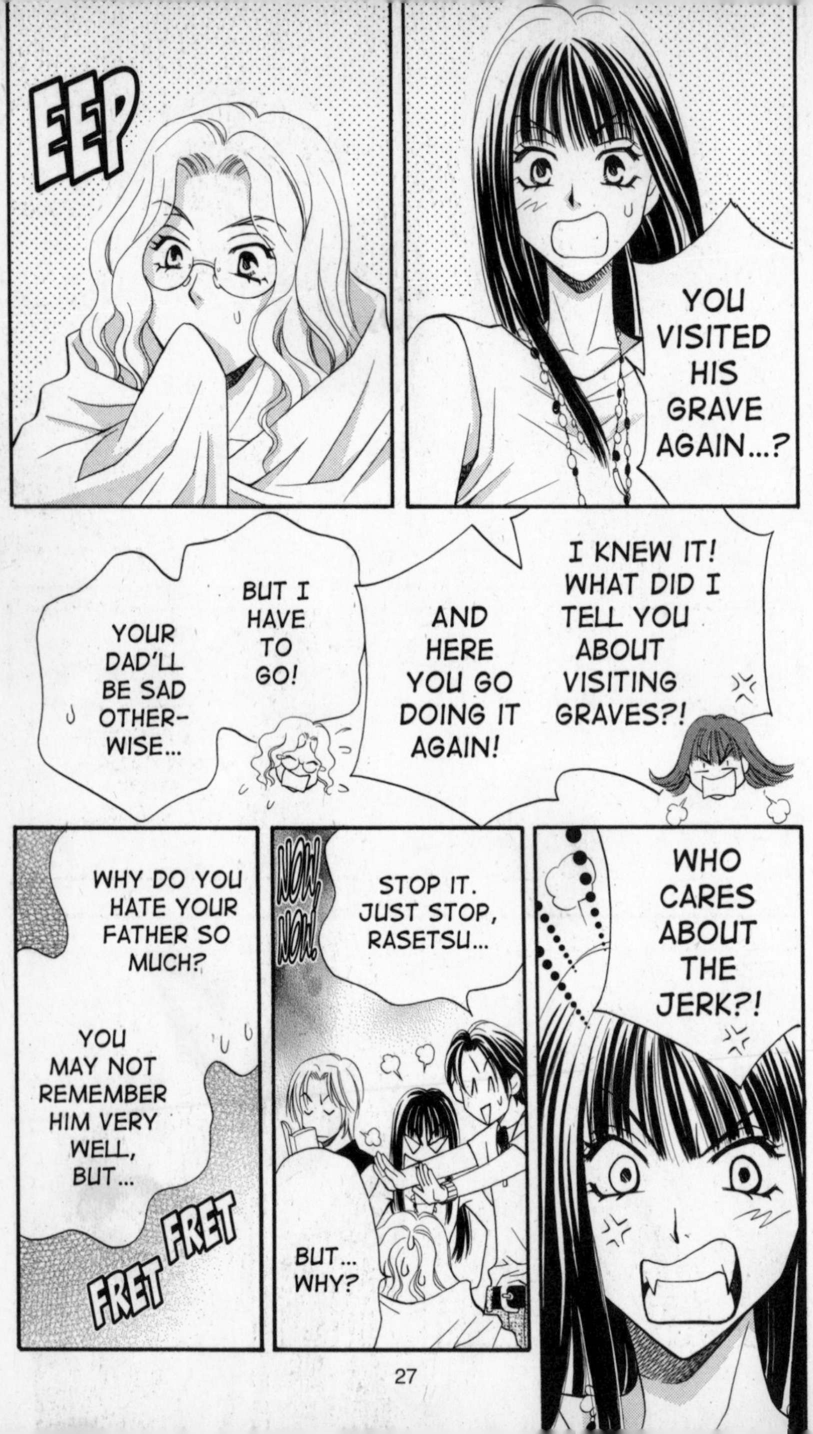
YOU VISITED HIS GRAVE AGAIN...?
EEP
I KNEW IT! WHAT DID I TELL YOU ABOUT VISITING GRAVES?!
AND HERE YOU GO DOING IT AGAIN!
BUT I HAVE TO GO!
YOUR DAD'LL BE SAD OTHER-WISE...
WHO CARES ABOUT THE JERK?!
NOW, NOW!
STOP IT. JUST STOP, RASETSU...
BUT... WHY?
WHY DO YOU HATE YOUR FATHER SO MUCH?
YOU MAY NOT REMEMBER HIM VERY WELL, BUT...
FRET FRET

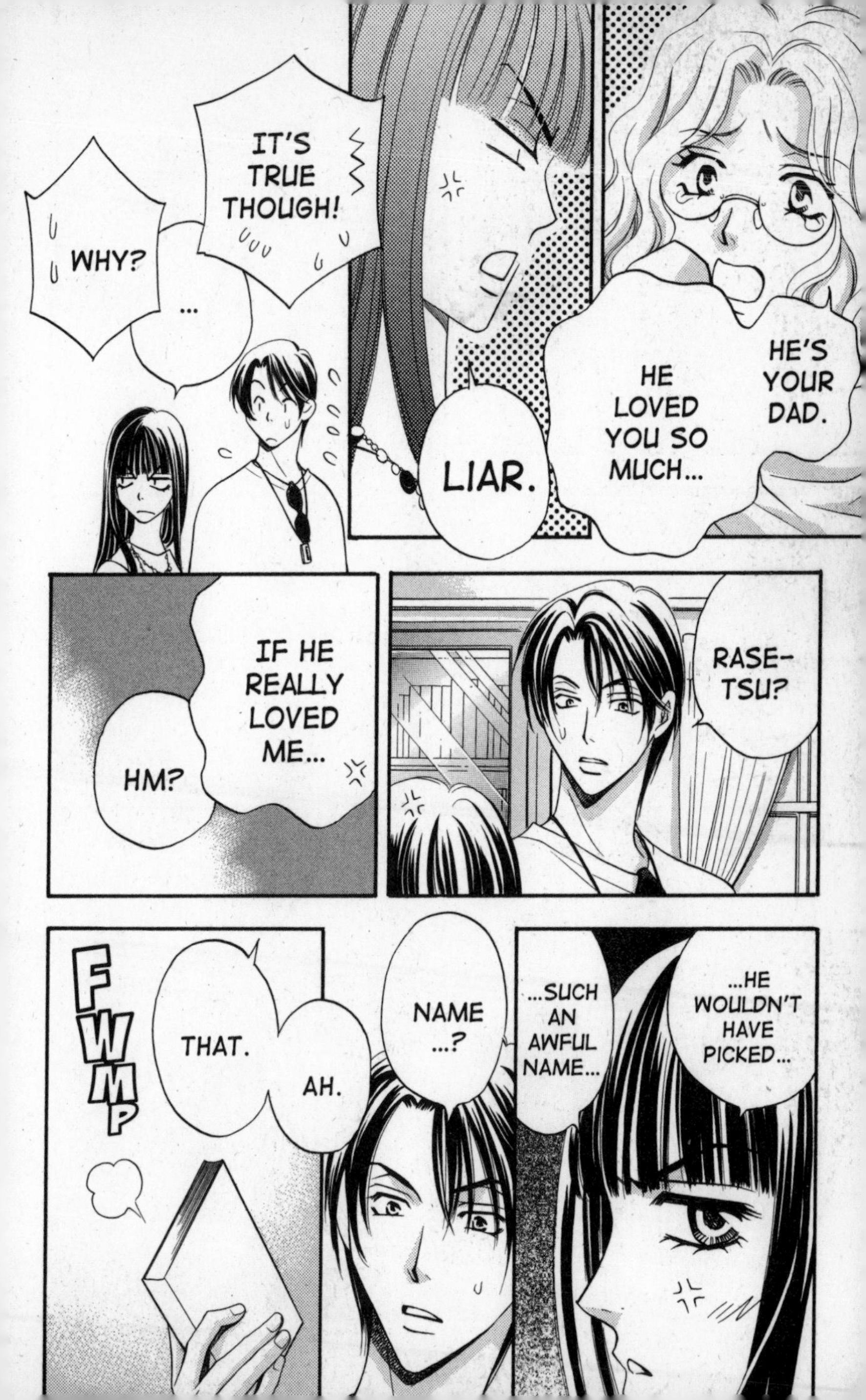

HE'S YOUR DAD.
HE LOVED YOU SO MUCH...
LIAR.
IT'S TRUE THOUGH!
WHY?
...
RASE-TSU?
IF HE REALLY LOVED ME...
HM?
...HE WOULDN'T HAVE PICKED...
...SUCH AN AWFUL NAME...
NAME ...?
AH.
THAT.
FWMP

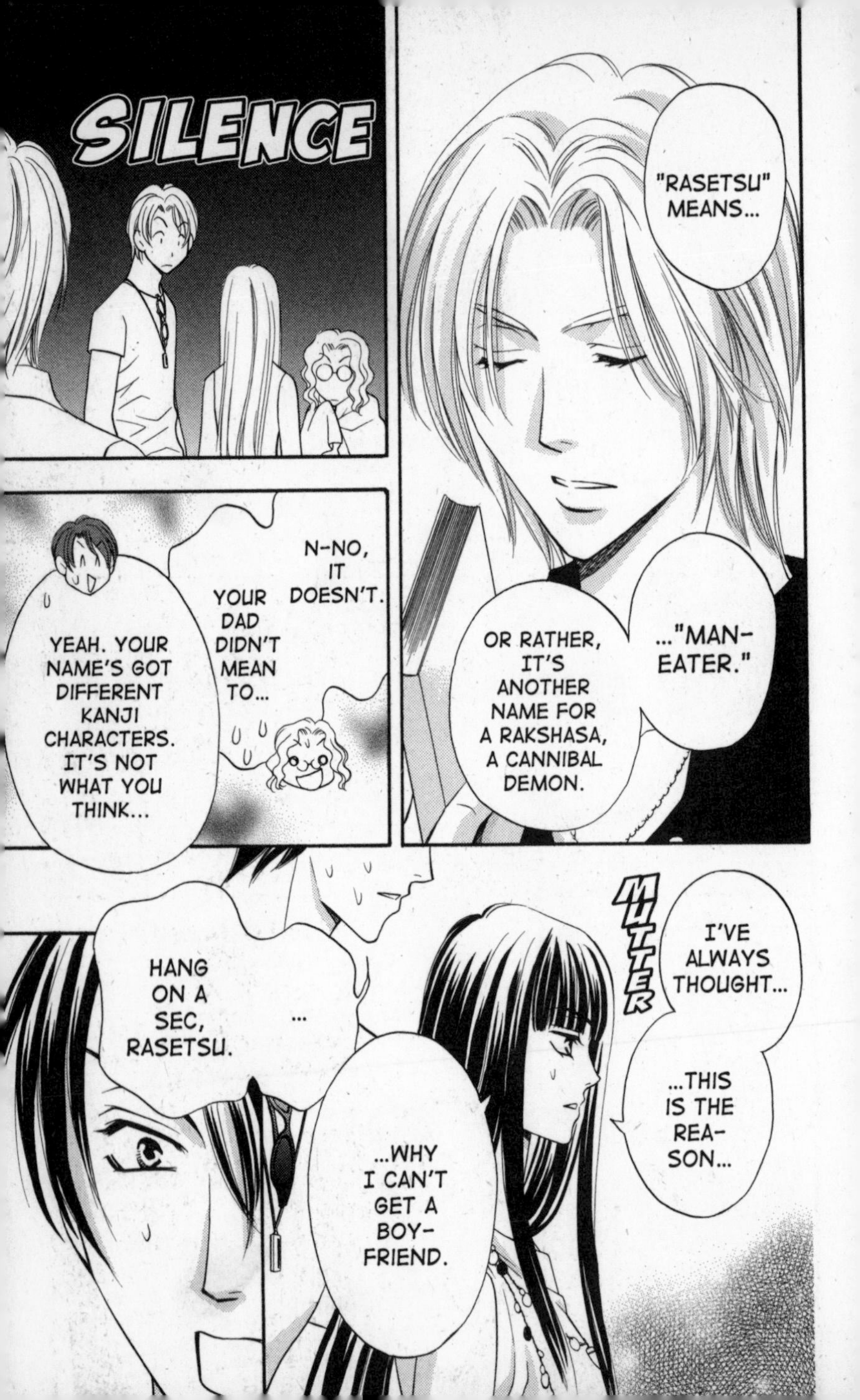
"RASETSU" MEANS...
..."MAN-EATER."
OR RATHER, IT'S ANOTHER NAME FOR A RAKSHASA, A CANNIBAL DEMON.
SILENCE
N-NO, IT DOESN'T.
YOUR DAD DIDN'T MEAN TO...
YEAH. YOUR NAME'S GOT DIFFERENT KANJI CHARACTERS. IT'S NOT WHAT YOU THINK...
MUTTER
I'VE ALWAYS THOUGHT...
...THIS IS THE REASON...
...WHY I CAN'T GET A BOYFRIEND.
...
HANG ON A SEC, RASETSU.

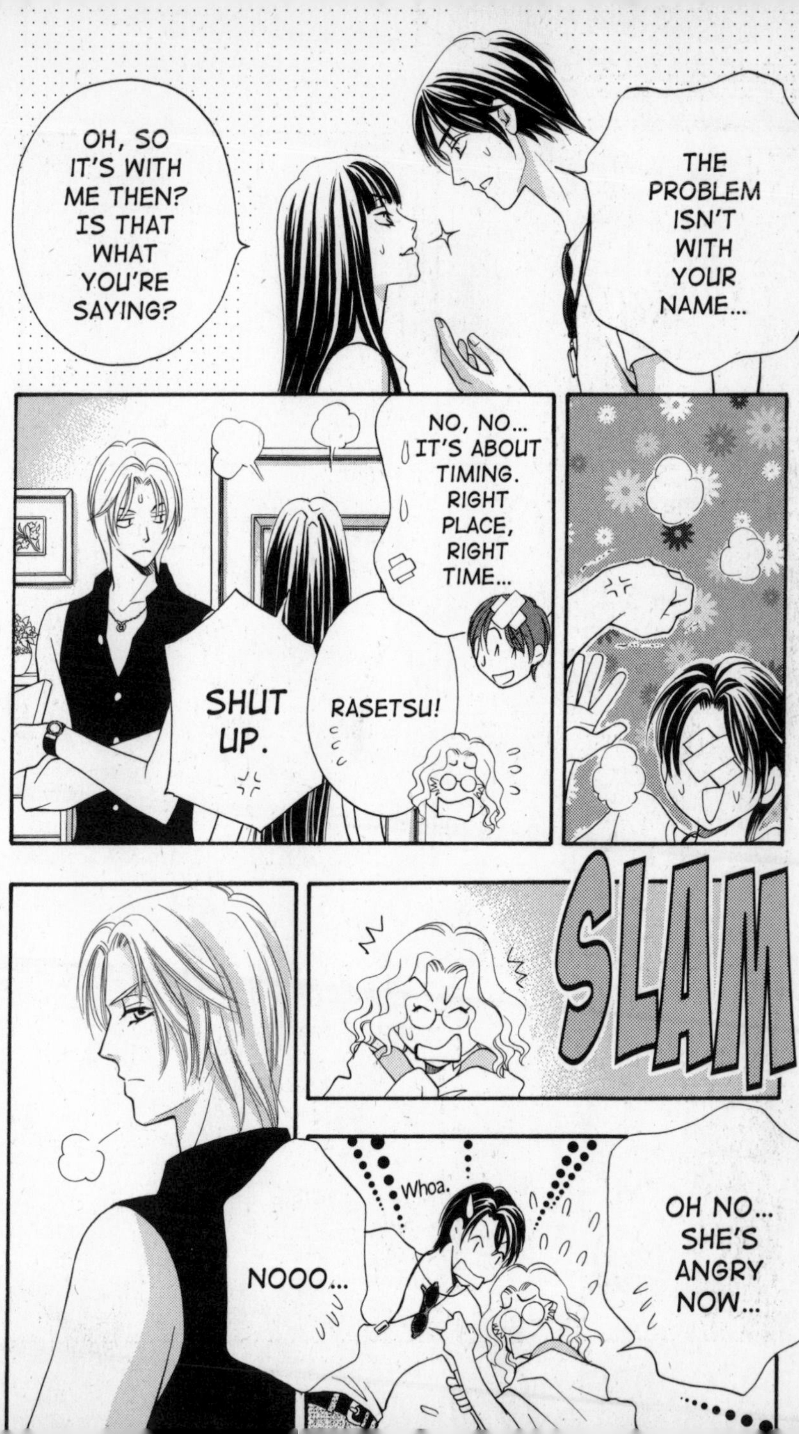
THE PROBLEM ISN'T WITH YOUR NAME...
OH, SO IT'S WITH ME THEN? IS THAT WHAT YOU'RE SAYING?
NO, NO... IT'S ABOUT TIMING. RIGHT PLACE, RIGHT TIME...
RASETSU!
SHUT UP.
SLAM
OH NO... SHE'S ANGRY NOW...
Whoa.
NOOO...

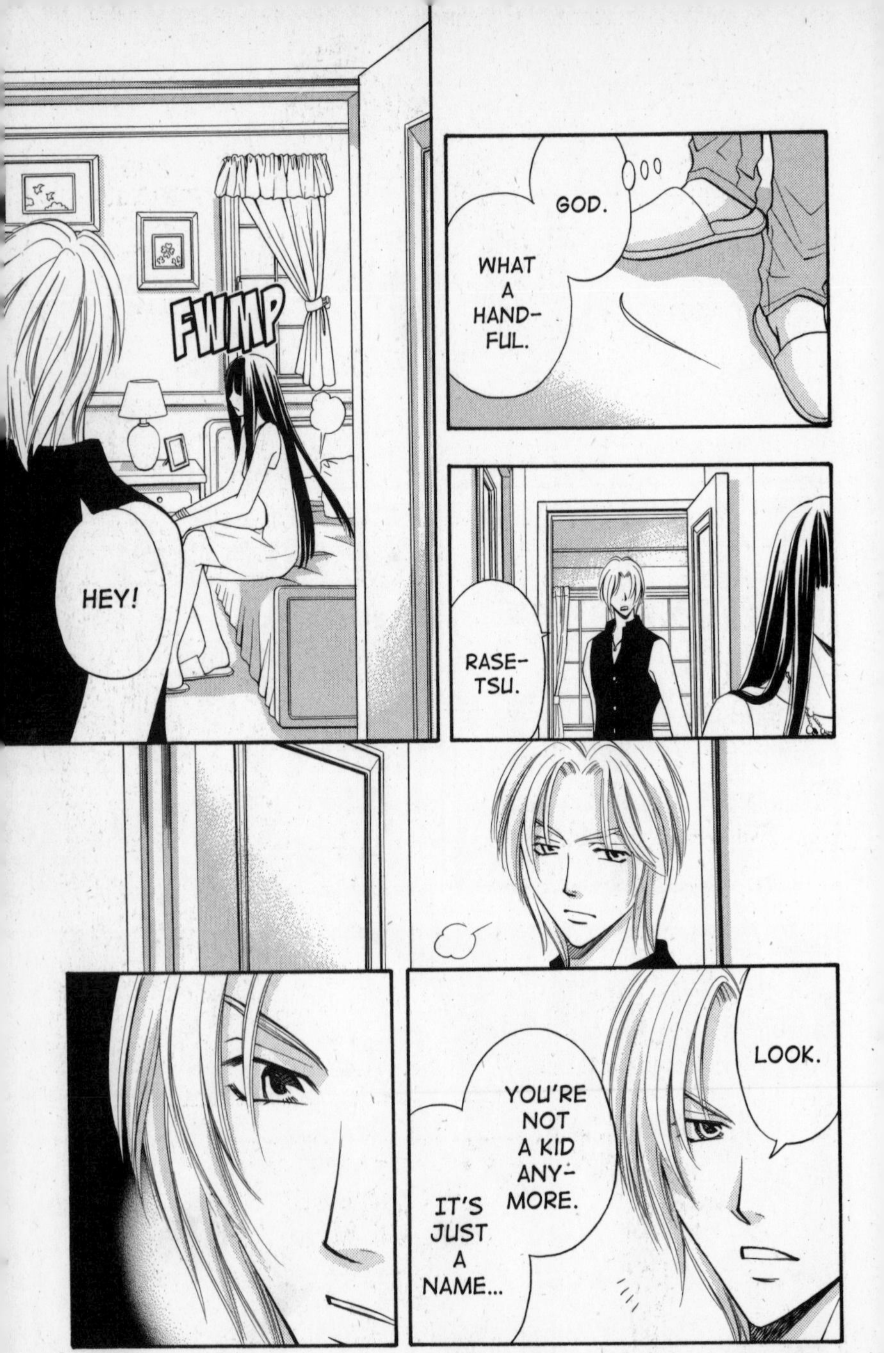
GOD.
WHAT A HANDFUL.
RASETSU.
FWMP
HEY!
LOOK.
YOU'RE NOT A KID ANYMORE.
IT'S JUST A NAME...

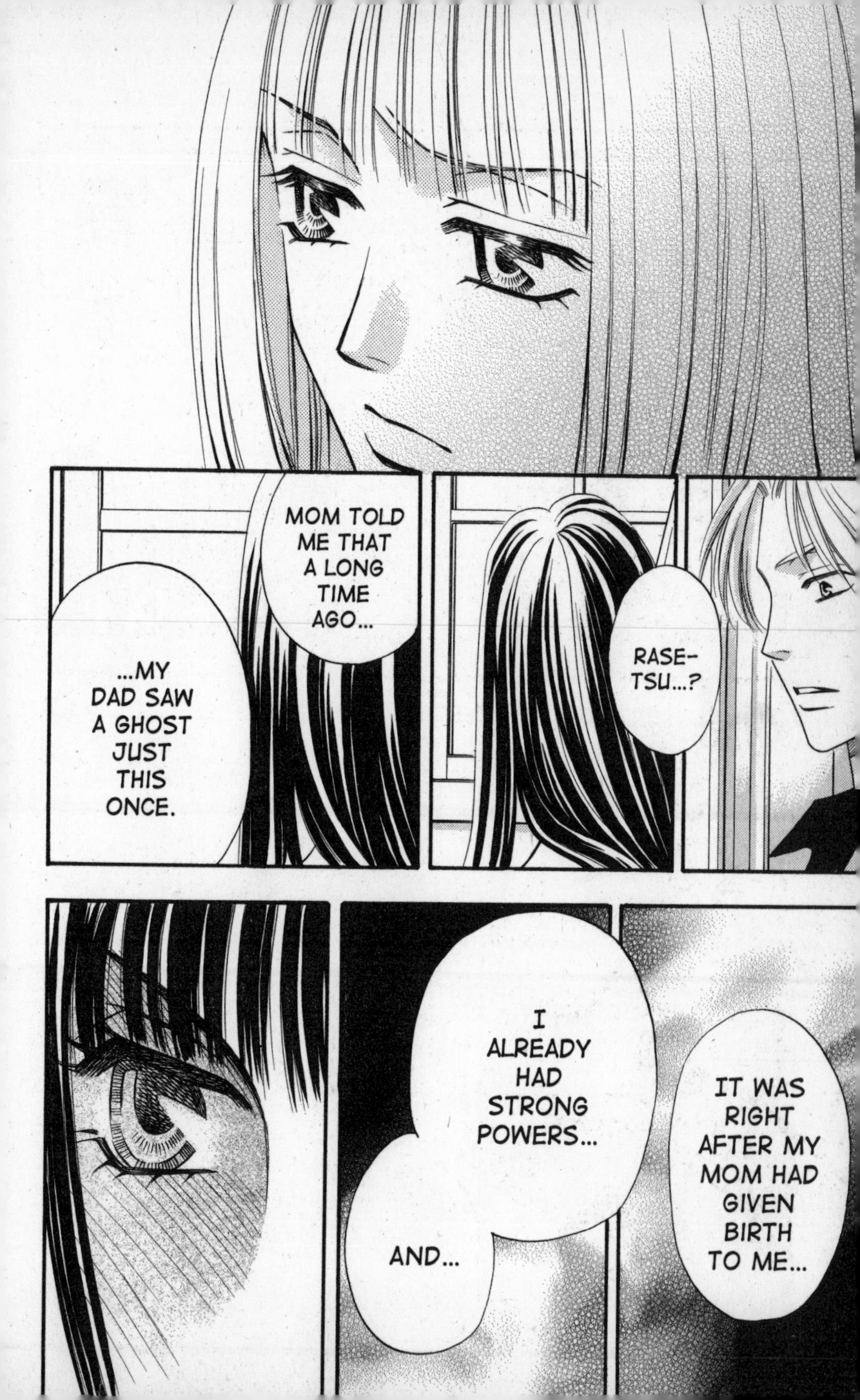
RASE-TSU...?
MOM TOLD ME THAT A LONG TIME AGO...
...MY DAD SAW A GHOST JUST THIS ONCE.
IT WAS RIGHT AFTER MY MOM HAD GIVEN BIRTH TO ME...
I ALREADY HAD STRONG POWERS...
AND...

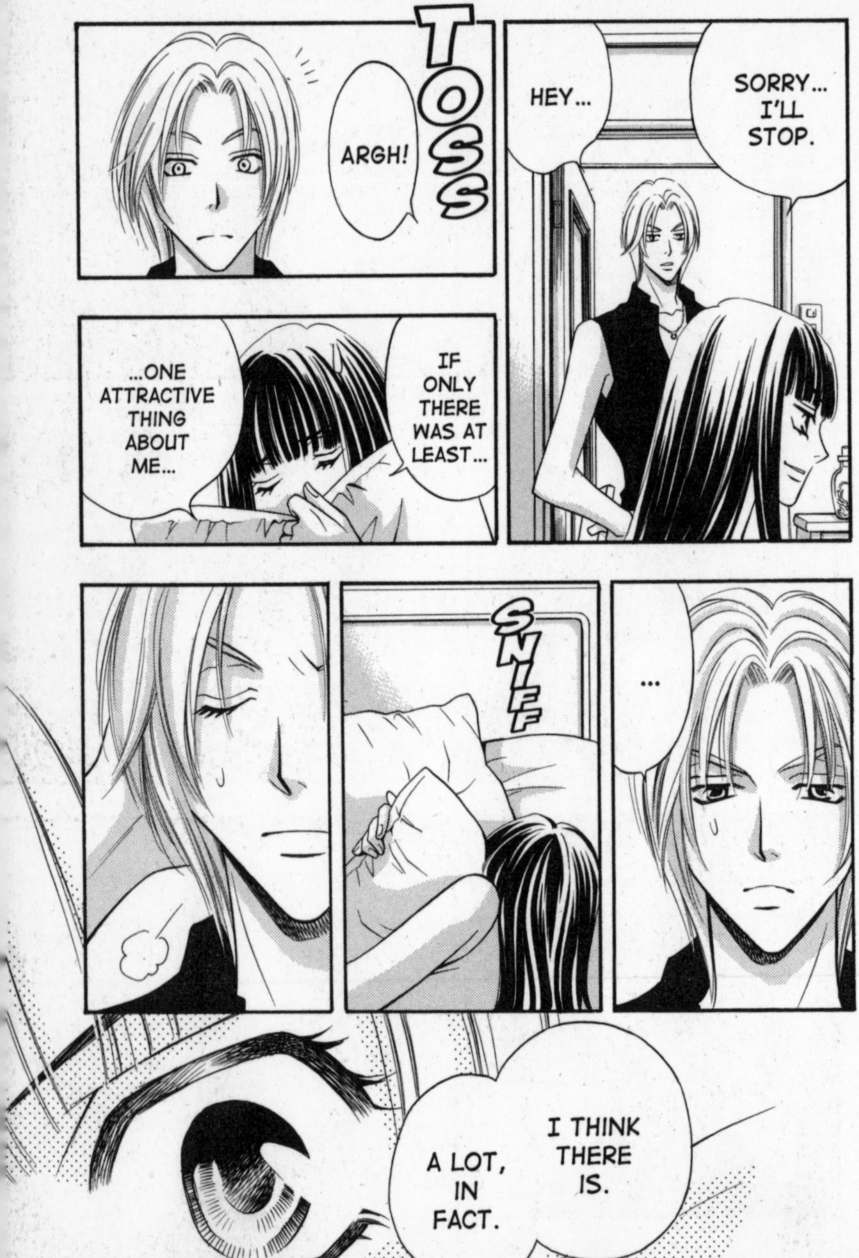
SORRY... I'LL STOP.
HEY...
TOSS
ARGH!
IF ONLY THERE WAS AT LEAST...
...ONE ATTRACTIVE THING ABOUT ME...
...
SNIFF
I THINK THERE IS.
A LOT, IN FACT.

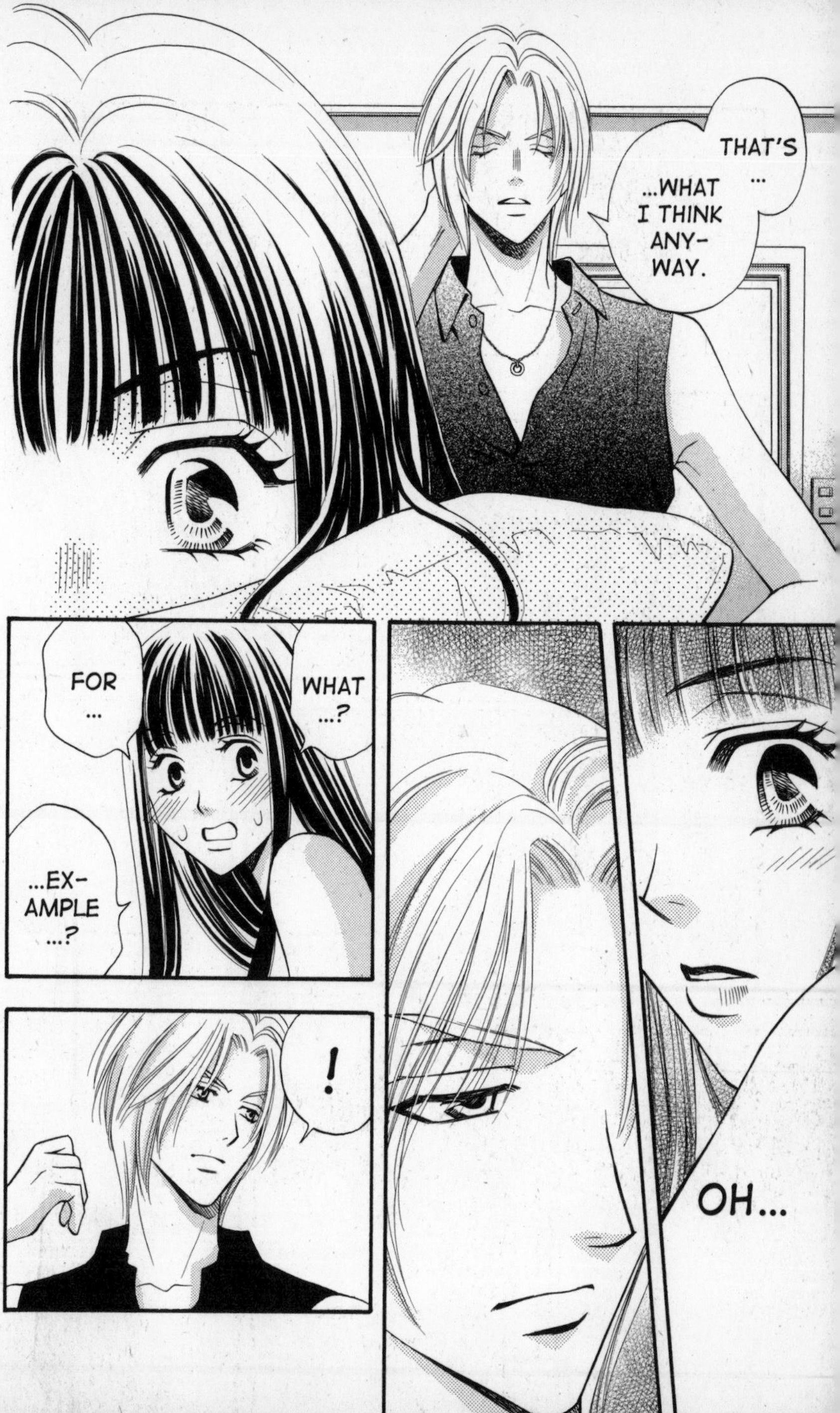
THAT'S ...
...WHAT I THINK ANY-WAY.
OH...
WHAT ...?
FOR ...
...EX-AMPLE ...?
!

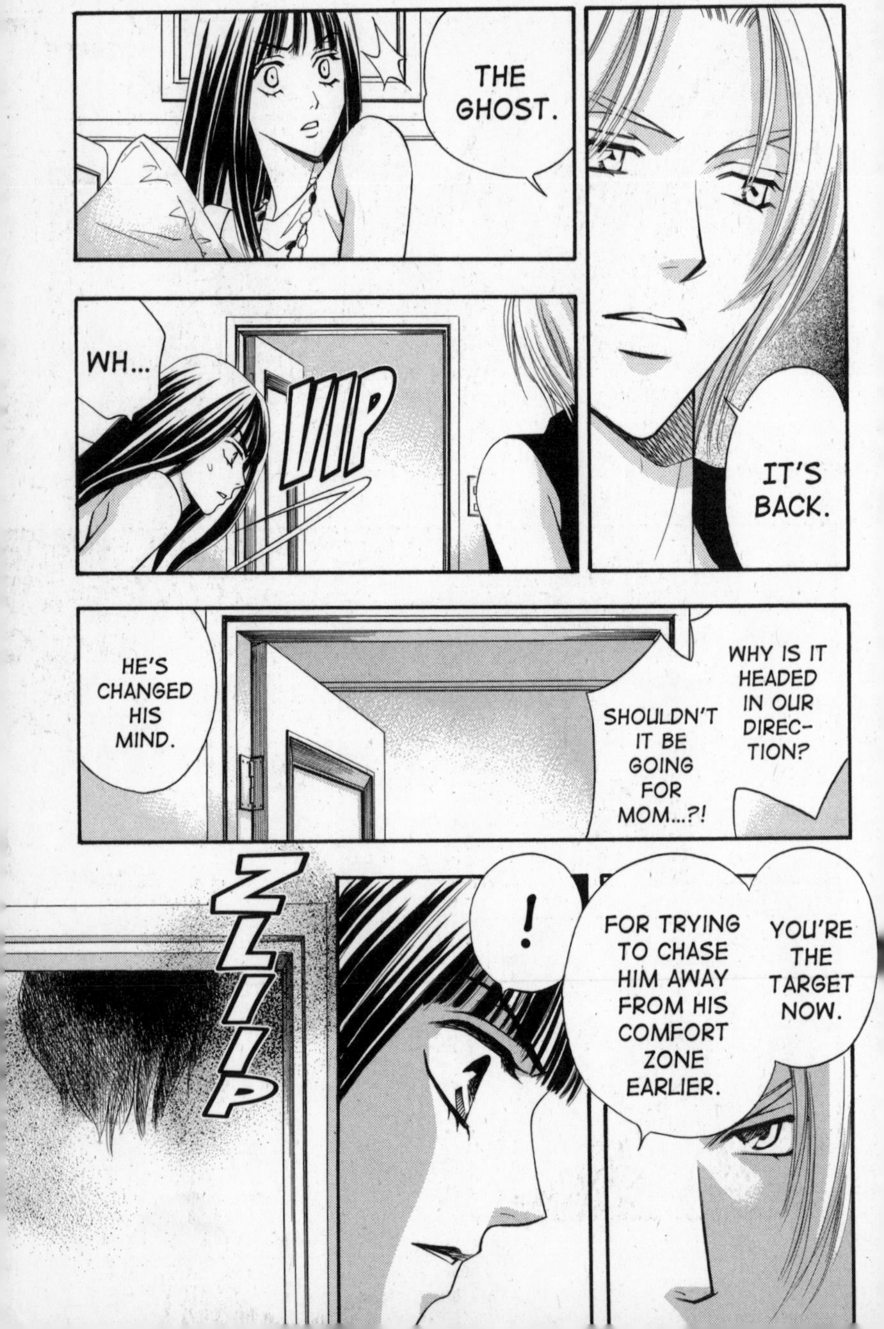
IT'S BACK.
THE GHOST.
WH...
VIIP
WHY IS IT HEADED IN OUR DIRECTION?
SHOULDN'T IT BE GOING FOR MOM...?!
HE'S CHANGED HIS MIND.
YOU'RE THE TARGET NOW.
FOR TRYING TO CHASE HIM AWAY FROM HIS COMFORT ZONE EARLIER.
!
ZLLIP

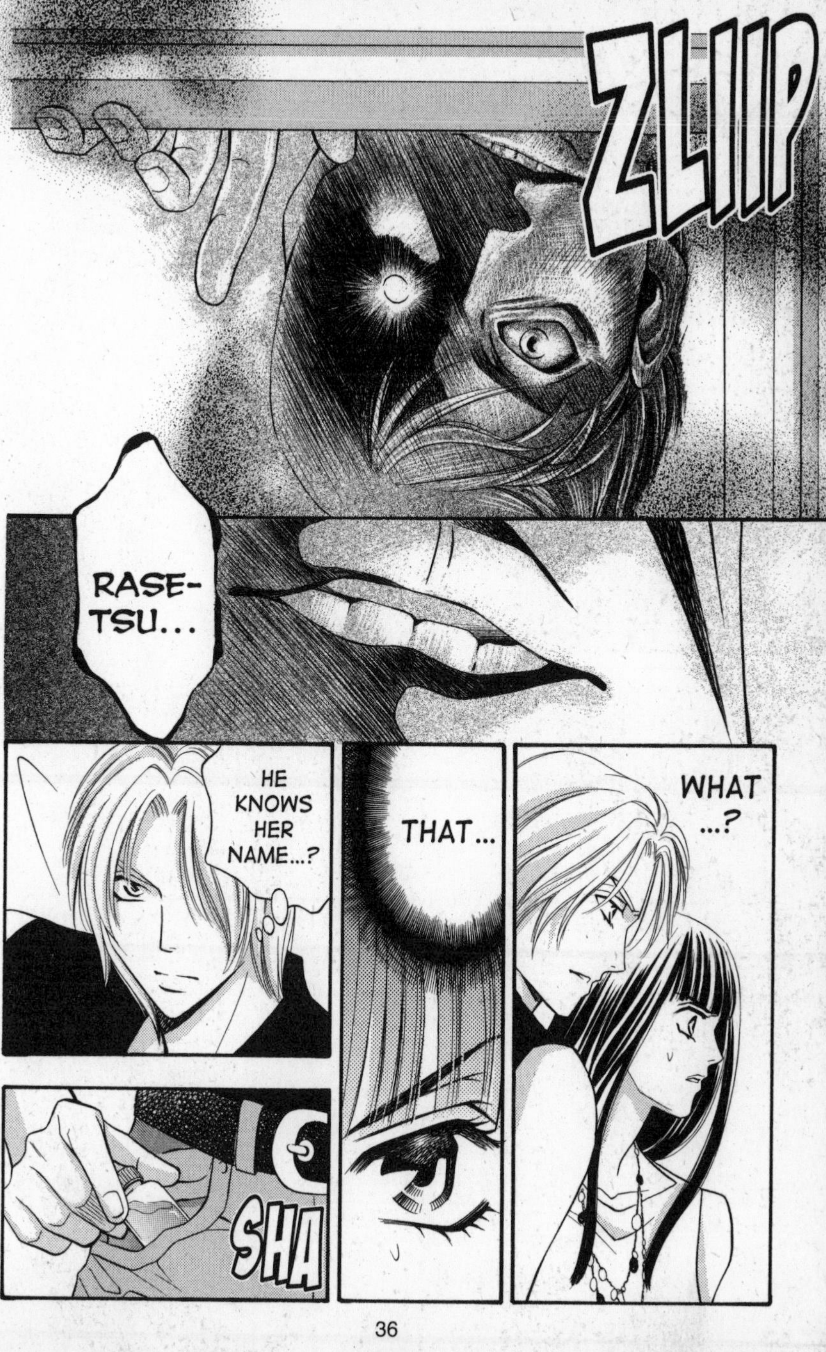
ZLIIP
RASE-TSU...
WHAT ...?
THAT...
HE KNOWS HER NAME...?
SHA

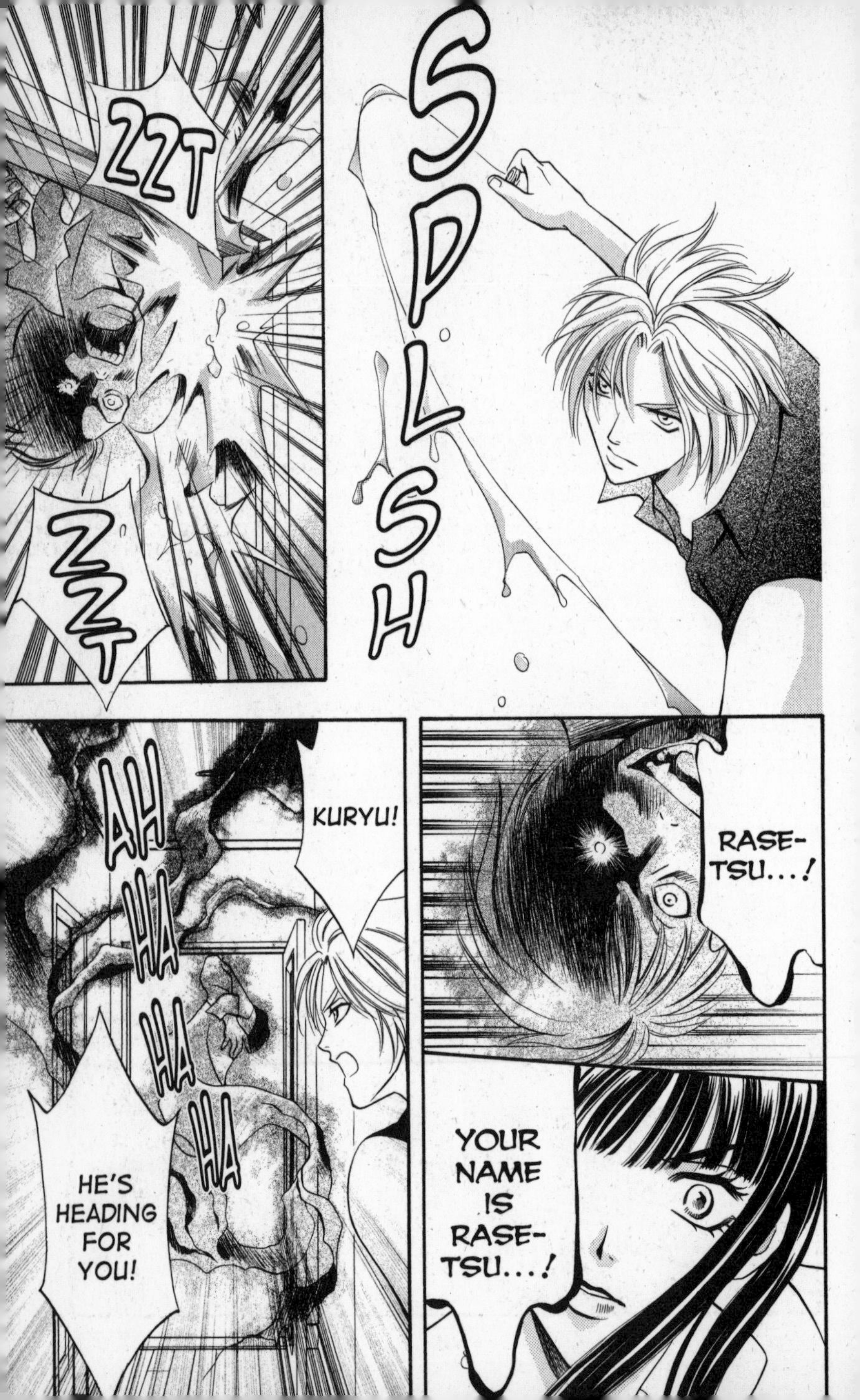
SPLSH
ZZT
ZZZT
RASE-TSU...!
YOUR NAME IS RASE-TSU...!
KURYU!
AH HA HA HA HA
HE'S HEADING FOR YOU!

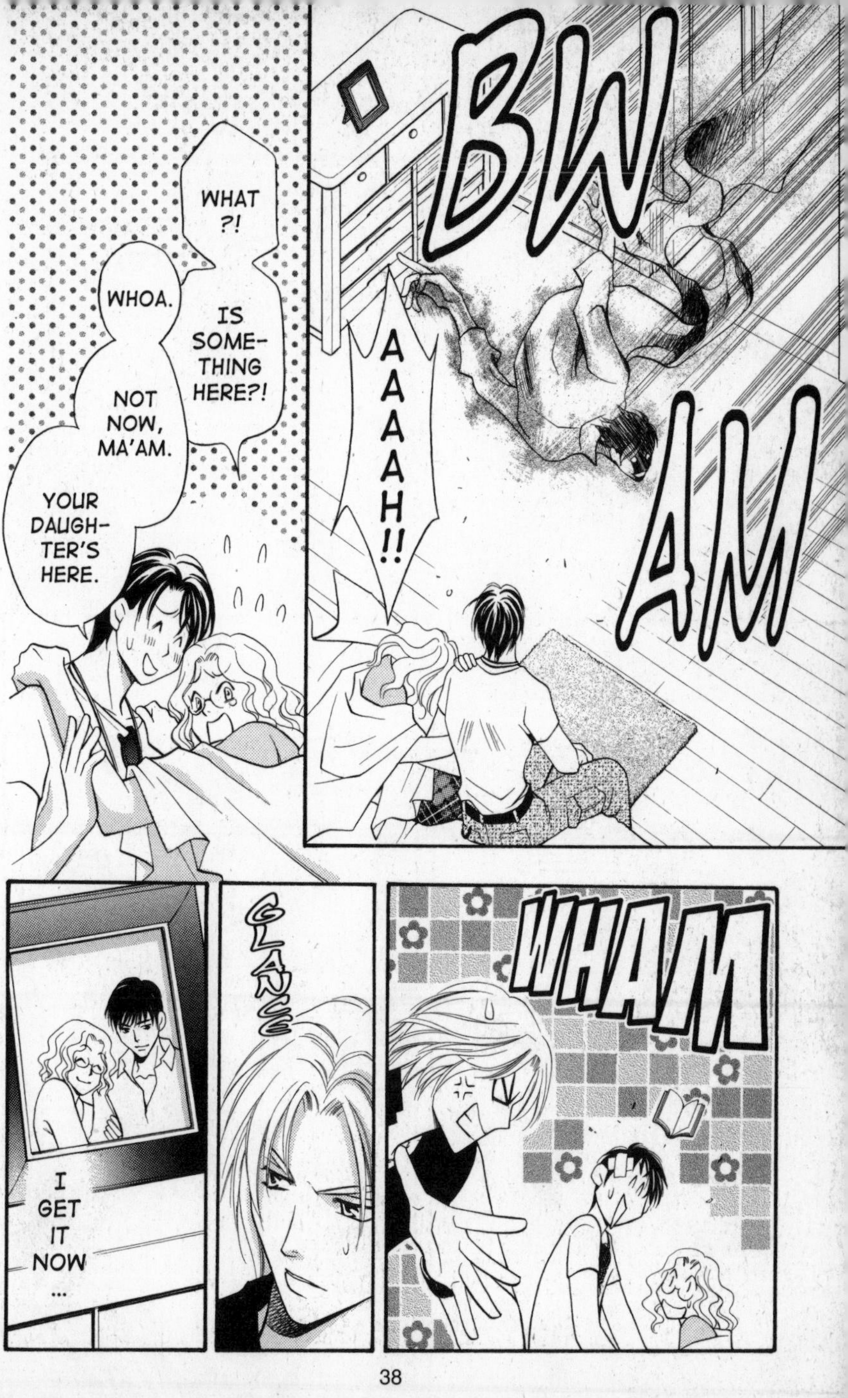
BWAM
AAAAAH!!
WHAT ?!
IS SOME-THING HERE?!
WHOA.
NOT NOW, MA'AM.
YOUR DAUGH-TER'S HERE.
WHAM
GLANCE
I GET IT NOW ...

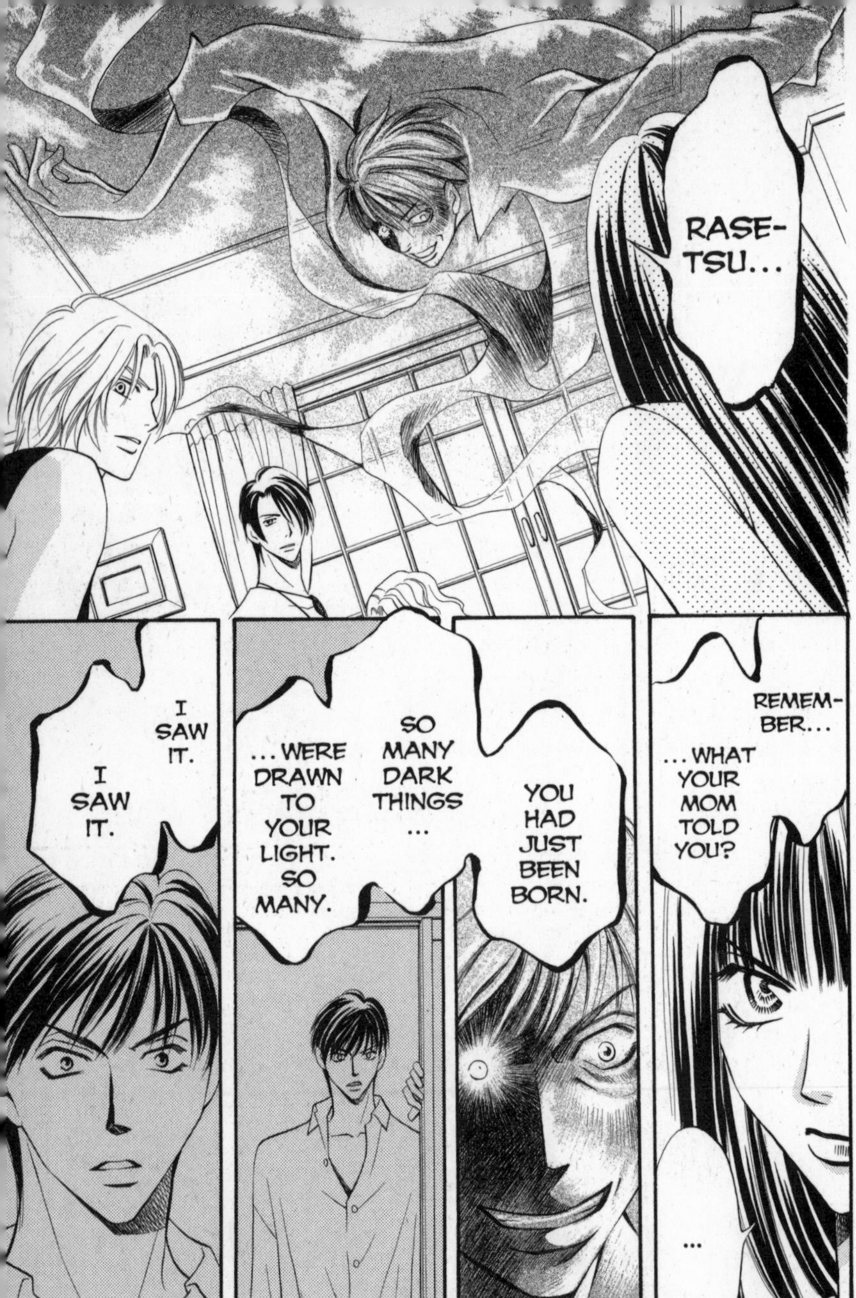
RASE-TSU...
REMEMBER...
...WHAT YOUR MOM TOLD YOU?
...
YOU HAD JUST BEEN BORN.
SO MANY DARK THINGS ...
...WERE DRAWN TO YOUR LIGHT. SO MANY.
I SAW IT.
I SAW IT.

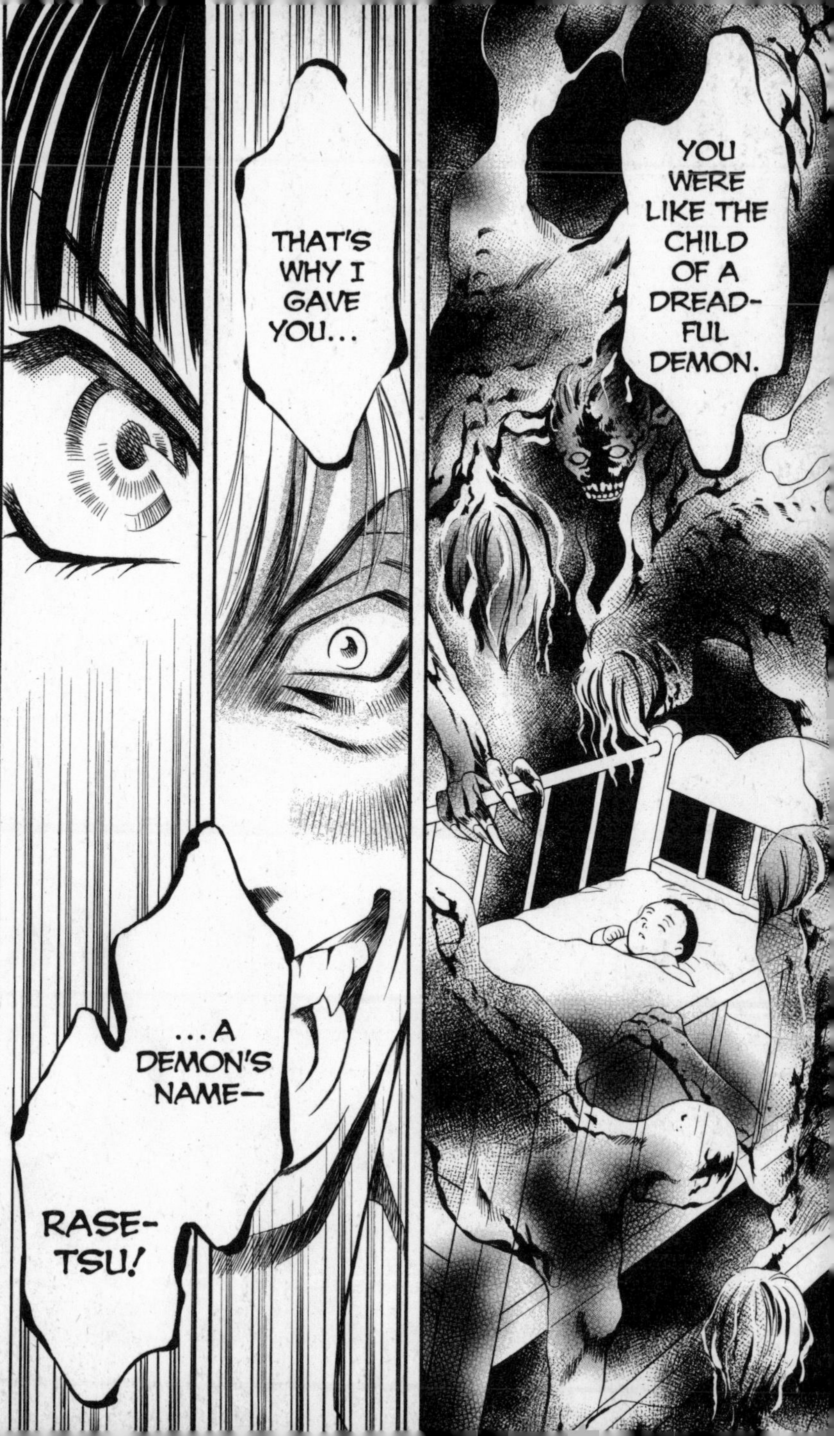
YOU WERE LIKE THE CHILD OF A DREAD-FUL DEMON.
THAT'S WHY I GAVE YOU...
...A DEMON'S NAME—
RASE-TSU!

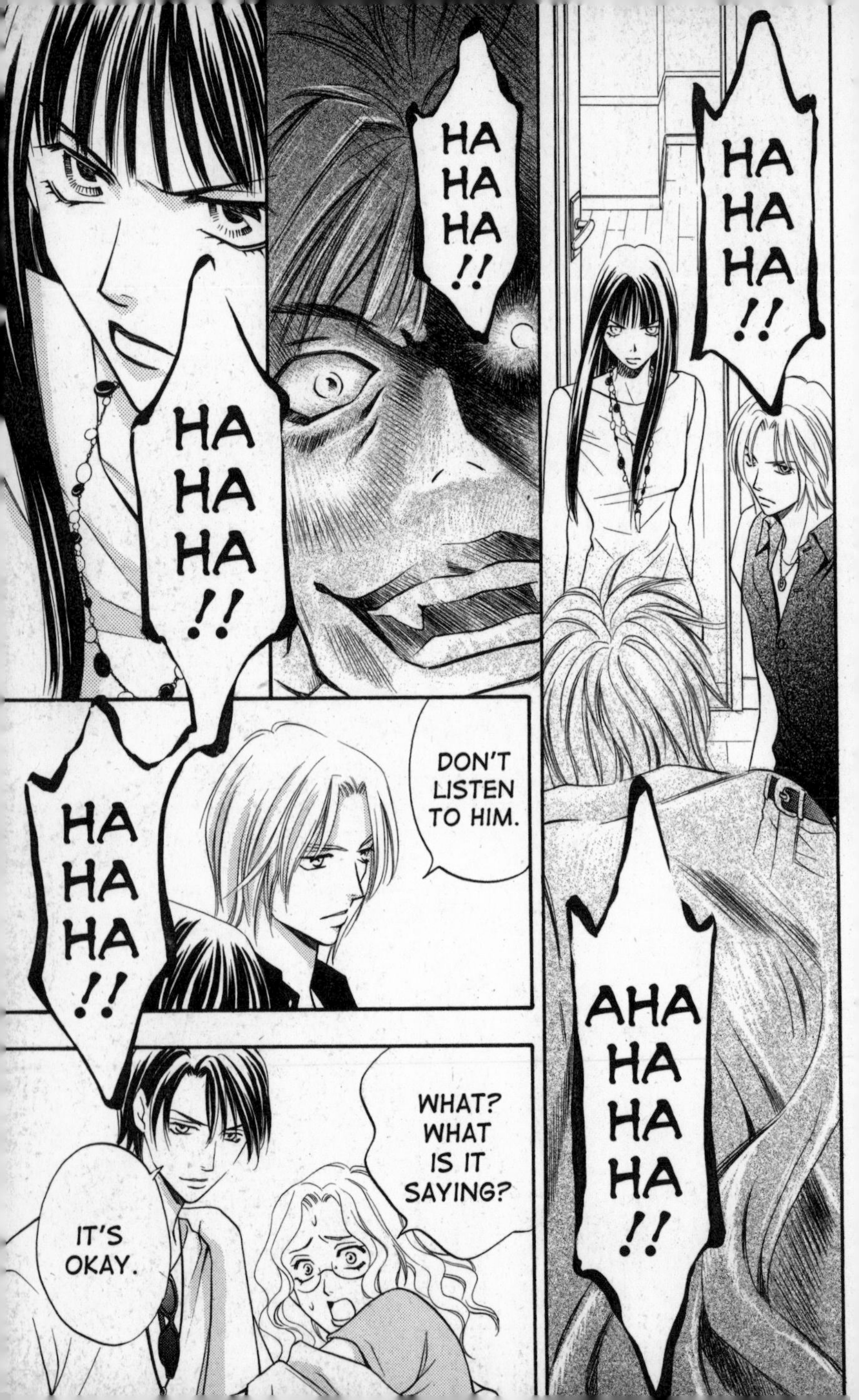
HA HA HA!!
AHA HA HA HA!!
HA HA HA!!
HA HA HA!!
DON'T LISTEN TO HIM.
HA HA HA!!
WHAT? WHAT IS IT SAYING?
IT'S OKAY.

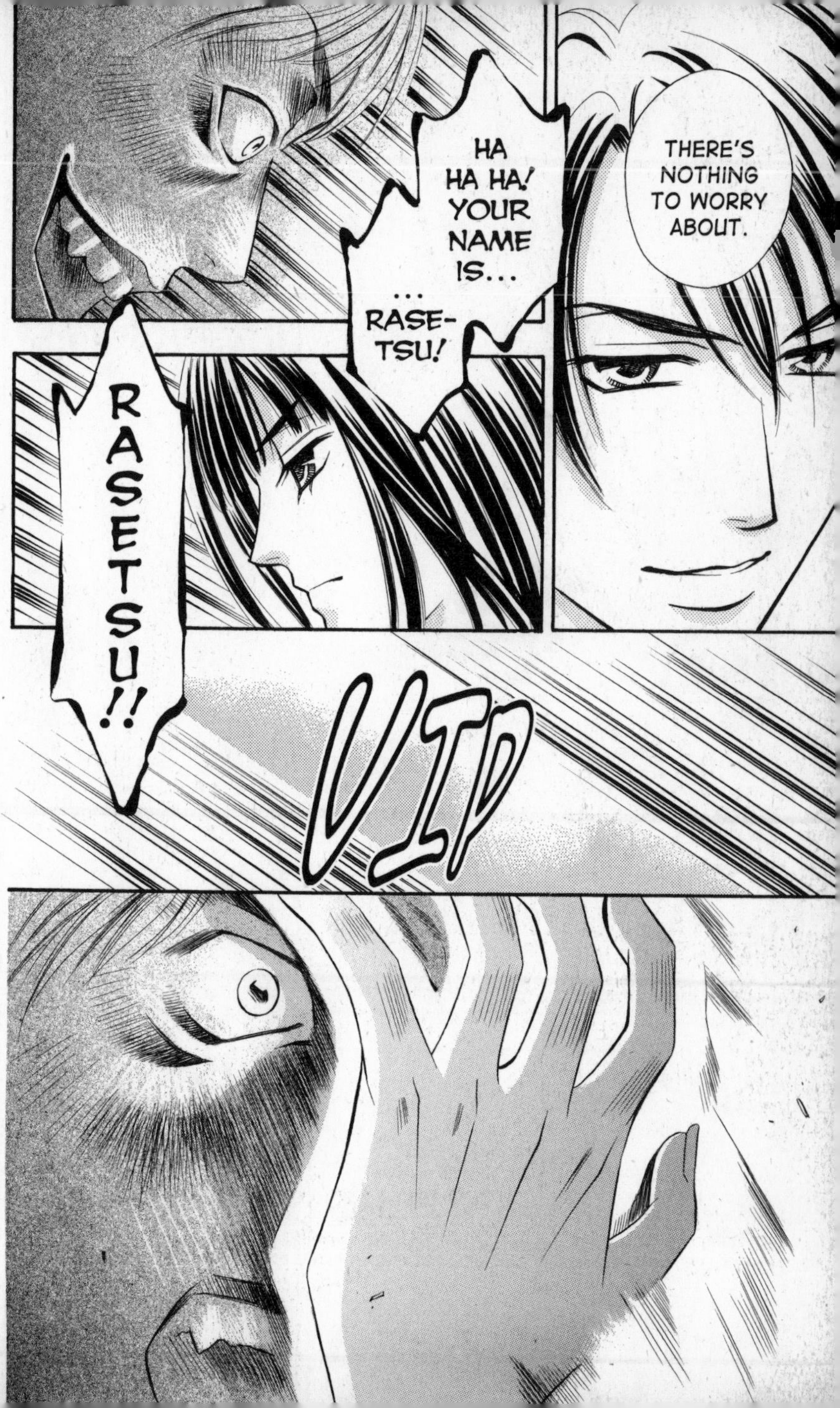
THERE'S NOTHING TO WORRY ABOUT.
HA HA HA! YOUR NAME IS...
...RASE-TSU!
RASETSU!!
VIP

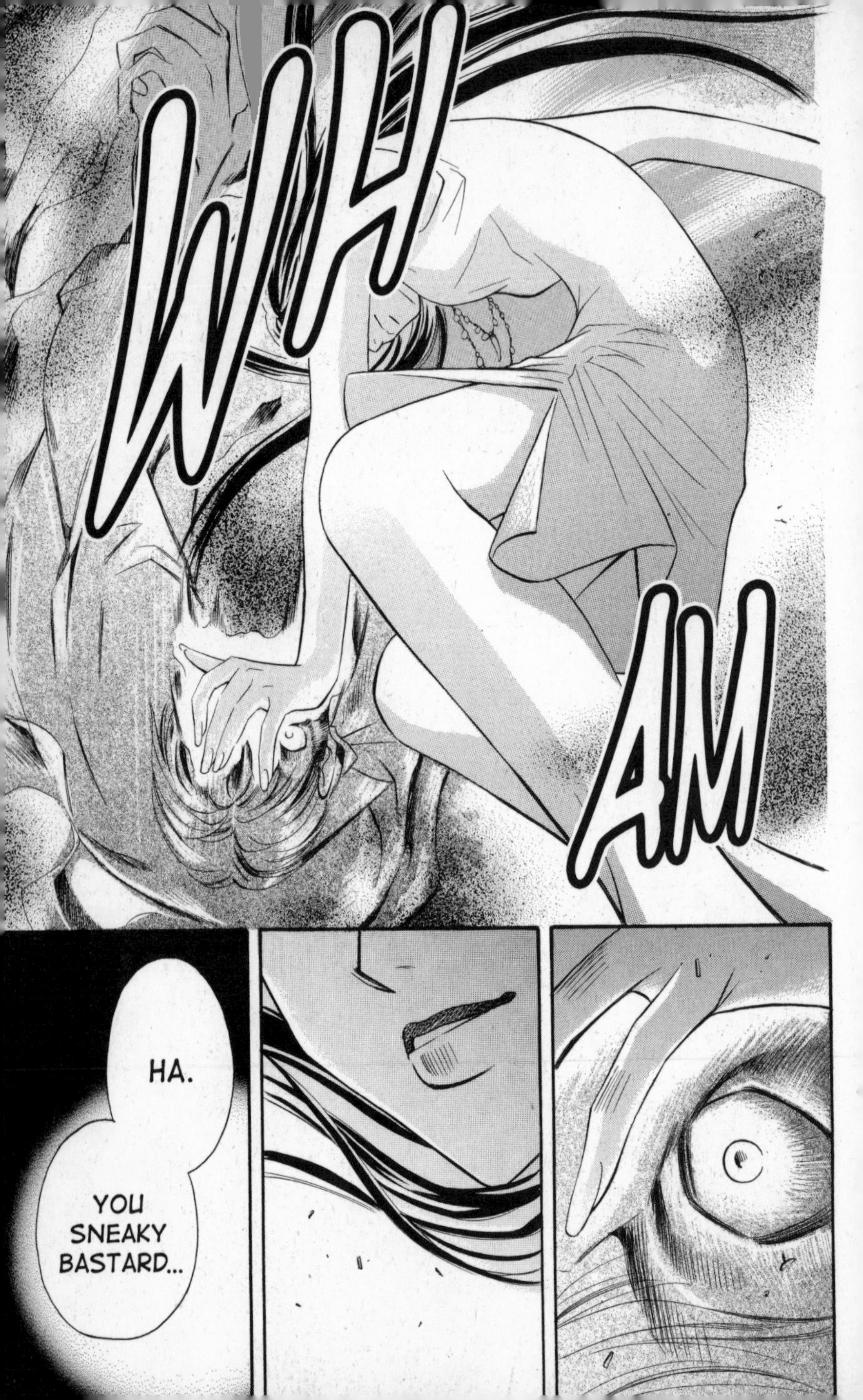
WH
AM
HA.
YOU SNEAKY BASTARD...

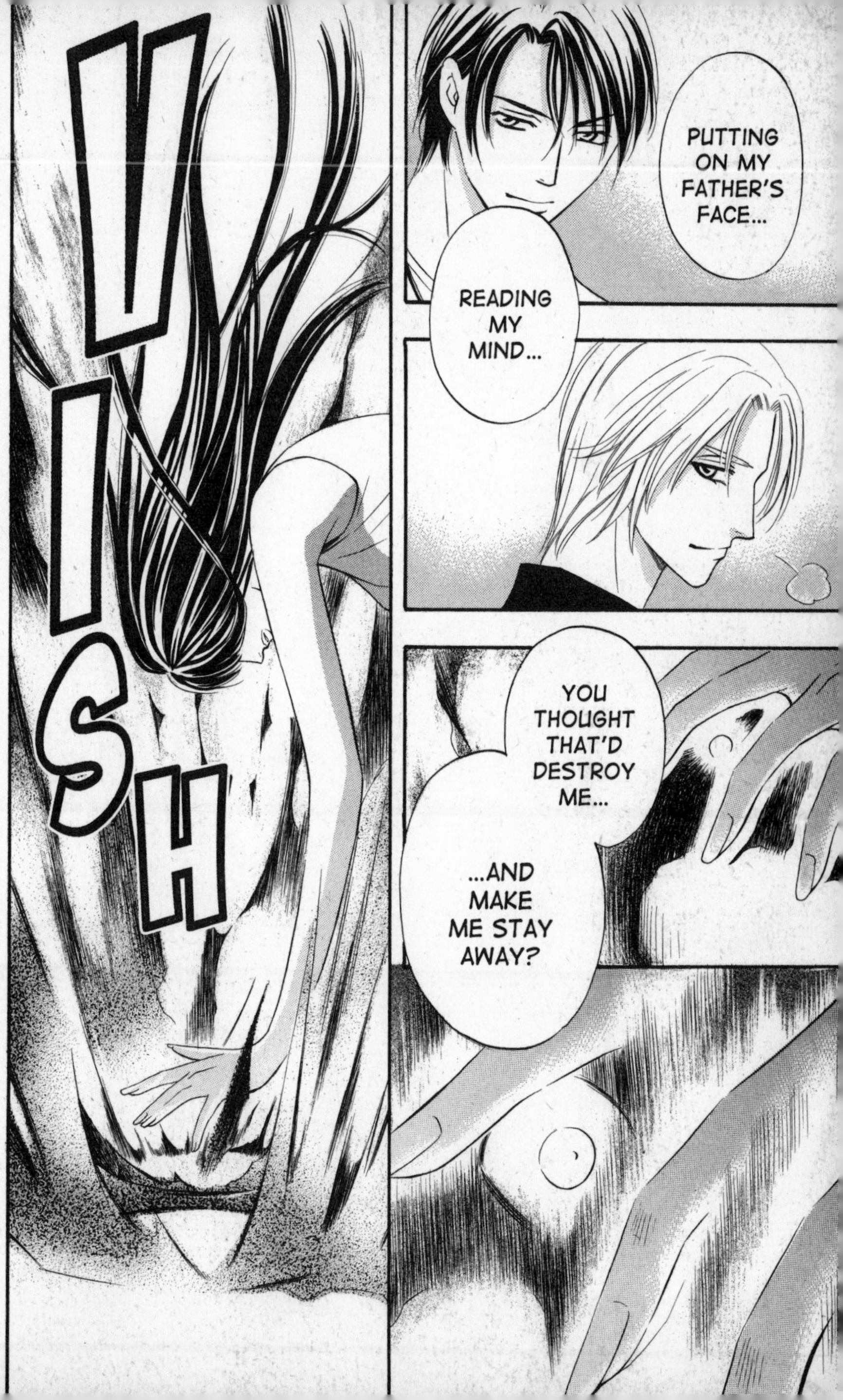
PUTTING ON MY FATHER'S FACE...
READING MY MIND...
YOU THOUGHT THAT'D DESTROY ME...
...AND MAKE ME STAY AWAY?
VISH

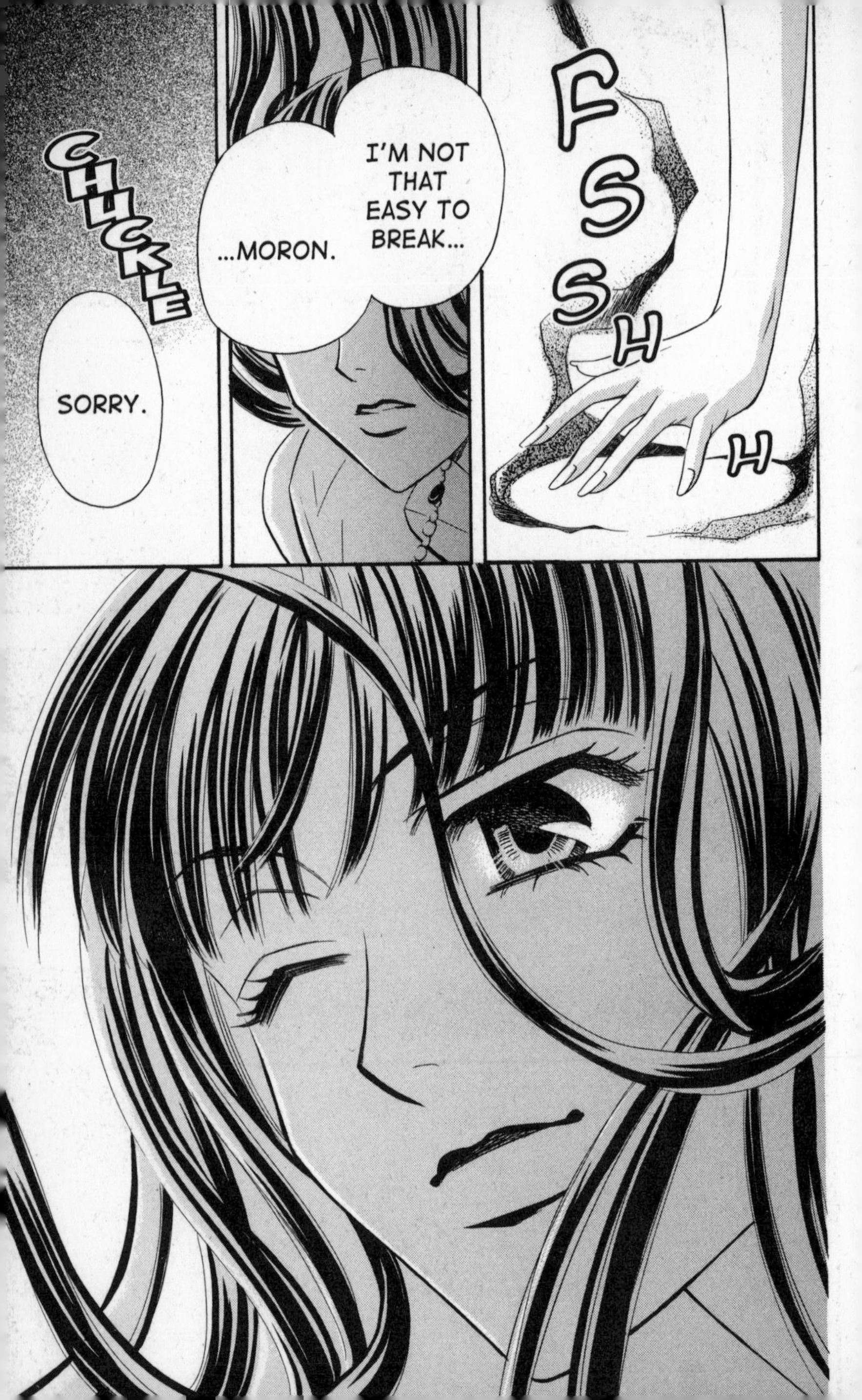
FSSHH
I'M NOT THAT EASY TO BREAK...
...MORON.
CHUCKLE
SORRY.

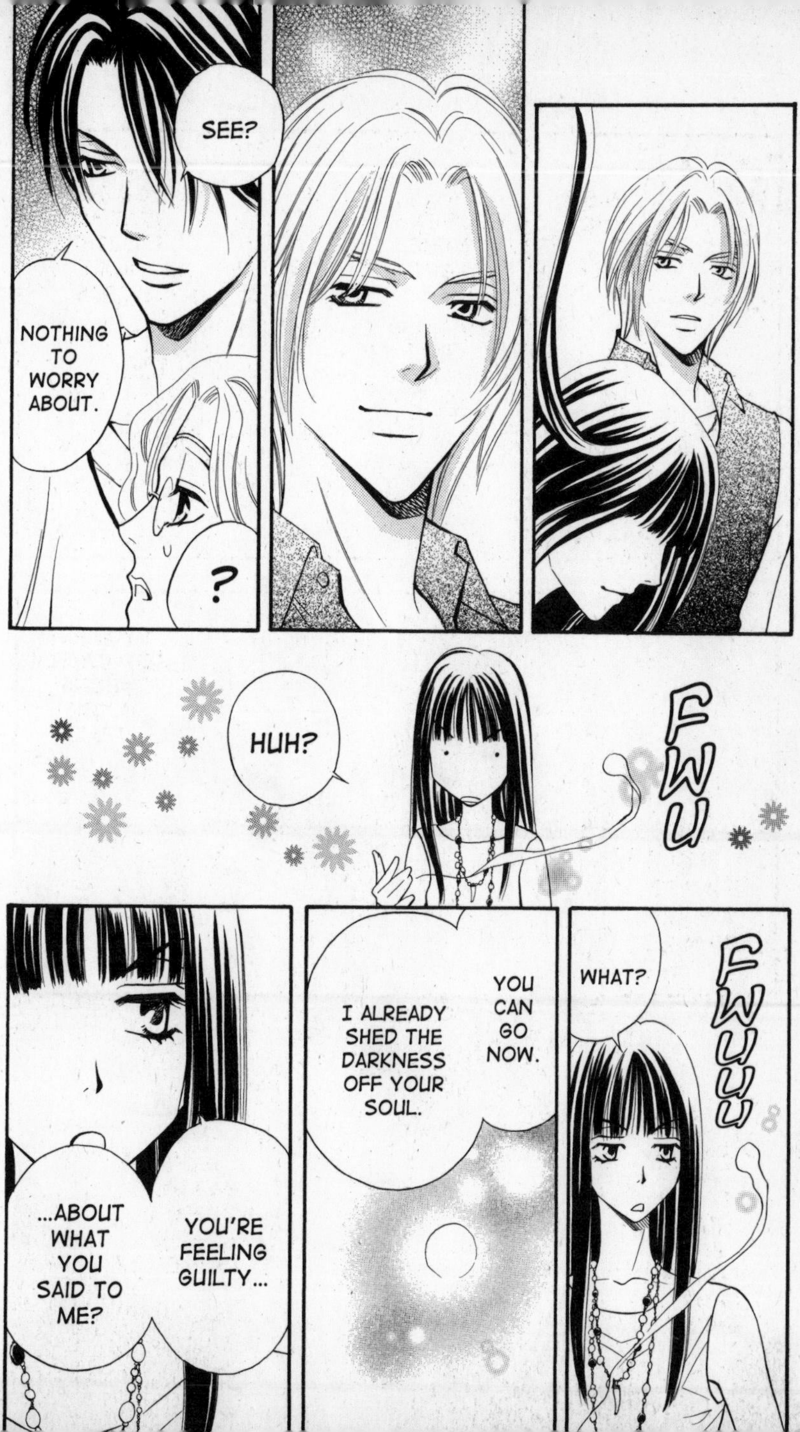
SEE?
NOTHING TO WORRY ABOUT.
?
FWU
HUH?
FWUUU
WHAT?
YOU CAN GO NOW.
I ALREADY SHED THE DARKNESS OFF YOUR SOUL.
YOU'RE FEELING GUILTY...
...ABOUT WHAT YOU SAID TO ME?

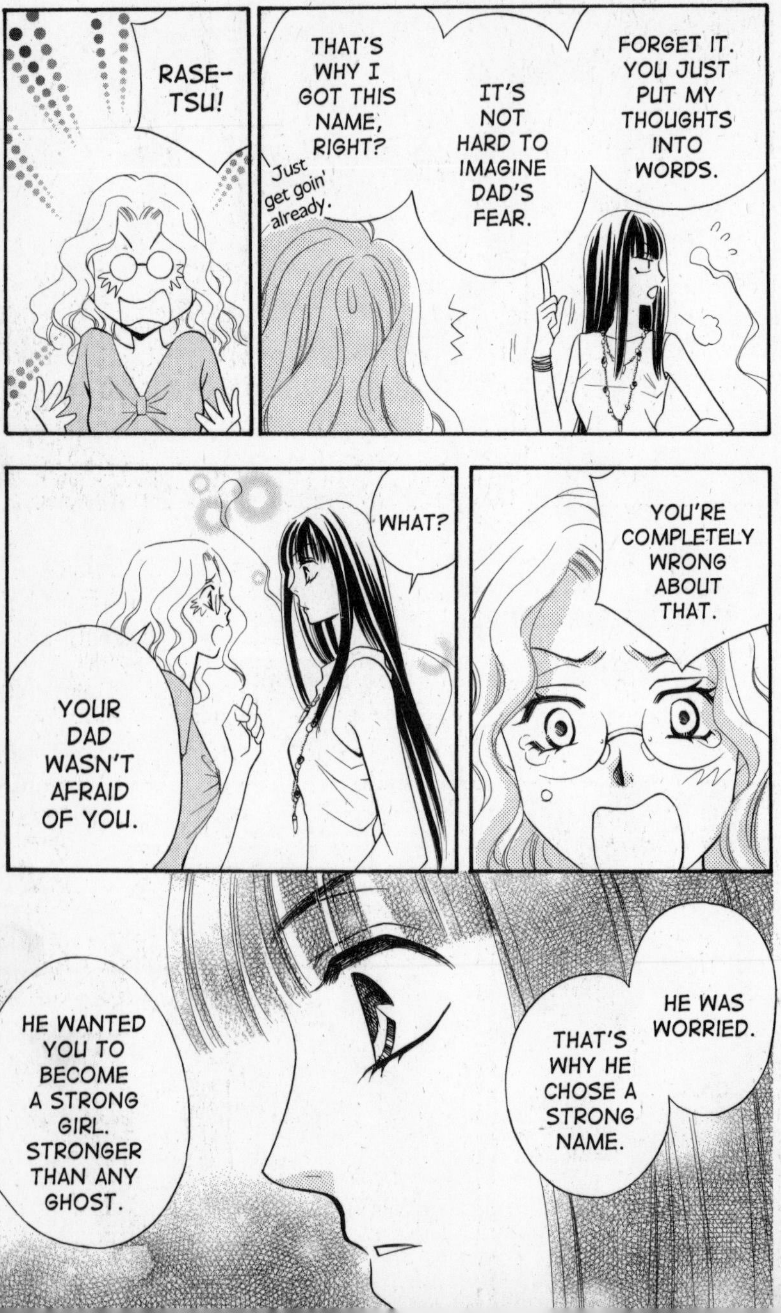
FORGET IT. YOU JUST PUT MY THOUGHTS INTO WORDS.
IT'S NOT HARD TO IMAGINE DAD'S FEAR.
THAT'S WHY I GOT THIS NAME, RIGHT?
Just get goin' already.
RASE-TSU!
YOU'RE COMPLETELY WRONG ABOUT THAT.
WHAT?
YOUR DAD WASN'T AFRAID OF YOU.
HE WAS WORRIED.
THAT'S WHY HE CHOSE A STRONG NAME.
HE WANTED YOU TO BECOME A STRONG GIRL. STRONGER THAN ANY GHOST.

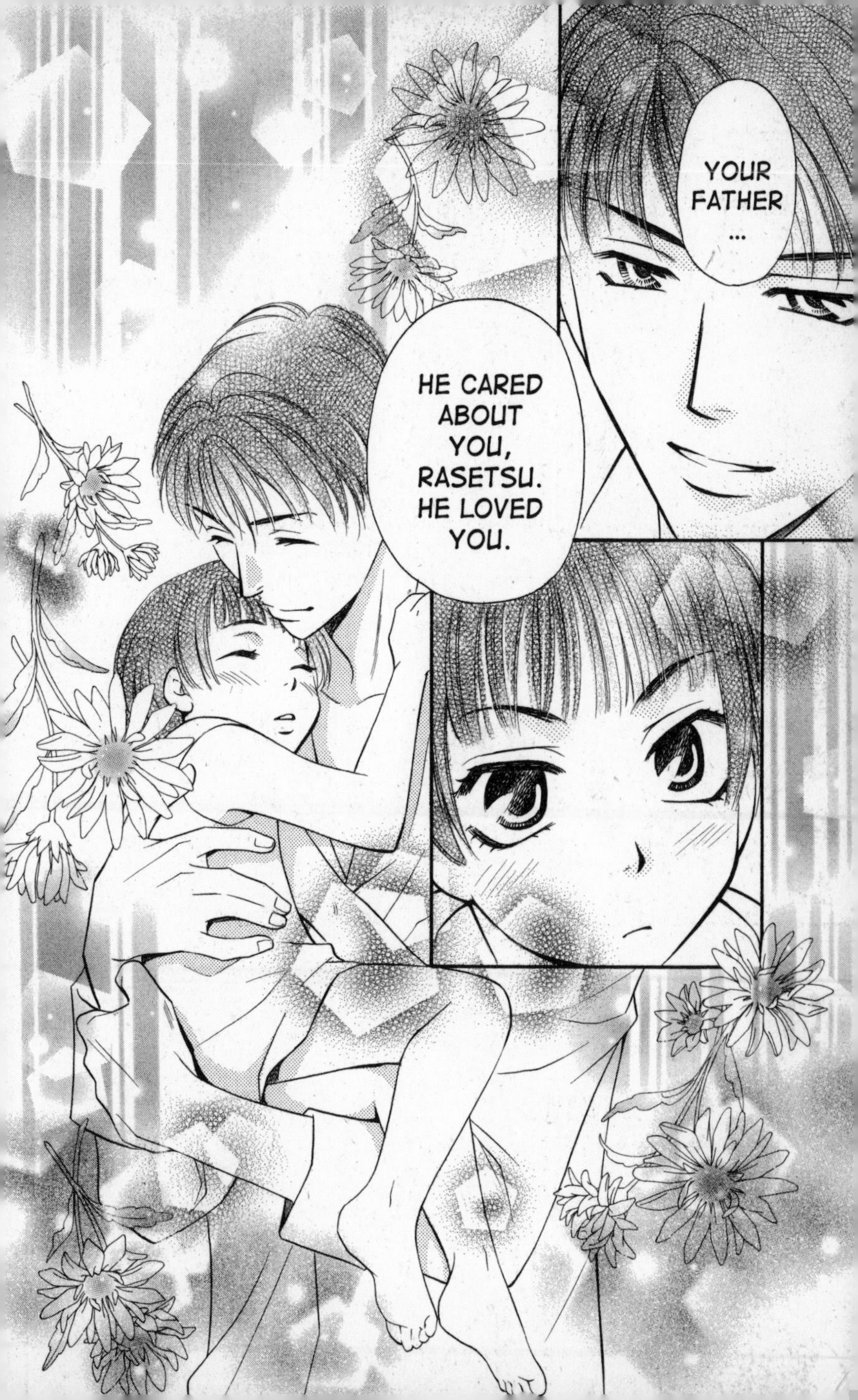
YOUR FATHER ...
HE CARED ABOUT YOU, RASETSU. HE LOVED YOU.

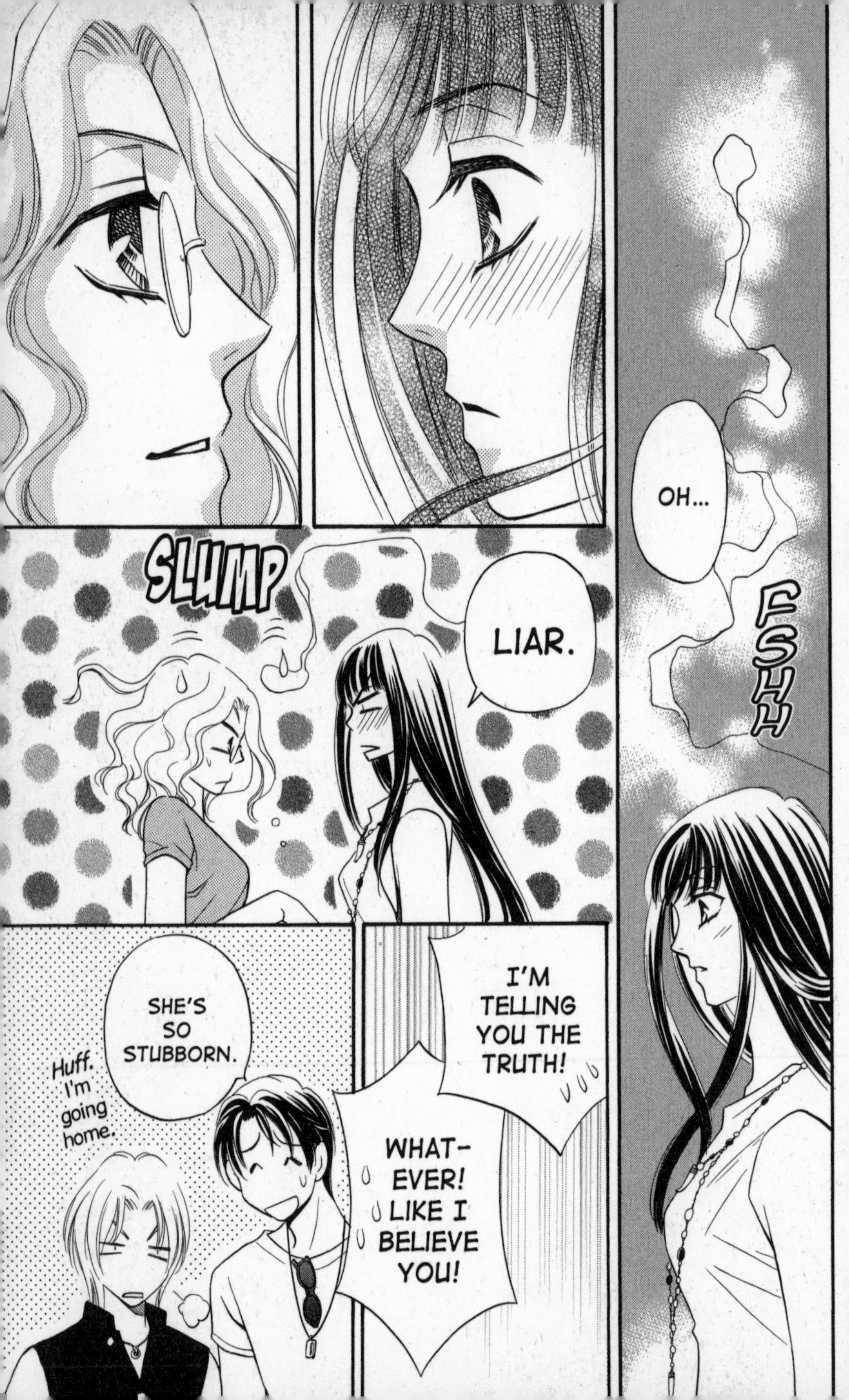
OH...
FSHH
LIAR.
SLUMP
I'M TELLING YOU THE TRUTH!
WHAT-EVER! LIKE I BELIEVE YOU!
SHE'S SO STUBBORN.
Huff. I'm going home.

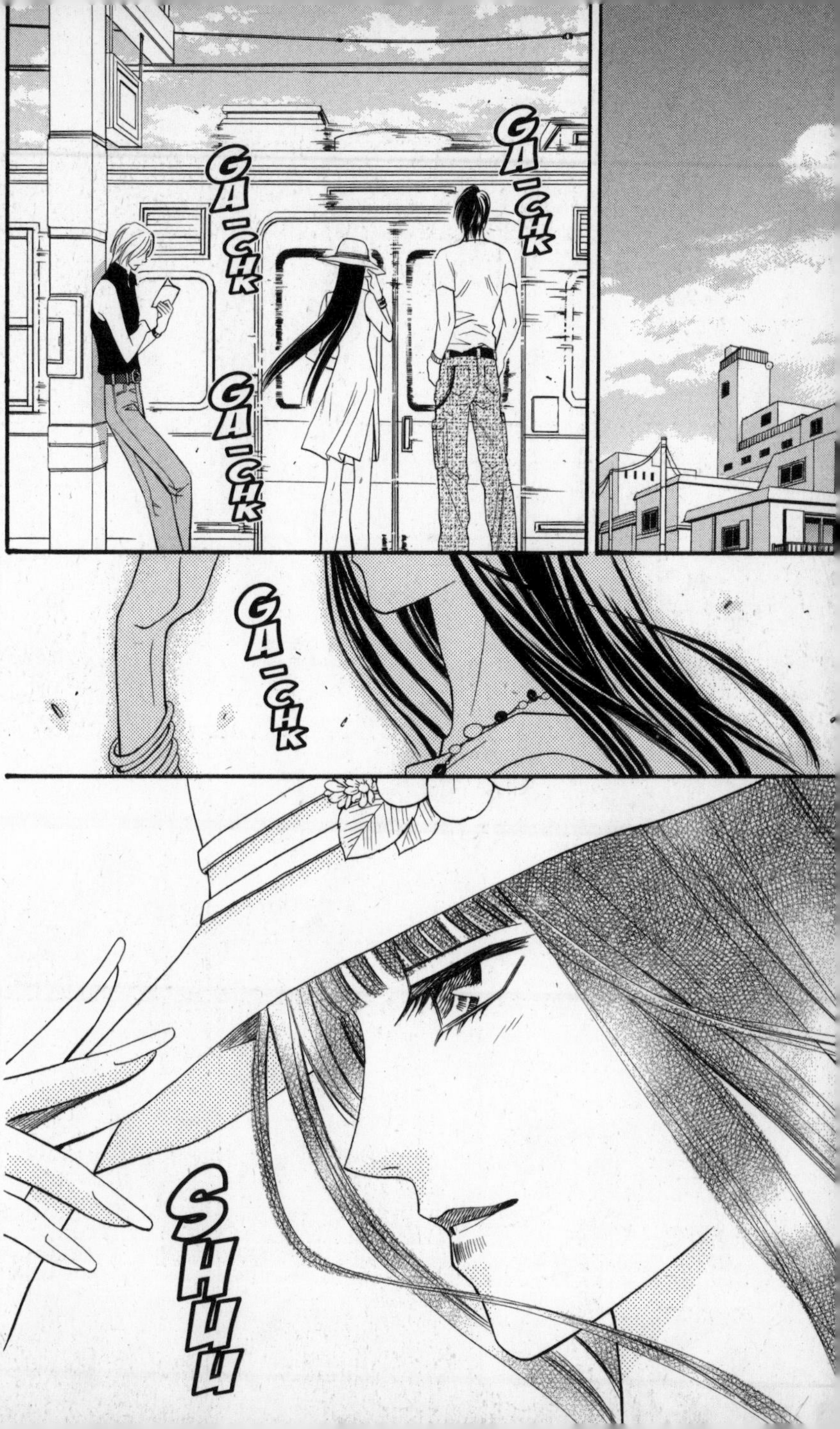
GA-CHK
GA-CHK
GA-CHK
GA-CHK
SHUU

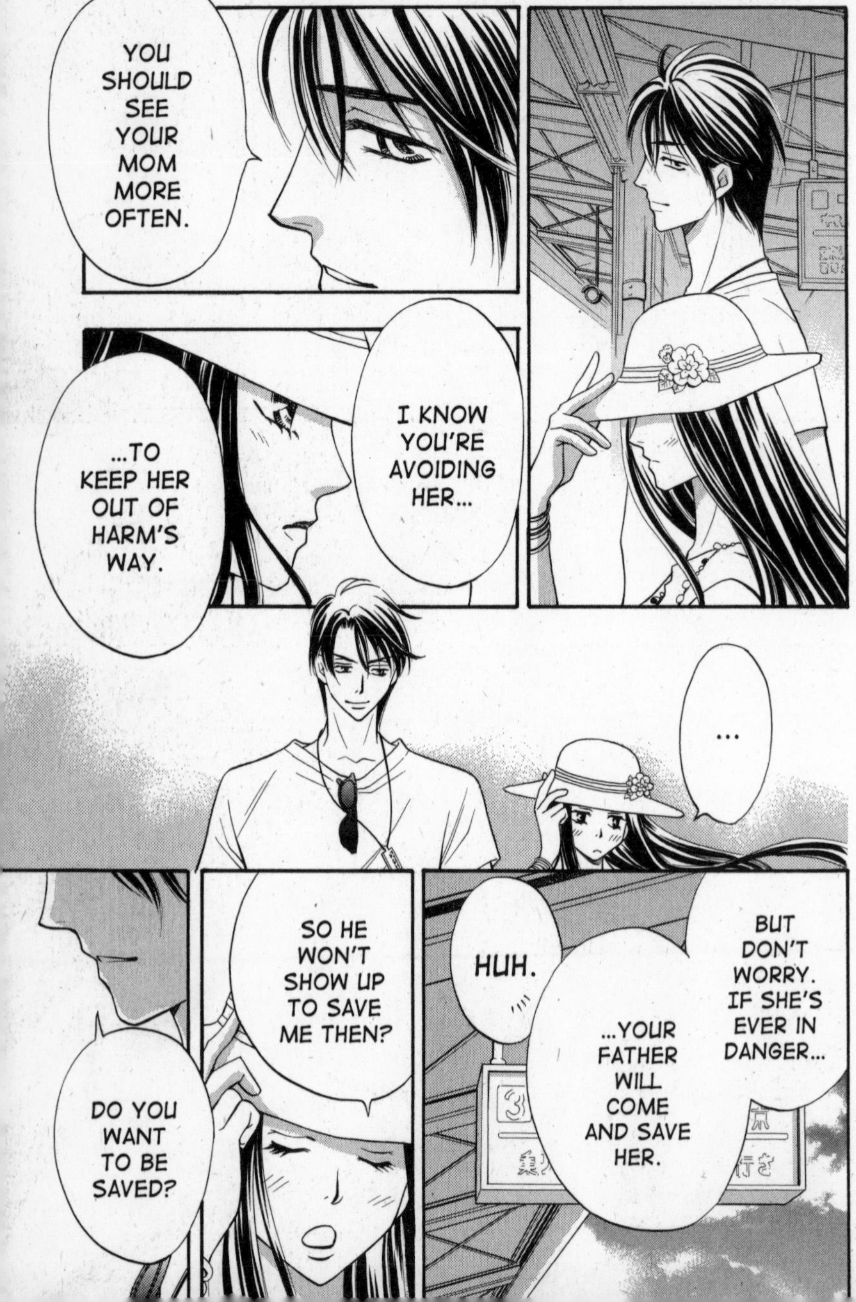
YOU SHOULD SEE YOUR MOM MORE OFTEN.
I KNOW YOU'RE AVOIDING HER...
...TO KEEP HER OUT OF HARM'S WAY.
...
BUT DON'T WORRY. IF SHE'S EVER IN DANGER...
...YOUR FATHER WILL COME AND SAVE HER.
HUH.
SO HE WON'T SHOW UP TO SAVE ME THEN?
DO YOU WANT TO BE SAVED?

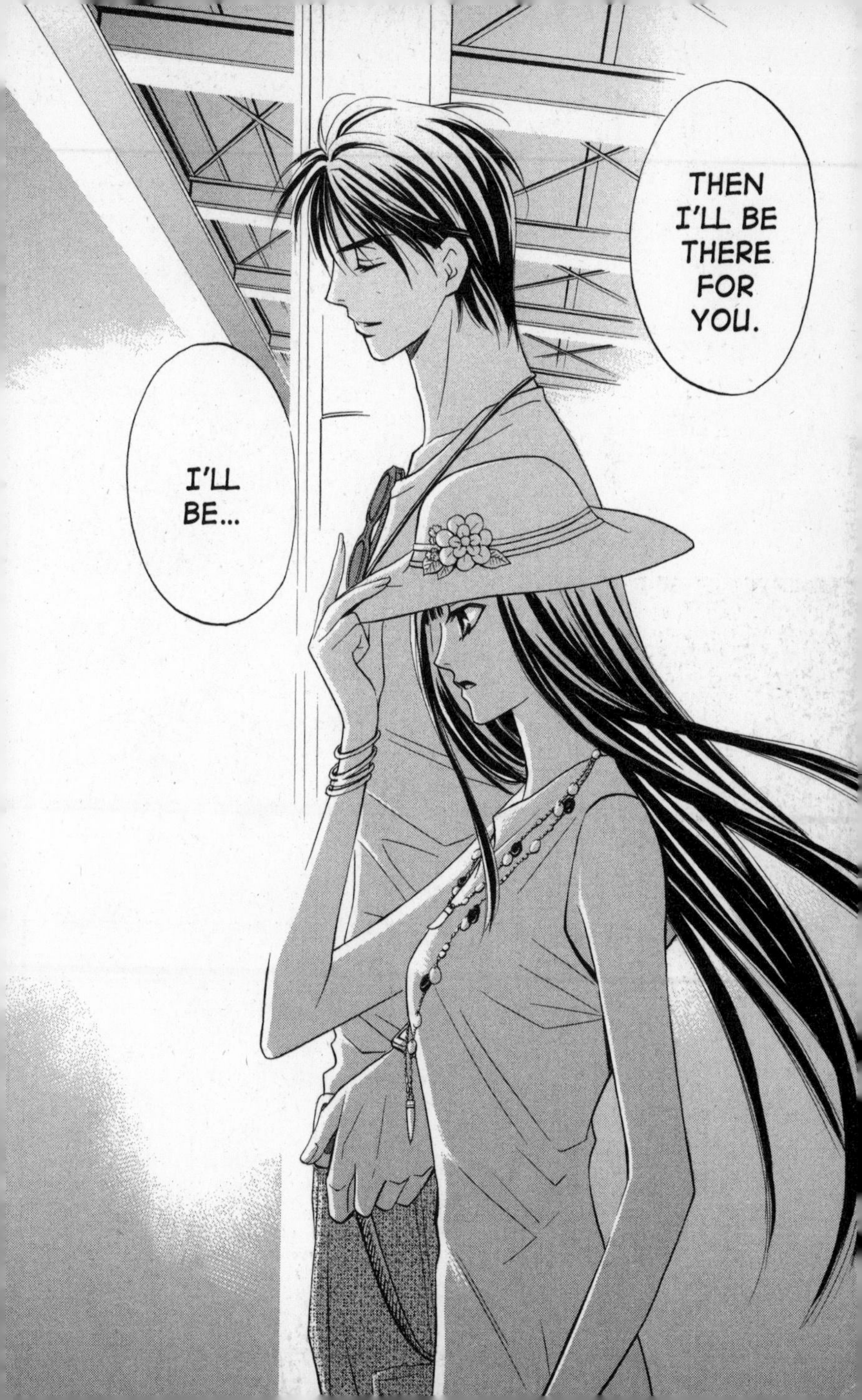
THEN I'LL BE THERE FOR YOU.
I'LL BE...

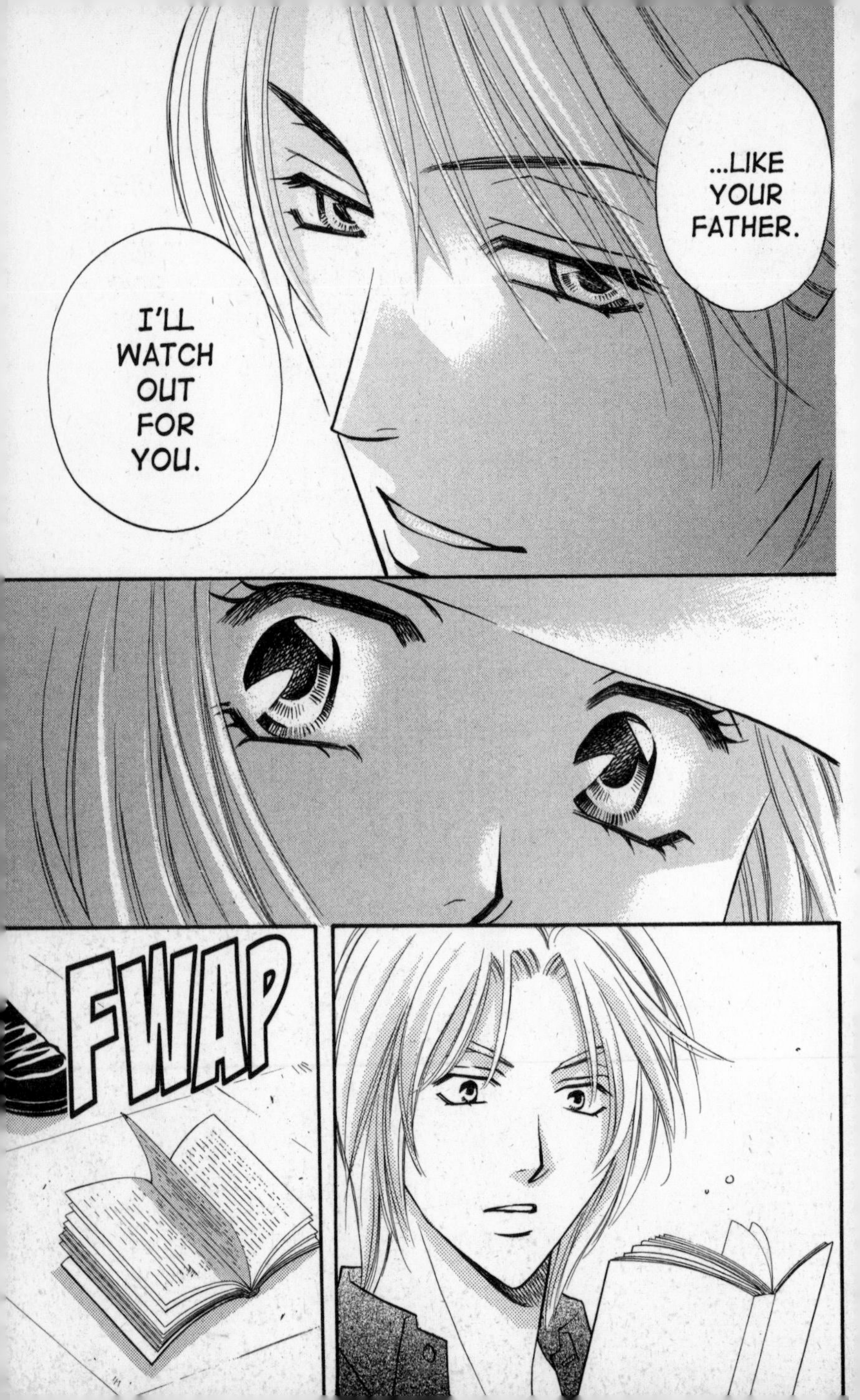
...LIKE YOUR FATHER.
I'LL WATCH OUT FOR YOU.
FWAP

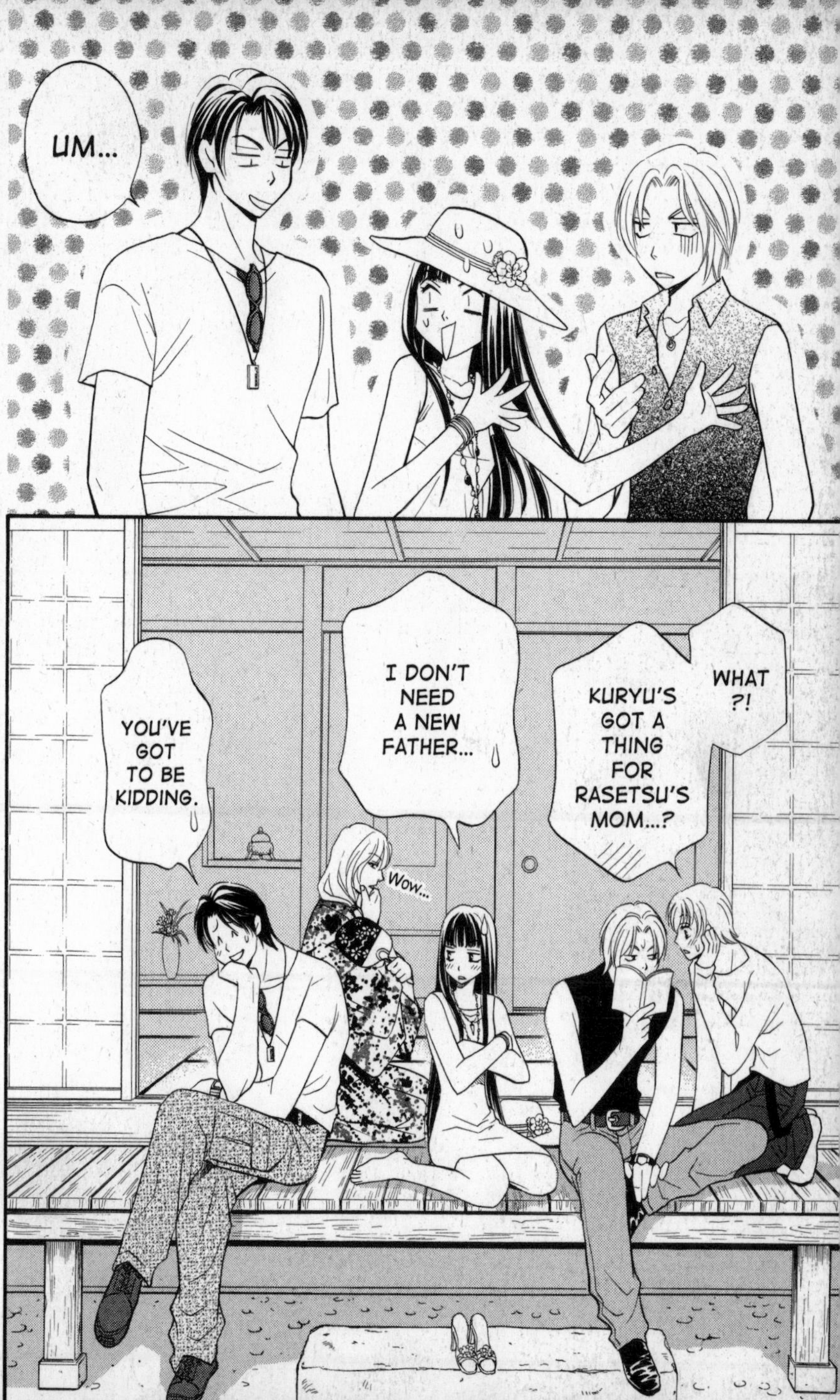
UM...
WHAT?!
KURYU'S GOT A THING FOR RASETSU'S MOM...?
I DON'T NEED A NEW FATHER...
Wow...
YOU'VE GOT TO BE KIDDING.

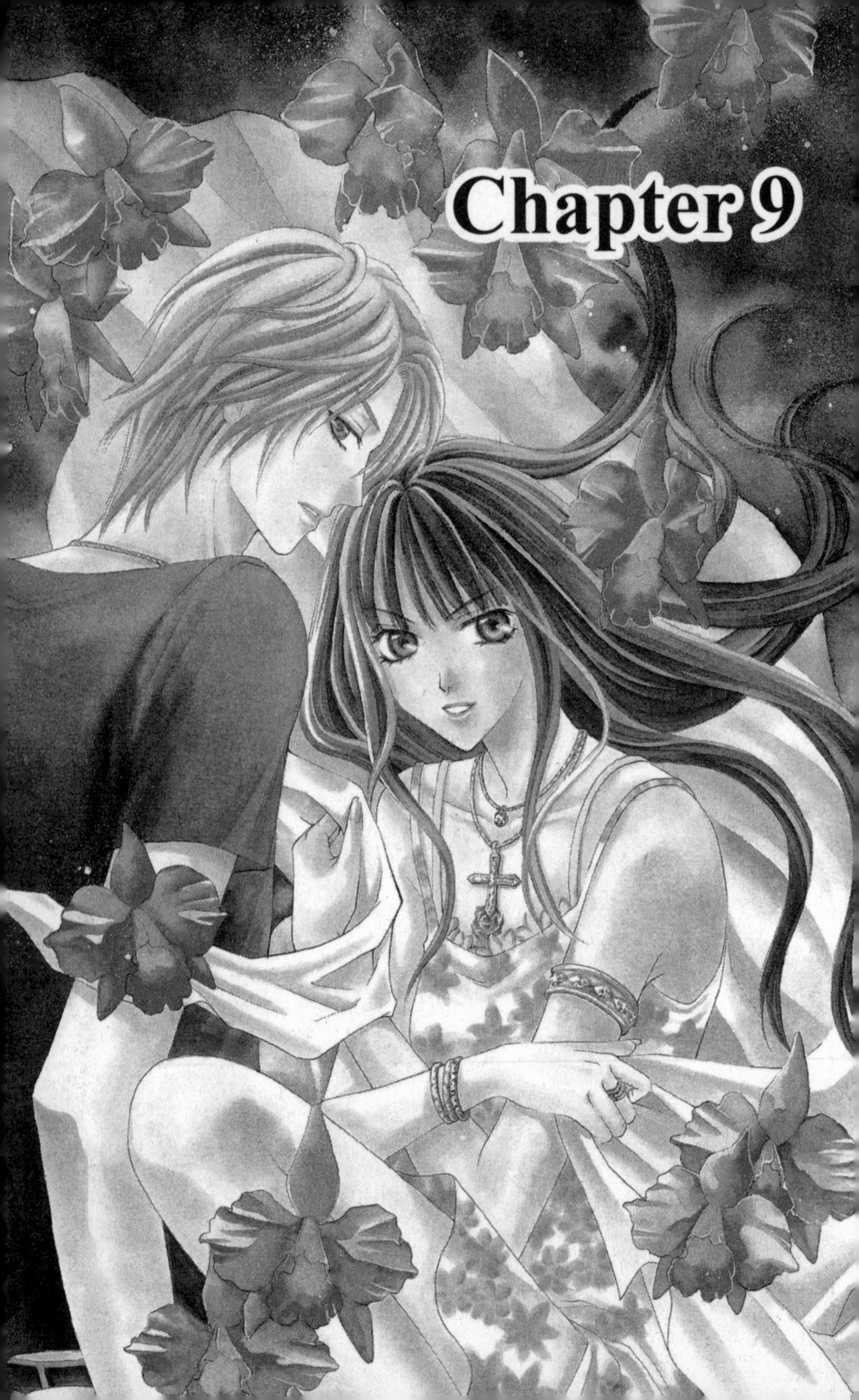
Chapter 9

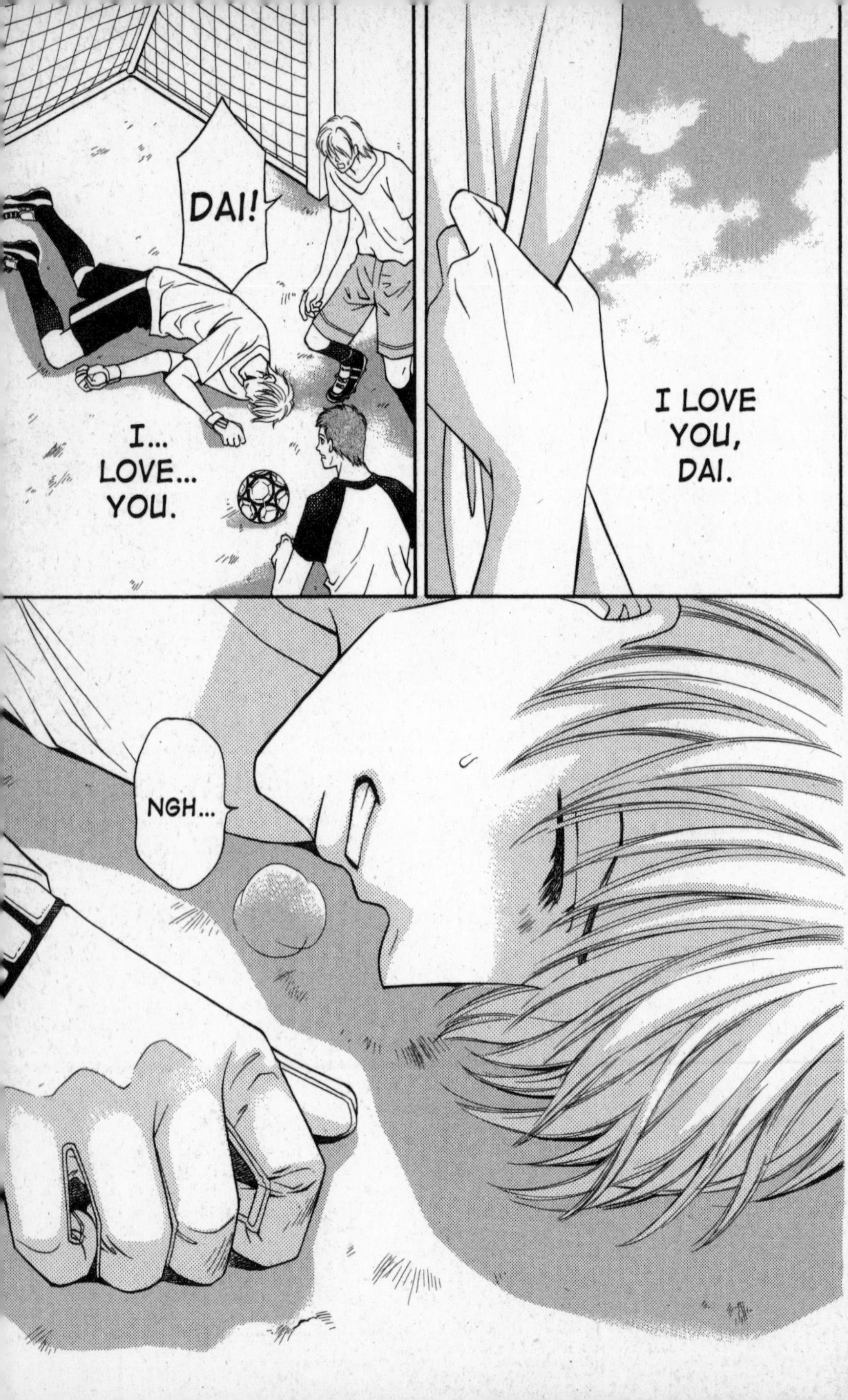
I LOVE YOU, DAI.
DAI!
I... LOVE... YOU.
NGH...

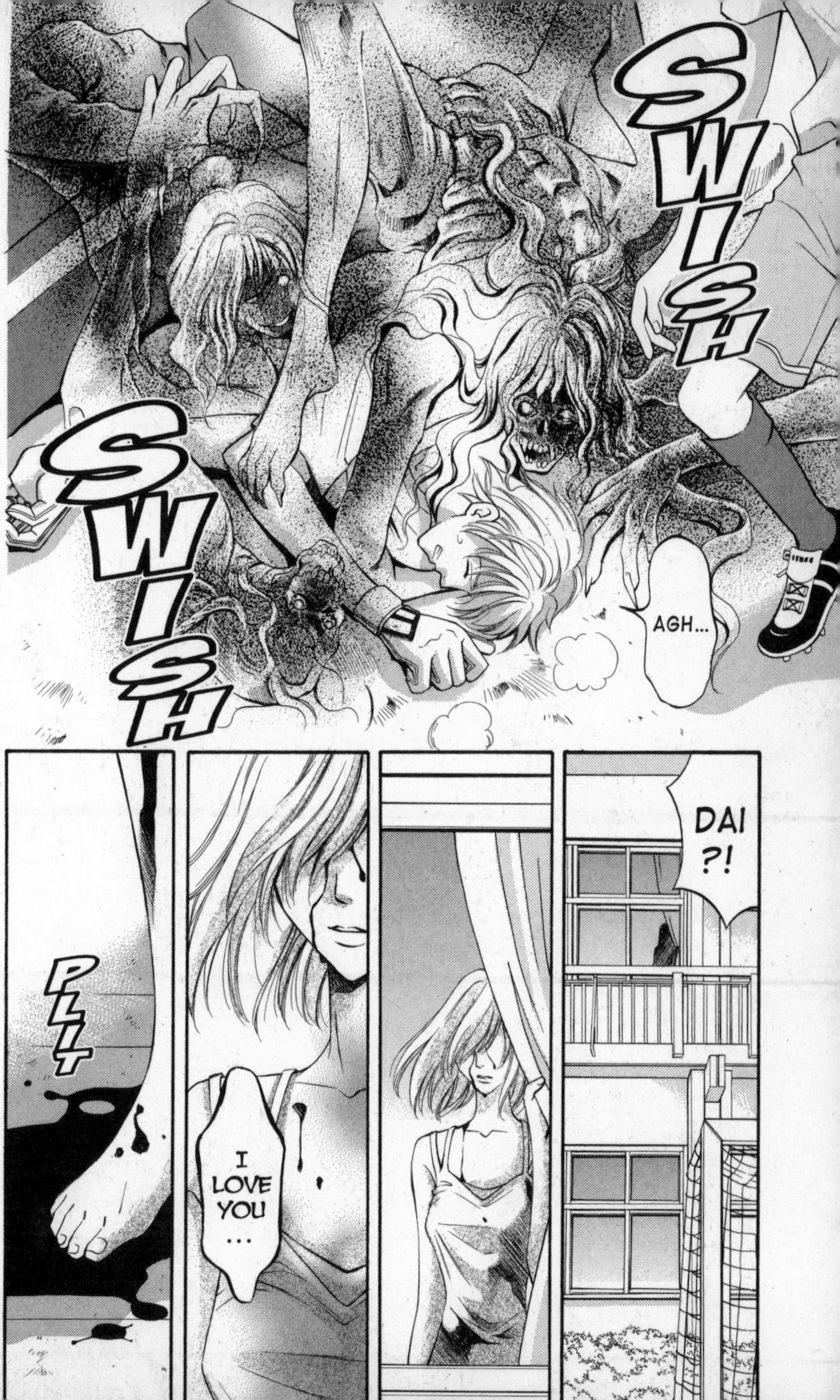
SWISH
SWISH
AGH...
DAI ?!
I LOVE YOU ...
PLIT

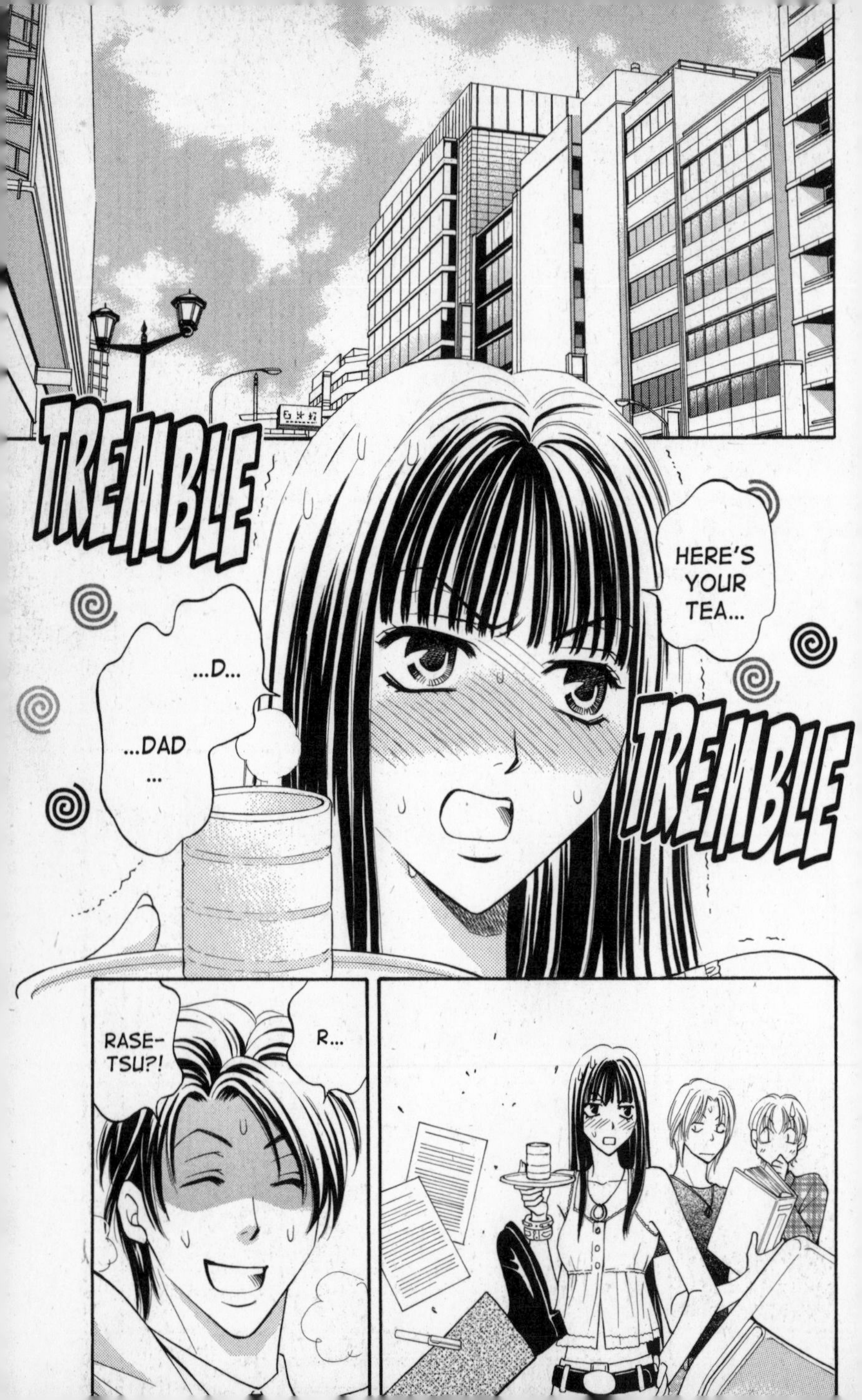
HERE'S YOUR TEA...
TREMBLE
TREMBLE
...D...
...DAD ...
R...
RASE-TSU?!

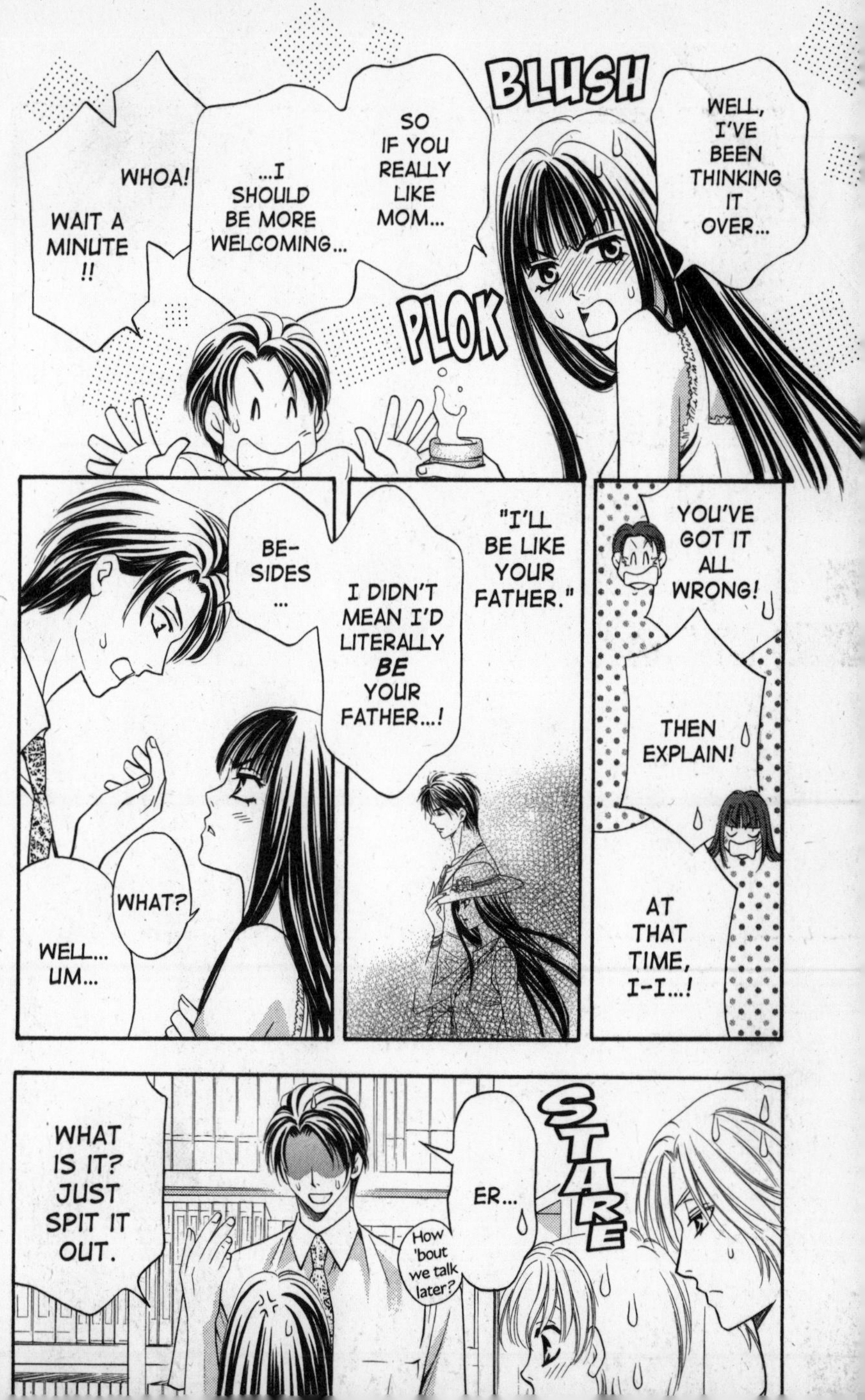
BLUSH
WELL, I'VE BEEN THINKING IT OVER...
SO IF YOU REALLY LIKE MOM...
...I SHOULD BE MORE WELCOMING...
WHOA!
WAIT A MINUTE !!
PLOK
YOU'VE GOT IT ALL WRONG!
THEN EXPLAIN!
AT THAT TIME, I-I...!
"I'LL BE LIKE YOUR FATHER."
BE-SIDES...
I DIDN'T MEAN I'D LITERALLY *BE* YOUR FATHER...!
WHAT?
WELL... UM...
STARE
ER...
How 'bout we talk later?
WHAT IS IT? JUST SPIT IT OUT.

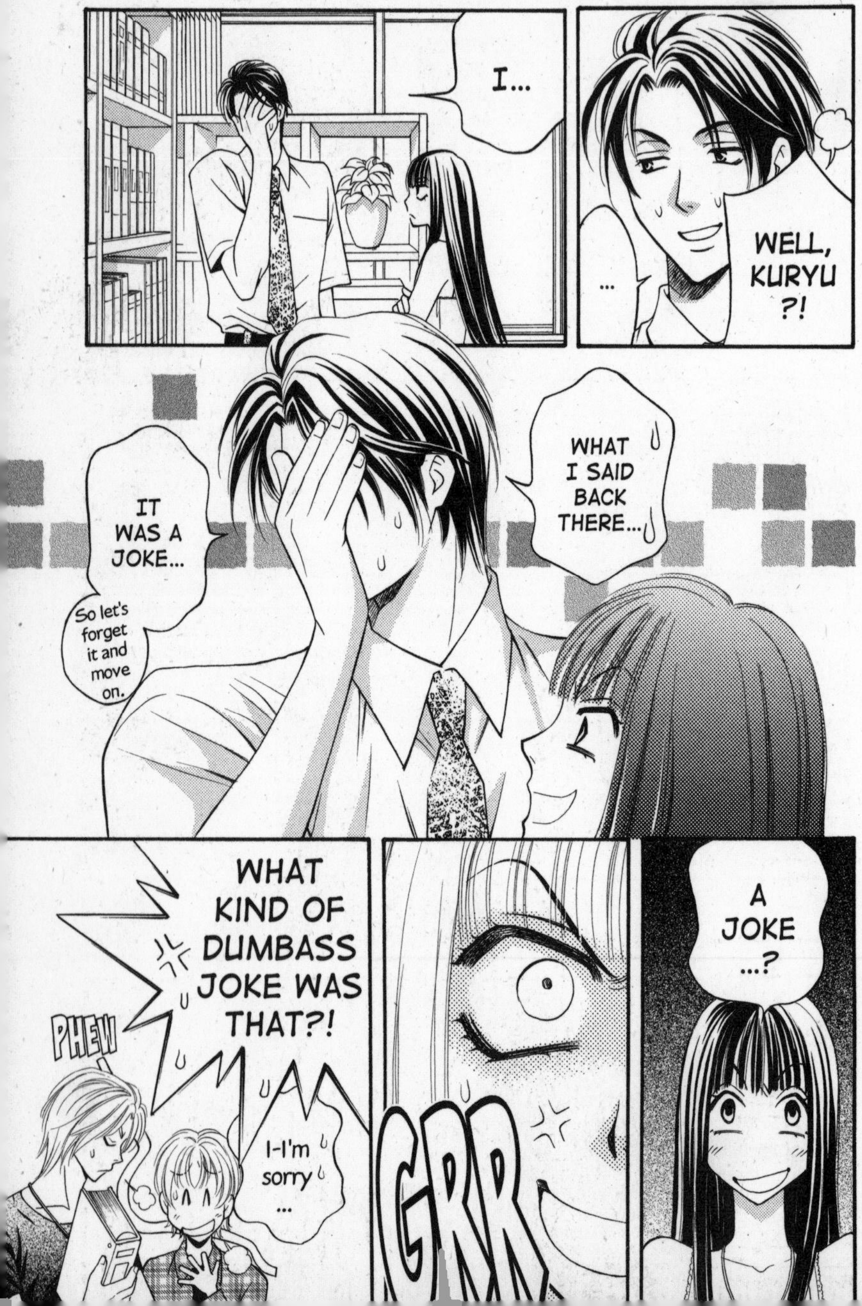
WELL, KURYU ?!
...
I...
WHAT I SAID BACK THERE...
IT WAS A JOKE...
So let's forget it and move on.
A JOKE ...?
GRR
WHAT KIND OF DUMBASS JOKE WAS THAT?!
PHEW
I-I'm sorry ...

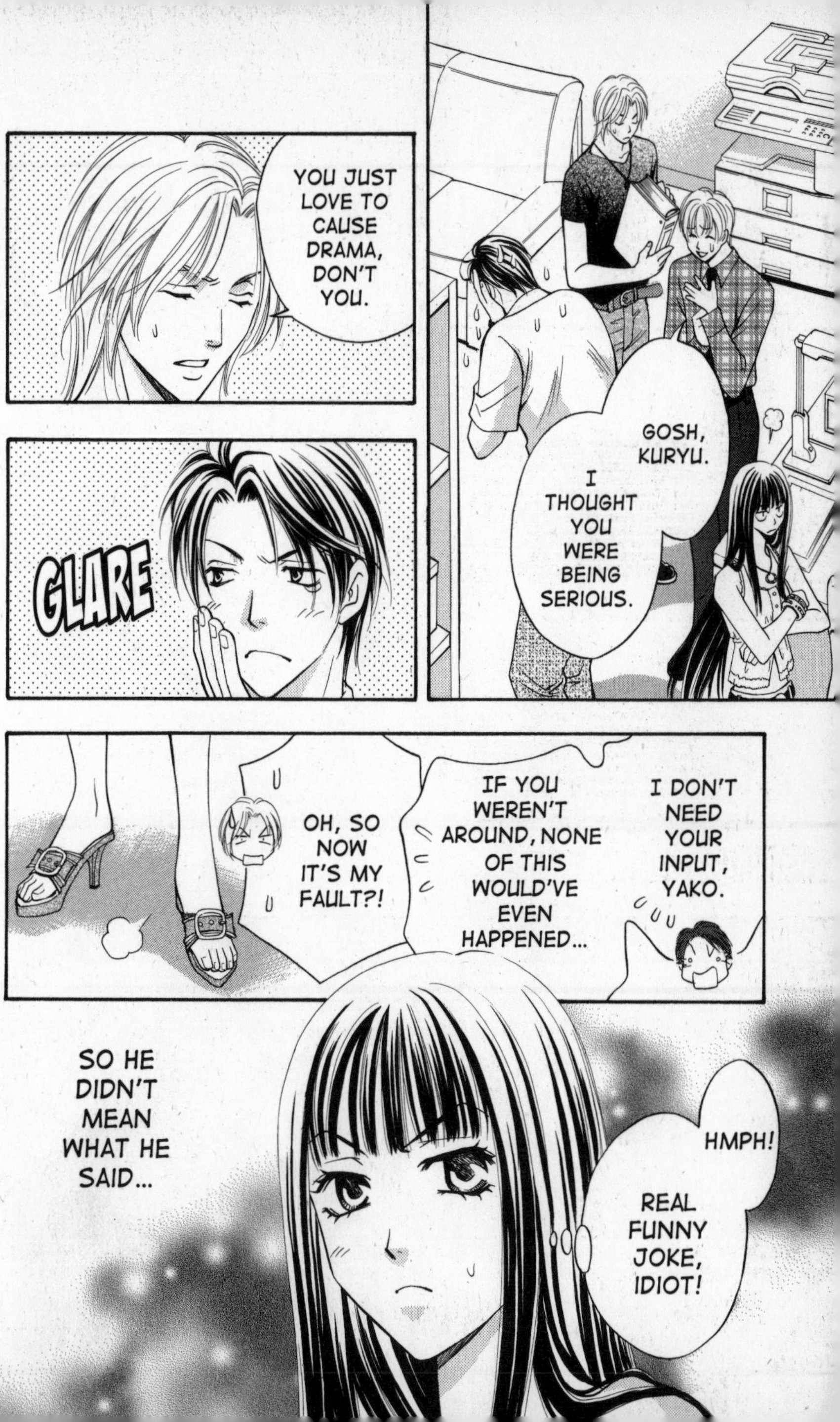
GOSH, KURYU. I THOUGHT YOU WERE BEING SERIOUS.
YOU JUST LOVE TO CAUSE DRAMA, DON'T YOU.
GLARE
I DON'T NEED YOUR INPUT, YAKO.
IF YOU WEREN'T AROUND, NONE OF THIS WOULD'VE EVEN HAPPENED...
OH, SO NOW IT'S MY FAULT?!
HMPH!
REAL FUNNY JOKE, IDIOT!
SO HE DIDN'T MEAN WHAT HE SAID...

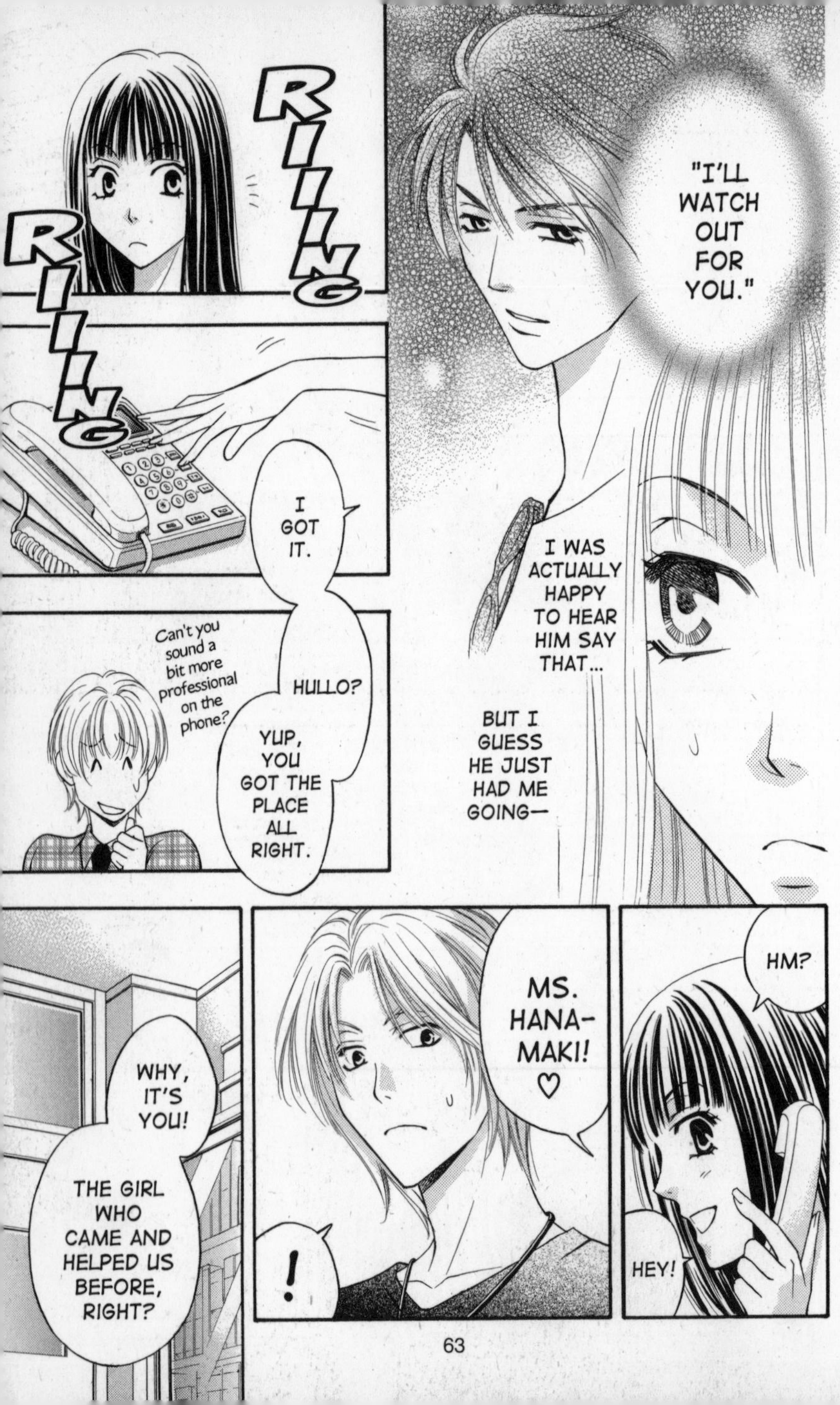
"I'LL WATCH OUT FOR YOU."
I WAS ACTUALLY HAPPY TO HEAR HIM SAY THAT...
BUT I GUESS HE JUST HAD ME GOING—
RIIING
RIIING
I GOT IT.
HULLO?
YUP, YOU GOT THE PLACE ALL RIGHT.
Can't you sound a bit more professional on the phone?
HM?
HEY!
MS. HANA-MAKI! ♡
!
WHY, IT'S YOU!
THE GIRL WHO CAME AND HELPED US BEFORE, RIGHT?

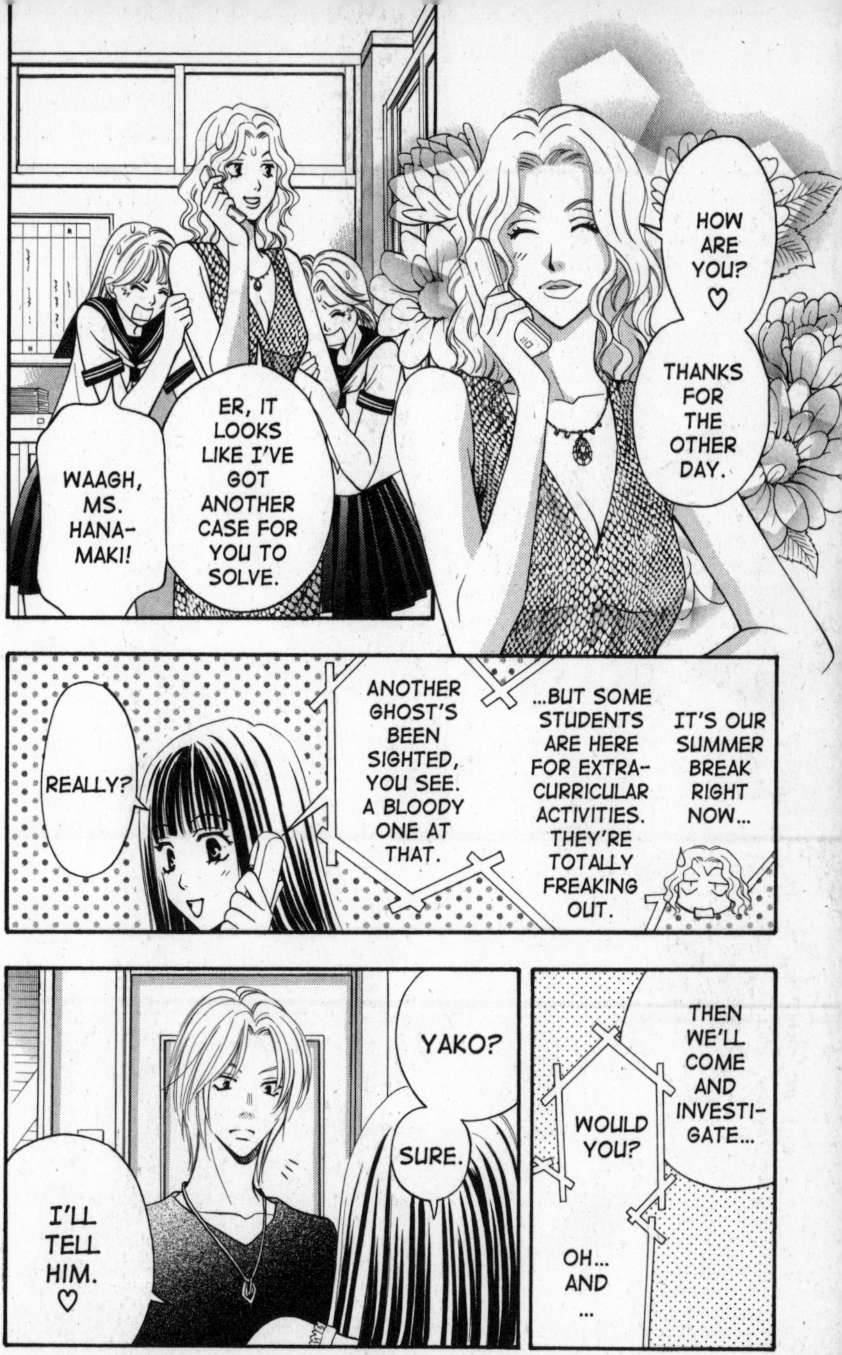
HOW ARE YOU? ♡
THANKS FOR THE OTHER DAY.
ER, IT LOOKS LIKE I'VE GOT ANOTHER CASE FOR YOU TO SOLVE.
WAAGH, MS. HANA-MAKI!
IT'S OUR SUMMER BREAK RIGHT NOW...
...BUT SOME STUDENTS ARE HERE FOR EXTRA-CURRICULAR ACTIVITIES. THEY'RE TOTALLY FREAKING OUT.
ANOTHER GHOST'S BEEN SIGHTED, YOU SEE. A BLOODY ONE AT THAT.
REALLY?
THEN WE'LL COME AND INVESTI-GATE...
WOULD YOU?
OH... AND ...
YAKO?
SURE.
I'LL TELL HIM. ♡

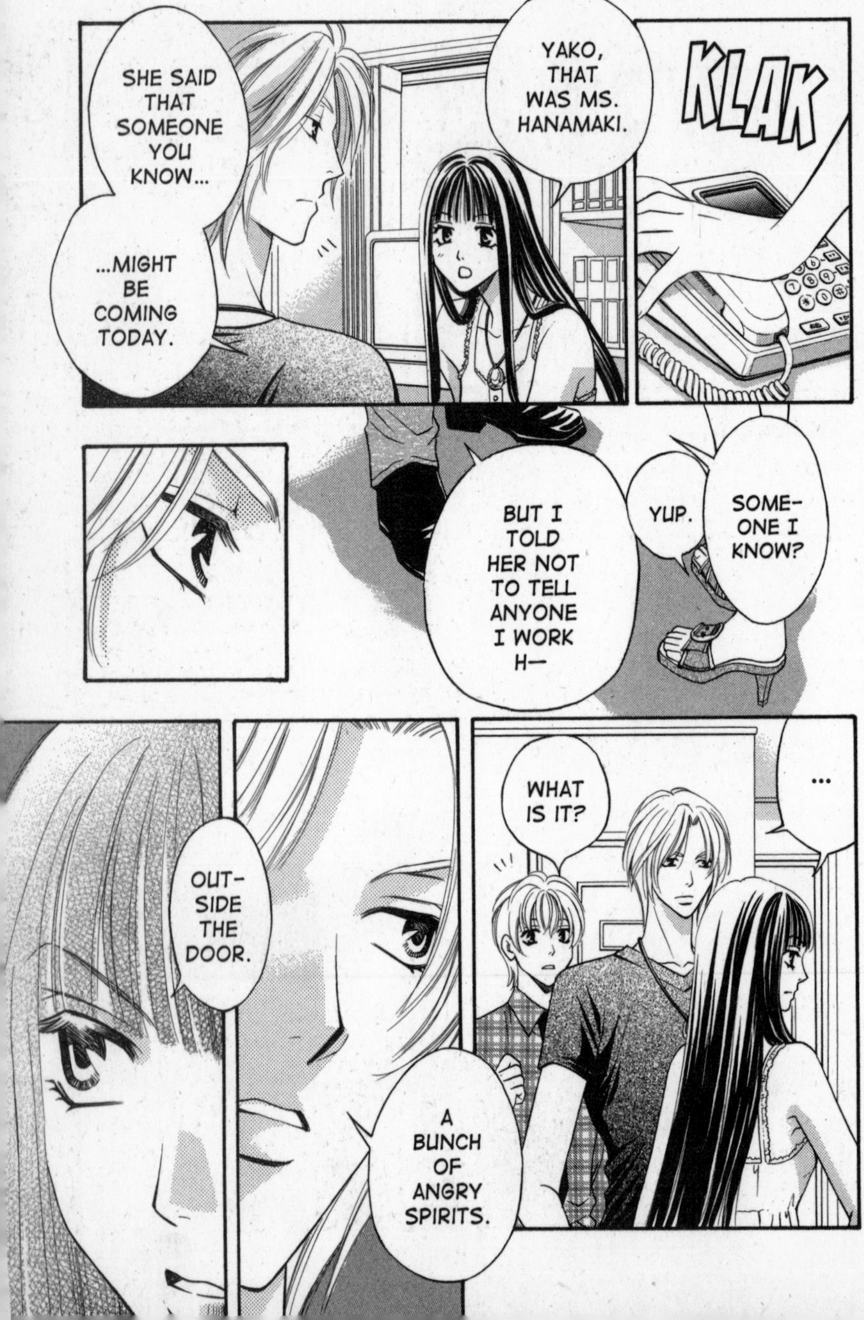
KLAK
YAKO, THAT WAS MS. HANAMAKI.
SHE SAID THAT SOMEONE YOU KNOW...
...MIGHT BE COMING TODAY.
SOME-ONE I KNOW?
YUP.
BUT I TOLD HER NOT TO TELL ANYONE I WORK H—
...
WHAT IS IT?
OUT-SIDE THE DOOR.
A BUNCH OF ANGRY SPIRITS.

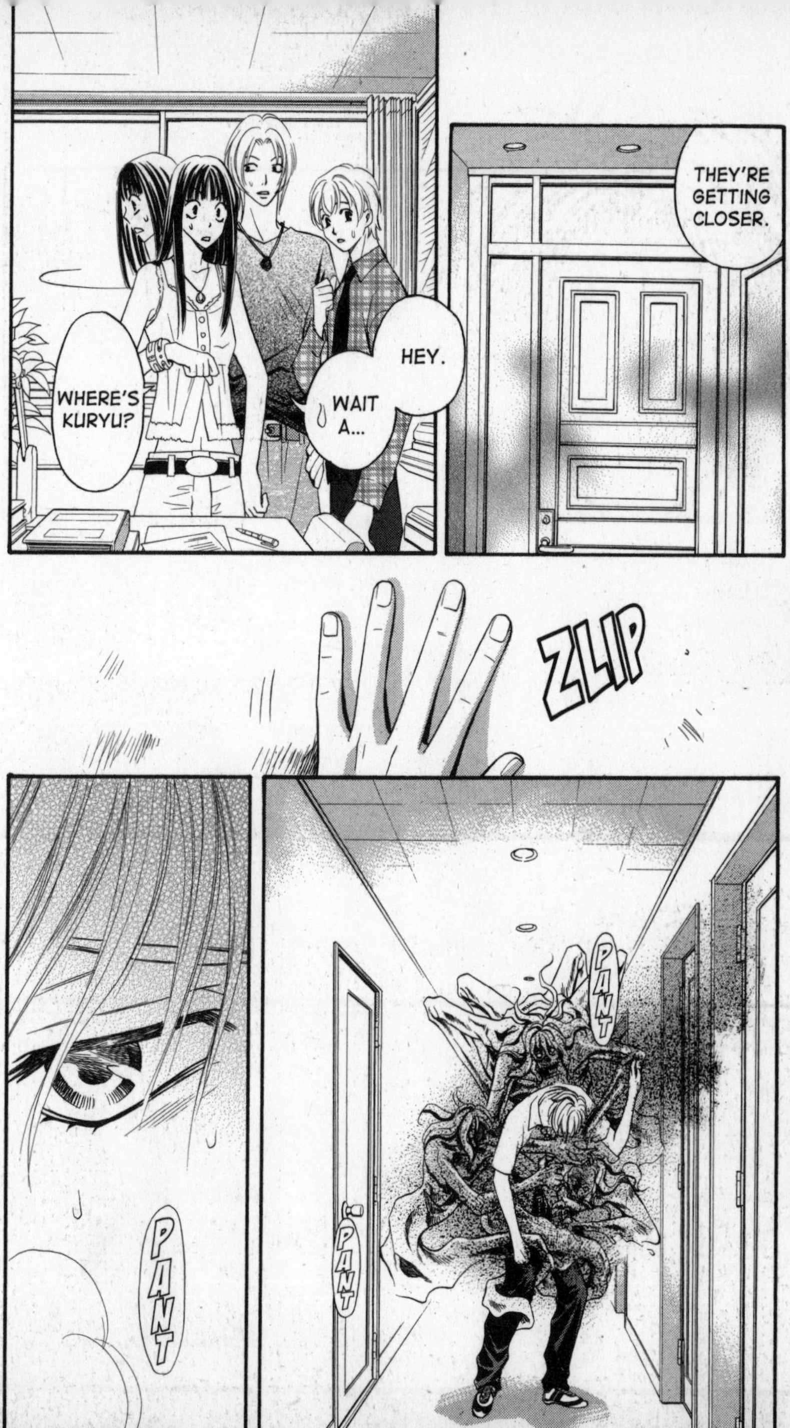
THEY'RE GETTING CLOSER.
HEY.
WAIT A...
WHERE'S KURYU?
ZLIP
PANT
PANT
PANT

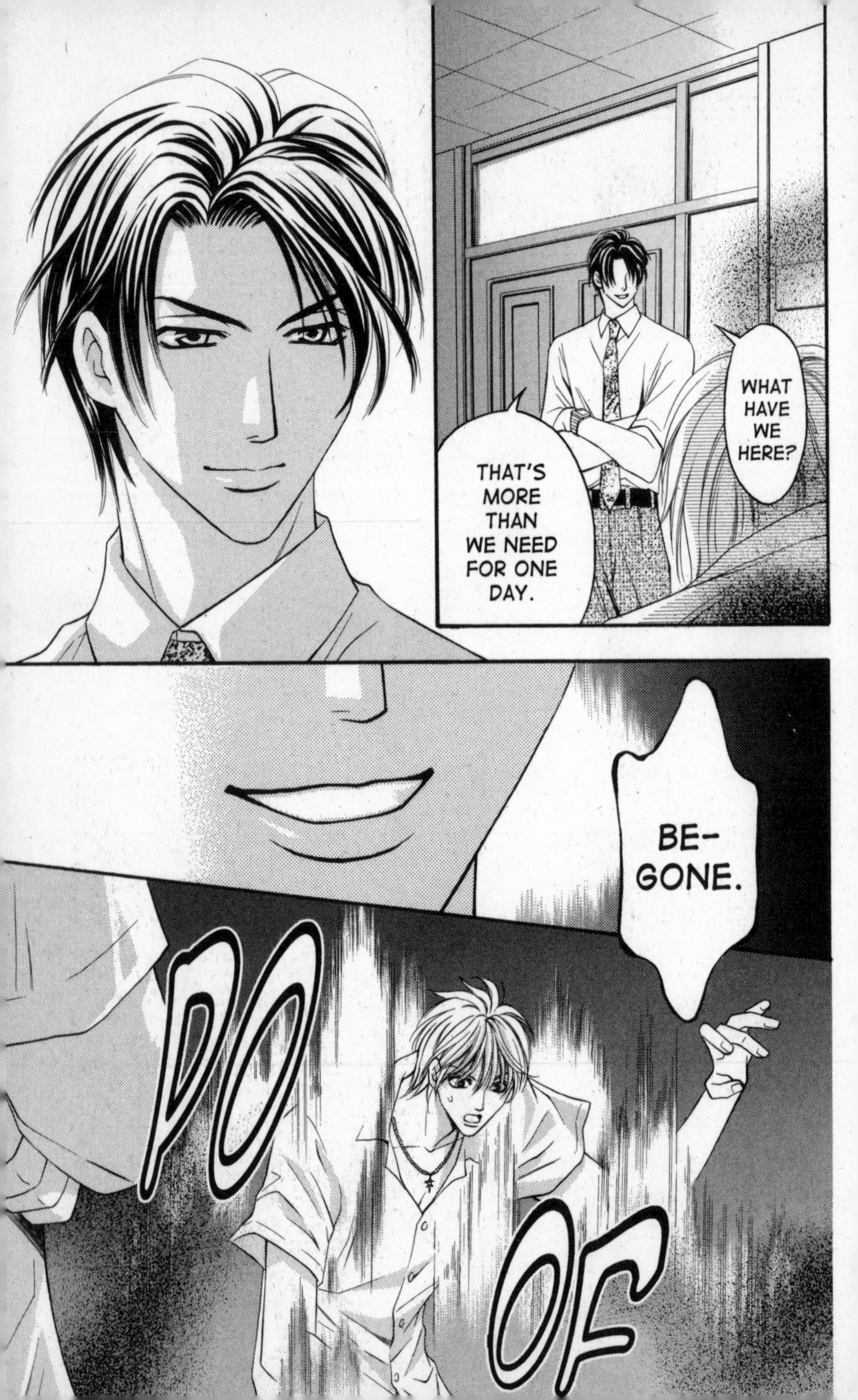
WHAT HAVE WE HERE?
THAT'S MORE THAN WE NEED FOR ONE DAY.
BE-GONE.
DO
OF

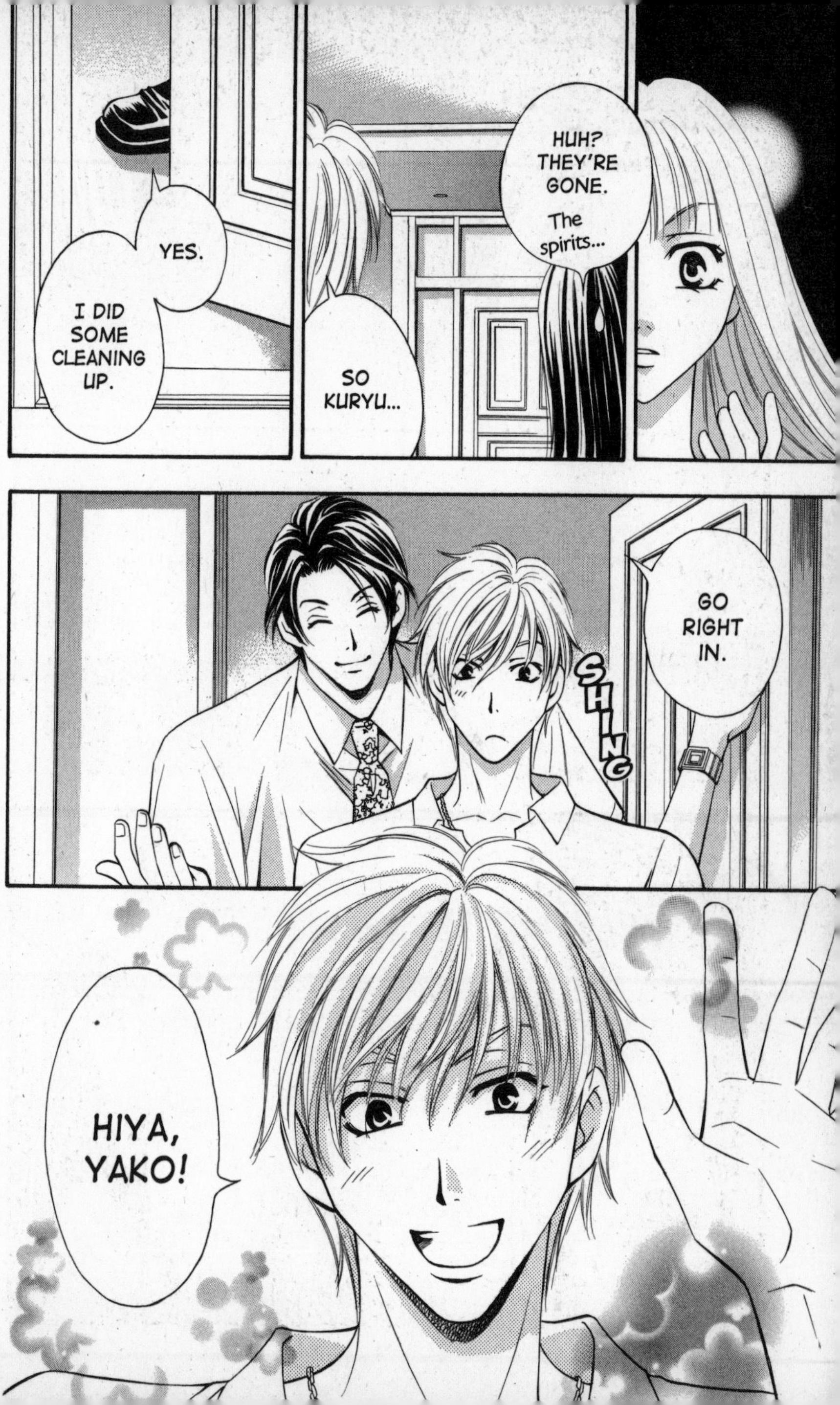
HUH? THEY'RE GONE.
The spirits...
SO KURYU...
YES.
I DID SOME CLEANING UP.
GO RIGHT IN.
SHING
HIYA, YAKO!

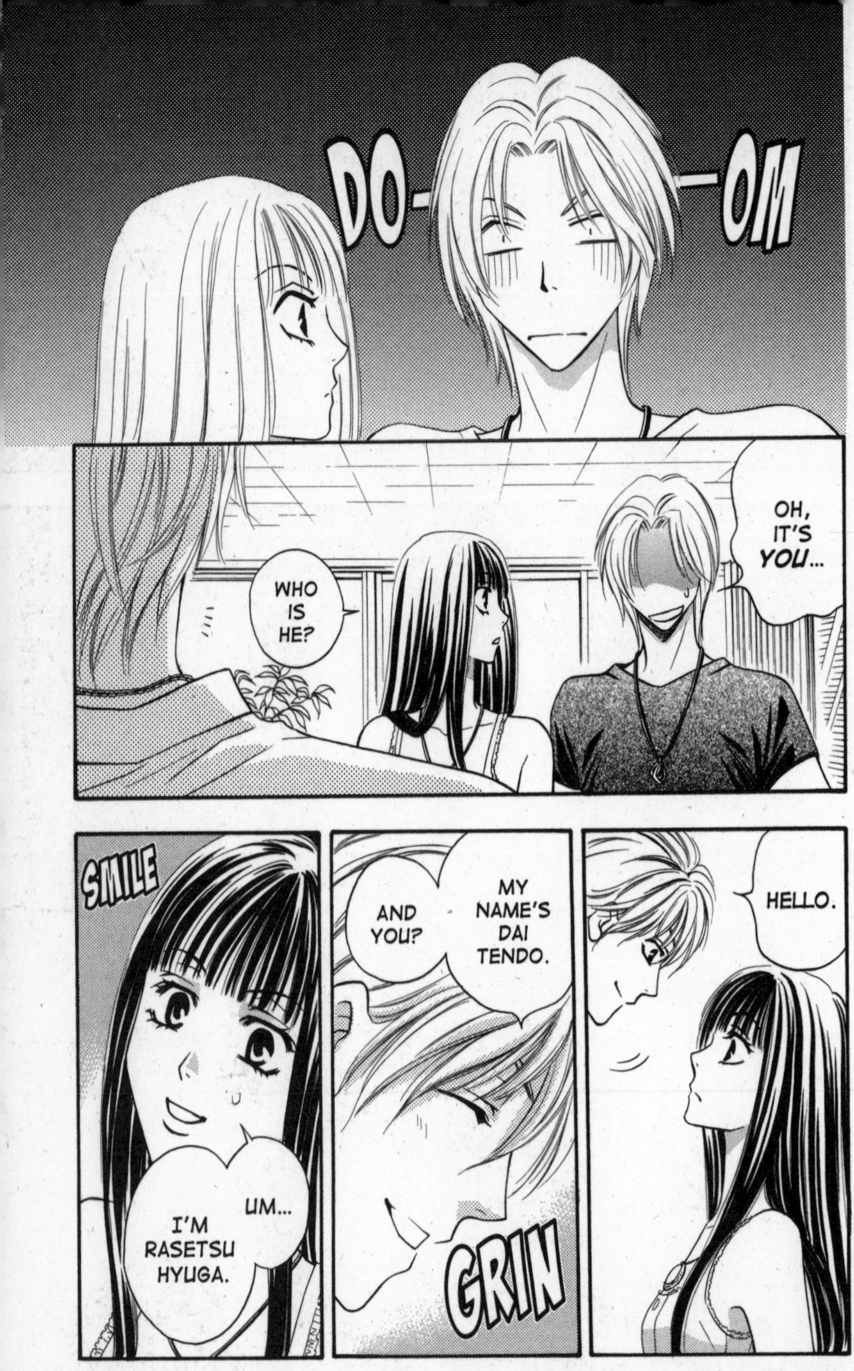
DO-OM
OH, IT'S *YOU*...
WHO IS HE?
HELLO.
MY NAME'S DAI TENDO.
AND YOU?
GRIN
SMILE
UM...
I'M RASETSU HYUGA.

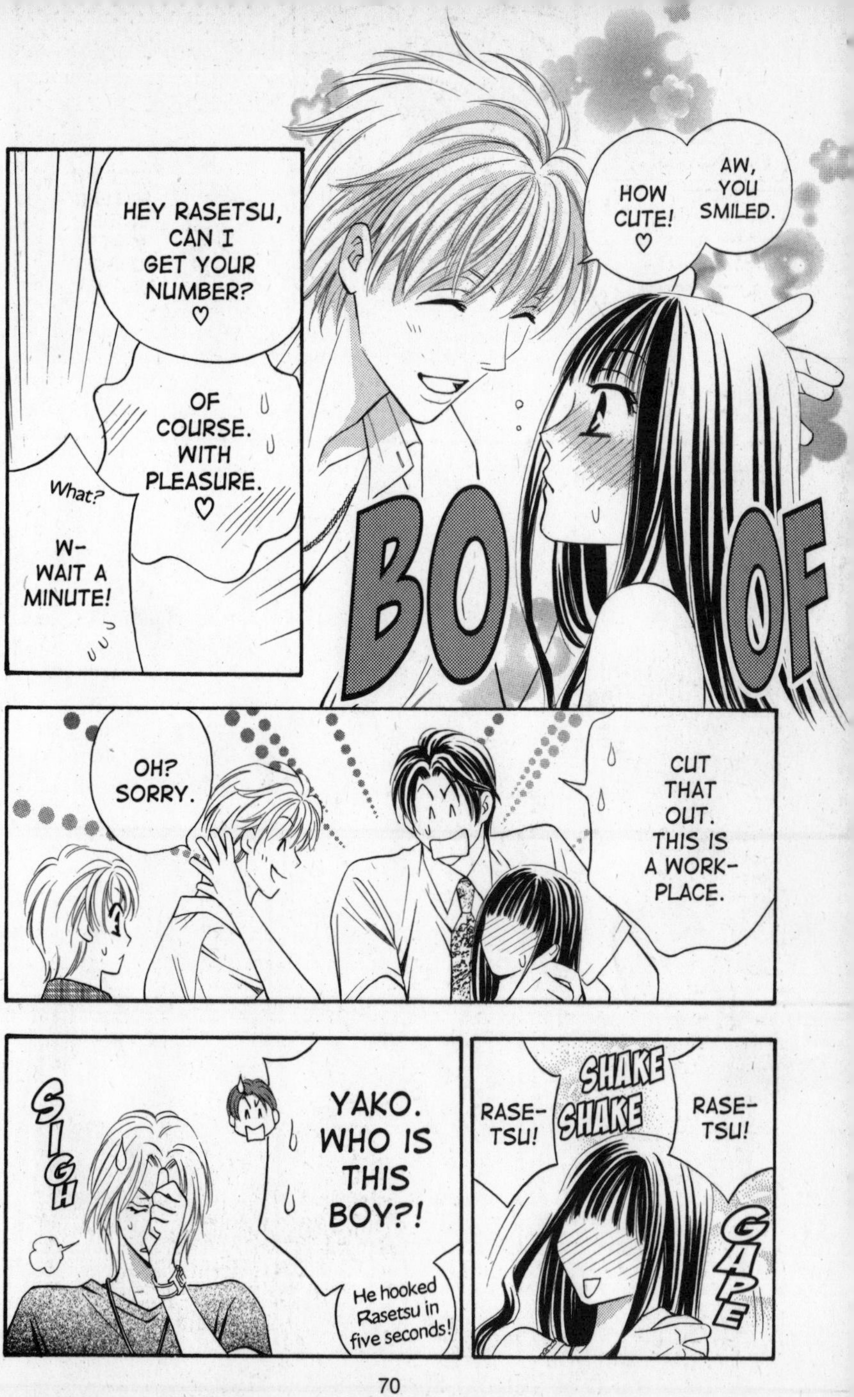
AW, YOU SMILED.
HOW CUTE! ♡
BO OF
HEY RASETSU, CAN I GET YOUR NUMBER? ♡
OF COURSE. WITH PLEASURE. ♡
What?
W-WAIT A MINUTE!
CUT THAT OUT. THIS IS A WORK-PLACE.
OH? SORRY.
RASE-TSU!
SHAKE SHAKE
RASE-TSU!
GAPE
YAKO. WHO IS THIS BOY?!
He hooked Rasetsu in five seconds!
SIGH

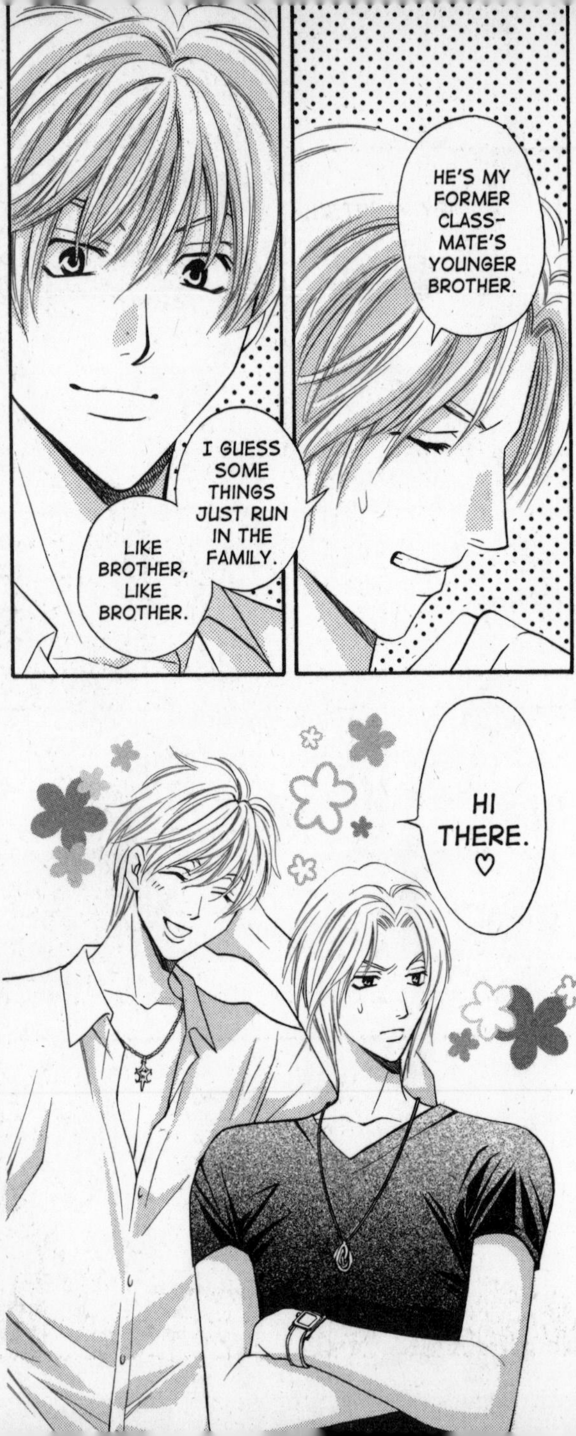
HE'S MY FORMER CLASS-MATE'S YOUNGER BROTHER.
I GUESS SOME THINGS JUST RUN IN THE FAMILY.
LIKE BROTHER, LIKE BROTHER.
HI THERE. ♡

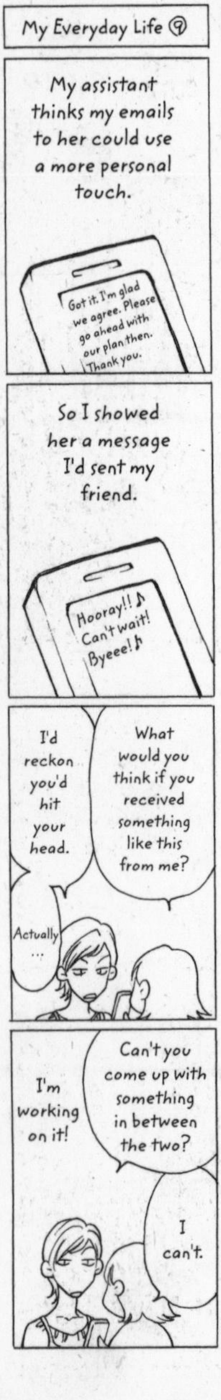
My Everyday Life 9
My assistant thinks my emails to her could use a more personal touch.
Got it. I'm glad we agree. Please go ahead with our plan then. Thank you.
So I showed her a message I'd sent my friend.
Hooray!! ♪ Can't wait! Byeee! ♪
What would you think if you received something like this from me?
I'd reckon you'd hit your head.
Actually...
Can't you come up with something in between the two?
I'm working on it!
I can't.

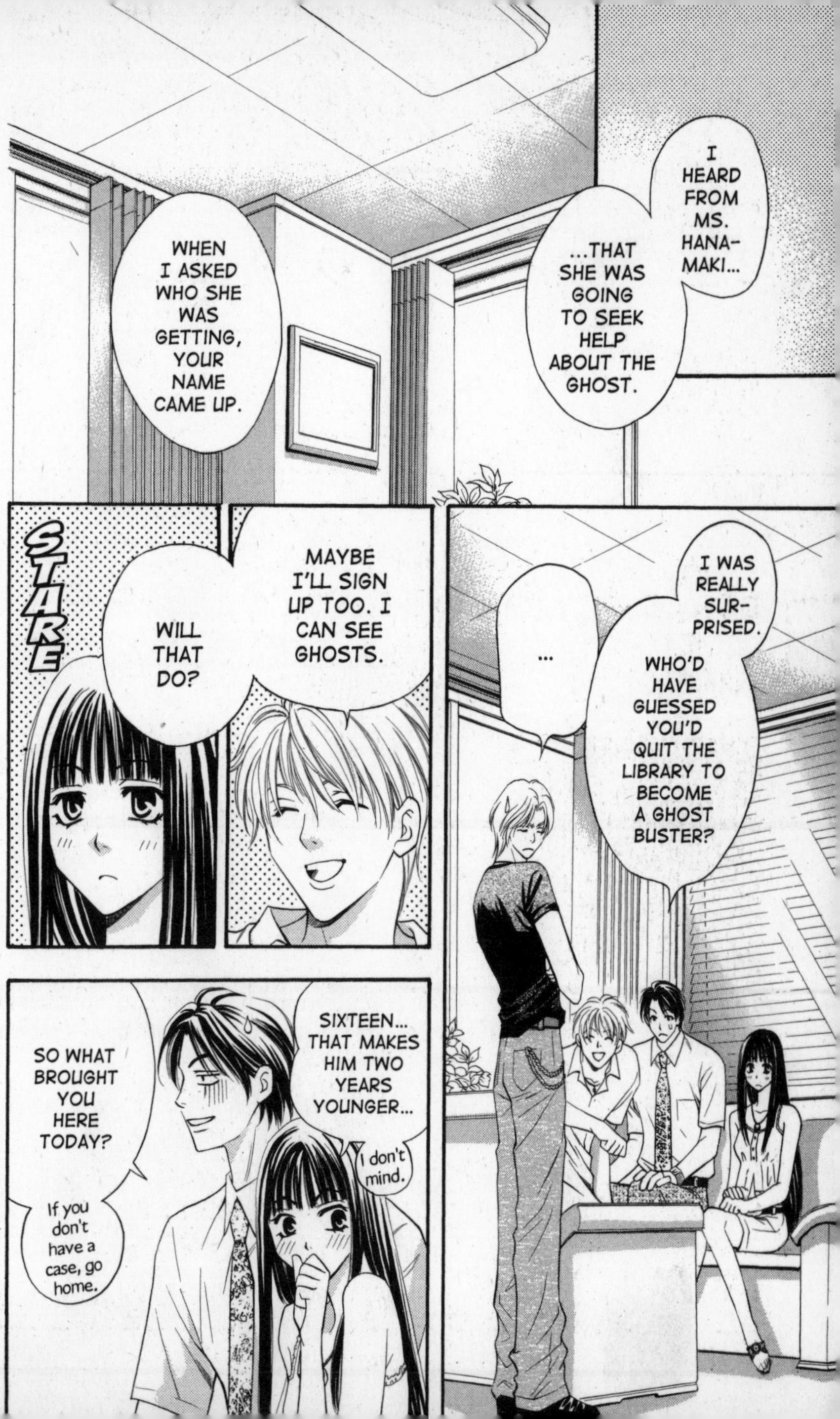
I HEARD FROM MS. HANAMAKI...
...THAT SHE WAS GOING TO SEEK HELP ABOUT THE GHOST.
WHEN I ASKED WHO SHE WAS GETTING, YOUR NAME CAME UP.
I WAS REALLY SURPRISED.
WHO'D HAVE GUESSED YOU'D QUIT THE LIBRARY TO BECOME A GHOST BUSTER?
...
MAYBE I'LL SIGN UP TOO. I CAN SEE GHOSTS.
WILL THAT DO?
STARE
SIXTEEN... THAT MAKES HIM TWO YEARS YOUNGER...
I don't mind.
SO WHAT BROUGHT YOU HERE TODAY?
If you don't have a case, go home.

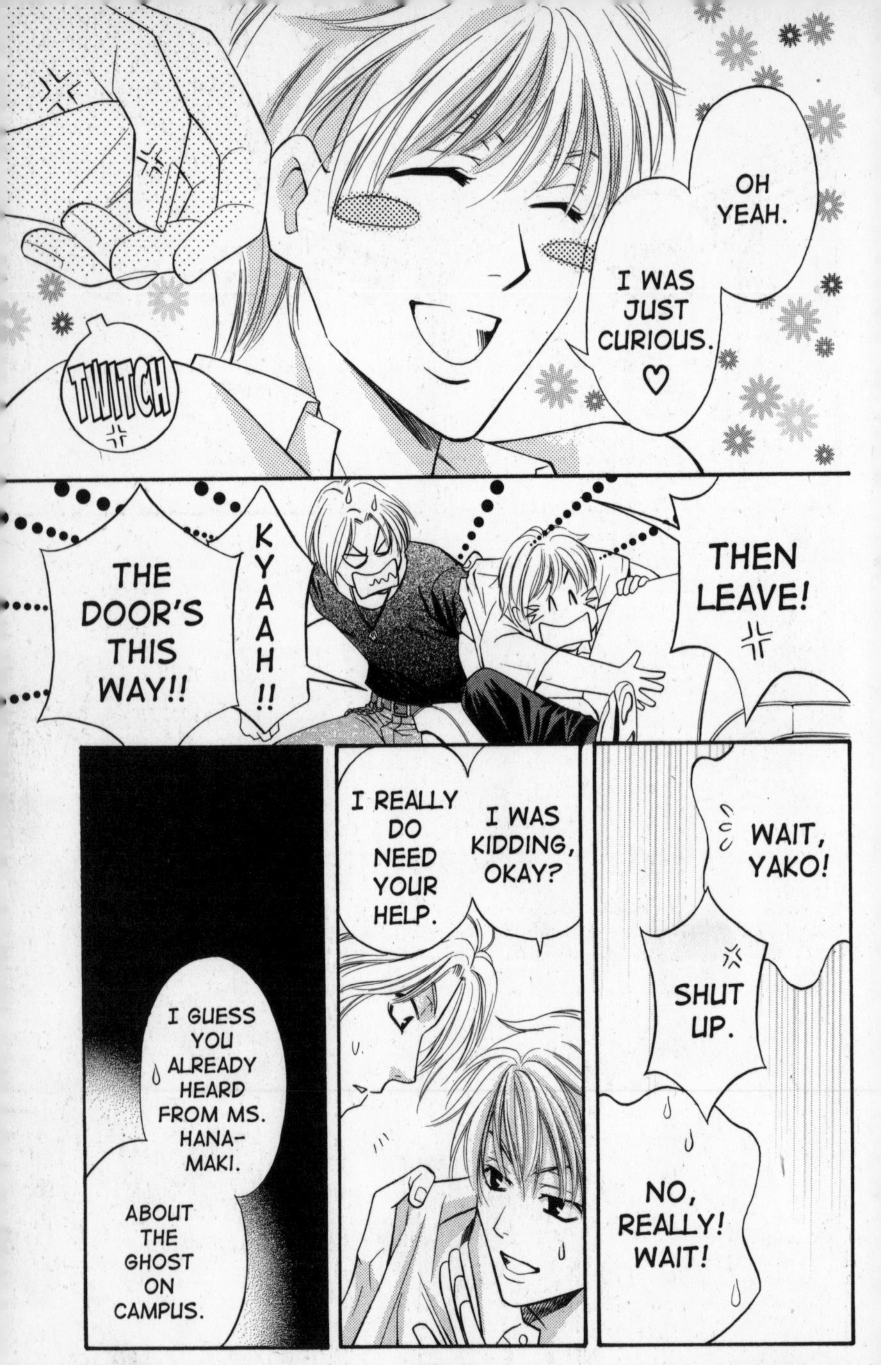
OH YEAH.
I WAS JUST CURIOUS. ♡
TWITCH
THEN LEAVE!
KYAAH!!
THE DOOR'S THIS WAY!!
WAIT, YAKO!
SHUT UP.
NO, REALLY! WAIT!
I WAS KIDDING, OKAY?
I REALLY DO NEED YOUR HELP.
I GUESS YOU ALREADY HEARD FROM MS. HANA-MAKI.
ABOUT THE GHOST ON CAMPUS.

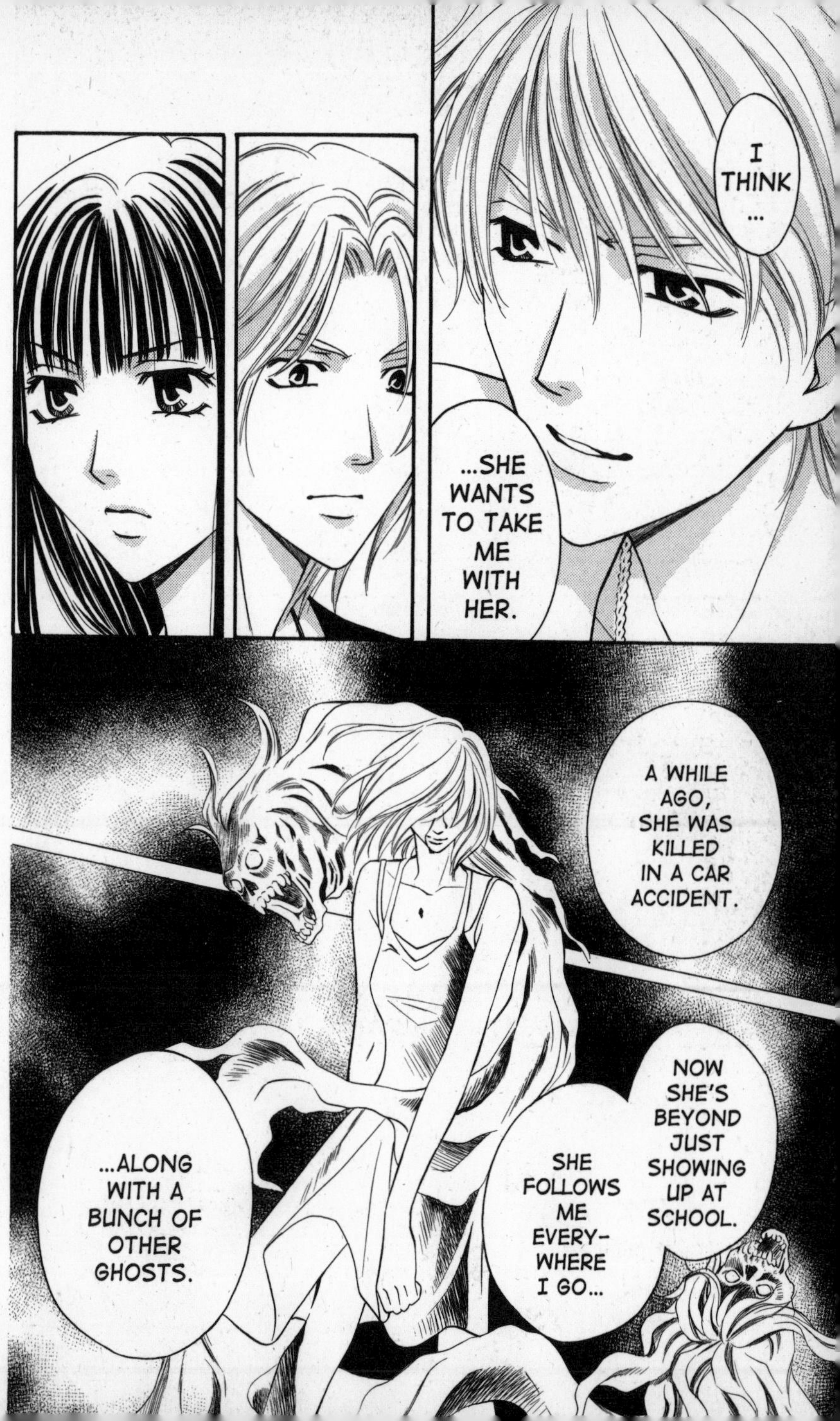
I THINK ...
...SHE WANTS TO TAKE ME WITH HER.
A WHILE AGO, SHE WAS KILLED IN A CAR ACCIDENT.
NOW SHE'S BEYOND JUST SHOWING UP AT SCHOOL.
SHE FOLLOWS ME EVERY-WHERE I GO...
...ALONG WITH A BUNCH OF OTHER GHOSTS.

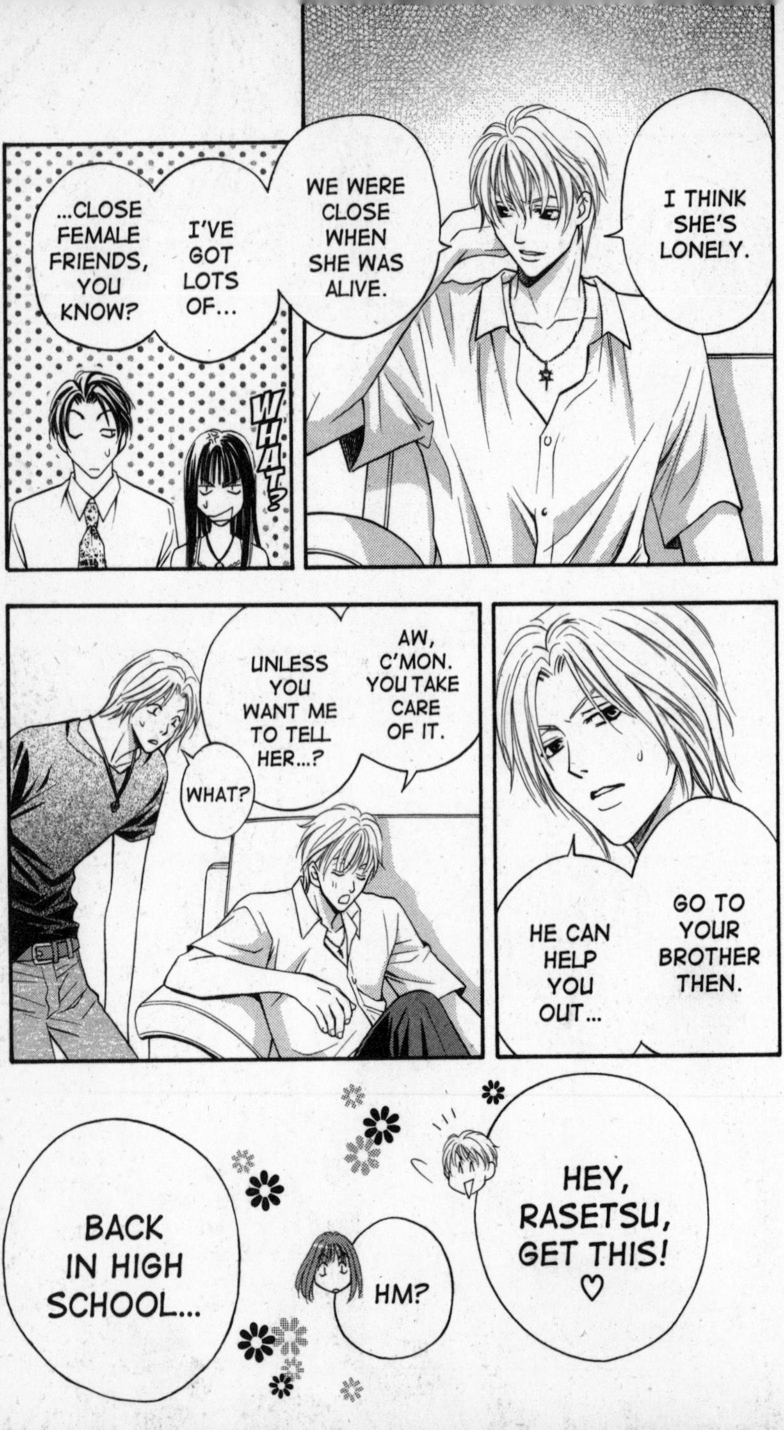
I THINK SHE'S LONELY.
WE WERE CLOSE WHEN SHE WAS ALIVE.
I'VE GOT LOTS OF...
...CLOSE FEMALE FRIENDS, YOU KNOW?
WHAT?!
GO TO YOUR BROTHER THEN.
HE CAN HELP YOU OUT...
AW, C'MON. YOU TAKE CARE OF IT.
UNLESS YOU WANT ME TO TELL HER...?
WHAT?
HEY, RASETSU, GET THIS! ♡
HM?
BACK IN HIGH SCHOOL...

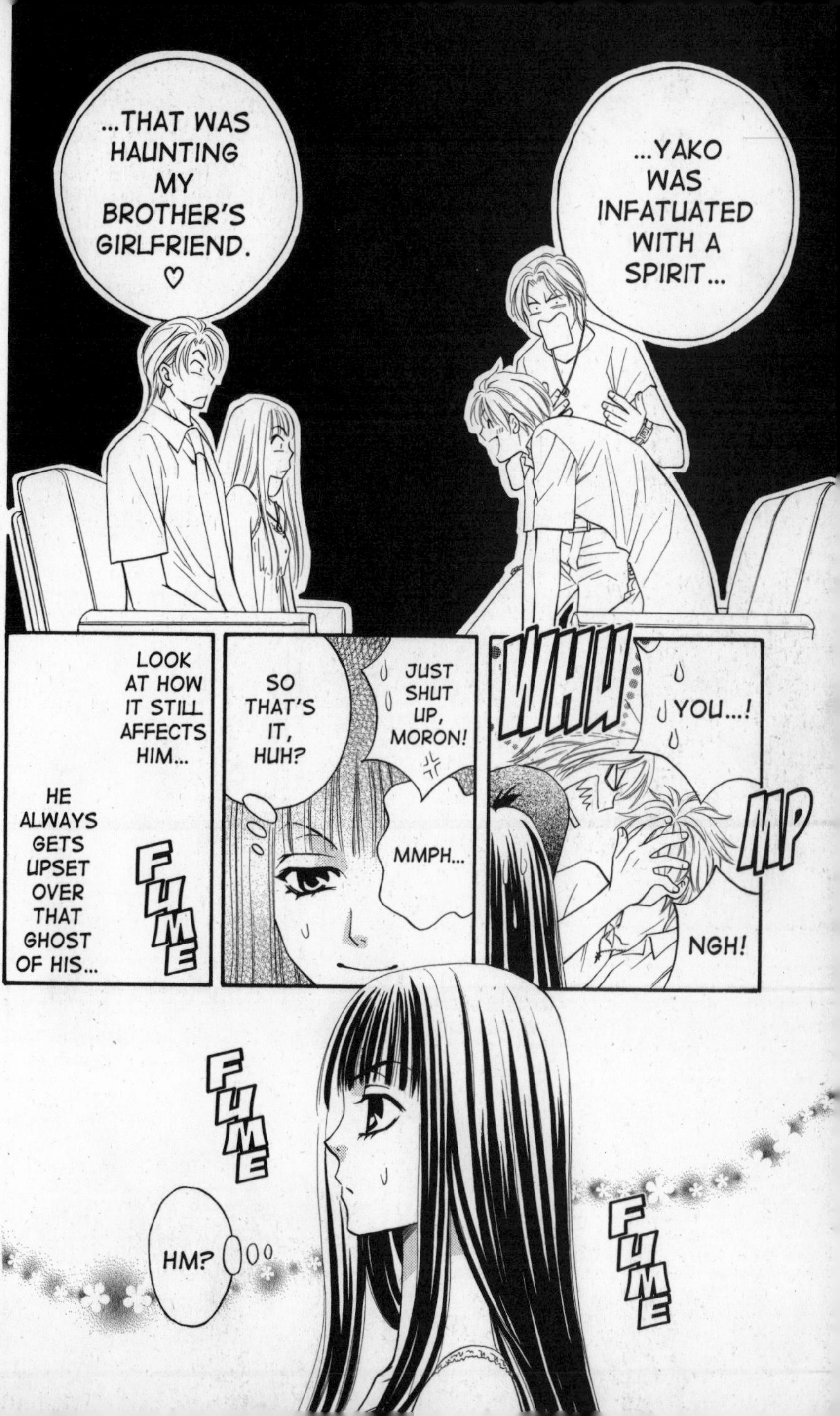
...YAKO WAS INFATUATED WITH A SPIRIT...
...THAT WAS HAUNTING MY BROTHER'S GIRLFRIEND. ♡
YOU...!
WHU
MP
NGH!
JUST SHUT UP, MORON!
SO THAT'S IT, HUH?
MMPH...
LOOK AT HOW IT STILL AFFECTS HIM...
HE ALWAYS GETS UPSET OVER THAT GHOST OF HIS...
FUME
FUME
FUME
HM?

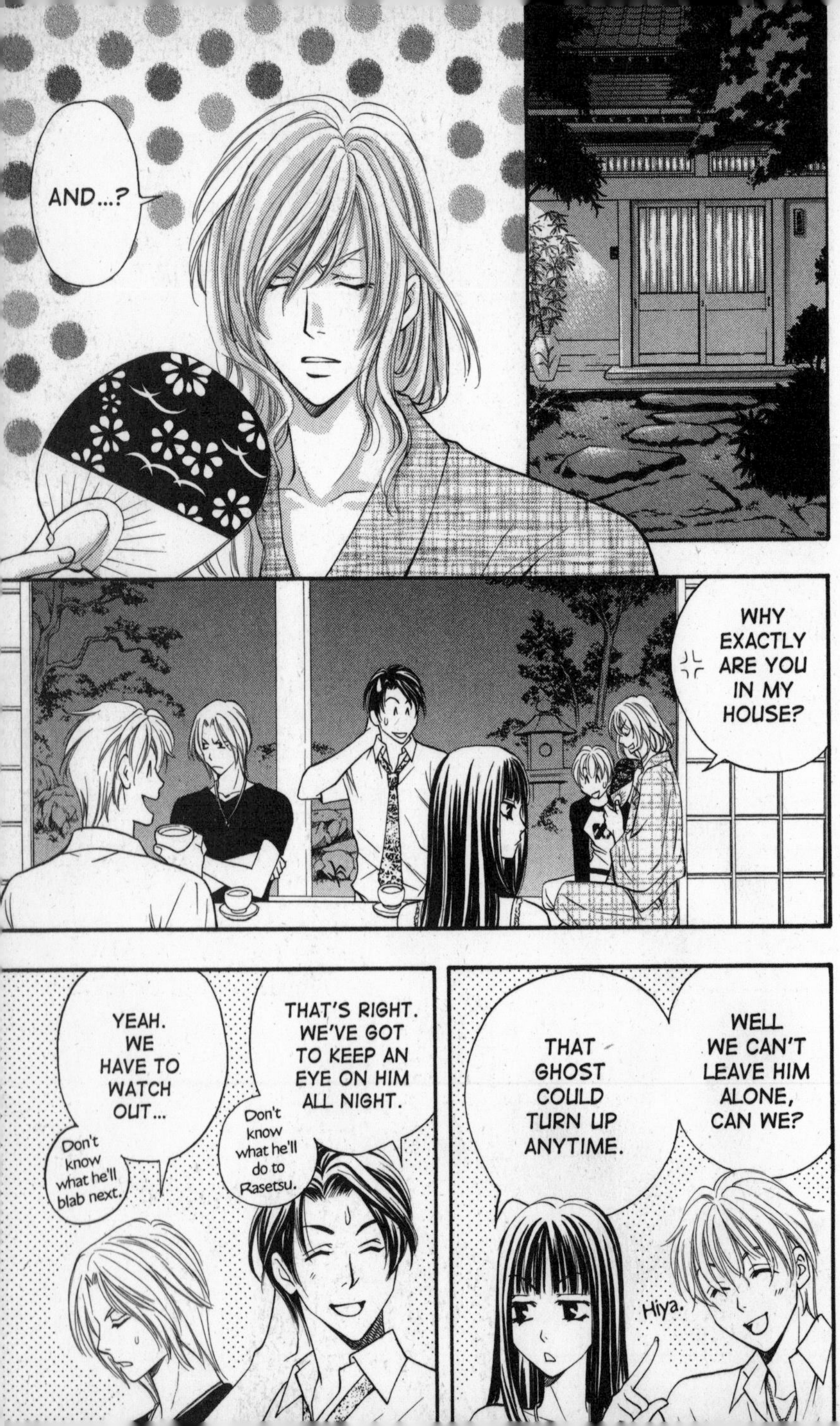
AND...?
WHY EXACTLY ARE YOU IN MY HOUSE?
WELL WE CAN'T LEAVE HIM ALONE, CAN WE?
THAT GHOST COULD TURN UP ANYTIME.
Hiya.
THAT'S RIGHT. WE'VE GOT TO KEEP AN EYE ON HIM ALL NIGHT.
Don't know what he'll do to Rasetsu.
YEAH. WE HAVE TO WATCH OUT...
Don't know what he'll blab next.

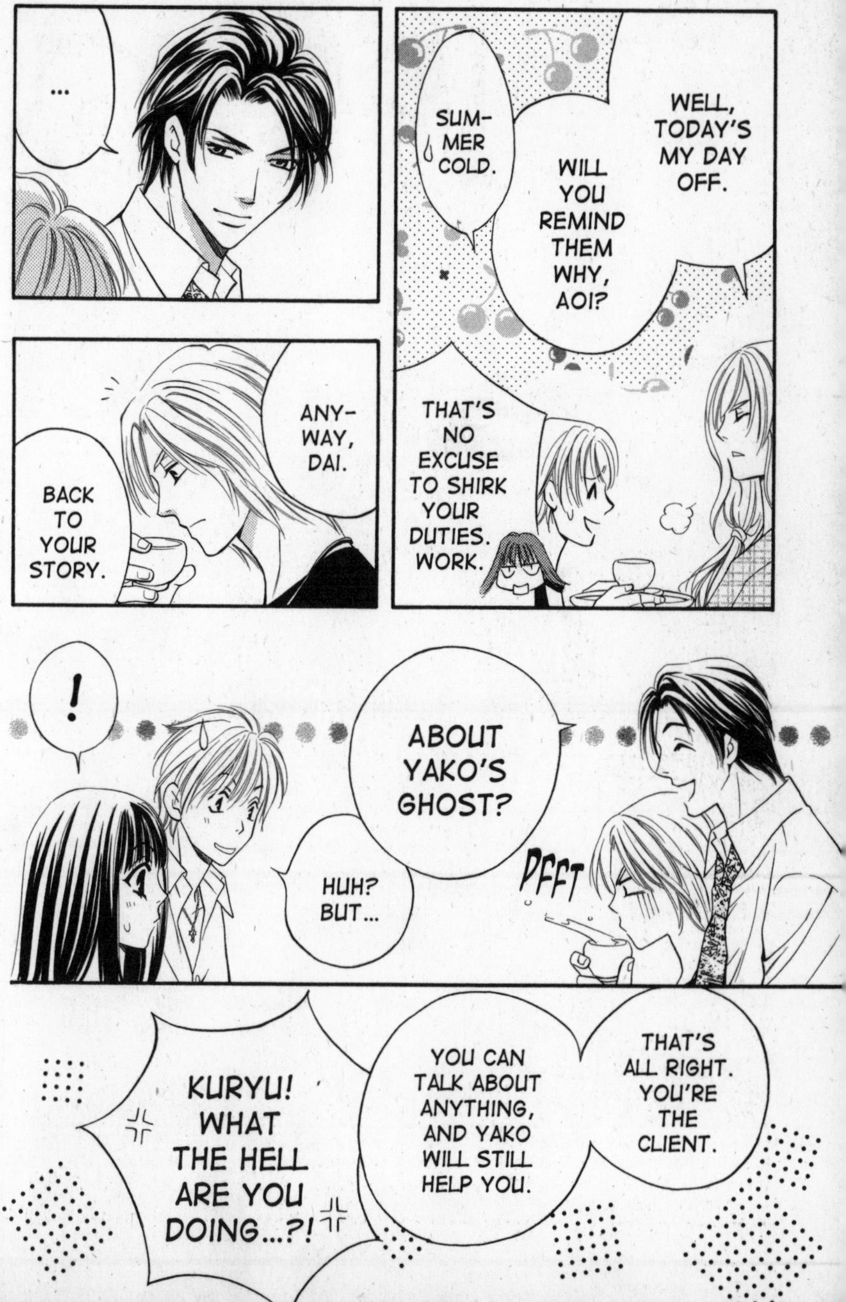
WELL, TODAY'S MY DAY OFF.
WILL YOU REMIND THEM WHY, AOI?
SUM-MER COLD.
THAT'S NO EXCUSE TO SHIRK YOUR DUTIES. WORK.
...
ANY-WAY, DAI.
BACK TO YOUR STORY.
ABOUT YAKO'S GHOST?
PFFT
!
HUH? BUT...
THAT'S ALL RIGHT. YOU'RE THE CLIENT.
YOU CAN TALK ABOUT ANYTHING, AND YAKO WILL STILL HELP YOU.
KURYU! WHAT THE HELL ARE YOU DOING...?!

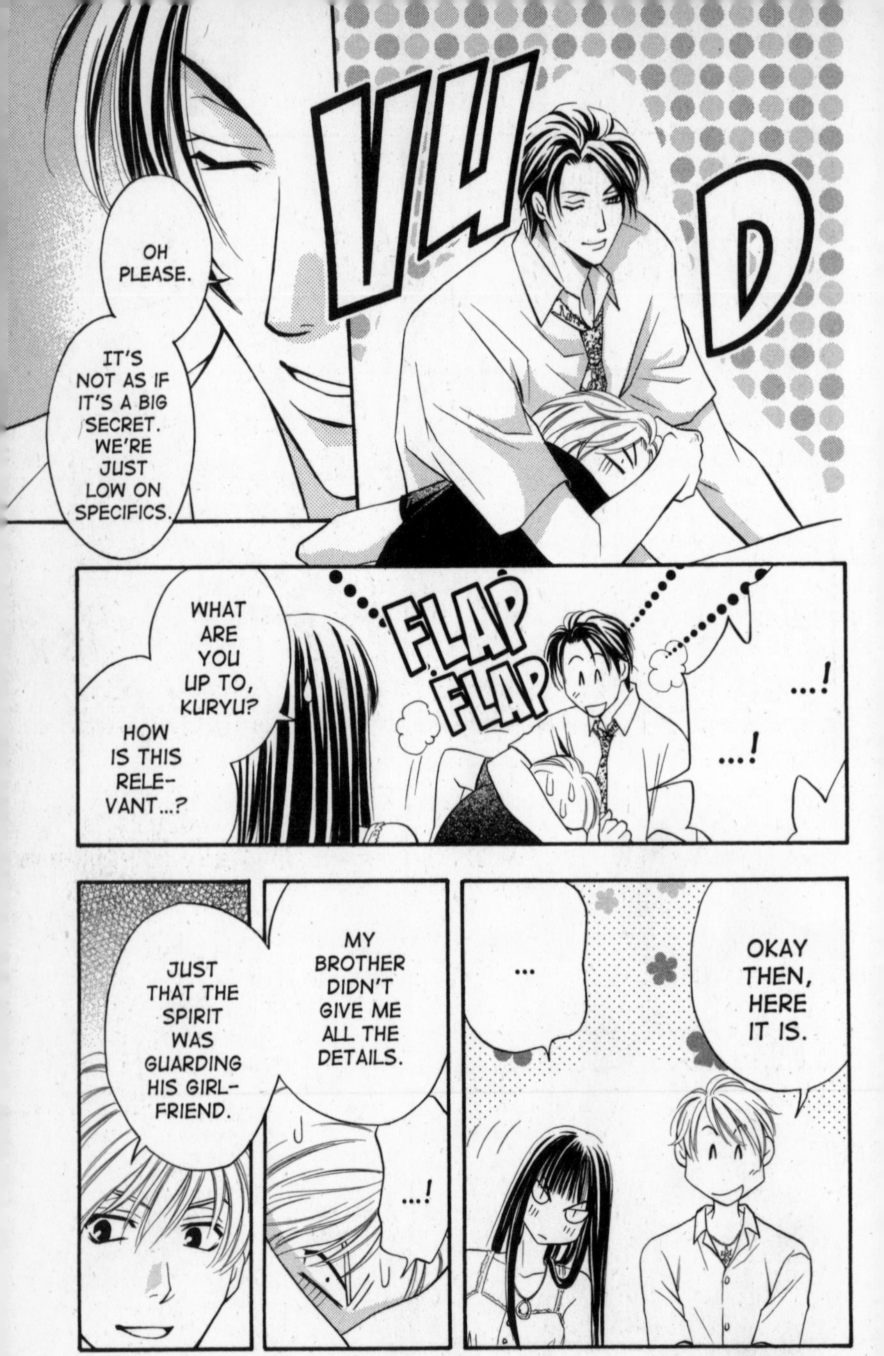
VUD
OH PLEASE.
IT'S NOT AS IF IT'S A BIG SECRET. WE'RE JUST LOW ON SPECIFICS.
...!
...!
FLAP FLAP
WHAT ARE YOU UP TO, KURYU?
HOW IS THIS RELE-VANT...?
OKAY THEN, HERE IT IS.
...
MY BROTHER DIDN'T GIVE ME ALL THE DETAILS.
...!
JUST THAT THE SPIRIT WAS GUARDING HIS GIRL-FRIEND.

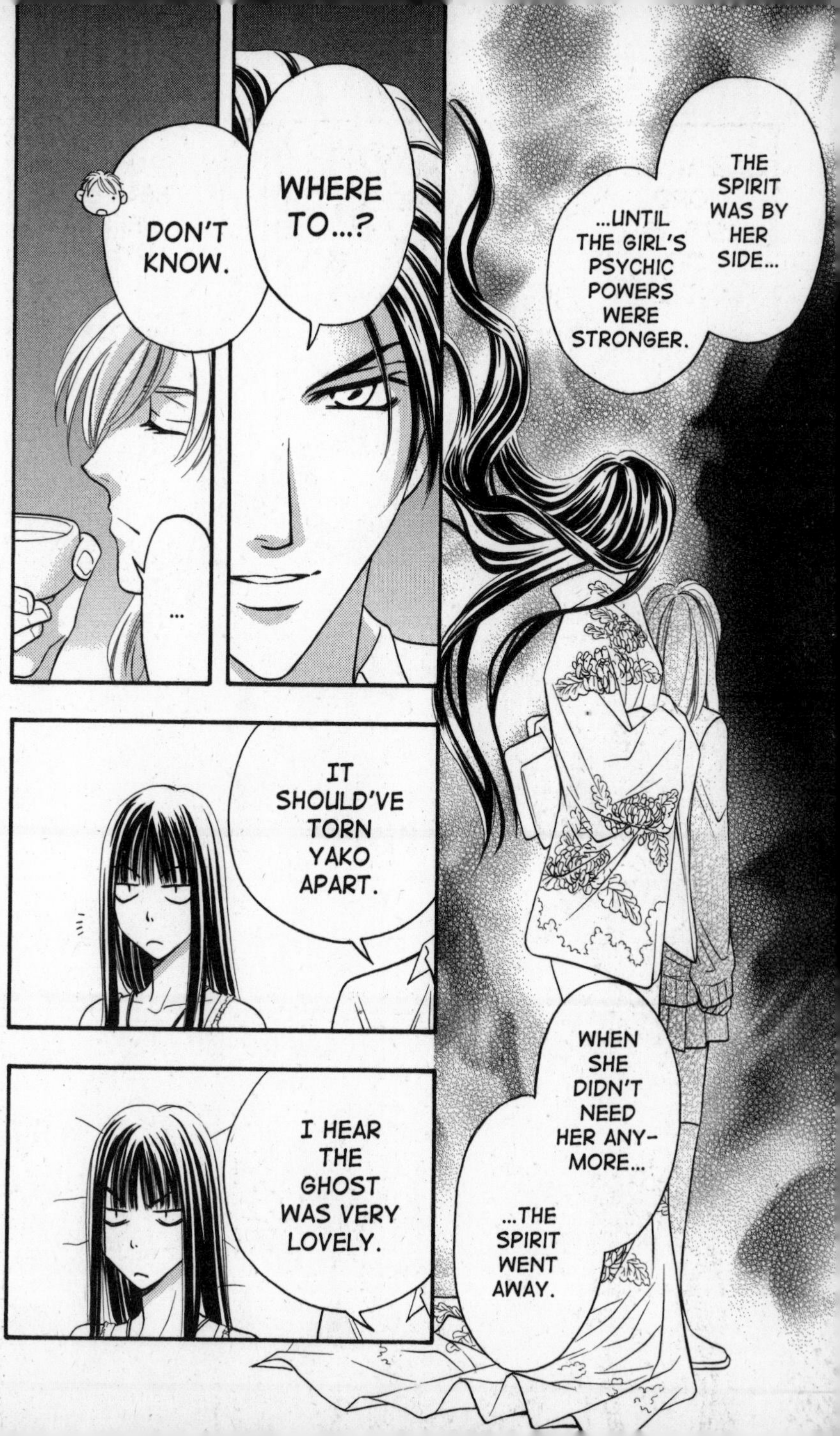
THE SPIRIT WAS BY HER SIDE...
...UNTIL THE GIRL'S PSYCHIC POWERS WERE STRONGER.
WHEN SHE DIDN'T NEED HER ANYMORE...
...THE SPIRIT WENT AWAY.
WHERE TO...?
DON'T KNOW.
...
IT SHOULD'VE TORN YAKO APART.
I HEAR THE GHOST WAS VERY LOVELY.

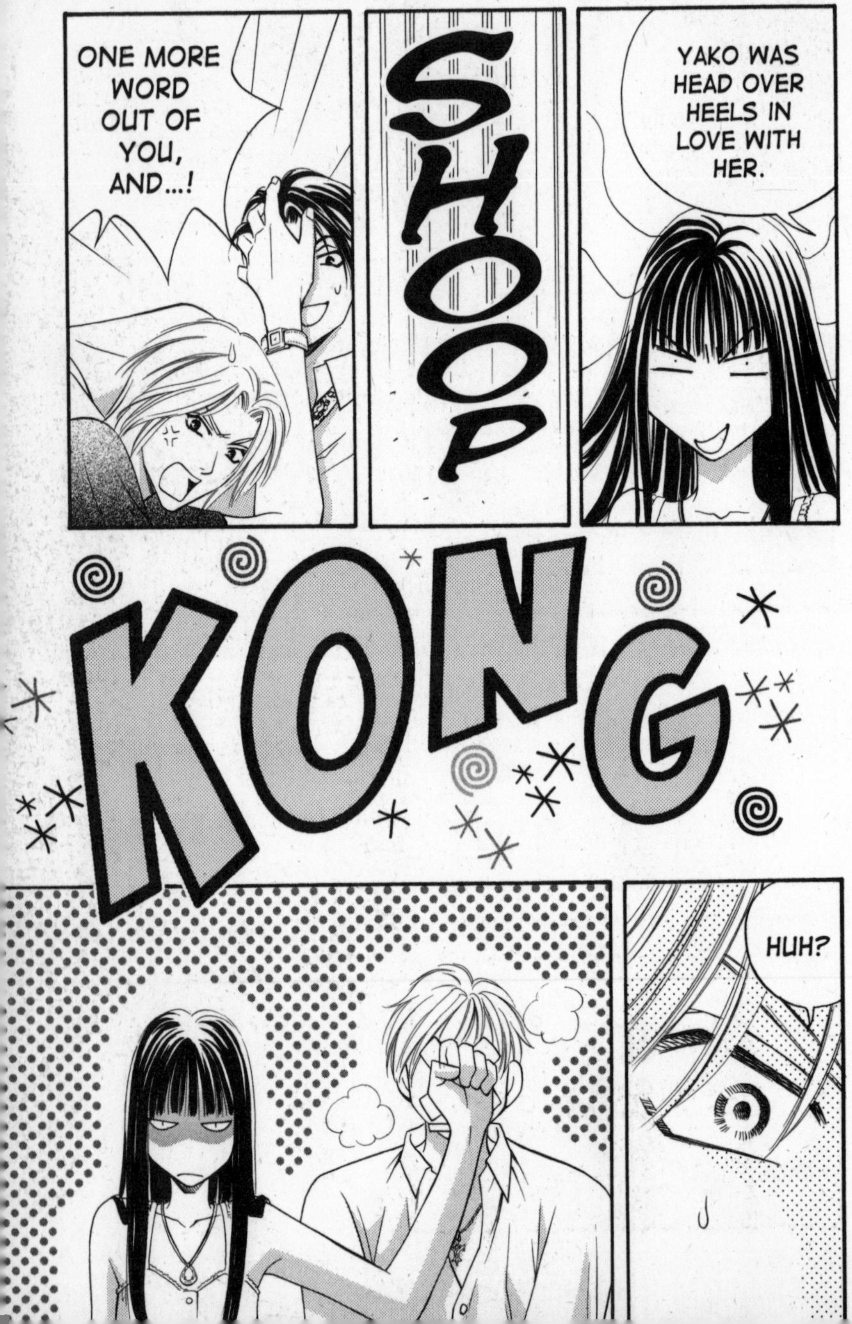
YAKO WAS HEAD OVER HEELS IN LOVE WITH HER.
SHOOP
ONE MORE WORD OUT OF YOU, AND...!
KONG
HUH?

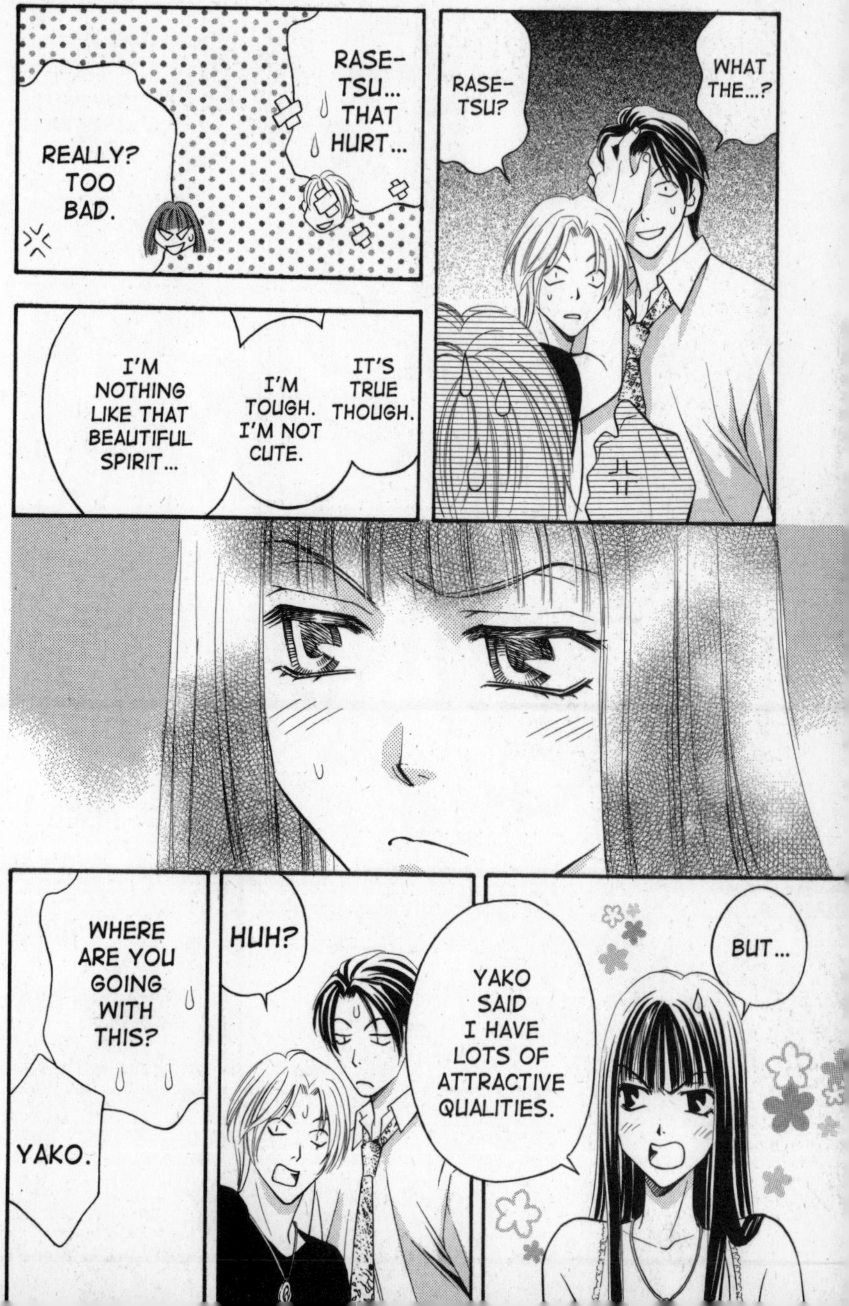
WHAT THE...?
RASE-TSU?
RASE-TSU... THAT HURT...
REALLY? TOO BAD.
IT'S TRUE THOUGH.
I'M TOUGH. I'M NOT CUTE.
I'M NOTHING LIKE THAT BEAUTIFUL SPIRIT...
BUT...
YAKO SAID I HAVE LOTS OF ATTRACTIVE QUALITIES.
HUH?
WHERE ARE YOU GOING WITH THIS?
YAKO.

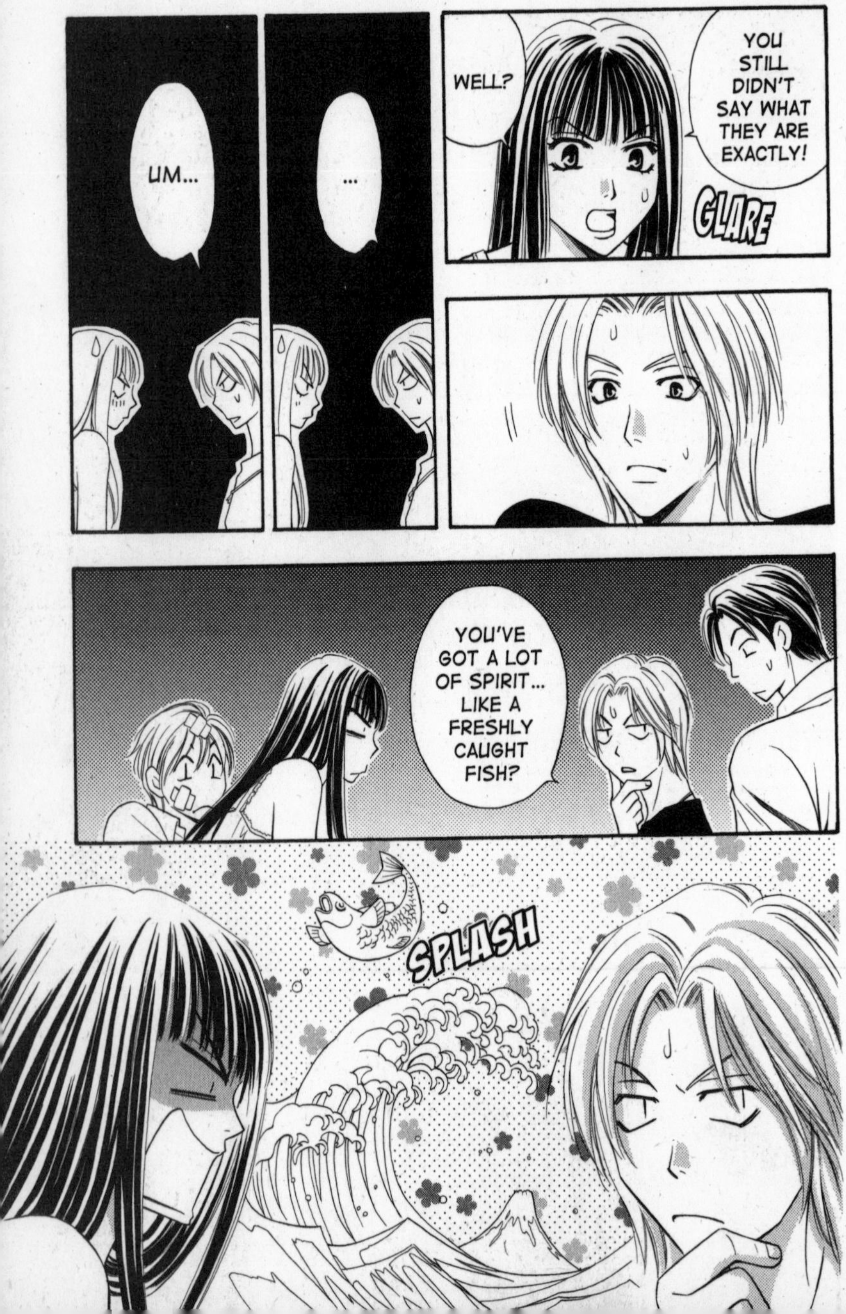
YOU STILL DIDN'T SAY WHAT THEY ARE EXACTLY!
WELL?
GLARE
...
UM...
YOU'VE GOT A LOT OF SPIRIT... LIKE A FRESHLY CAUGHT FISH?
SPLASH

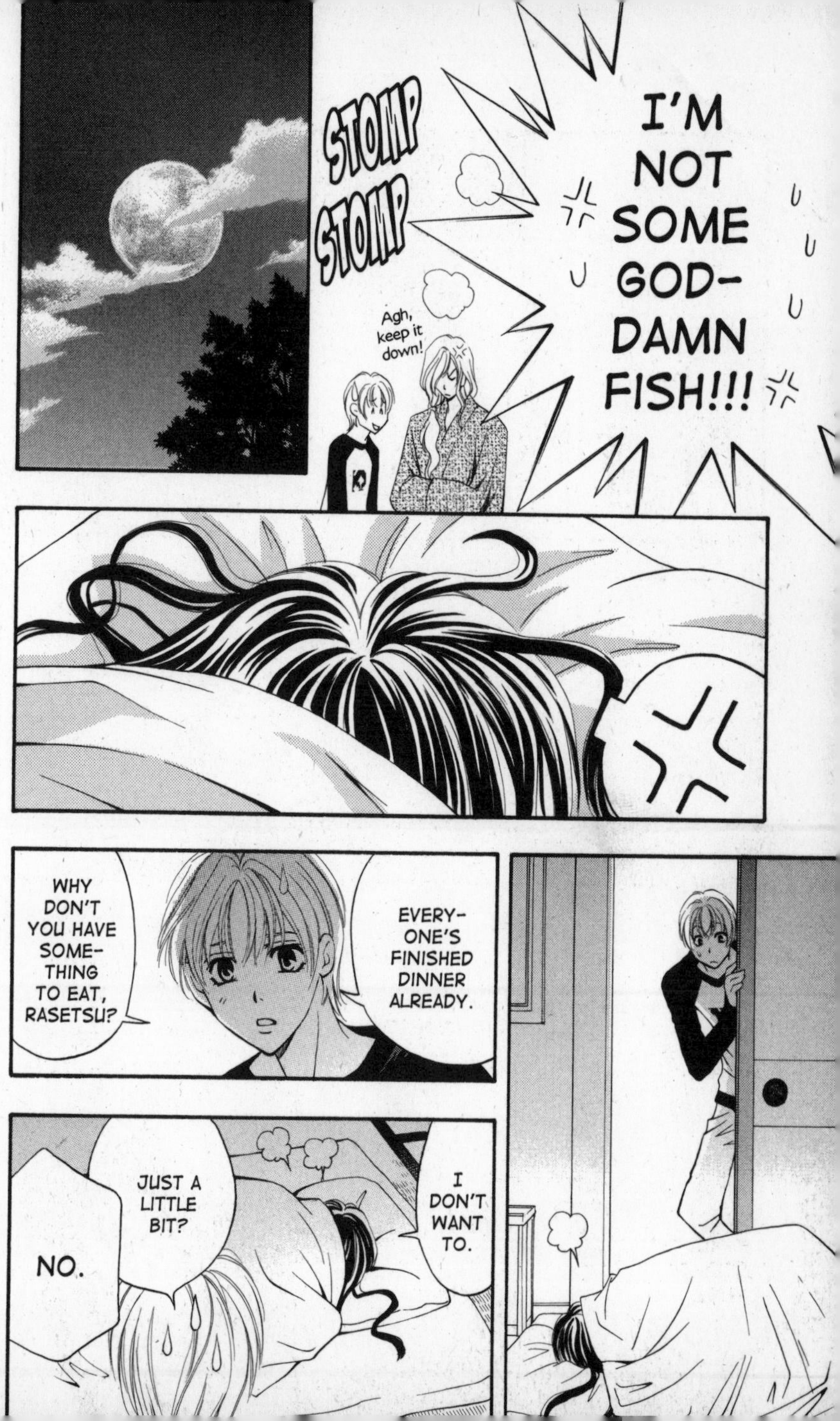
I'M NOT SOME GOD-DAMN FISH!!!
STOMP STOMP
Agh, keep it down!
EVERY-ONE'S FINISHED DINNER ALREADY.
WHY DON'T YOU HAVE SOME-THING TO EAT, RASETSU?
I DON'T WANT TO.
JUST A LITTLE BIT?
NO.

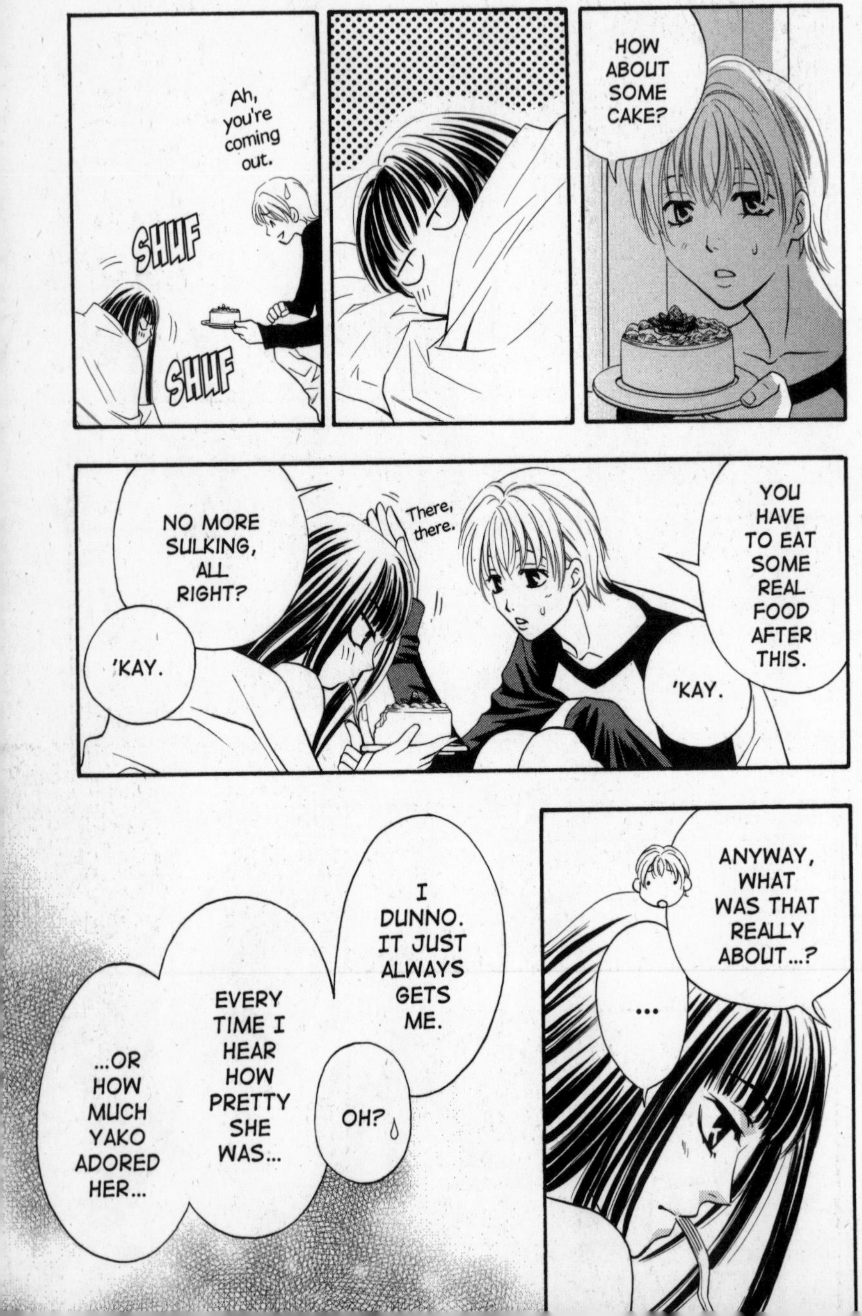
HOW ABOUT SOME CAKE?
Ah, you're coming out.
SHUF
SHUF
YOU HAVE TO EAT SOME REAL FOOD AFTER THIS.
'KAY.
There, there.
NO MORE SULKING, ALL RIGHT?
'KAY.
ANYWAY, WHAT WAS THAT REALLY ABOUT...?
...
I DUNNO. IT JUST ALWAYS GETS ME.
EVERY TIME I HEAR HOW PRETTY SHE WAS...
OH?
...OR HOW MUCH YAKO ADORED HER...

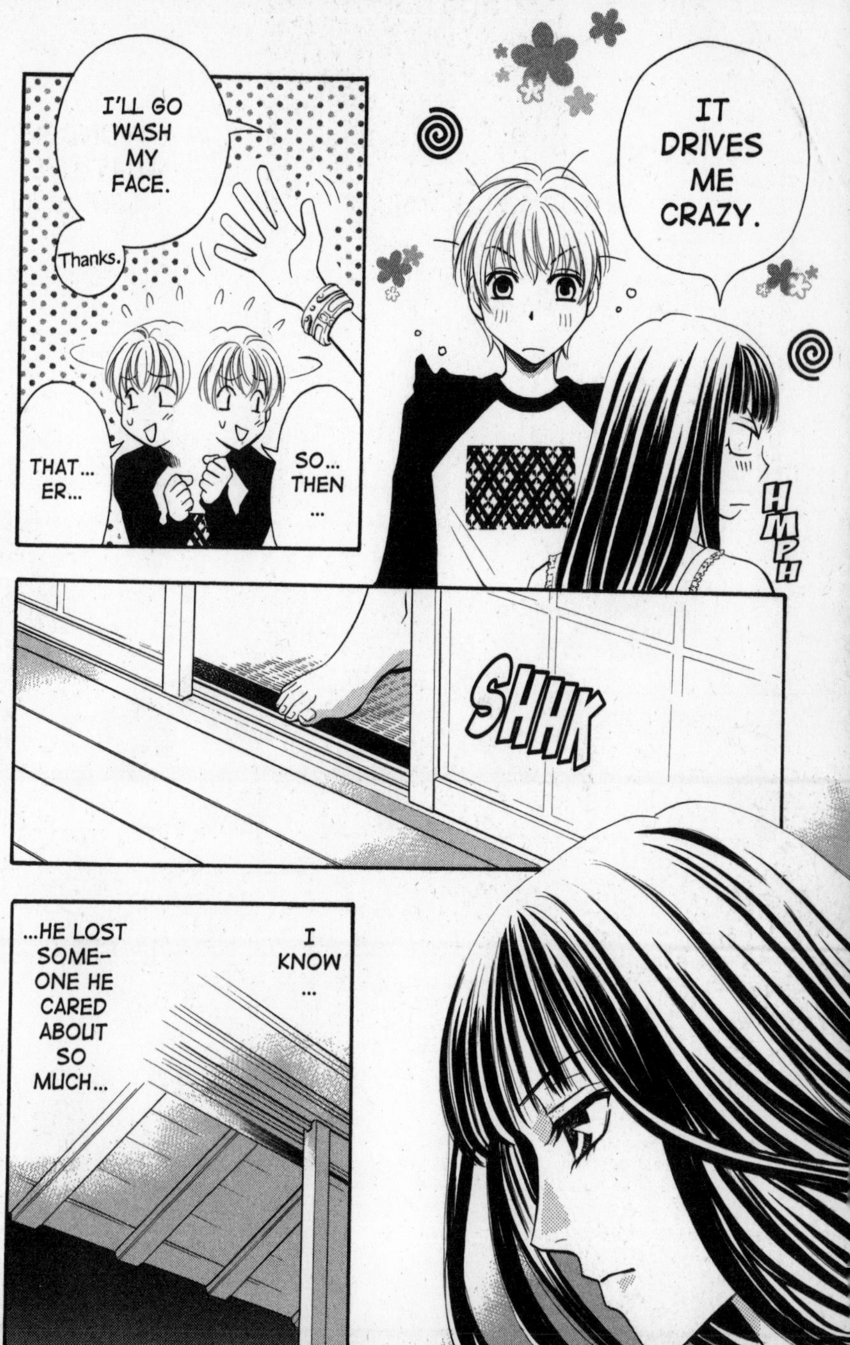
IT DRIVES ME CRAZY.
HMPH
I'LL GO WASH MY FACE.
Thanks.
SO... THEN ...
THAT... ER...
SHHK
I KNOW ...
...HE LOST SOMEONE HE CARED ABOUT SO MUCH...

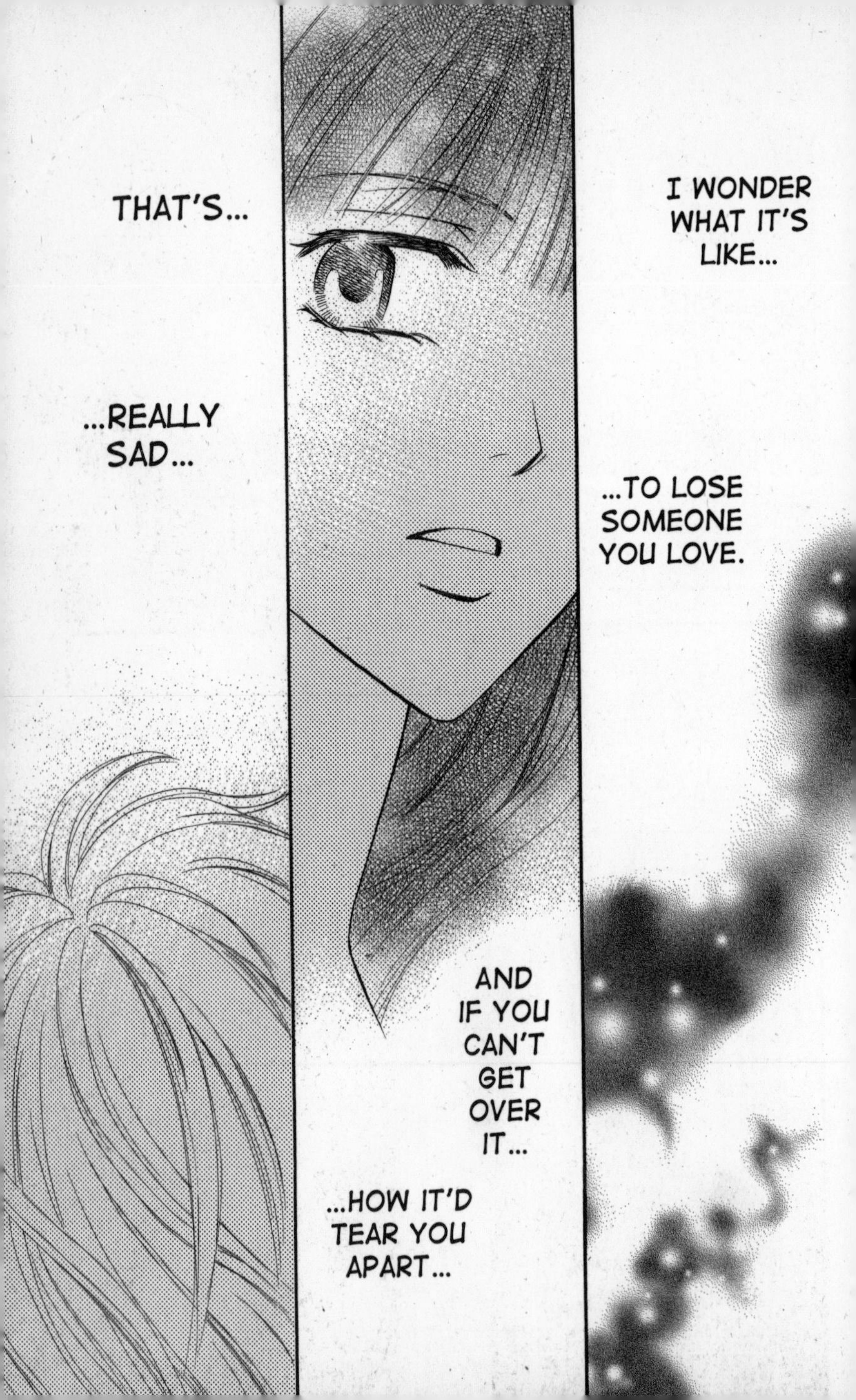
I WONDER WHAT IT'S LIKE...
...TO LOSE SOMEONE YOU LOVE.
AND IF YOU CAN'T GET OVER IT...
...HOW IT'D TEAR YOU APART...
THAT'S...
...REALLY SAD...

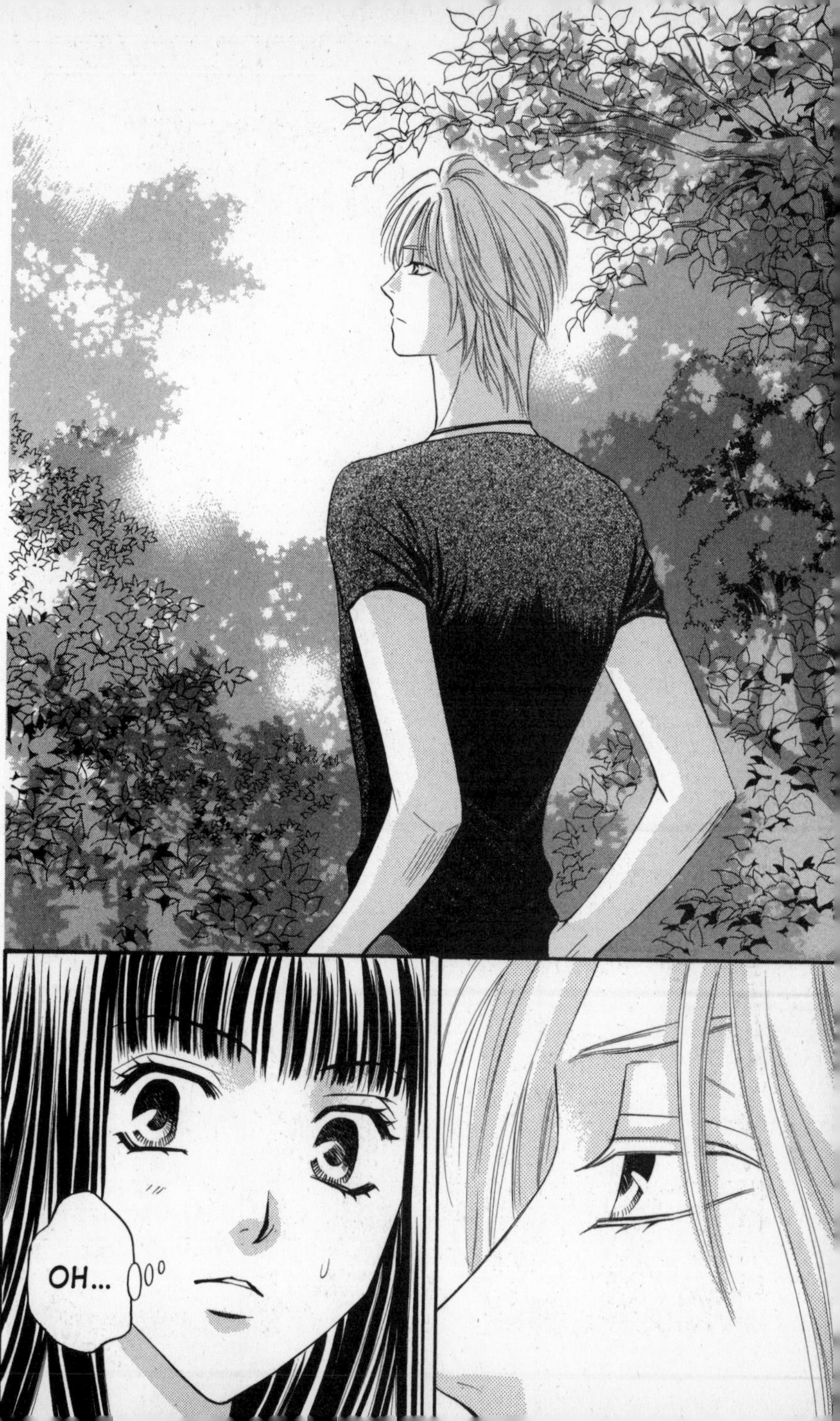
OH...

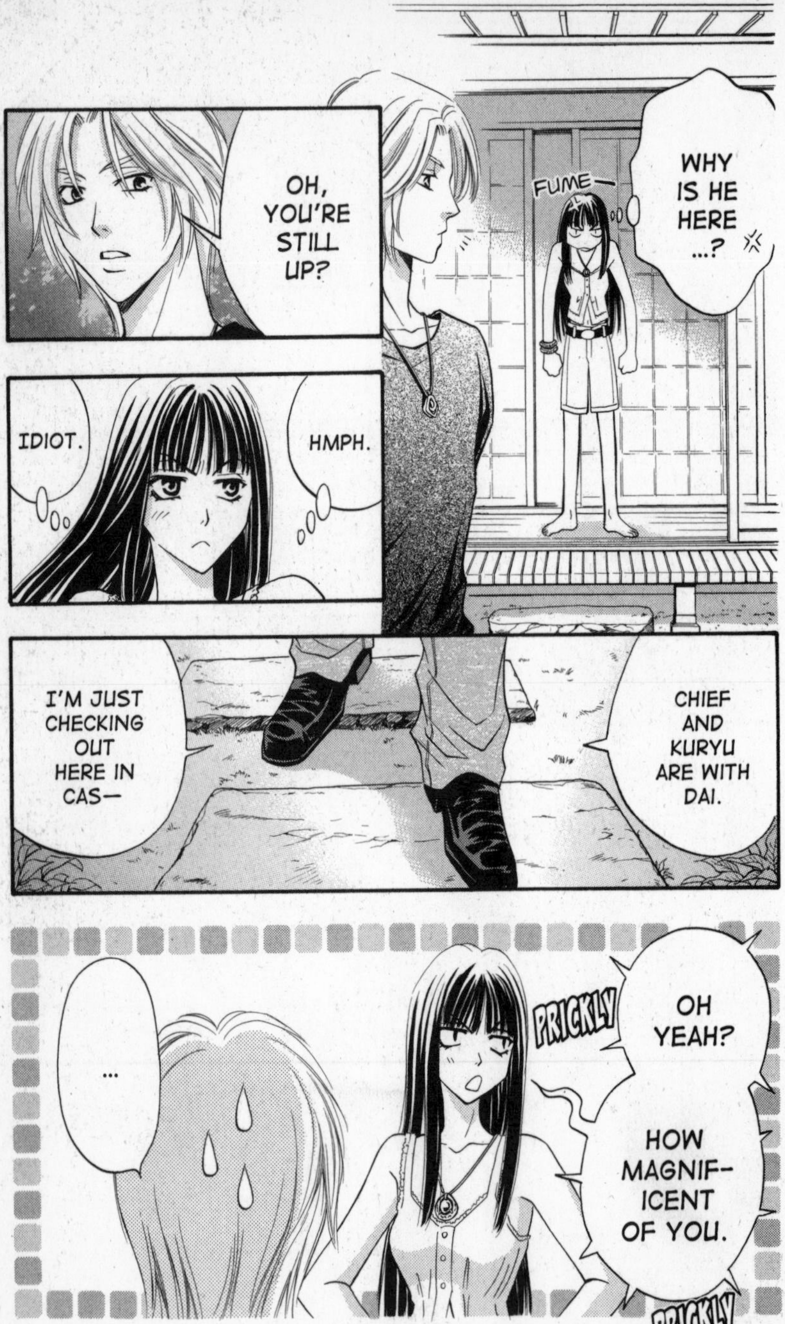
WHY IS HE HERE ...?
FUME—
OH, YOU'RE STILL UP?
HMPH.
IDIOT.
CHIEF AND KURYU ARE WITH DAI.
I'M JUST CHECKING OUT HERE IN CAS—
PRICKLY
OH YEAH?
HOW MAGNIF-ICENT OF YOU.
PRICKLY
...

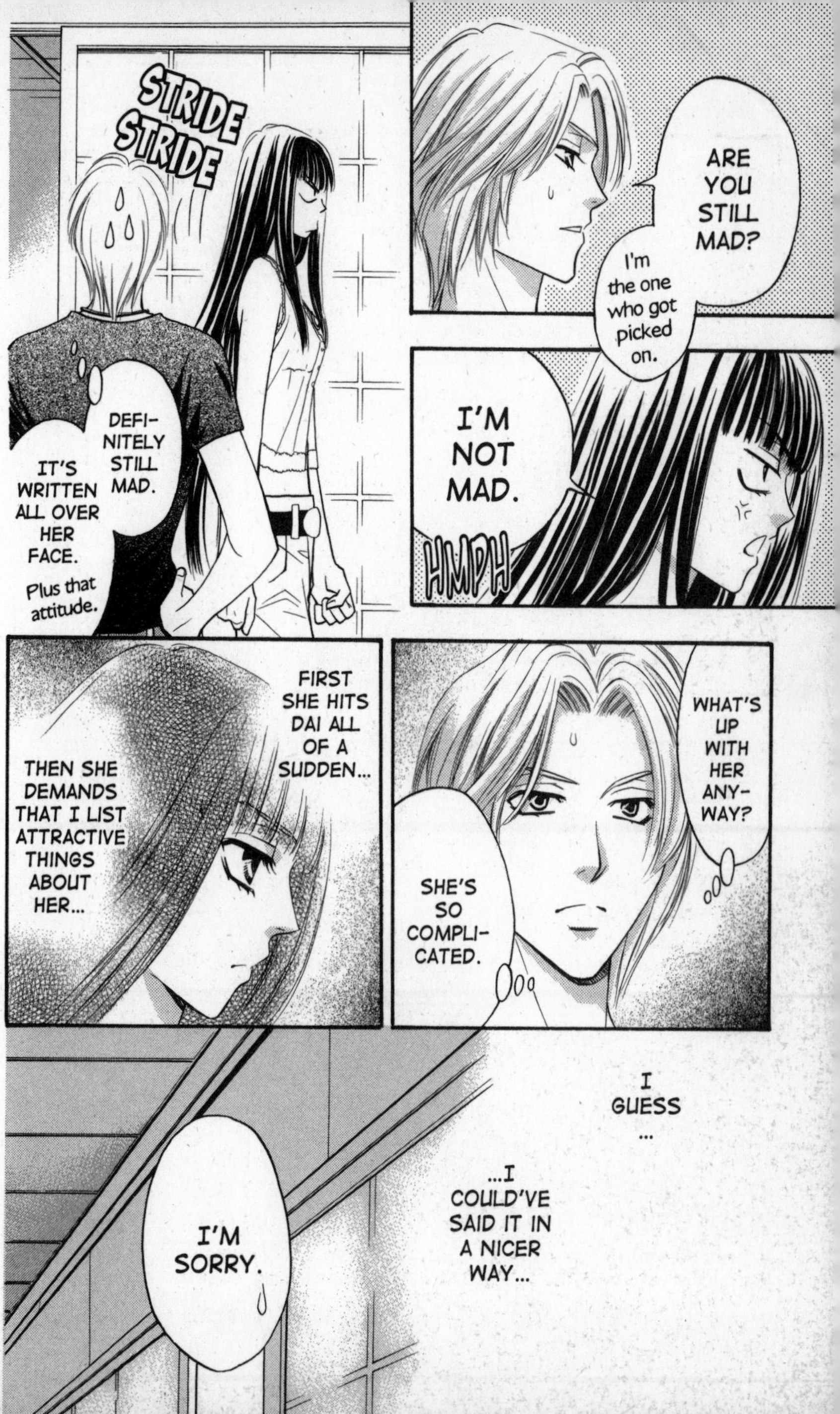
ARE YOU STILL MAD?
I'm the one who got picked on.
I'M NOT MAD.
HMPH
STRIDE STRIDE
DEFI-NITELY STILL MAD.
IT'S WRITTEN ALL OVER HER FACE.
Plus that attitude.
WHAT'S UP WITH HER ANY-WAY?
SHE'S SO COMPLI-CATED.
FIRST SHE HITS DAI ALL OF A SUDDEN...
THEN SHE DEMANDS THAT I LIST ATTRACTIVE THINGS ABOUT HER...
I GUESS...
...I COULD'VE SAID IT IN A NICER WAY...
I'M SORRY.

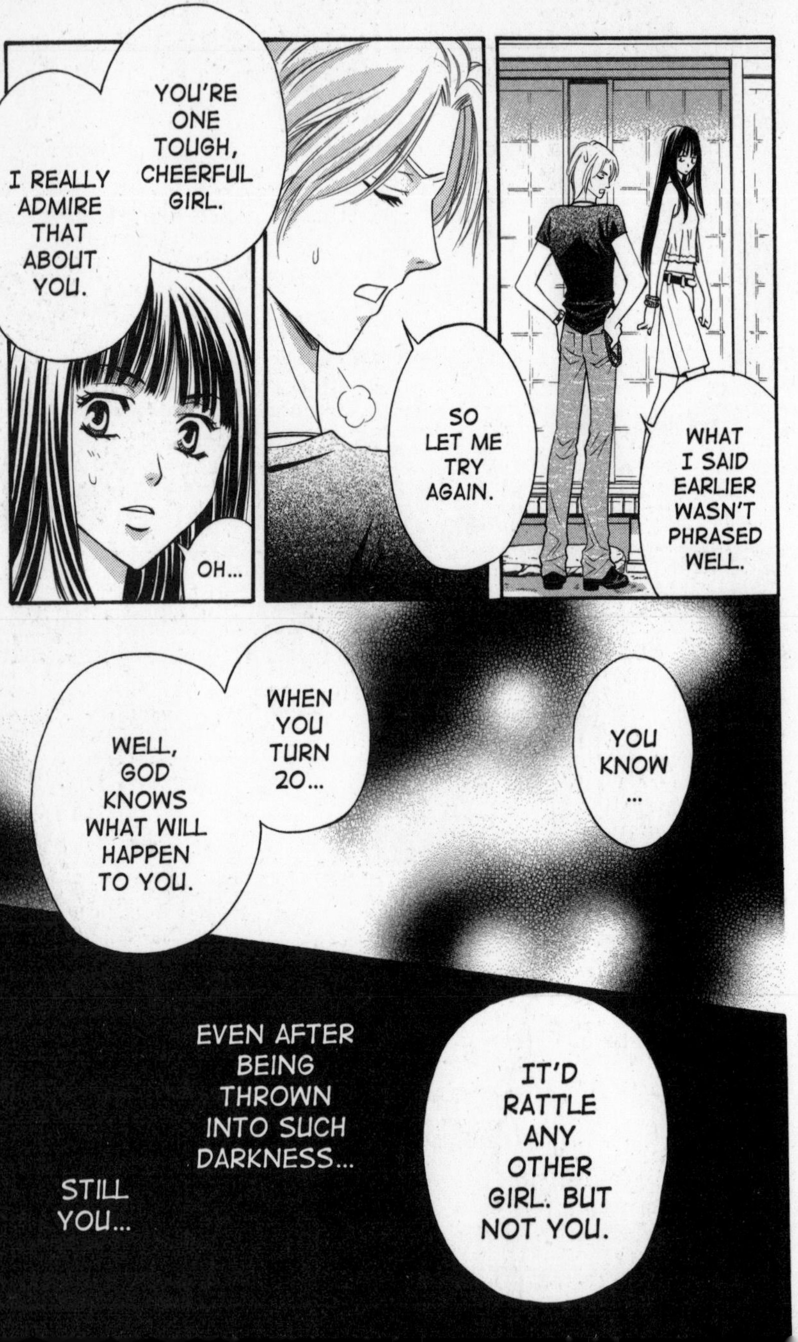
WHAT I SAID EARLIER WASN'T PHRASED WELL.
SO LET ME TRY AGAIN.
YOU'RE ONE TOUGH, CHEERFUL GIRL.
I REALLY ADMIRE THAT ABOUT YOU.
OH...
YOU KNOW ...
WHEN YOU TURN 20...
WELL, GOD KNOWS WHAT WILL HAPPEN TO YOU.
IT'D RATTLE ANY OTHER GIRL. BUT NOT YOU.
EVEN AFTER BEING THROWN INTO SUCH DARKNESS...
STILL YOU...

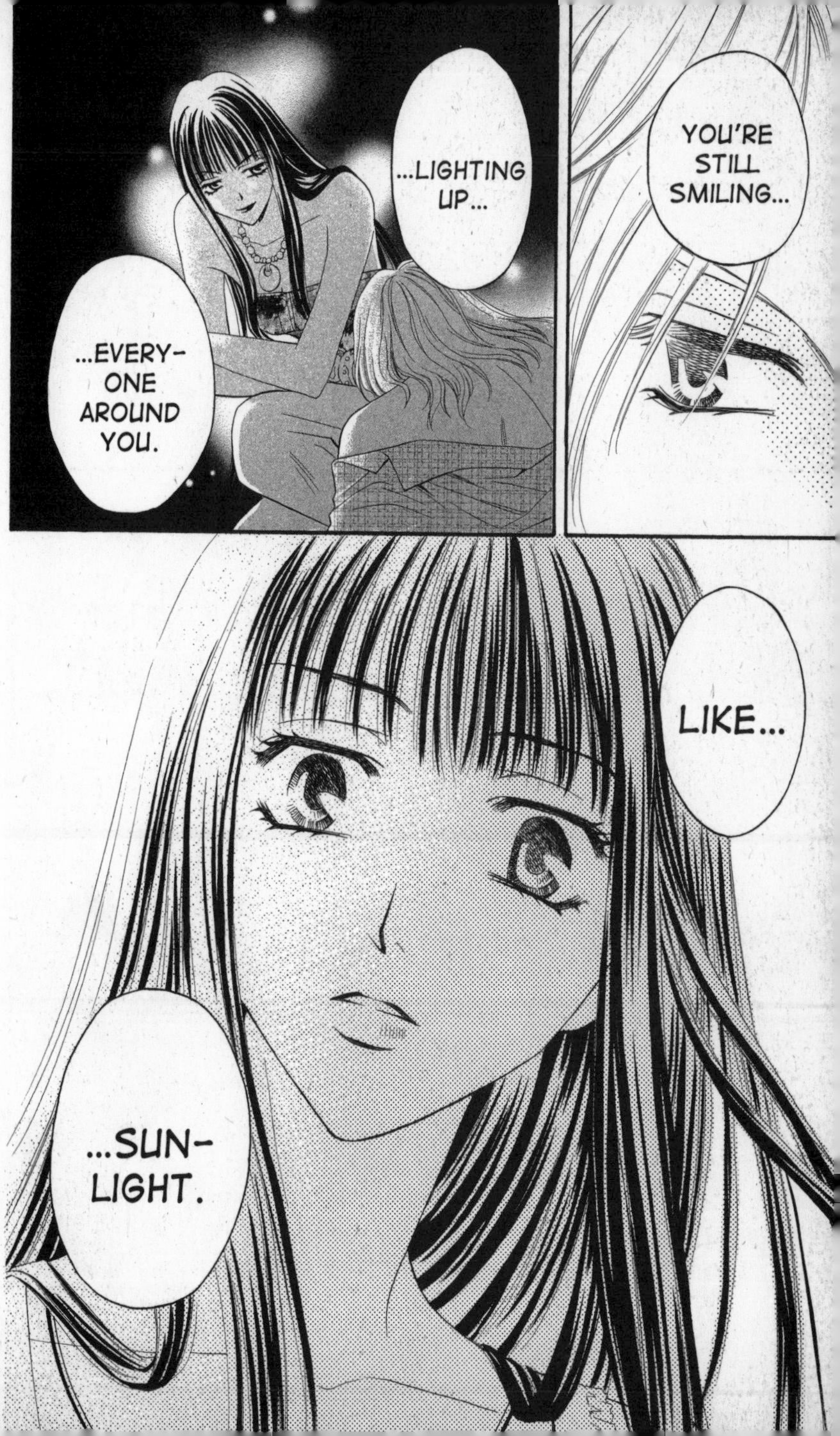
YOU'RE STILL SMILING...
...LIGHTING UP...
...EVERY-ONE AROUND YOU.
LIKE...
...SUN-LIGHT.

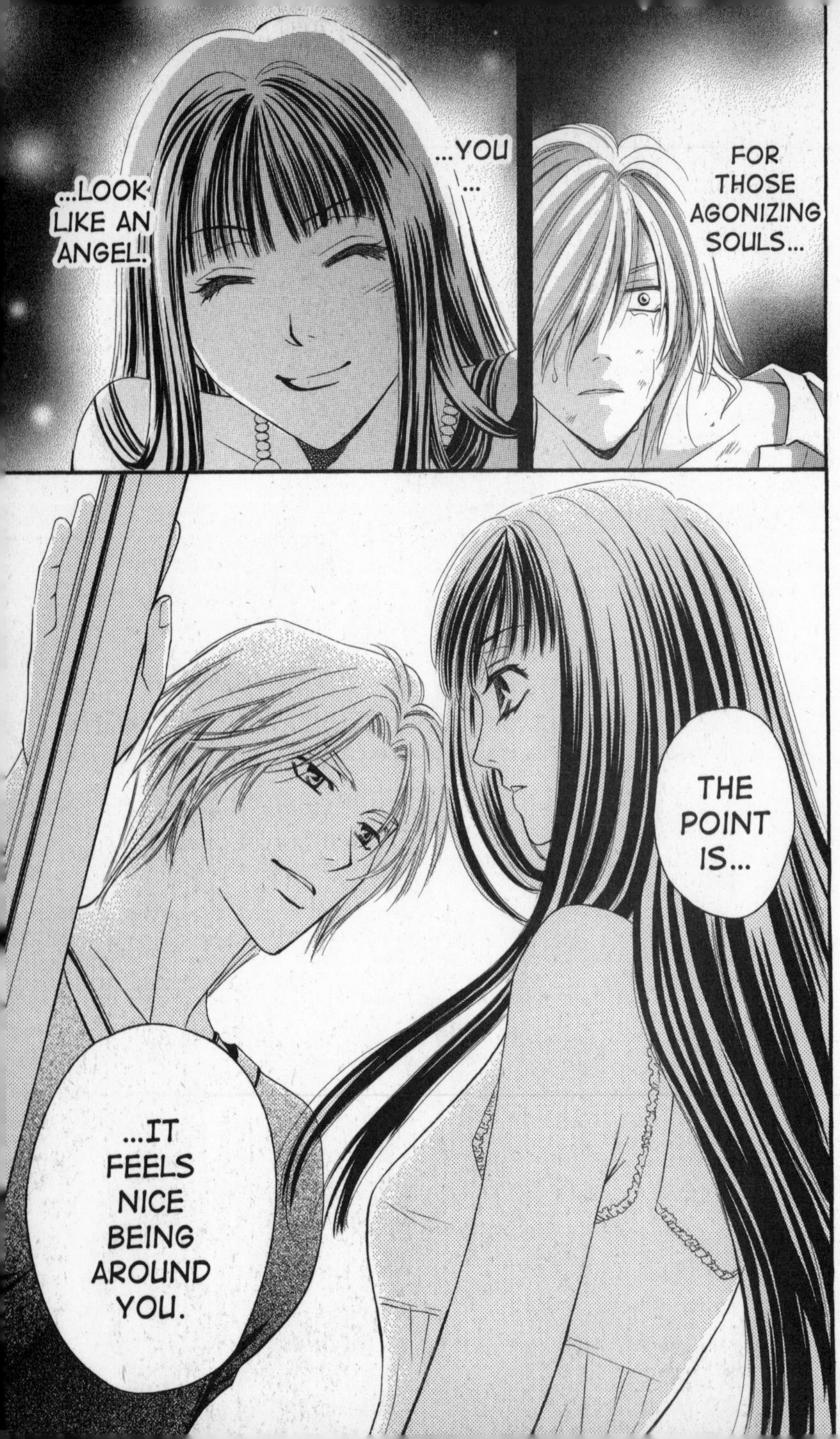
FOR THOSE AGONIZING SOULS...
...YOU ...
...LOOK LIKE AN ANGEL.
THE POINT IS...
...IT FEELS NICE BEING AROUND YOU.

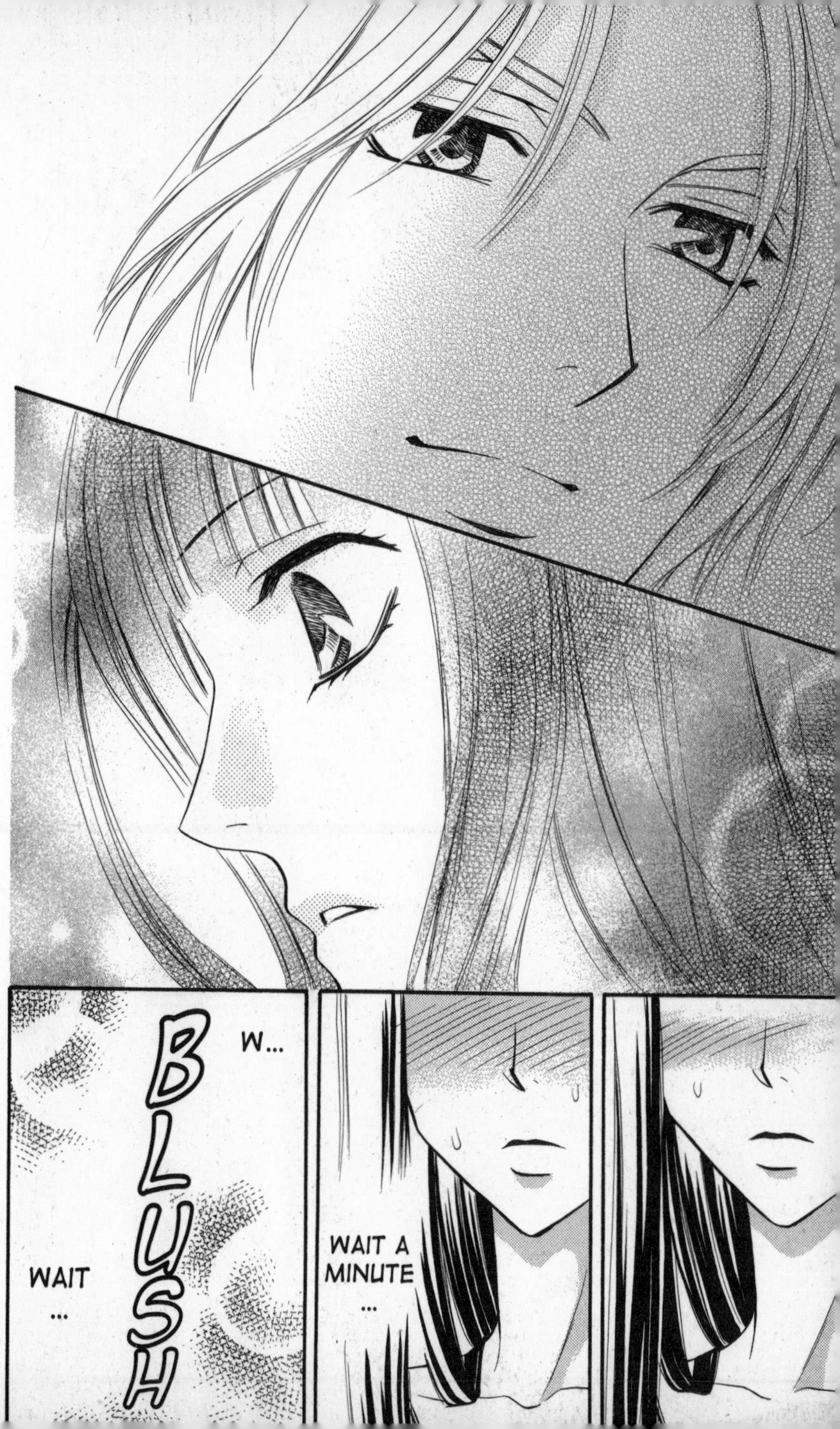
WAIT A MINUTE ...
W...
BLUSH
WAIT ...

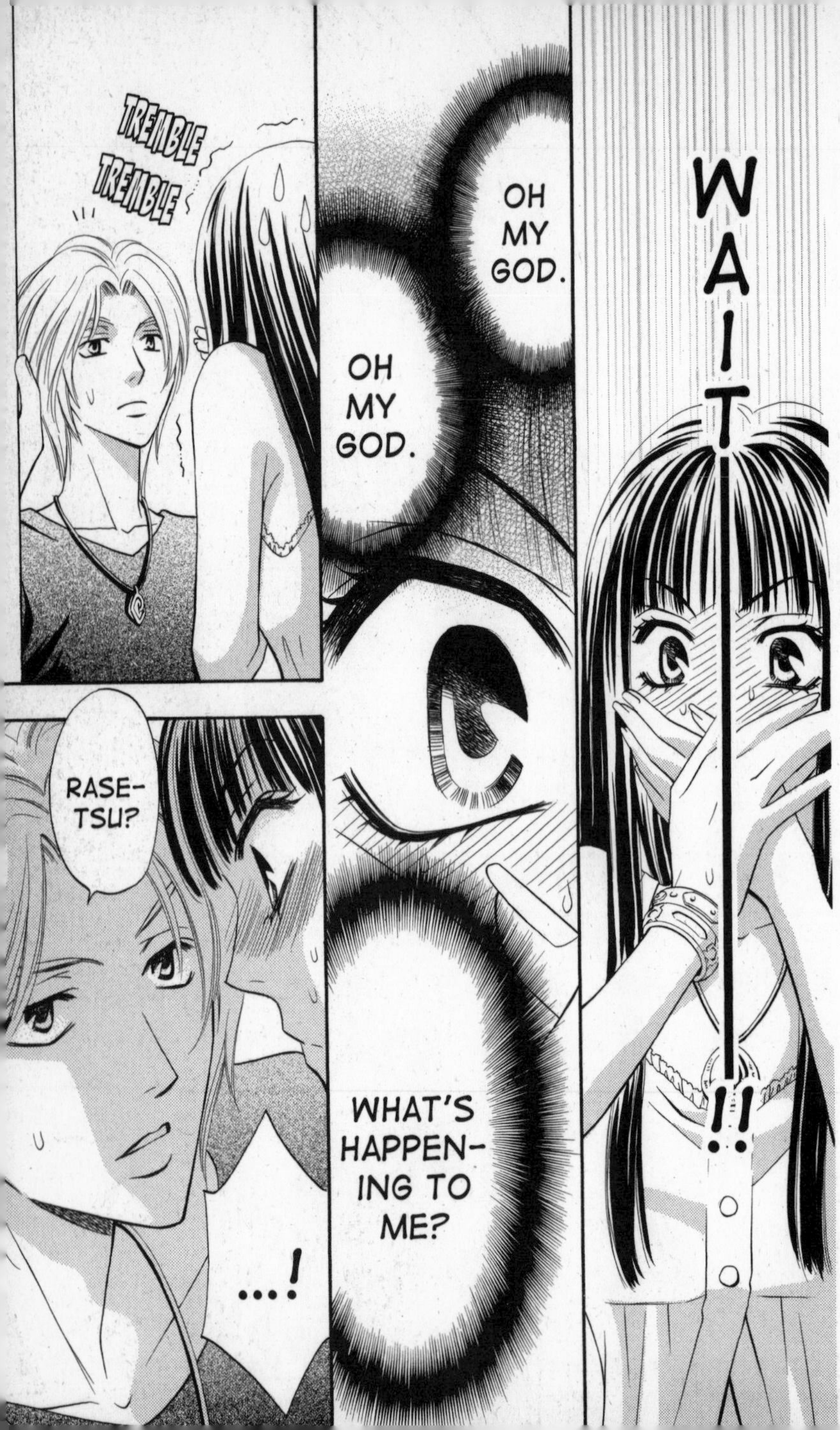
WAIT!!
OH MY GOD.
OH MY GOD.
WHAT'S HAPPEN-ING TO ME?
TREMBLE TREMBLE
RASE-TSU?
...!

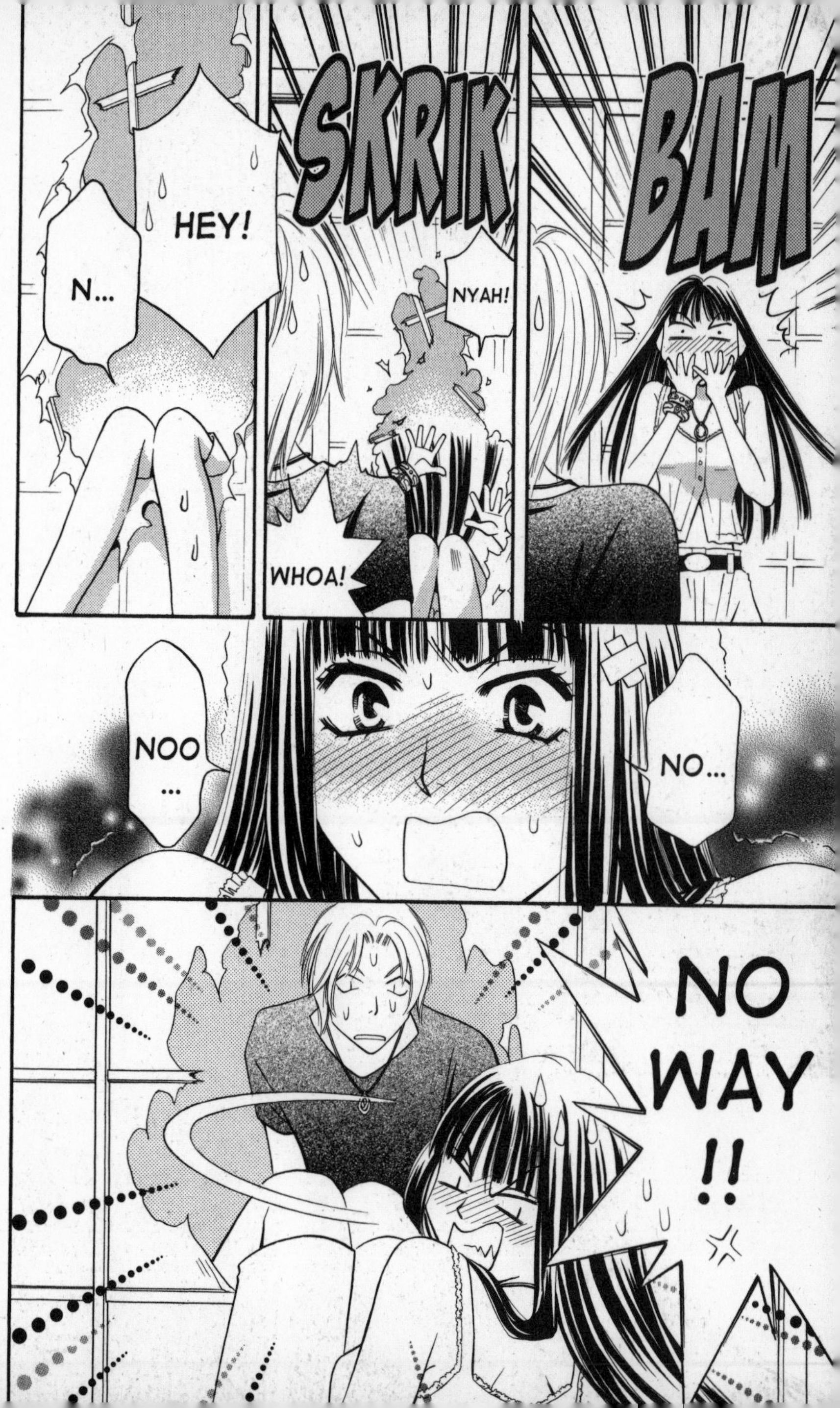
BAM
SKRIK
NYAH!
WHOA!
HEY!
N...
NO...
NOO ...
NO WAY !!

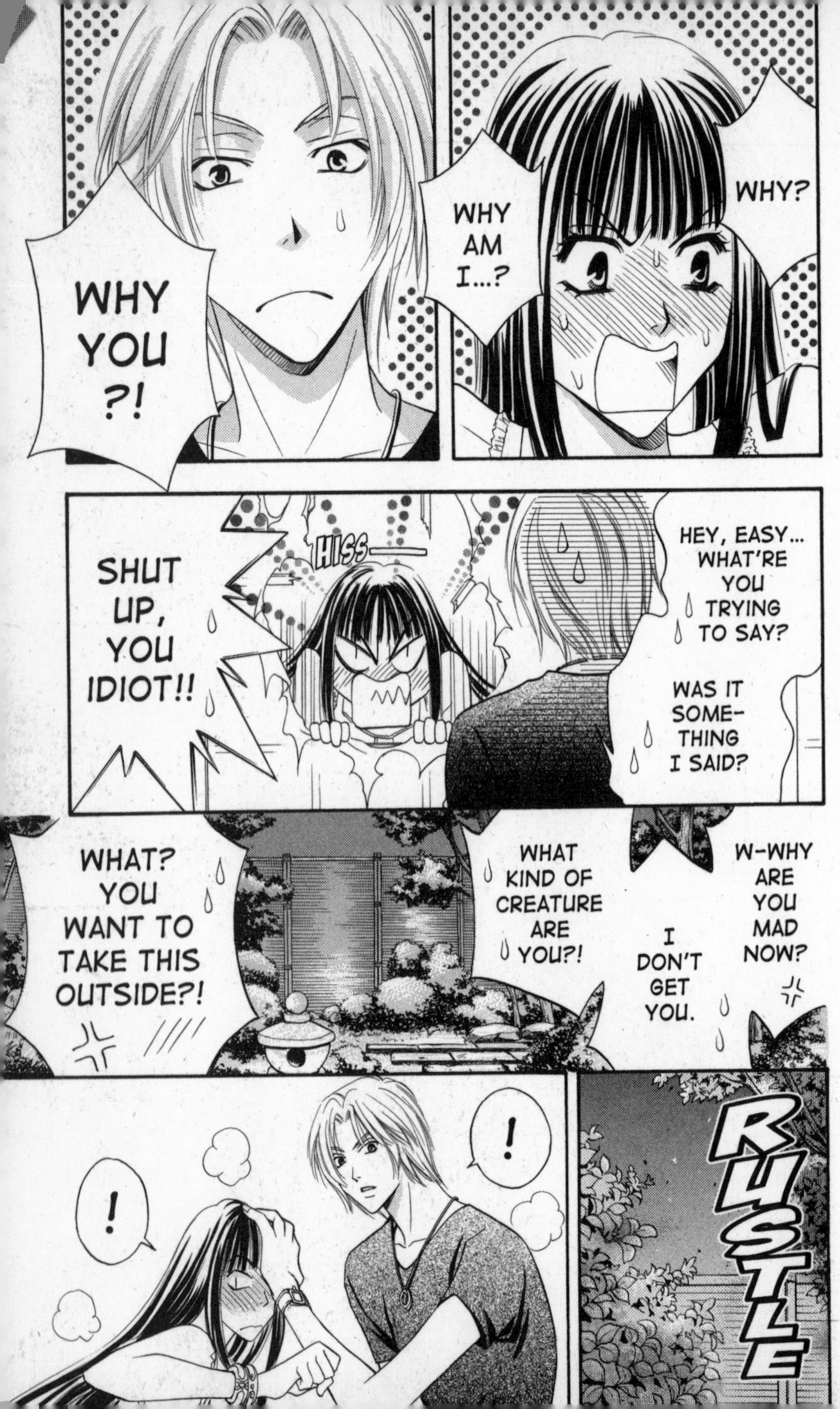
WHY?
WHY AM I...?
WHY YOU ?!
HEY, EASY... WHAT'RE YOU TRYING TO SAY?
WAS IT SOME-THING I SAID?
HISS—
SHUT UP, YOU IDIOT!!
W-WHY ARE YOU MAD NOW?
I DON'T GET YOU.
WHAT KIND OF CREATURE ARE YOU?!
WHAT? YOU WANT TO TAKE THIS OUTSIDE?!
RUSTLE
!
!

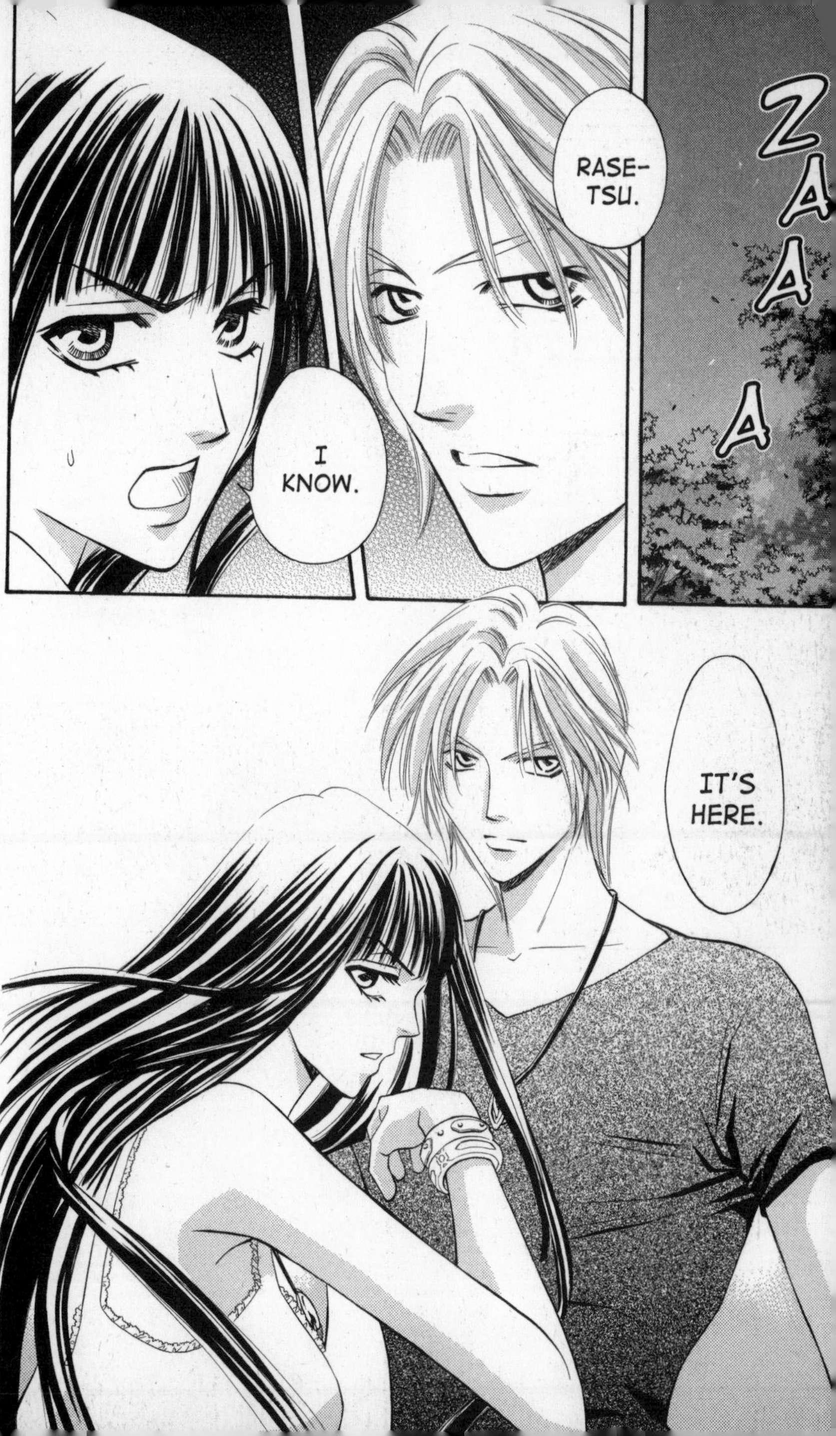
ZAAAA
RASE-TSU.
I KNOW.
IT'S HERE.

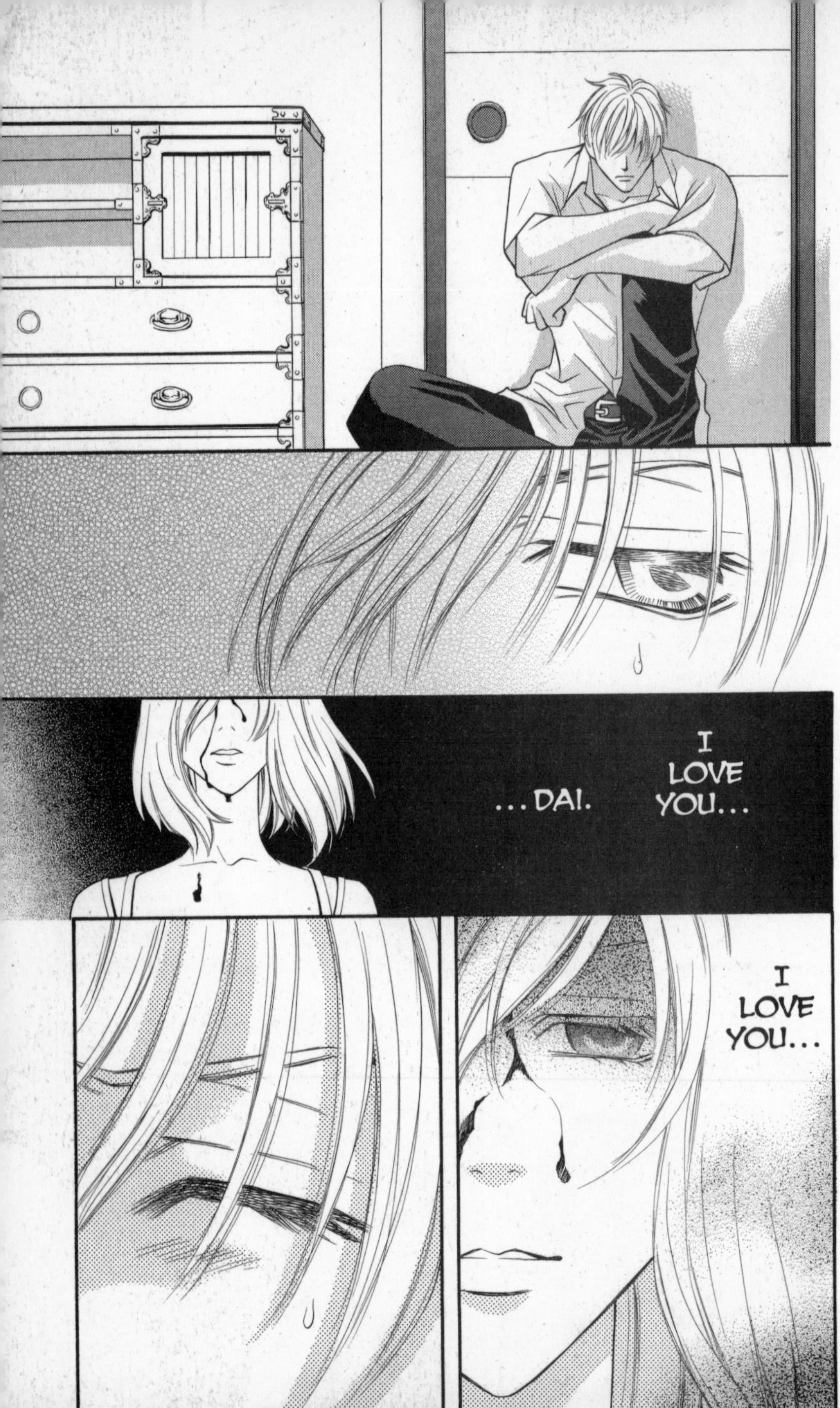
I LOVE YOU...
...DAI.
I LOVE YOU...

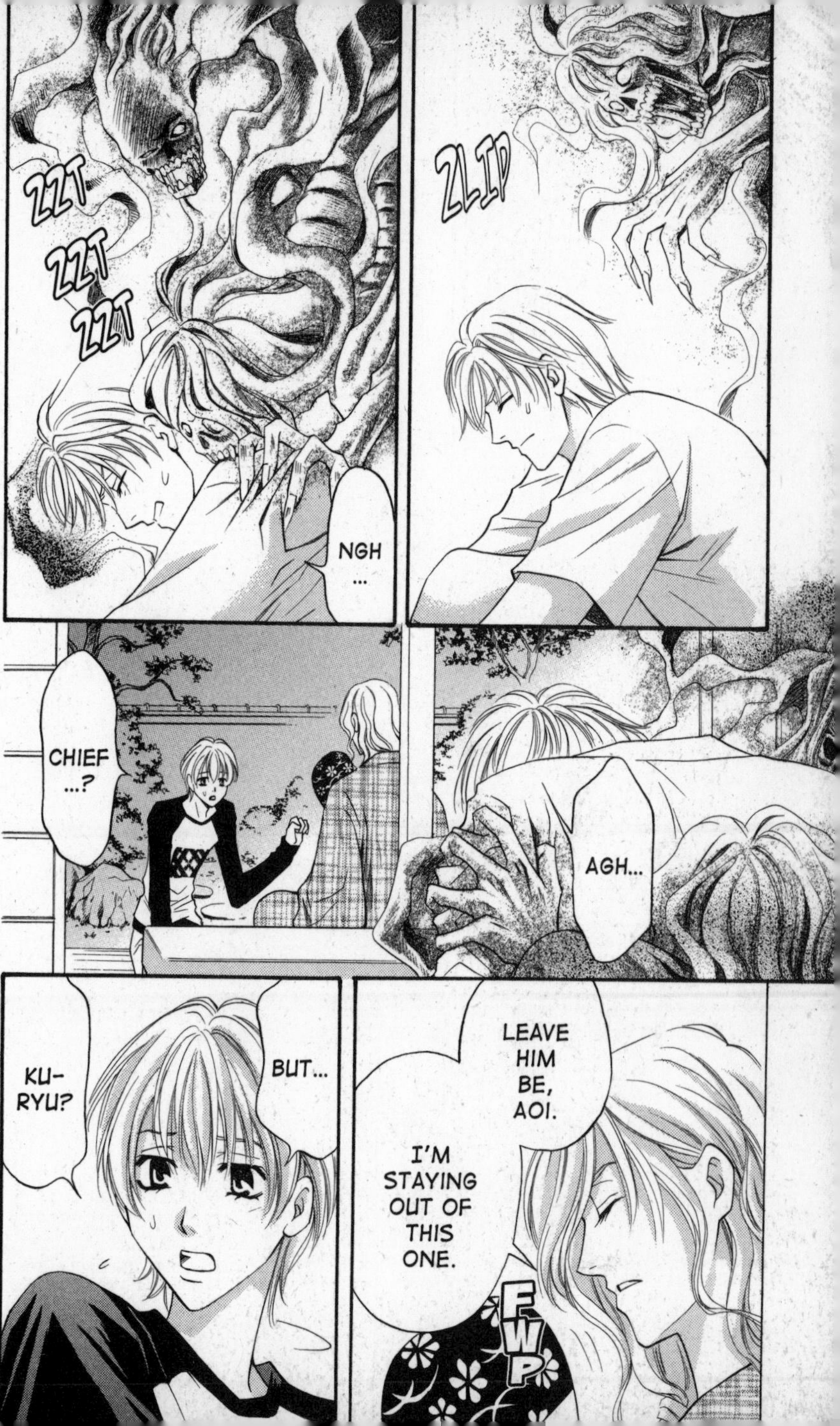
ZLIP
ZZT
ZZT
ZZT
NGH ...
AGH...
CHIEF ...?
LEAVE HIM BE, AOI.
I'M STAYING OUT OF THIS ONE.
FWP
BUT...
KU-RYU?

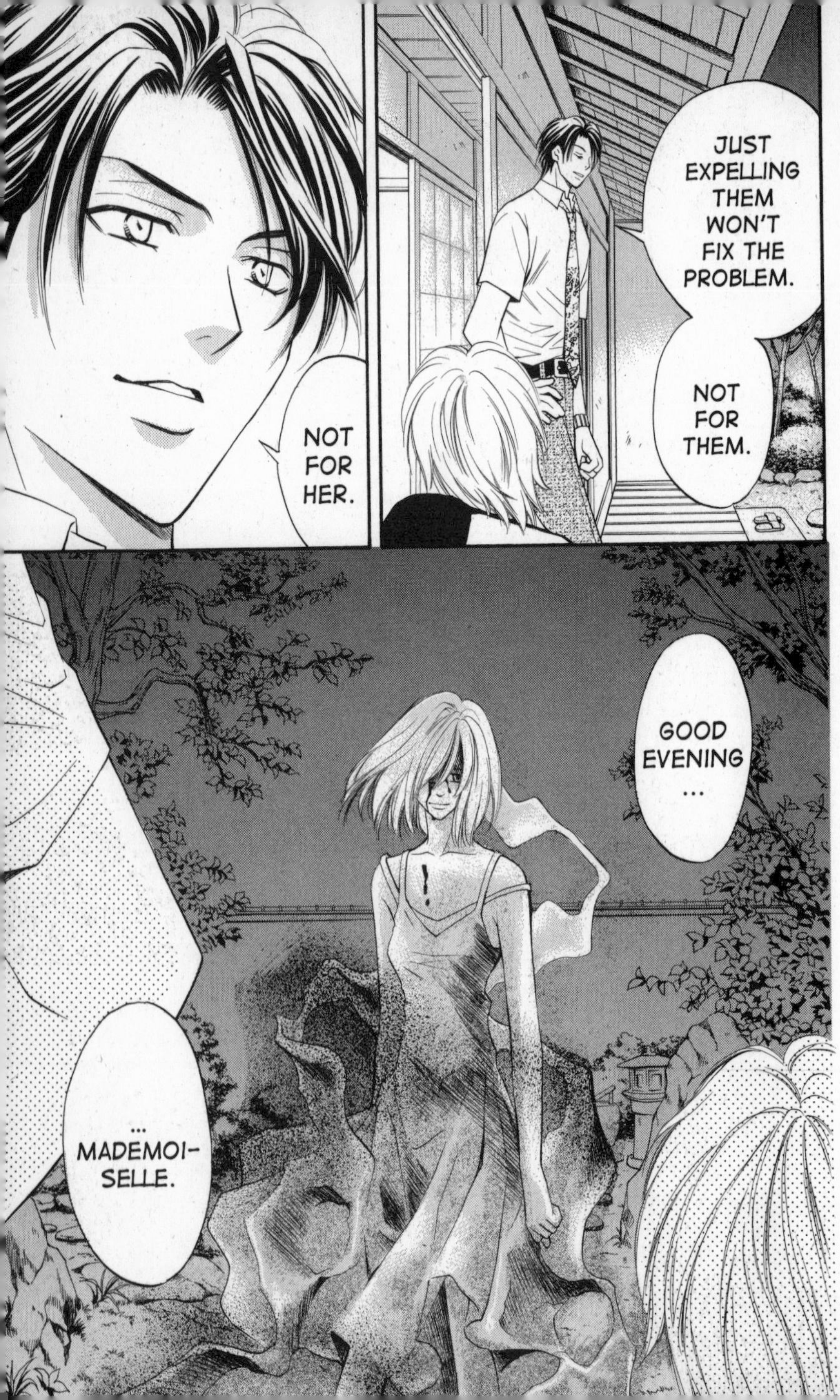
JUST EXPELLING THEM WON'T FIX THE PROBLEM.
NOT FOR THEM.
NOT FOR HER.
GOOD EVENING ...
... MADEMOI-SELLE.

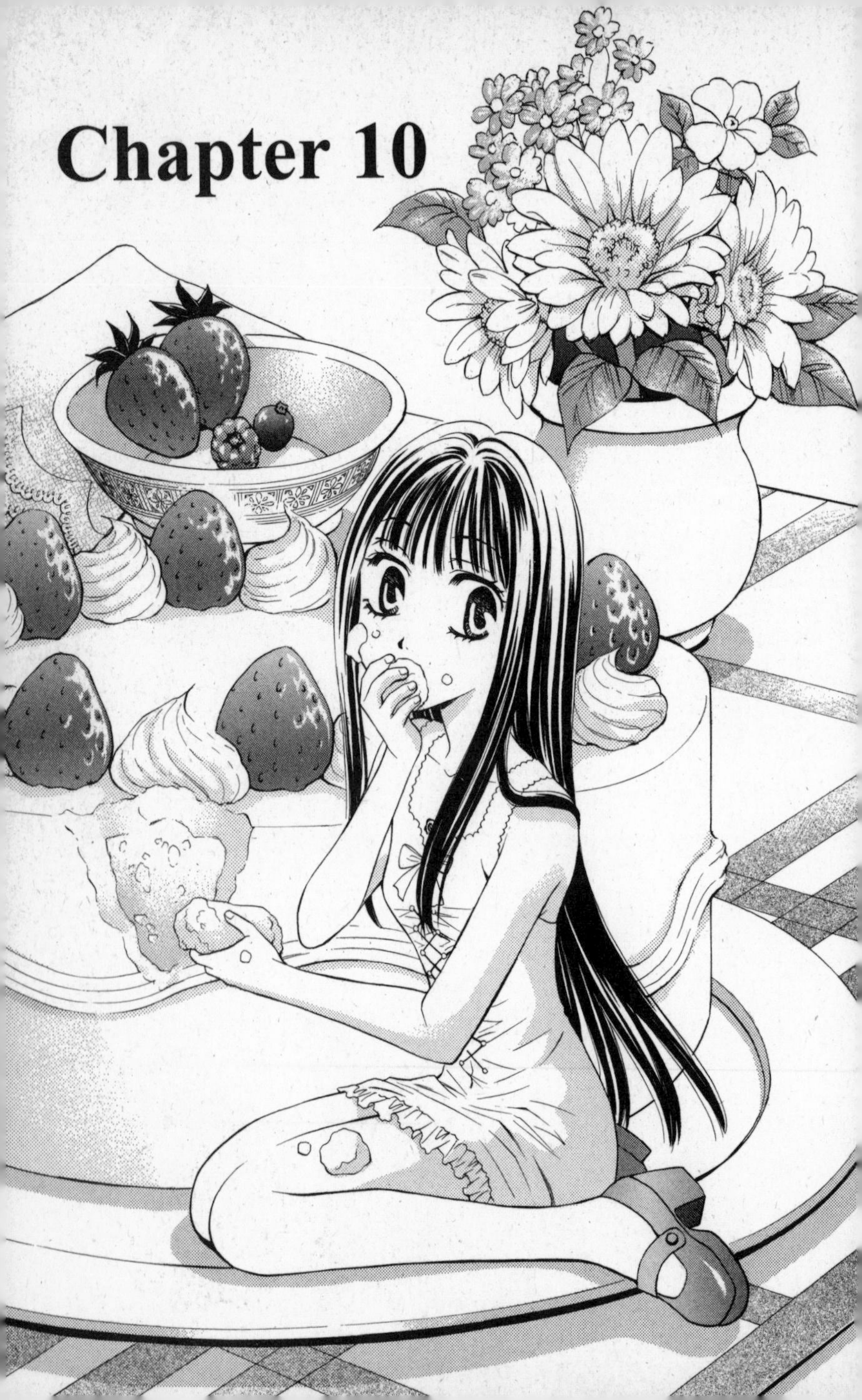
Chapter 10

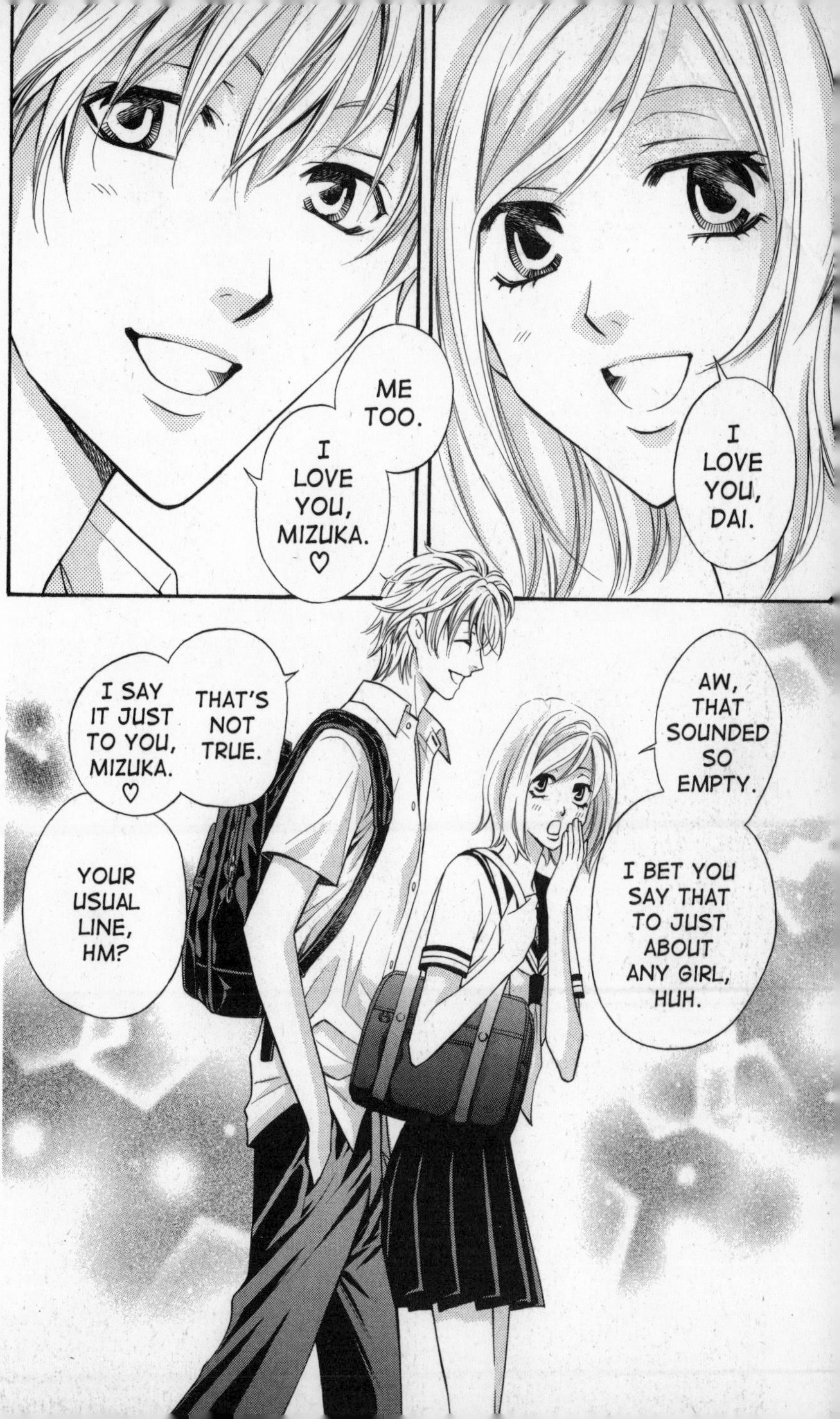
I LOVE YOU, DAI.
ME TOO.
I LOVE YOU, MIZUKA. ♡
AW, THAT SOUNDED SO EMPTY.
I BET YOU SAY THAT TO JUST ABOUT ANY GIRL, HUH.
THAT'S NOT TRUE.
I SAY IT JUST TO YOU, MIZUKA. ♡
YOUR USUAL LINE, HM?

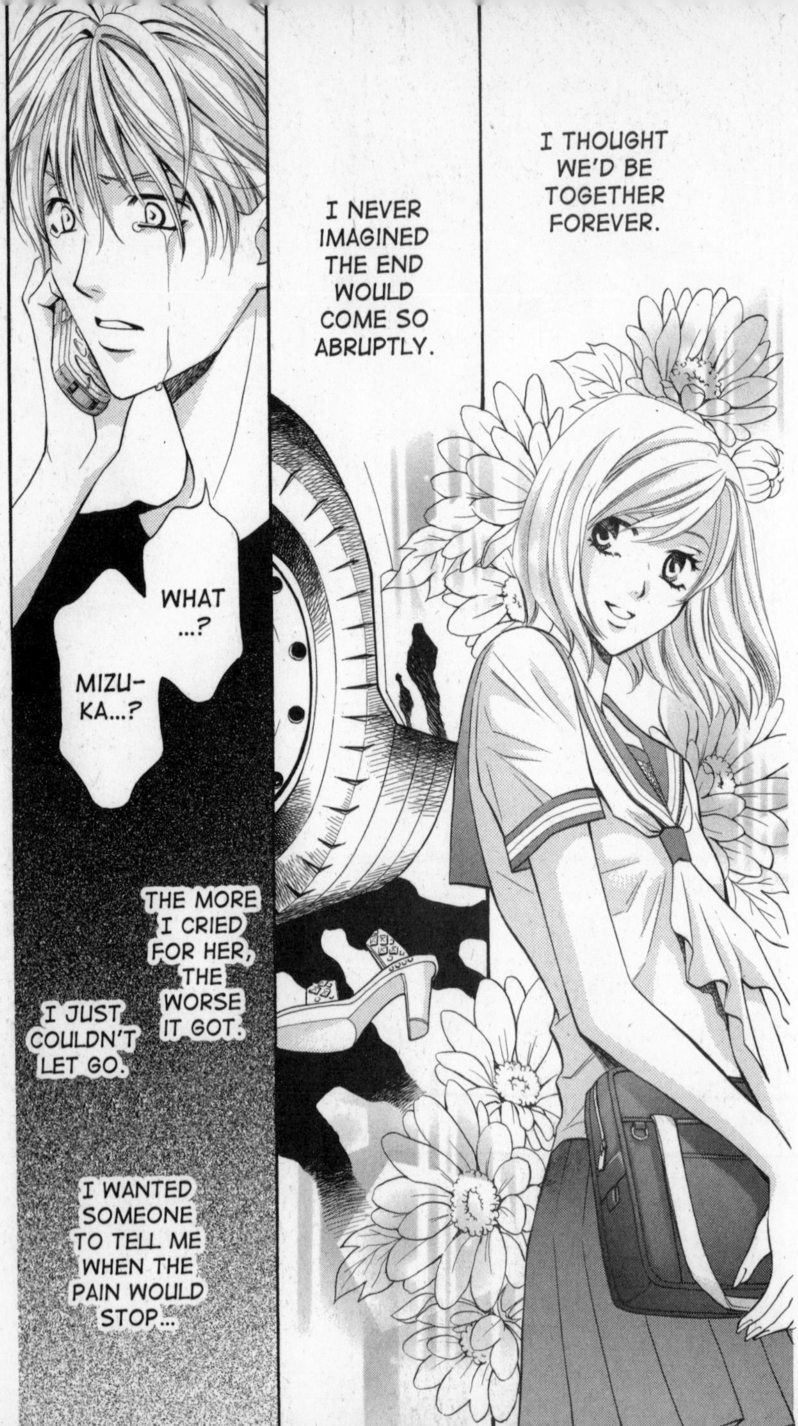
I THOUGHT WE'D BE TOGETHER FOREVER.
I NEVER IMAGINED THE END WOULD COME SO ABRUPTLY.
WHAT ...?
MIZUKA...?
THE MORE I CRIED FOR HER, THE WORSE IT GOT.
I JUST COULDN'T LET GO.
I WANTED SOMEONE TO TELL ME WHEN THE PAIN WOULD STOP...

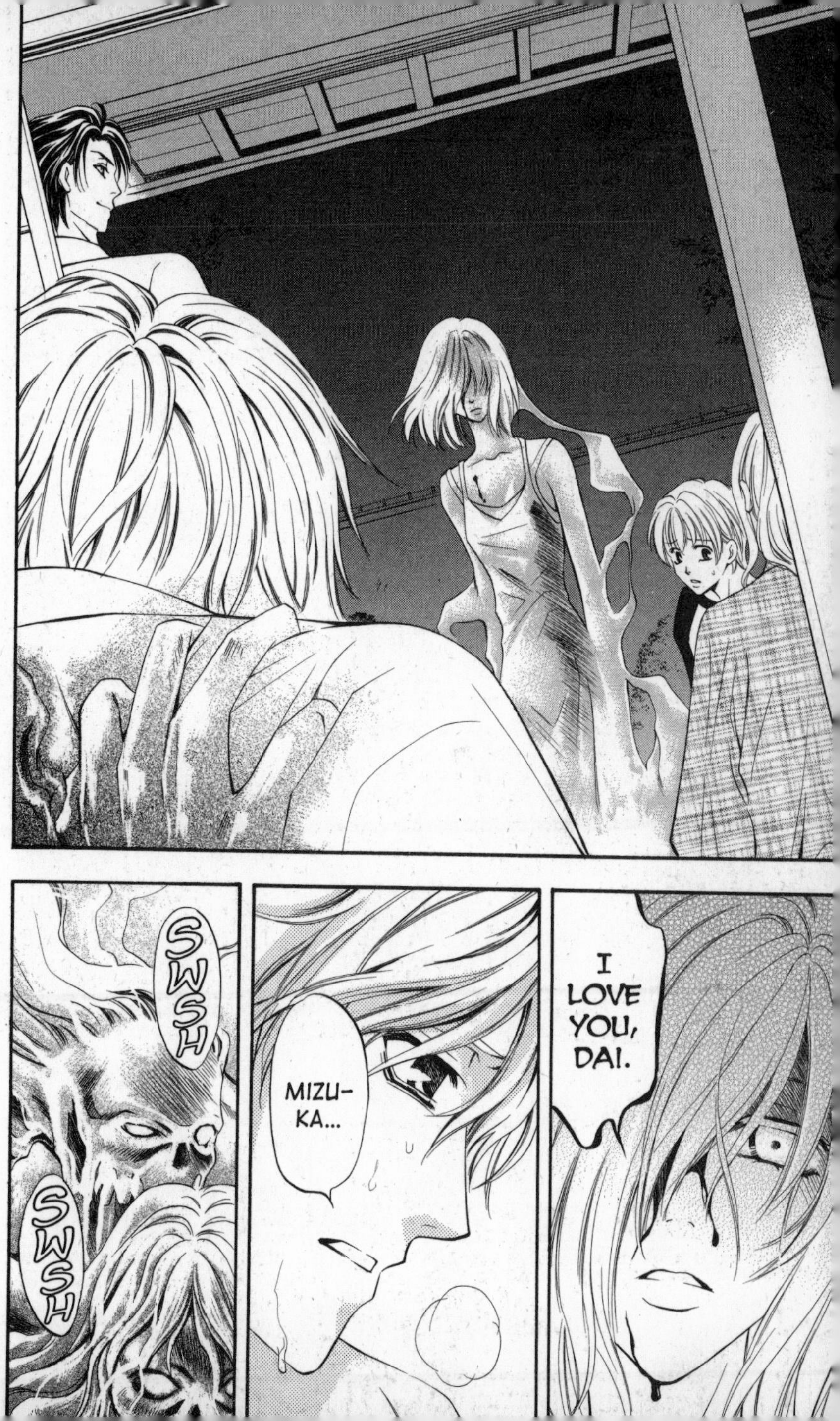
I LOVE YOU, DAI.
MIZU-KA...
SWSH
SWSH

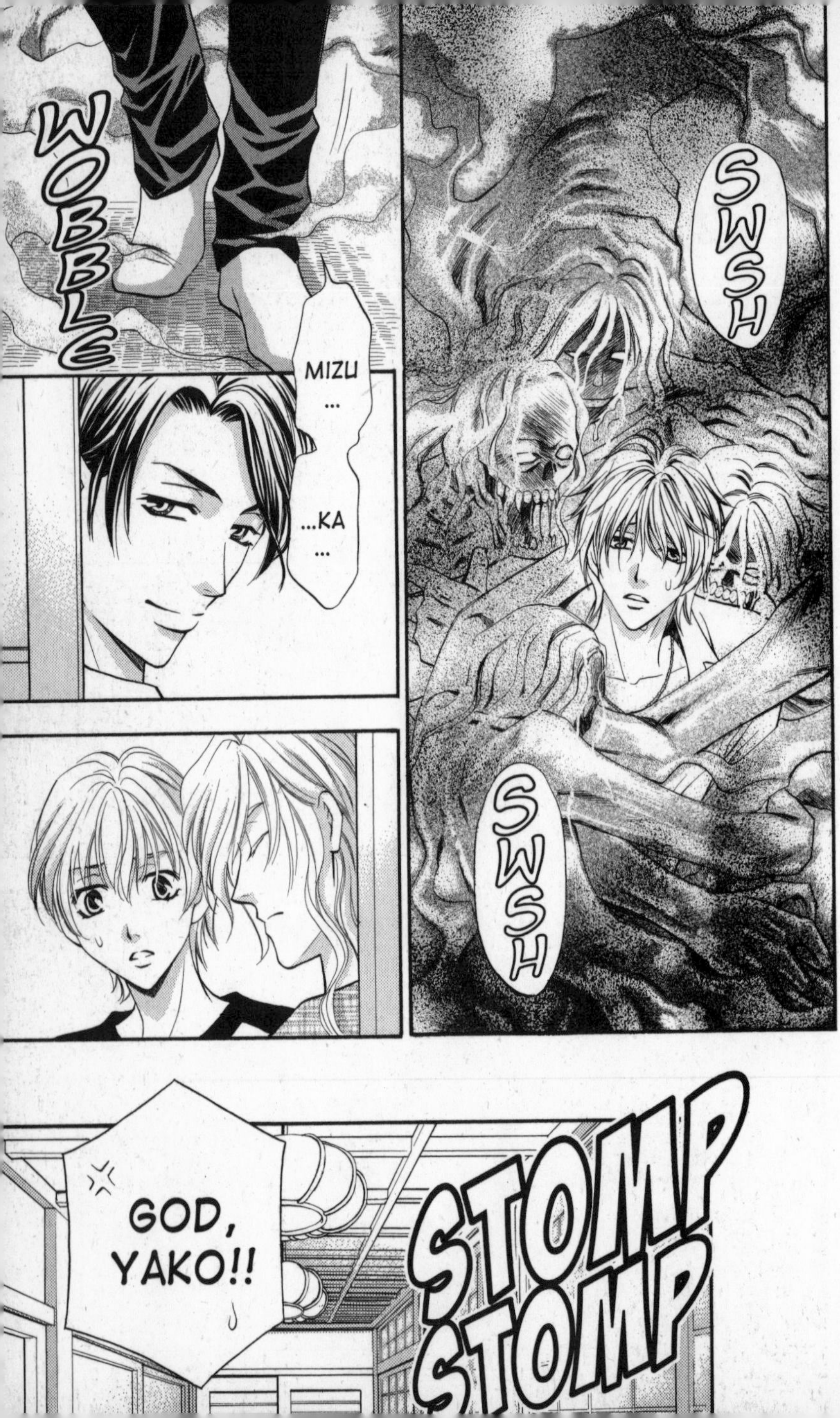
SWSH
SWSH
WOBBLE
MIZU ...
...KA ...
STOMP STOMP
GOD, YAKO!!

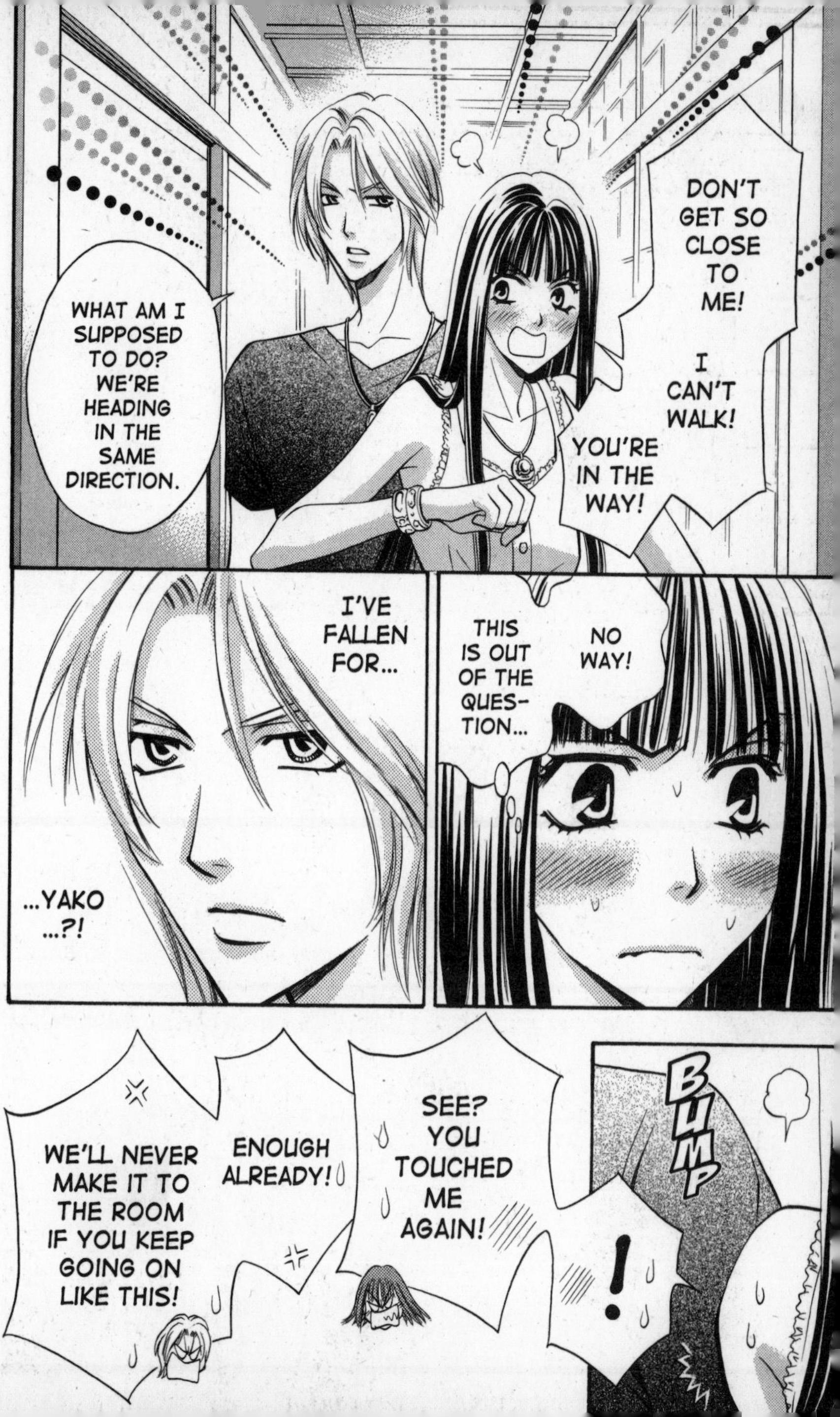
DON'T GET SO CLOSE TO ME!
I CAN'T WALK!
YOU'RE IN THE WAY!
WHAT AM I SUPPOSED TO DO? WE'RE HEADING IN THE SAME DIRECTION.
NO WAY!
THIS IS OUT OF THE QUES-TION...
I'VE FALLEN FOR...
...YAKO ...?!
BUMP
!
SEE? YOU TOUCHED ME AGAIN!
ENOUGH ALREADY!
WE'LL NEVER MAKE IT TO THE ROOM IF YOU KEEP GOING ON LIKE THIS!

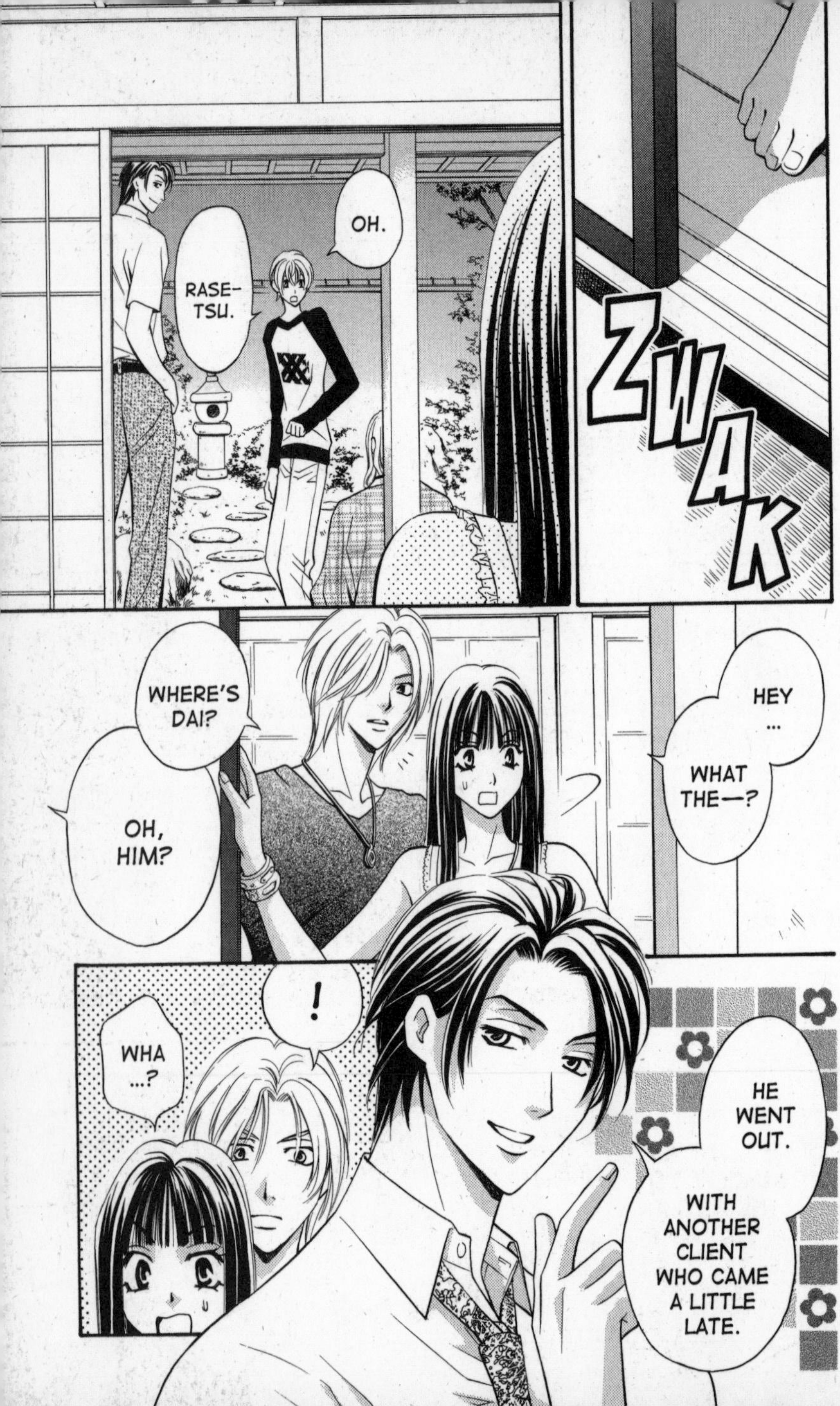
ZWAK
OH.
RASE-TSU.
HEY ... WHAT THE—?
WHERE'S DAI?
OH, HIM?
HE WENT OUT.
WITH ANOTHER CLIENT WHO CAME A LITTLE LATE.
!
WHA ...?

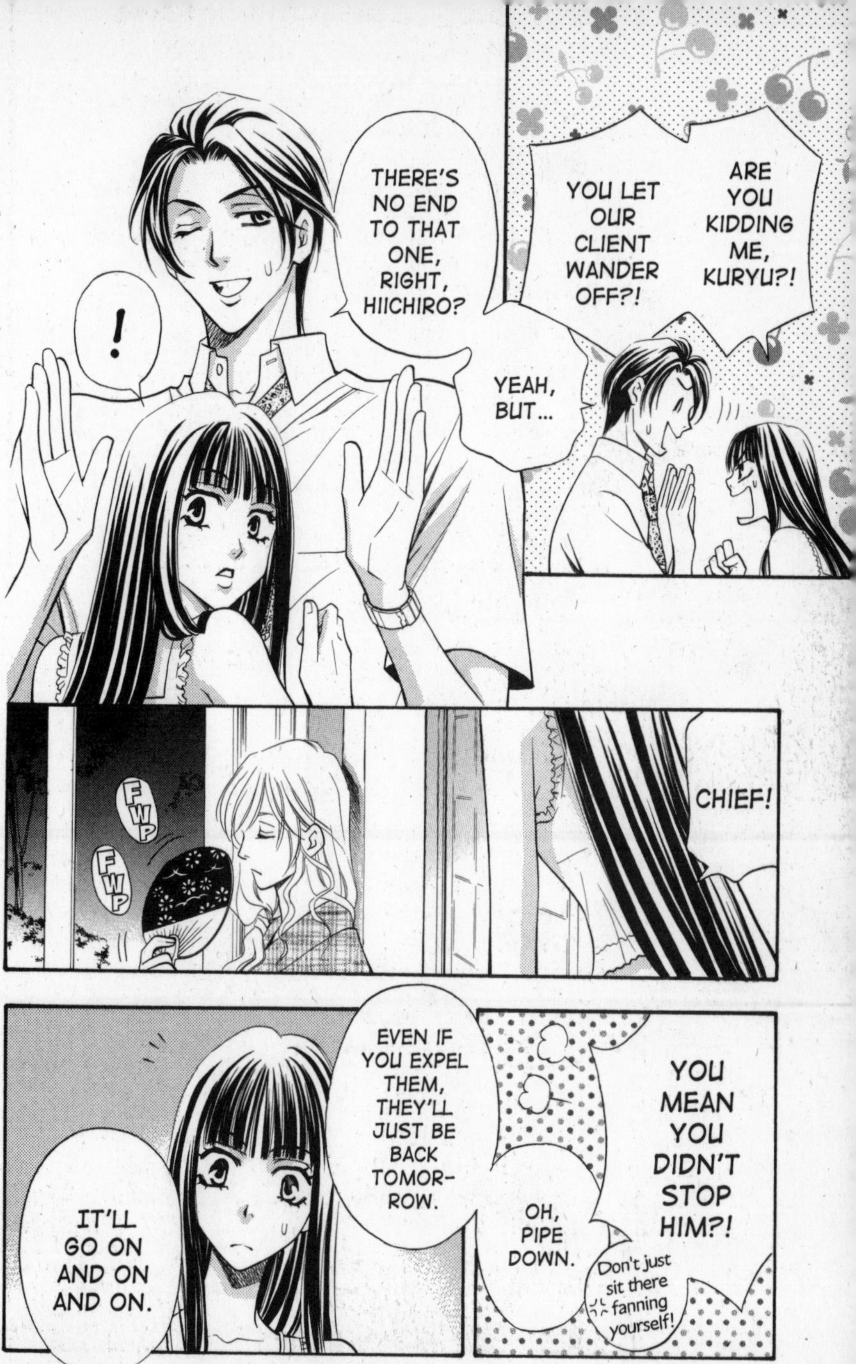
ARE YOU KIDDING ME, KURYU?!
YOU LET OUR CLIENT WANDER OFF?!
YEAH, BUT...
THERE'S NO END TO THAT ONE, RIGHT, HIICHIRO?
!
CHIEF!
FWP
FWP
YOU MEAN YOU DIDN'T STOP HIM?!
Don't just sit there fanning yourself!
OH, PIPE DOWN.
EVEN IF YOU EXPEL THEM, THEY'LL JUST BE BACK TOMOR-ROW.
IT'LL GO ON AND ON AND ON.

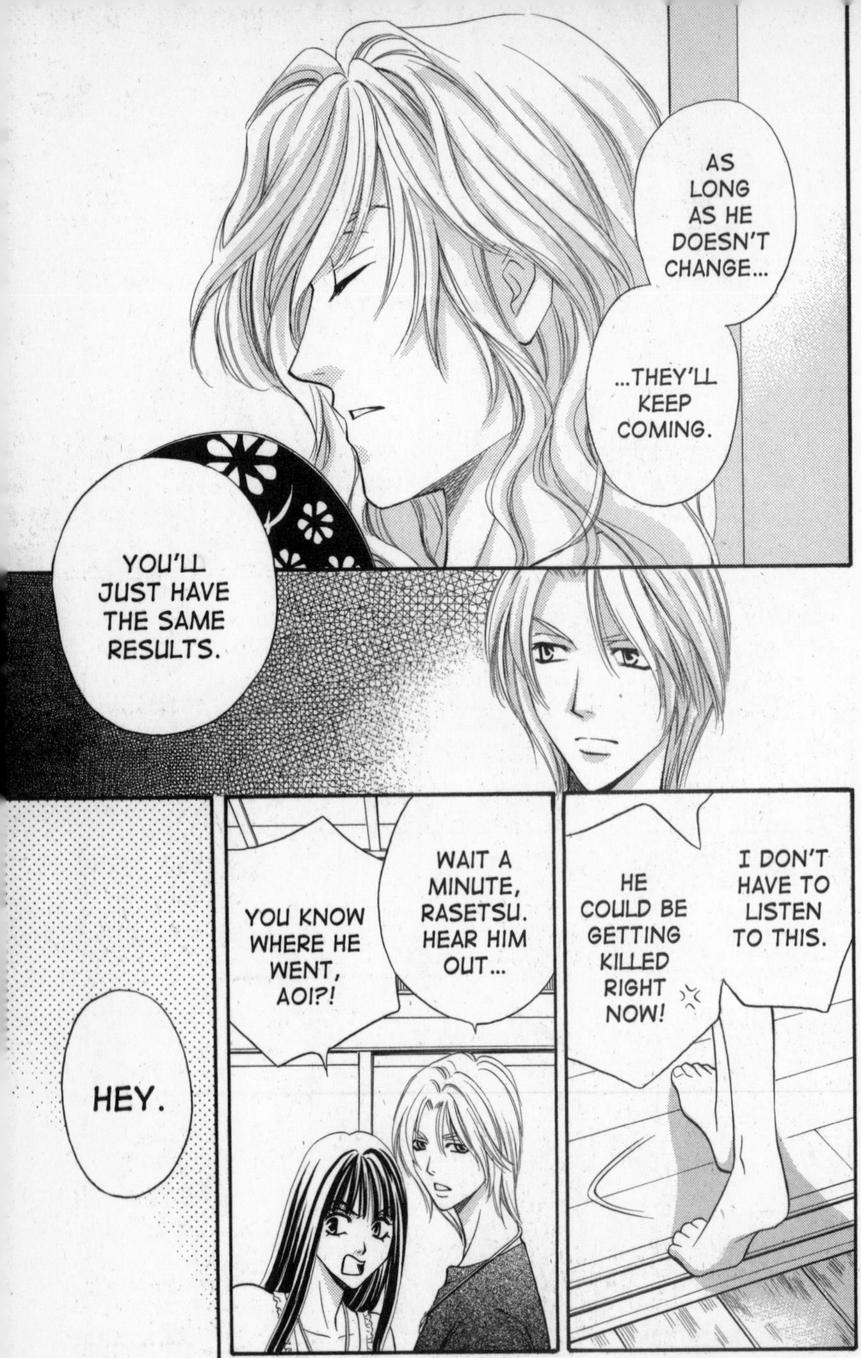
AS LONG AS HE DOESN'T CHANGE...
...THEY'LL KEEP COMING.
YOU'LL JUST HAVE THE SAME RESULTS.
I DON'T HAVE TO LISTEN TO THIS.
HE COULD BE GETTING KILLED RIGHT NOW!
WAIT A MINUTE, RASETSU. HEAR HIM OUT...
YOU KNOW WHERE HE WENT, AOI?!
HEY.

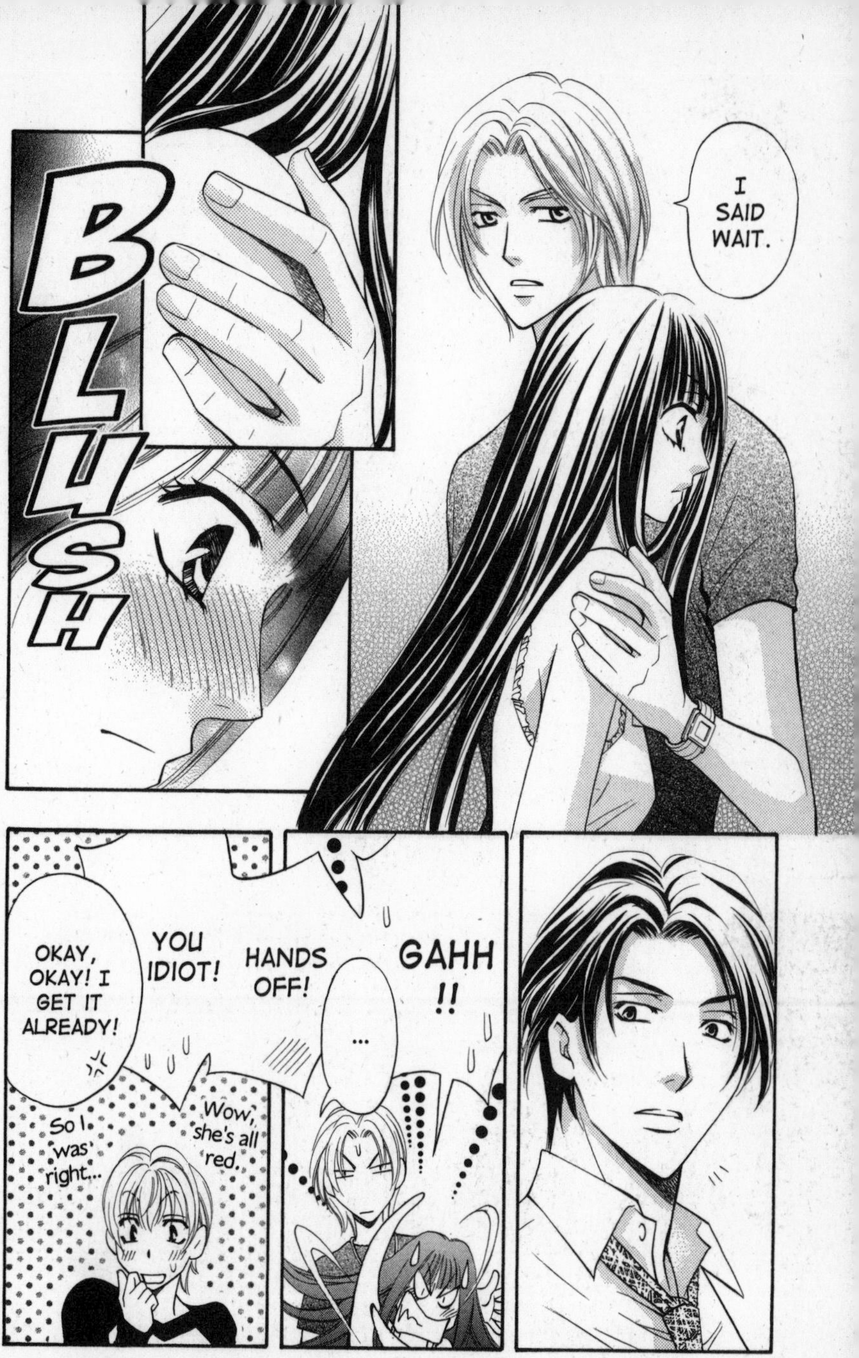
I SAID WAIT.
BLUSH
GAHH !!
HANDS OFF!
YOU IDIOT!
...
OKAY, OKAY! I GET IT ALREADY!
Wow, she's all red..
So I was right...

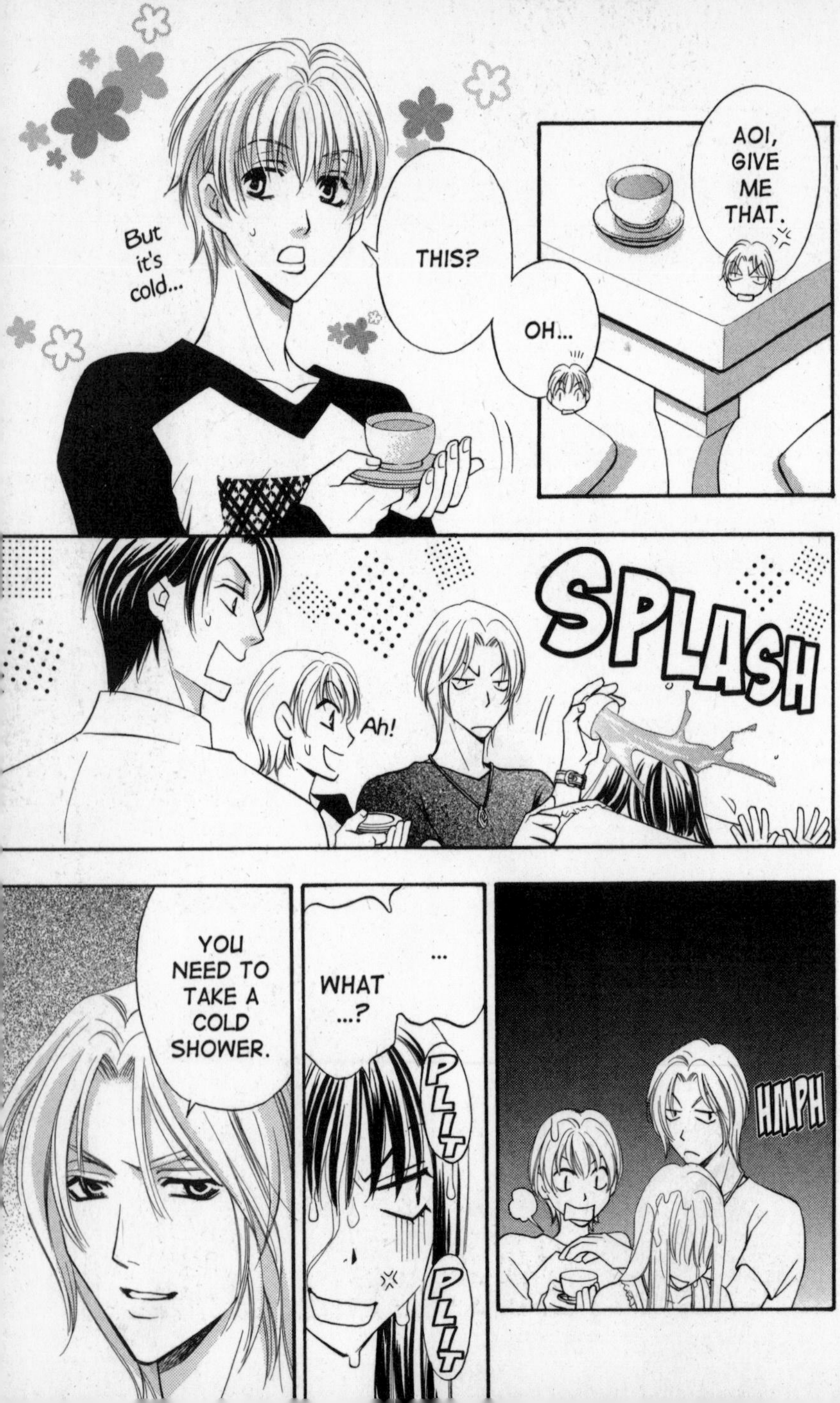
AOI, GIVE ME THAT.
THIS?
OH...
But it's cold...
SPLASH
Ah!
HMPH
...
WHAT ...?
PLIT
PLIT
YOU NEED TO TAKE A COLD SHOWER.

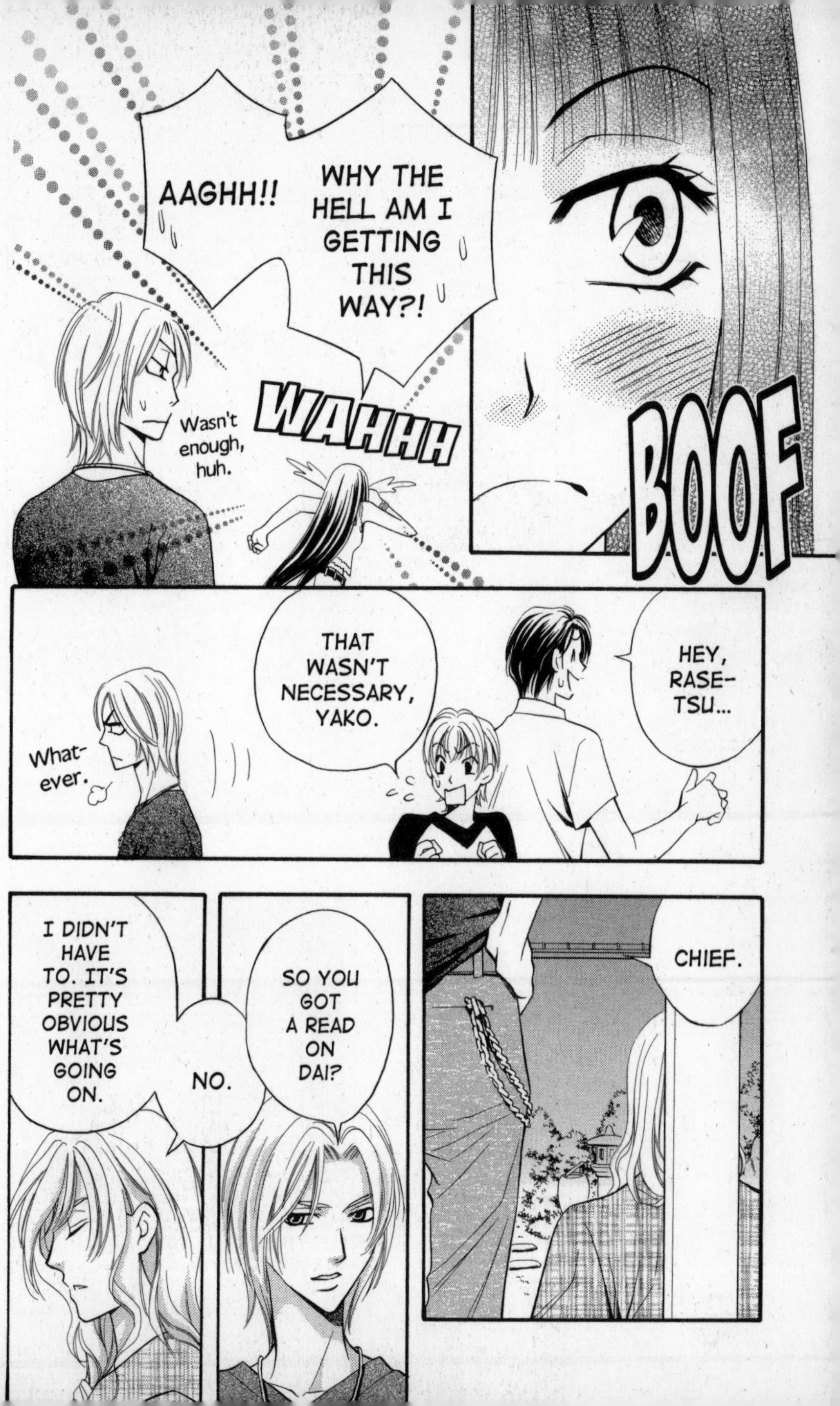
BOOF
AAGHH!!
WHY THE HELL AM I GETTING THIS WAY?!
WAHHH
Wasn't enough, huh.
HEY, RASE-TSU...
THAT WASN'T NECESSARY, YAKO.
What-ever.
CHIEF.
SO YOU GOT A READ ON DAI?
NO.
I DIDN'T HAVE TO. IT'S PRETTY OBVIOUS WHAT'S GOING ON.

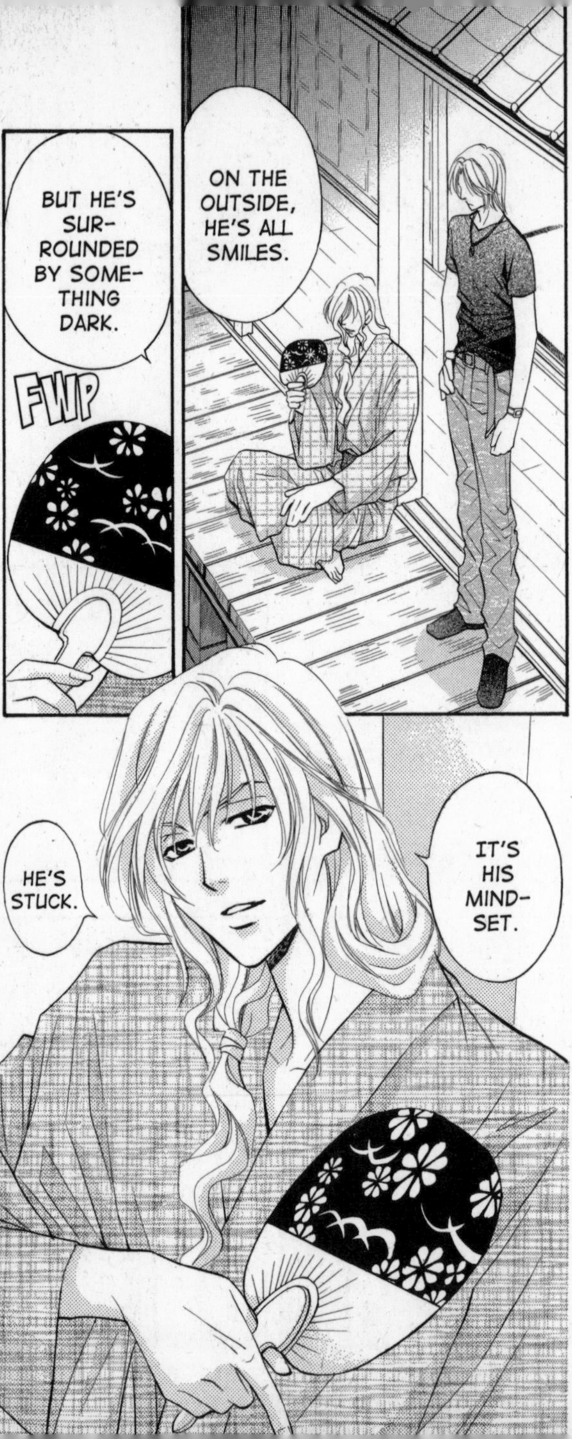
ON THE OUTSIDE, HE'S ALL SMILES.
BUT HE'S SUR-ROUNDED BY SOME-THING DARK.
FWP
IT'S HIS MIND-SET.
HE'S STUCK.

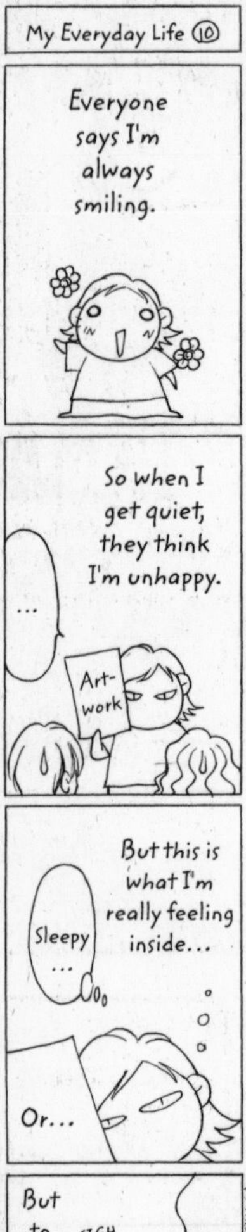
My Everyday Life ⑩
Everyone says I'm always smiling.
So when I get quiet, they think I'm unhappy.
...
Art-work
But this is what I'm really feeling inside...
Sleepy ...
Or...
But to them ...
SIGH
Tired ...
She doesn't like it...
She's examin-ing my work ...
FRET FRET

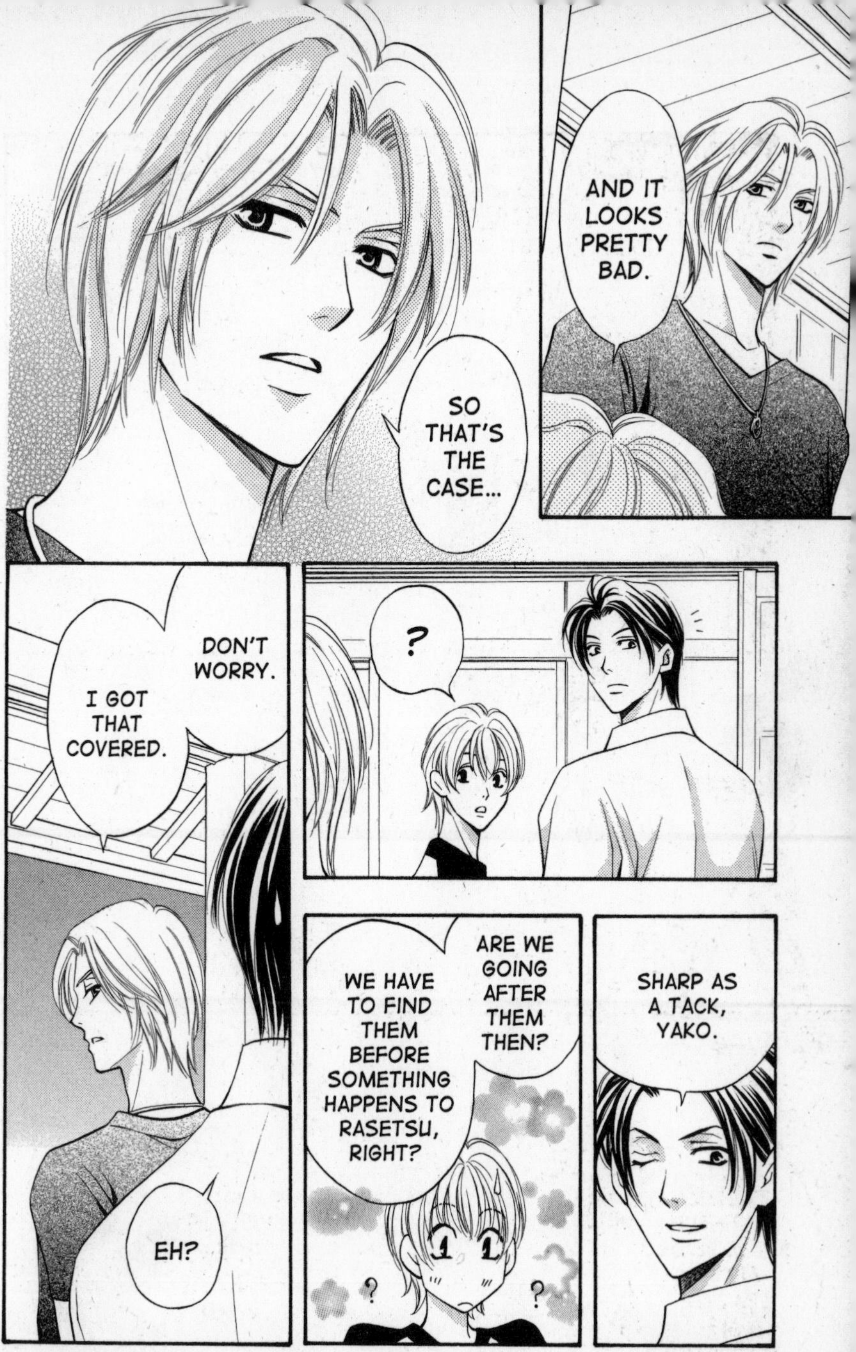
AND IT LOOKS PRETTY BAD.
SO THAT'S THE CASE...
?
SHARP AS A TACK, YAKO.
ARE WE GOING AFTER THEM THEN?
WE HAVE TO FIND THEM BEFORE SOMETHING HAPPENS TO RASETSU, RIGHT?
? ?
DON'T WORRY.
I GOT THAT COVERED.
EH?

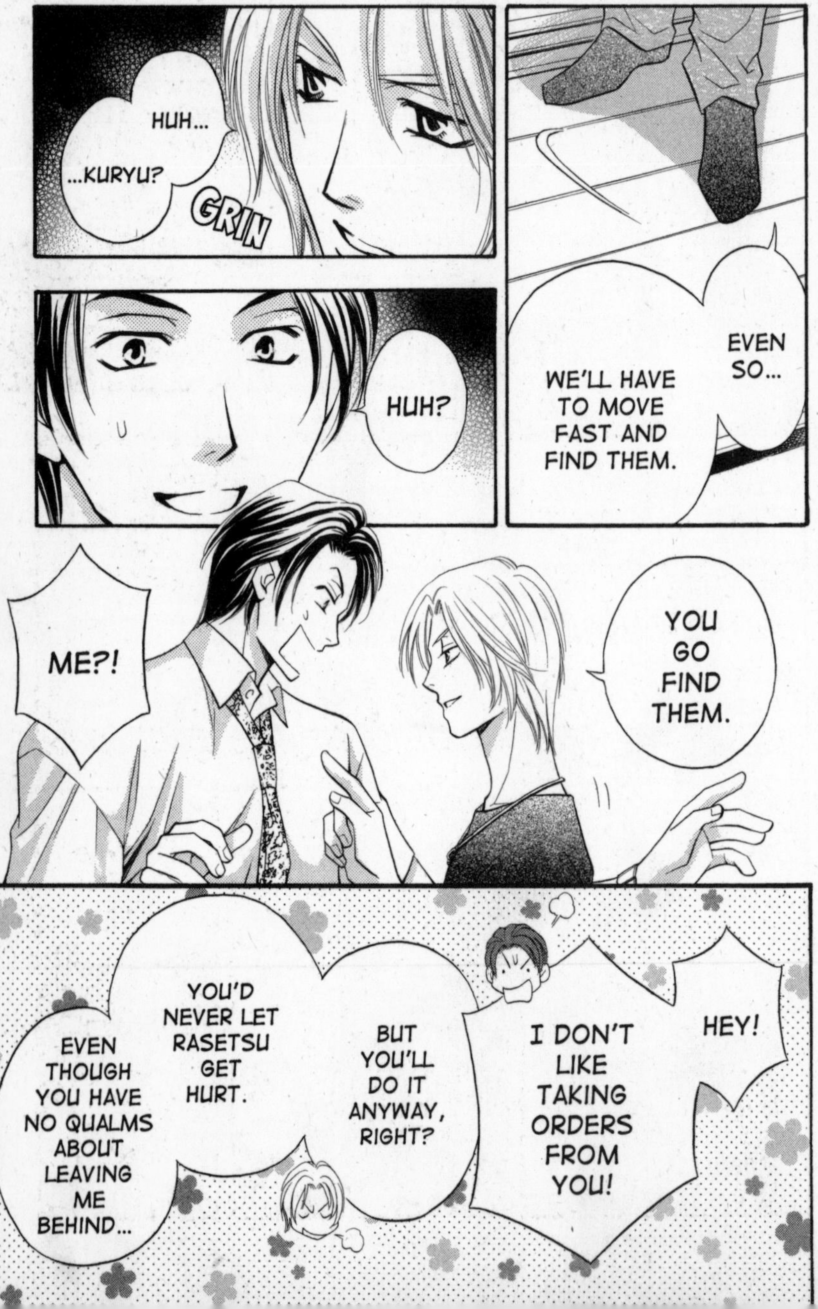
EVEN SO...
WE'LL HAVE TO MOVE FAST AND FIND THEM.
HUH... ...KURYU?
GRIN
HUH?
YOU GO FIND THEM.
ME?!
HEY!
I DON'T LIKE TAKING ORDERS FROM YOU!
BUT YOU'LL DO IT ANYWAY, RIGHT?
YOU'D NEVER LET RASETSU GET HURT.
EVEN THOUGH YOU HAVE NO QUALMS ABOUT LEAVING ME BEHIND...

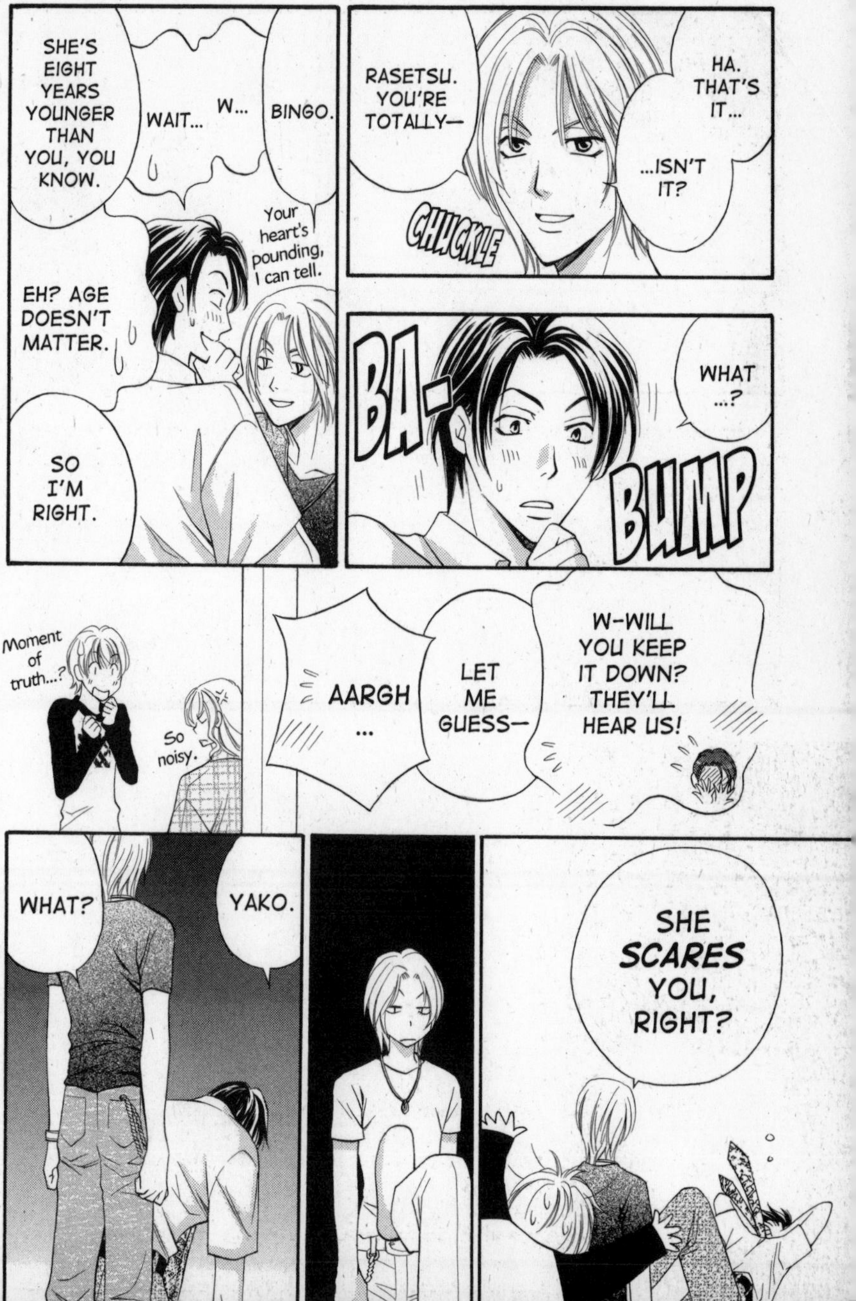
RASETSU. YOU'RE TOTALLY—
HA. THAT'S IT...
...ISN'T IT?
CHUCKLE
WHAT ...?
BA-BUMP
BINGO.
W...
WAIT...
SHE'S EIGHT YEARS YOUNGER THAN YOU, YOU KNOW.
Your heart's pounding, I can tell.
EH? AGE DOESN'T MATTER.
SO I'M RIGHT.
W-WILL YOU KEEP IT DOWN? THEY'LL HEAR US!
LET ME GUESS—
AARGH ...
So noisy.
Moment of truth...?
SHE *SCARES* YOU, RIGHT?
YAKO.
WHAT?

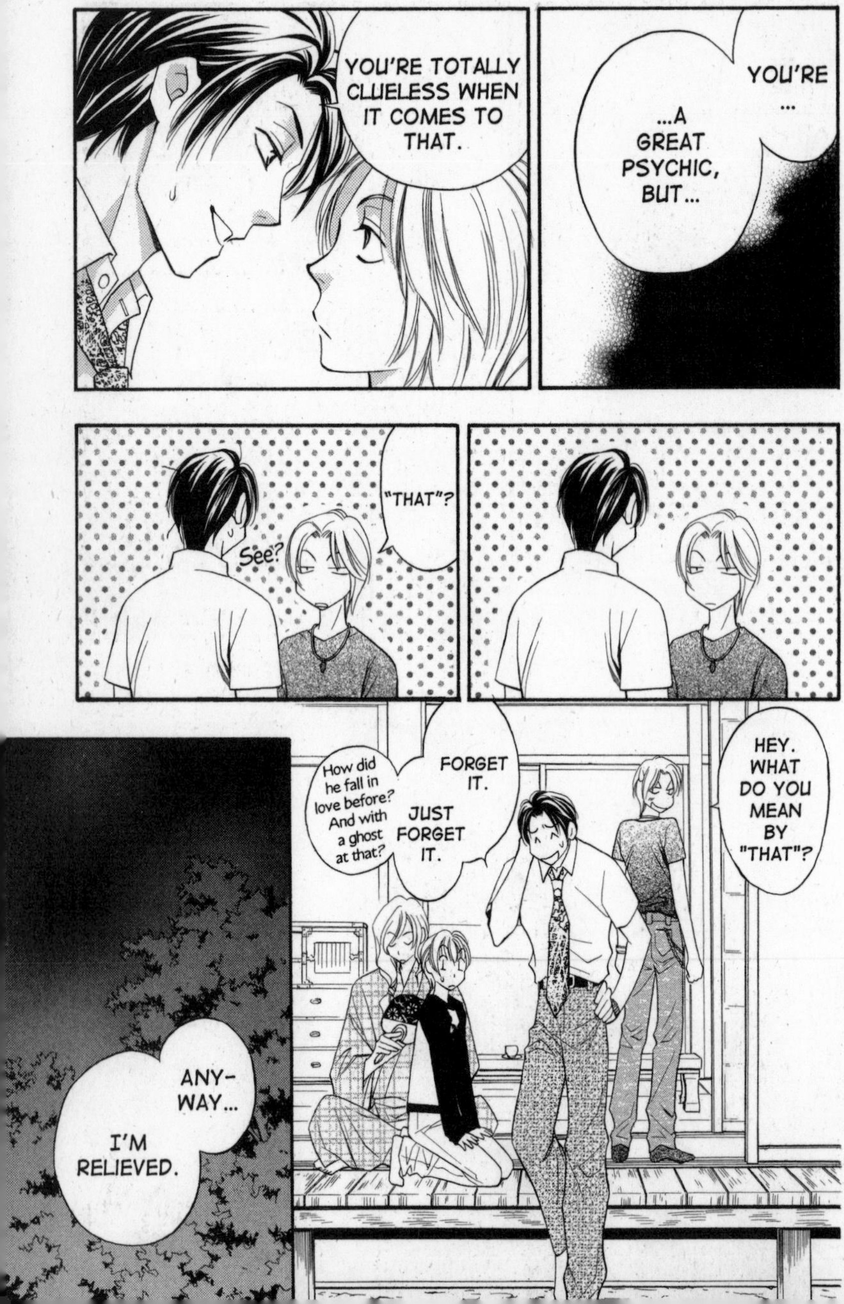
YOU'RE ...
...A GREAT PSYCHIC, BUT...
YOU'RE TOTALLY CLUELESS WHEN IT COMES TO THAT.
"THAT"?
See?
HEY. WHAT DO YOU MEAN BY "THAT"?
FORGET IT. JUST FORGET IT.
How did he fall in love before? And with a ghost at that?
ANY-WAY...
I'M RELIEVED.

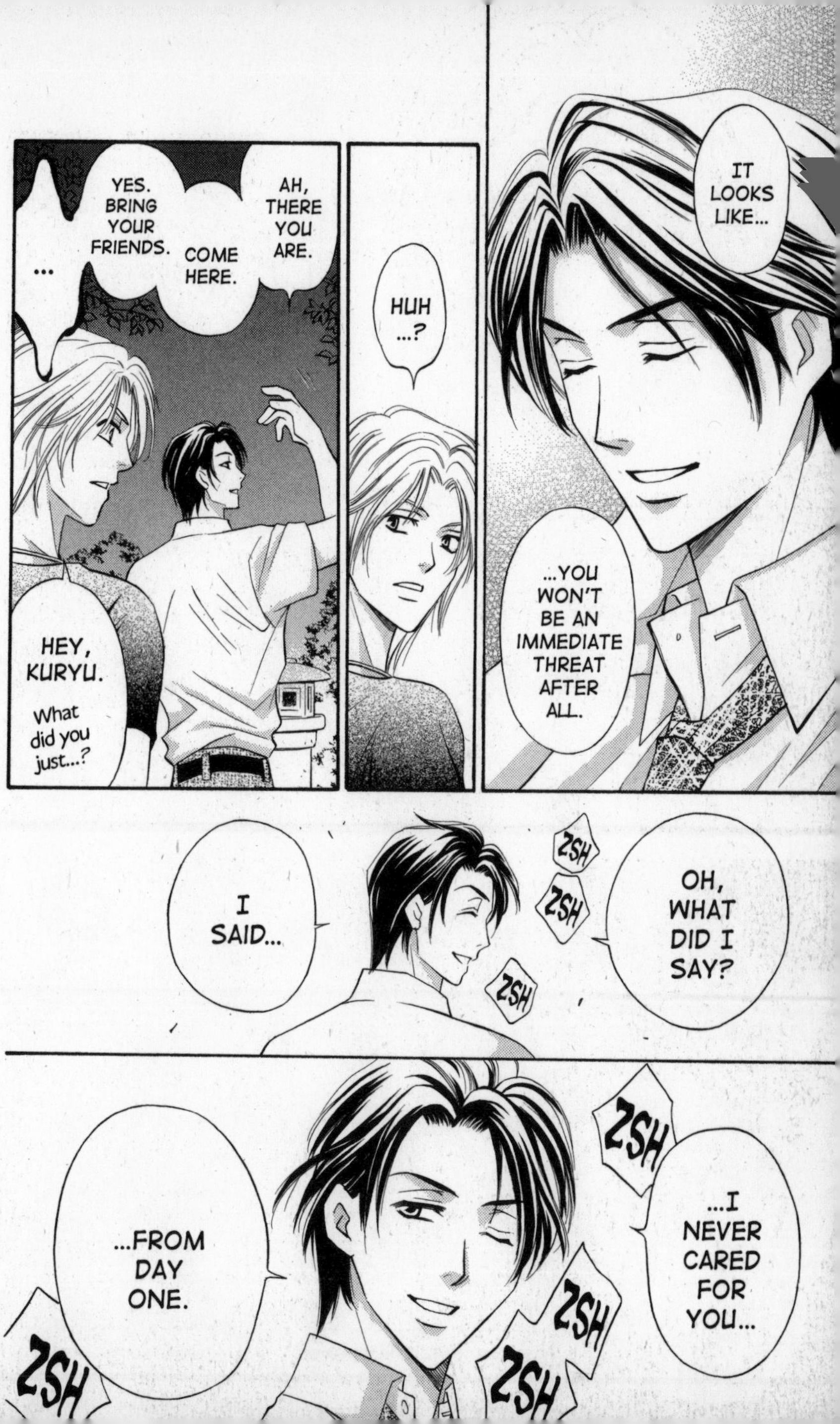
IT LOOKS LIKE...
...YOU WON'T BE AN IMMEDIATE THREAT AFTER ALL.
HUH ...?
AH, THERE YOU ARE.
COME HERE.
YES. BRING YOUR FRIENDS.
...
HEY, KURYU.
What did you just...?
OH, WHAT DID I SAY?
ZSH
ZSH
ZSH
I SAID...
ZSH
...I NEVER CARED FOR YOU...
ZSH
ZSH
...FROM DAY ONE.
ZSH

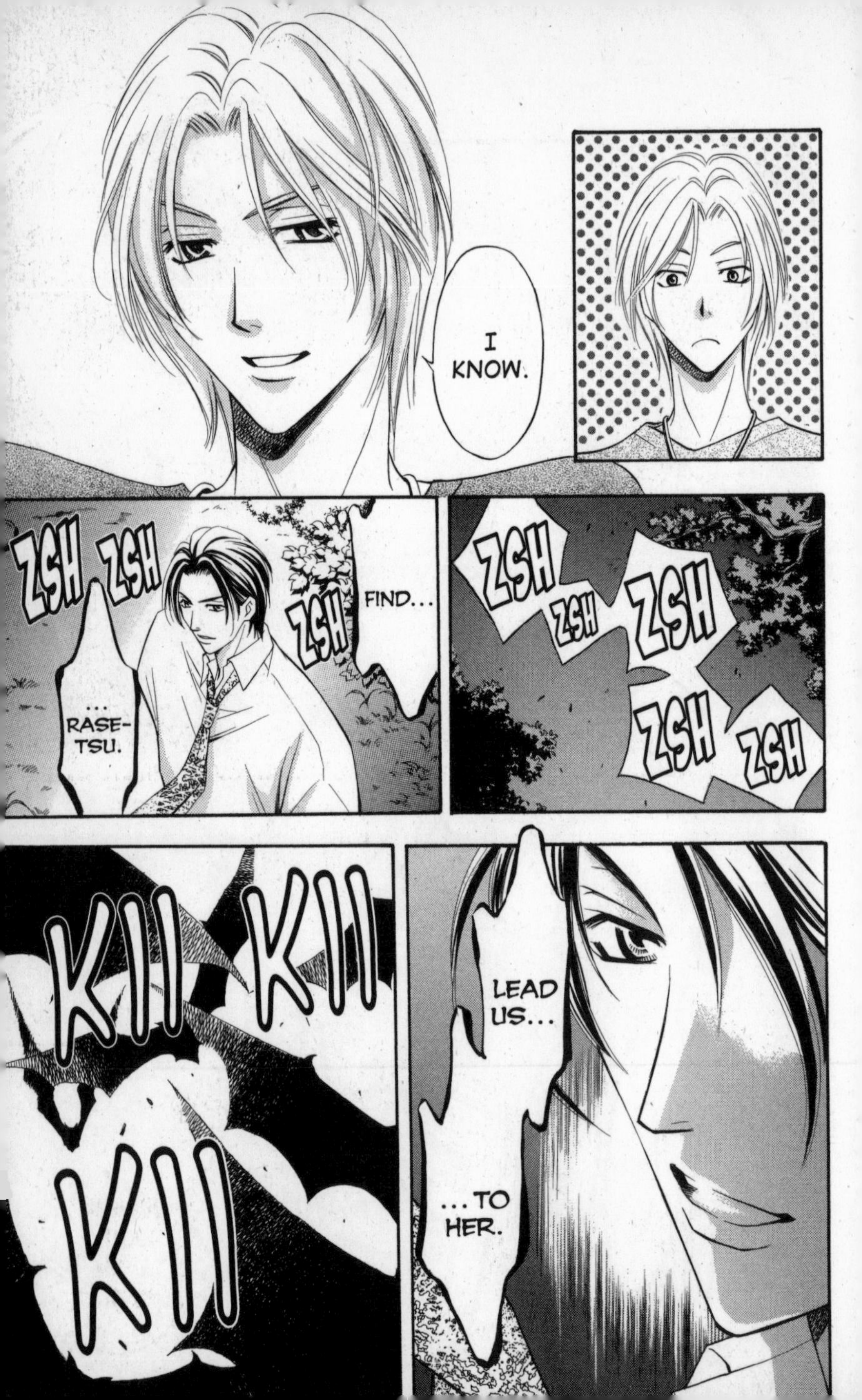
I KNOW.
ZSH
ZSH
ZSH
ZSH
ZSH
ZSH ZSH
ZSH
FIND...
...RASE-TSU.
LEAD US...
...TO HER.
KII KII
KII

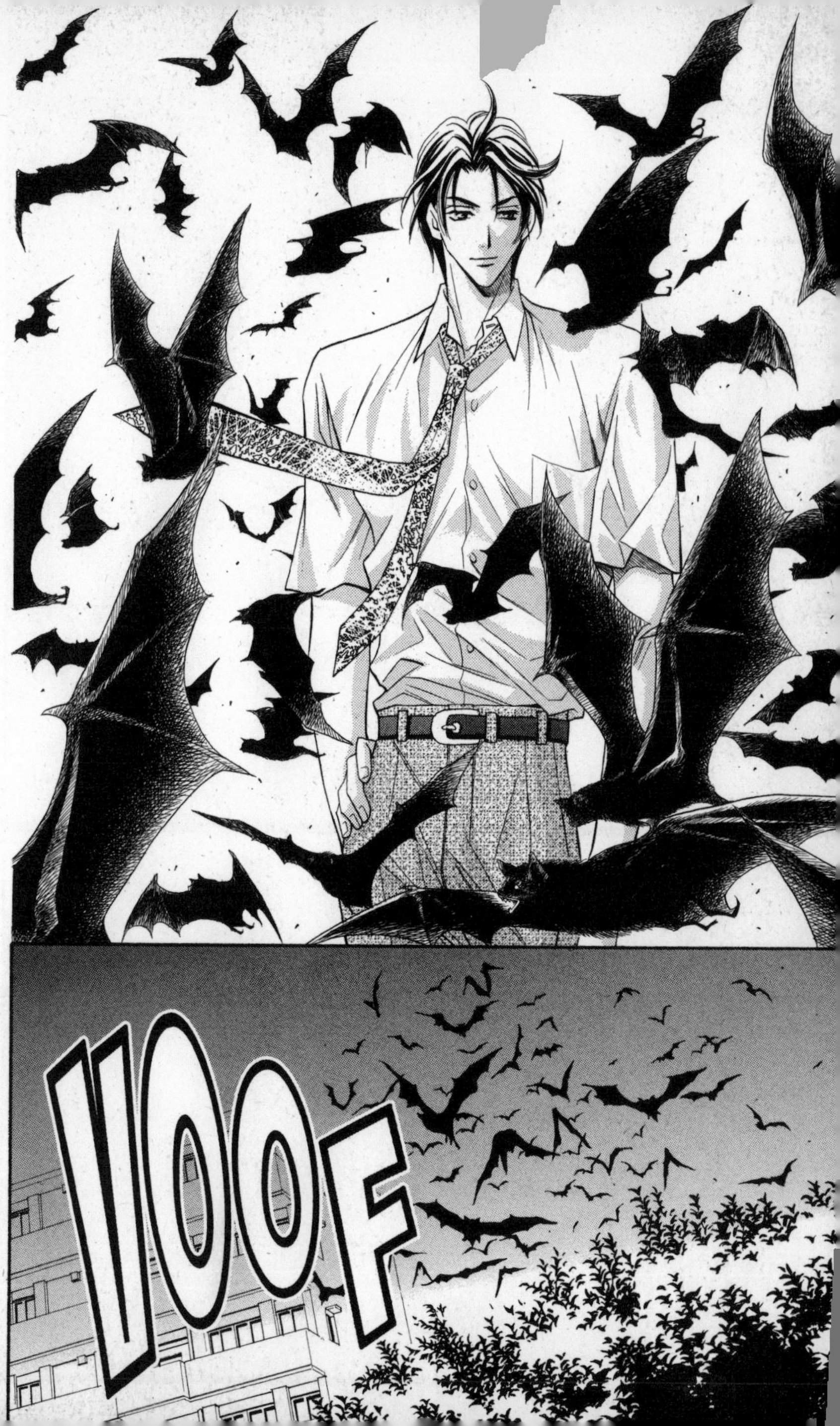
VOOF

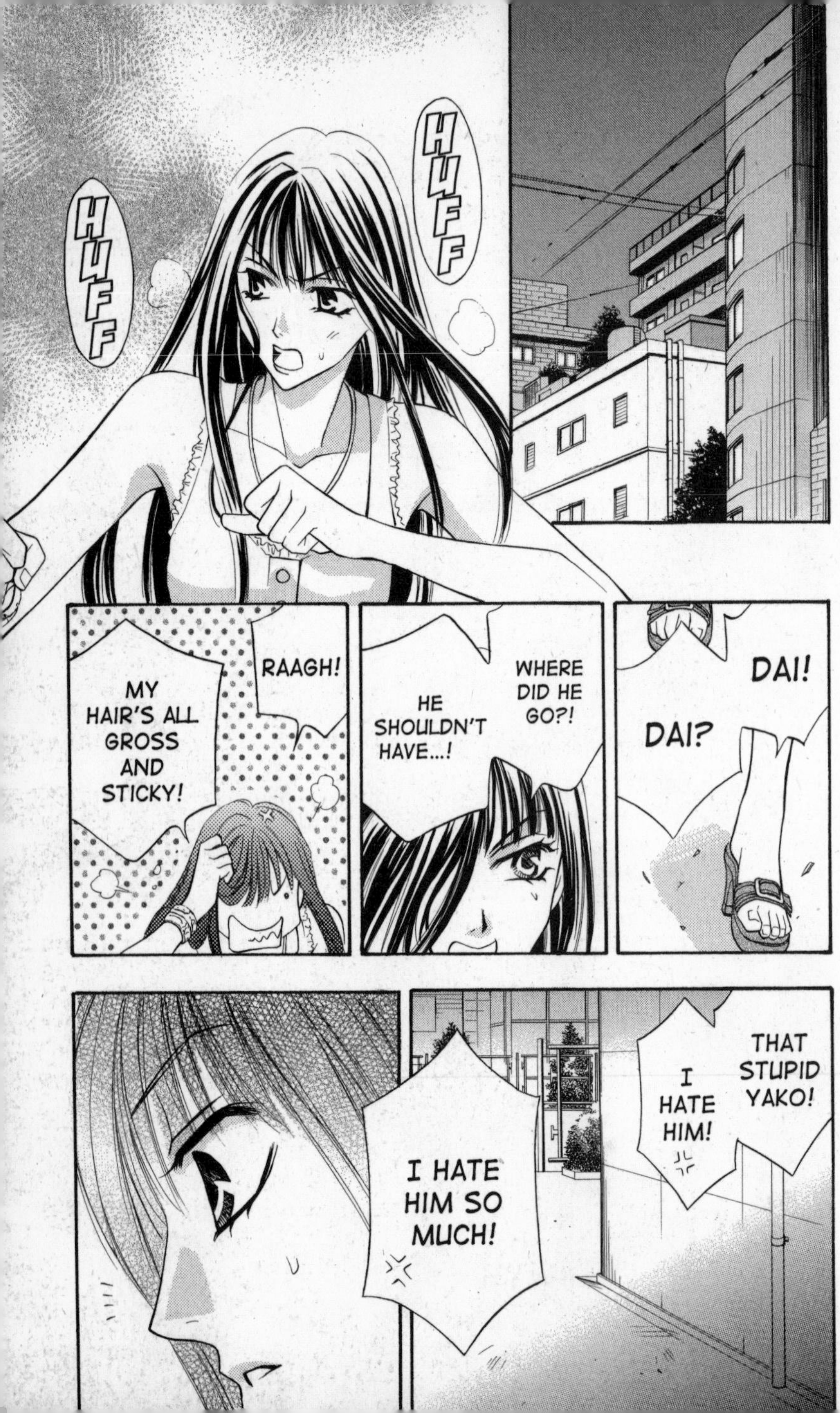
HUFF
HUFF
DAI!
DAI?
WHERE DID HE GO?!
HE SHOULDN'T HAVE...!
RAAGH!
MY HAIR'S ALL GROSS AND STICKY!
THAT STUPID YAKO!
I HATE HIM!
I HATE HIM SO MUCH!

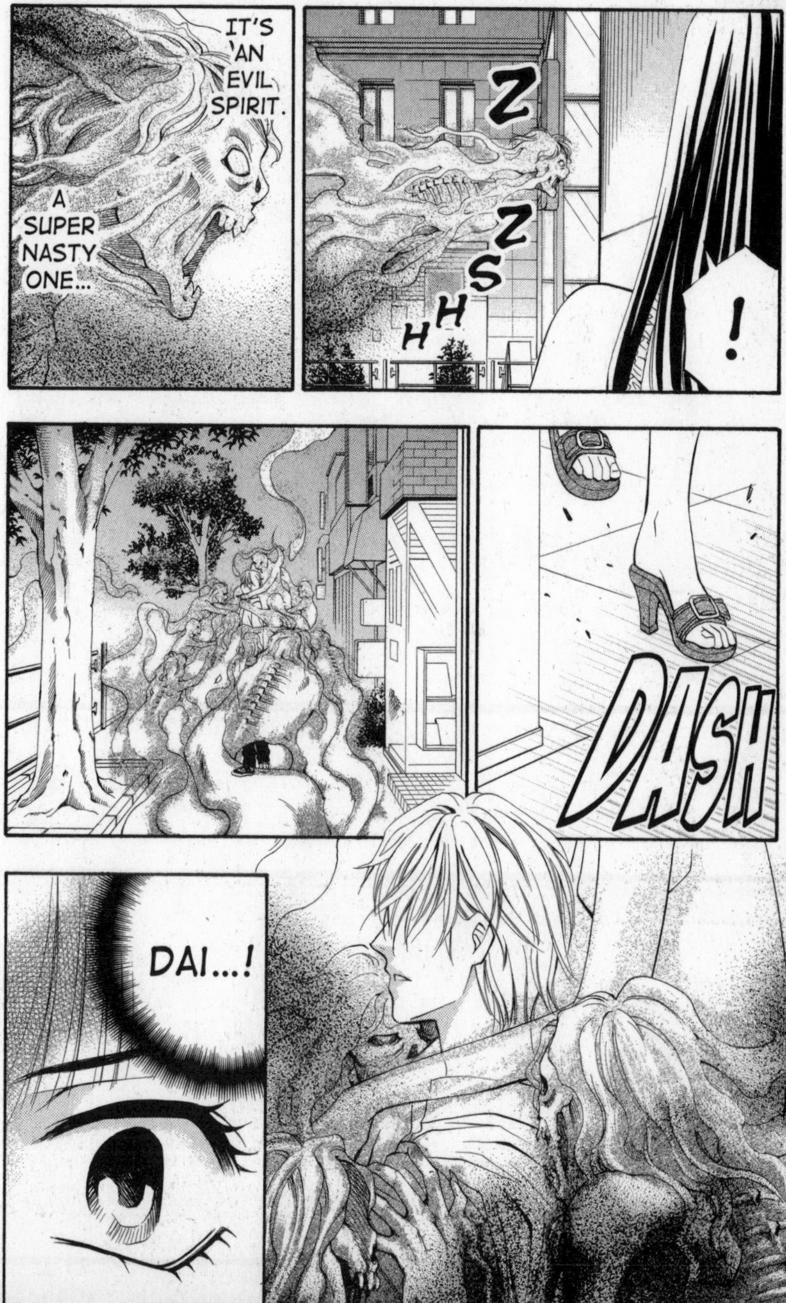
!
ZZSHH
IT'S AN EVIL SPIRIT.
A SUPER NASTY ONE...
DASH
DAI...!

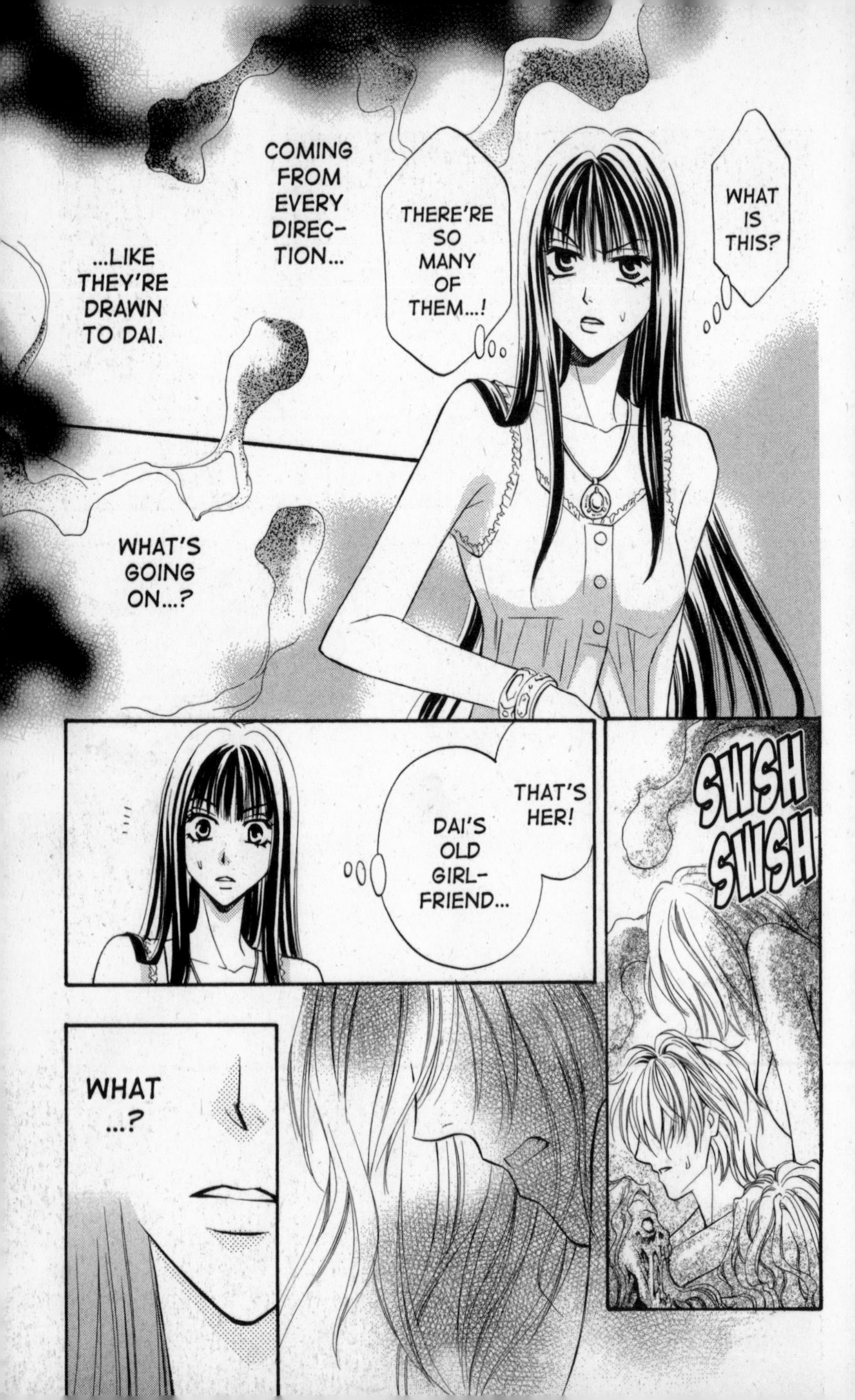
WHAT IS THIS?
THERE'RE SO MANY OF THEM...!
COMING FROM EVERY DIREC- TION...
...LIKE THEY'RE DRAWN TO DAI.
WHAT'S GOING ON...?
SWSH SWSH
THAT'S HER!
DAI'S OLD GIRL- FRIEND...
WHAT ...?

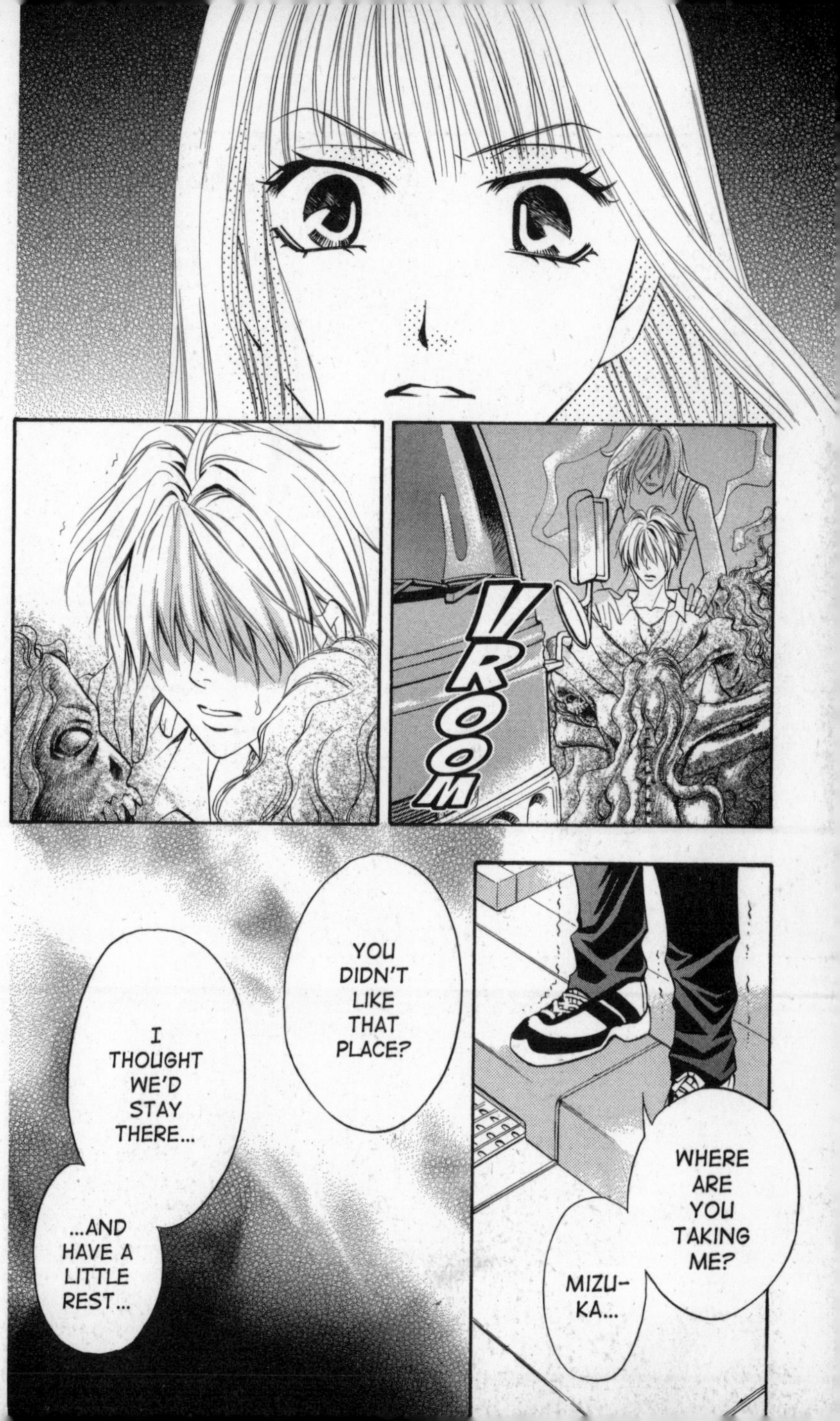
VROOM
WHERE ARE YOU TAKING ME?
MIZU-KA...
YOU DIDN'T LIKE THAT PLACE?
I THOUGHT WE'D STAY THERE...
...AND HAVE A LITTLE REST...

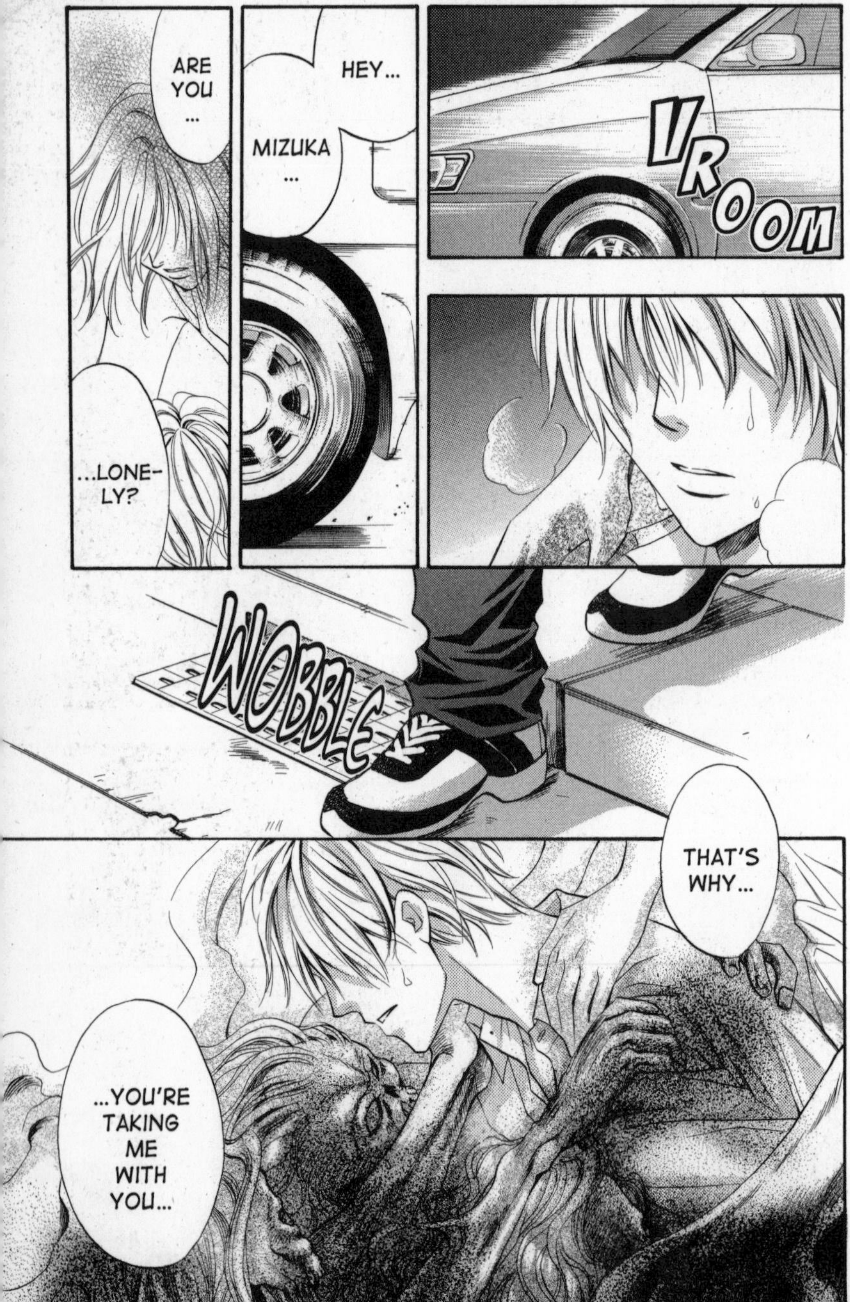
VROOM
HEY... MIZUKA...
ARE YOU ...
...LONE-LY?
WOBBLE
THAT'S WHY...
...YOU'RE TAKING ME WITH YOU...

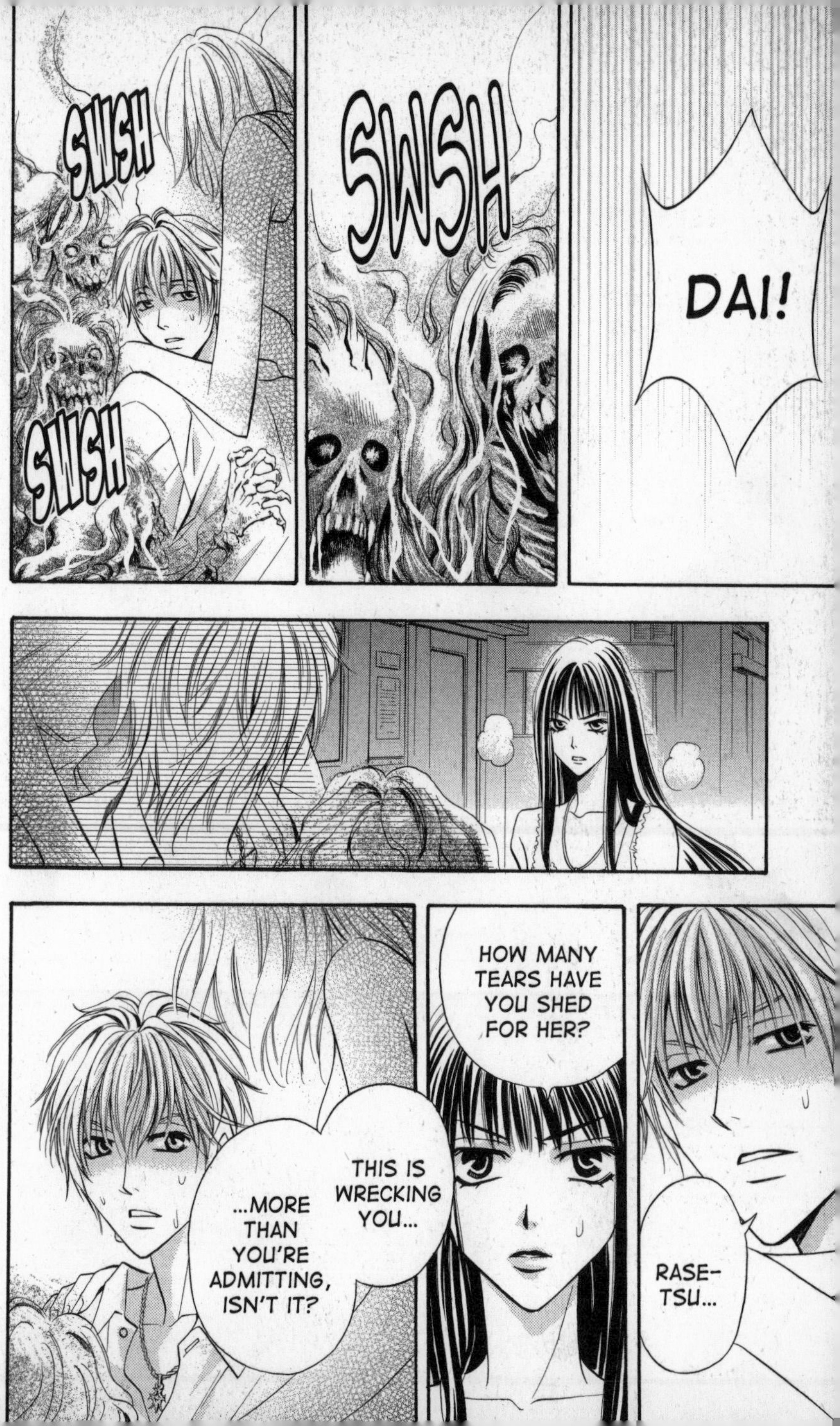
DAI!
SWSH
SWSH
SWSH
RASE-TSU...
HOW MANY TEARS HAVE YOU SHED FOR HER?
THIS IS WRECKING YOU...
...MORE THAN YOU'RE ADMITTING, ISN'T IT?

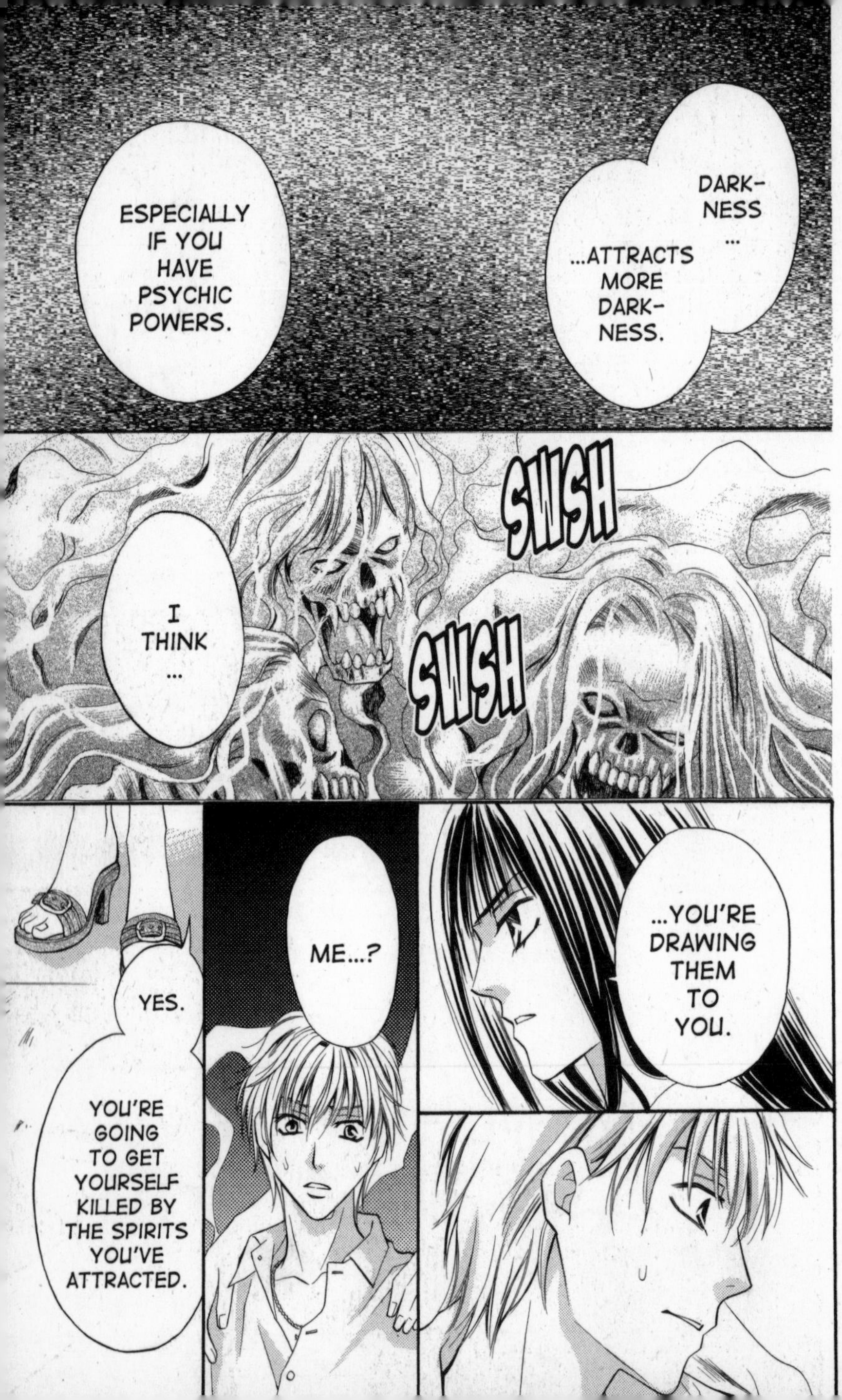
DARKNESS... ...ATTRACTS MORE DARKNESS.
ESPECIALLY IF YOU HAVE PSYCHIC POWERS.
SWSH
SWSH
I THINK...
...YOU'RE DRAWING THEM TO YOU.
ME...?
YES.
YOU'RE GOING TO GET YOURSELF KILLED BY THE SPIRITS YOU'VE ATTRACTED.

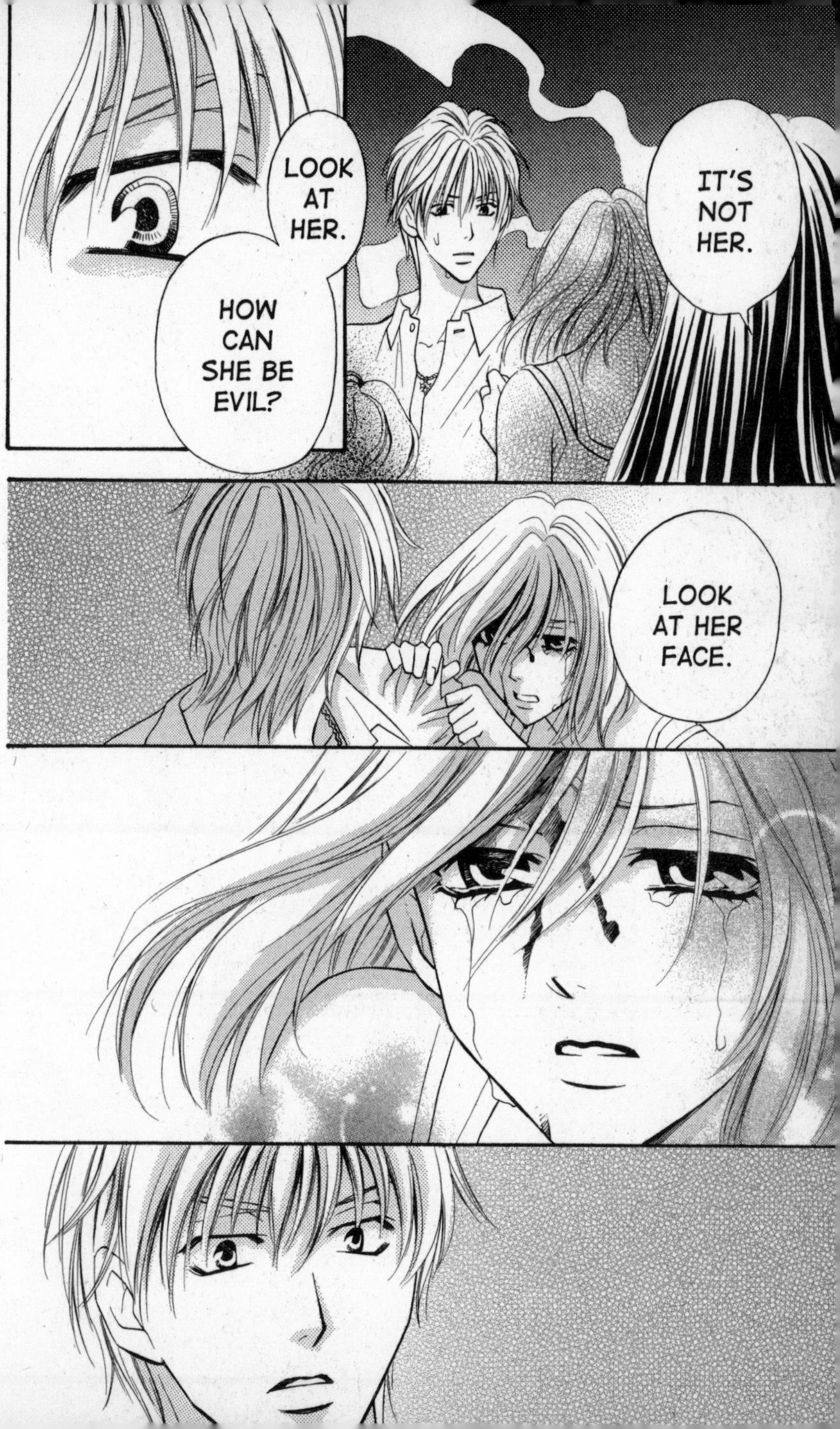
IT'S NOT HER.
LOOK AT HER.
HOW CAN SHE BE EVIL?
LOOK AT HER FACE.

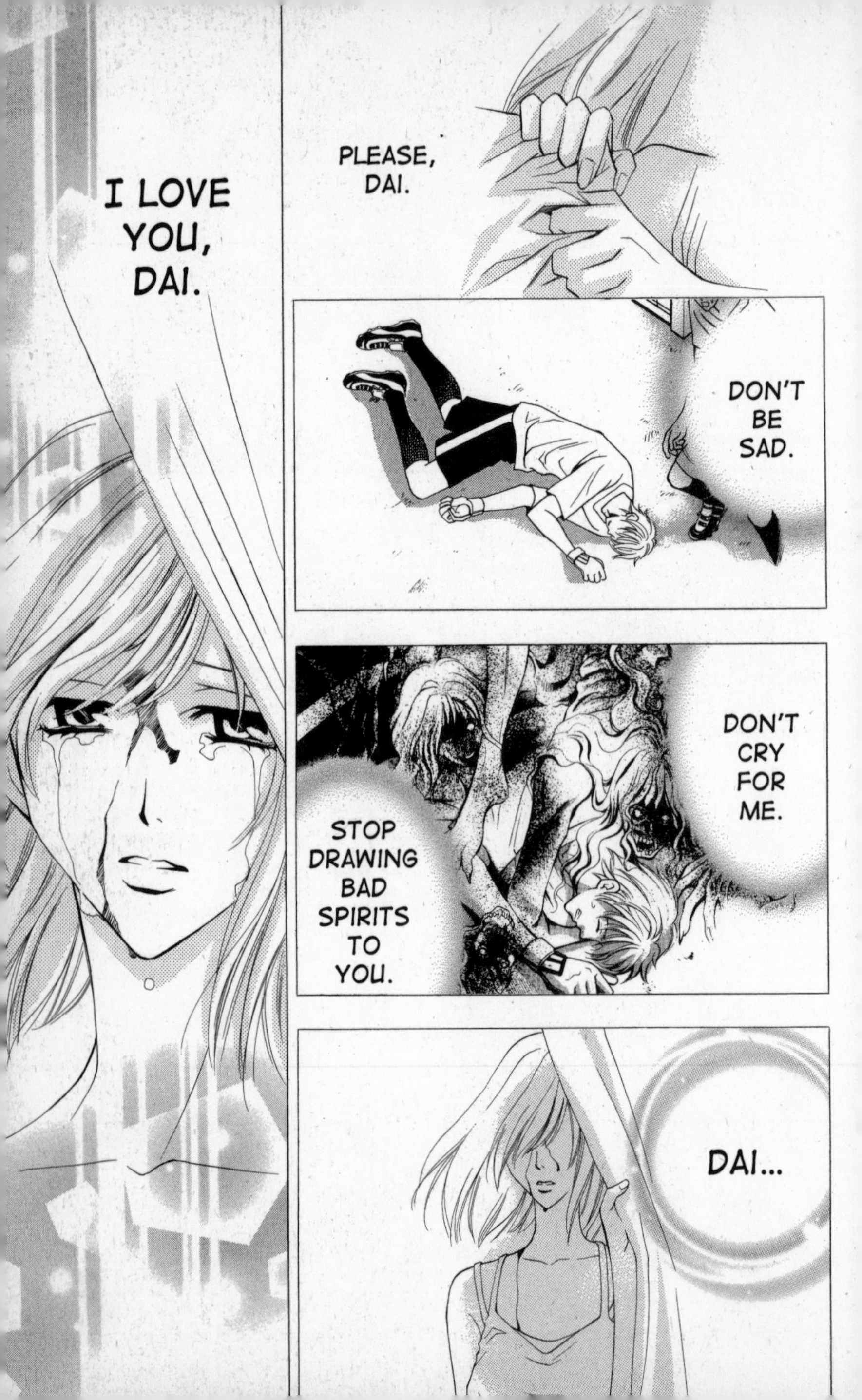
PLEASE, DAI.
DON'T BE SAD.
DON'T CRY FOR ME.
STOP DRAWING BAD SPIRITS TO YOU.
DAI...
I LOVE YOU, DAI.

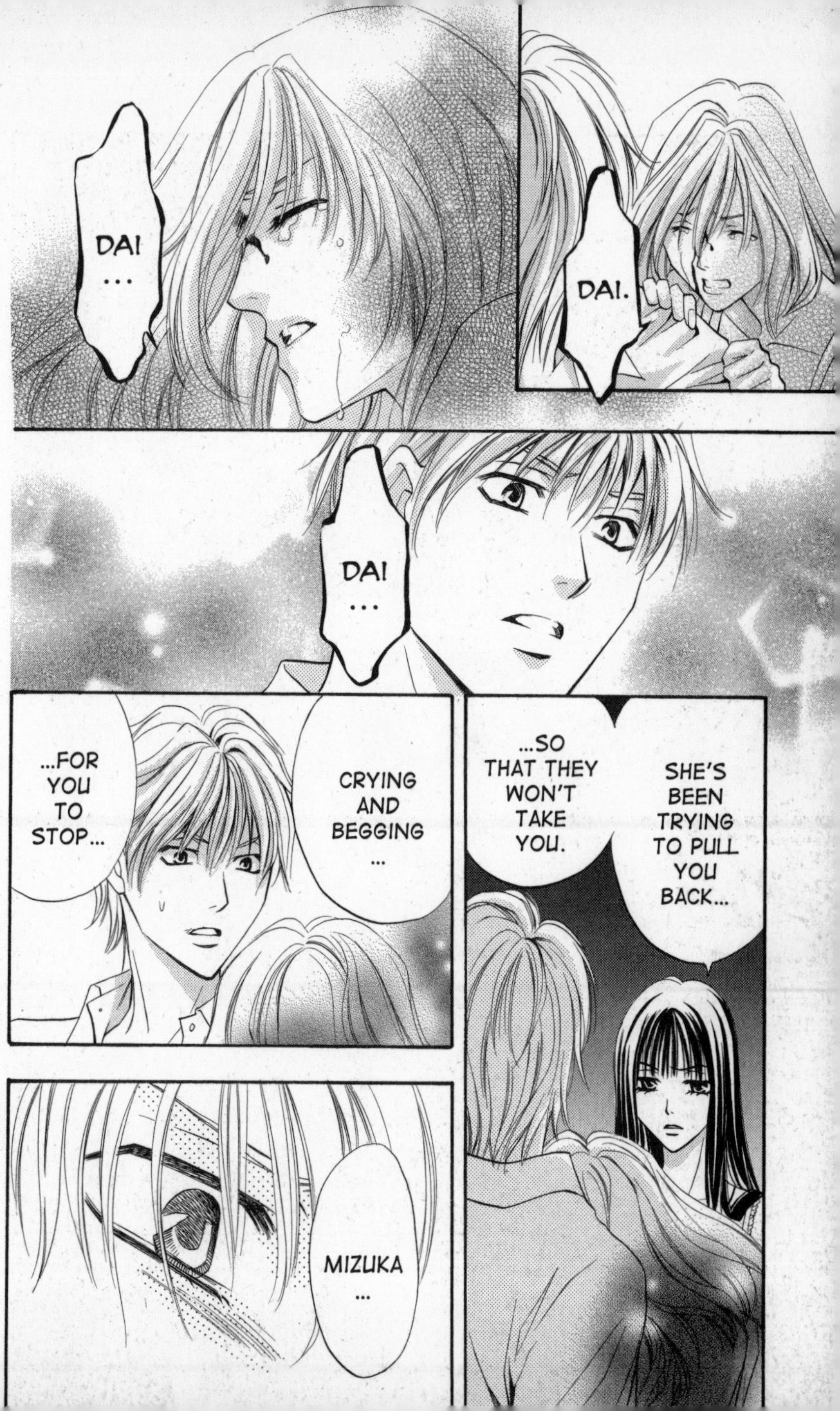
DAI.
DAI ...
DAI ...
SHE'S BEEN TRYING TO PULL YOU BACK...
...SO THAT THEY WON'T TAKE YOU.
CRYING AND BEGGING ...
...FOR YOU TO STOP...
MIZUKA ...

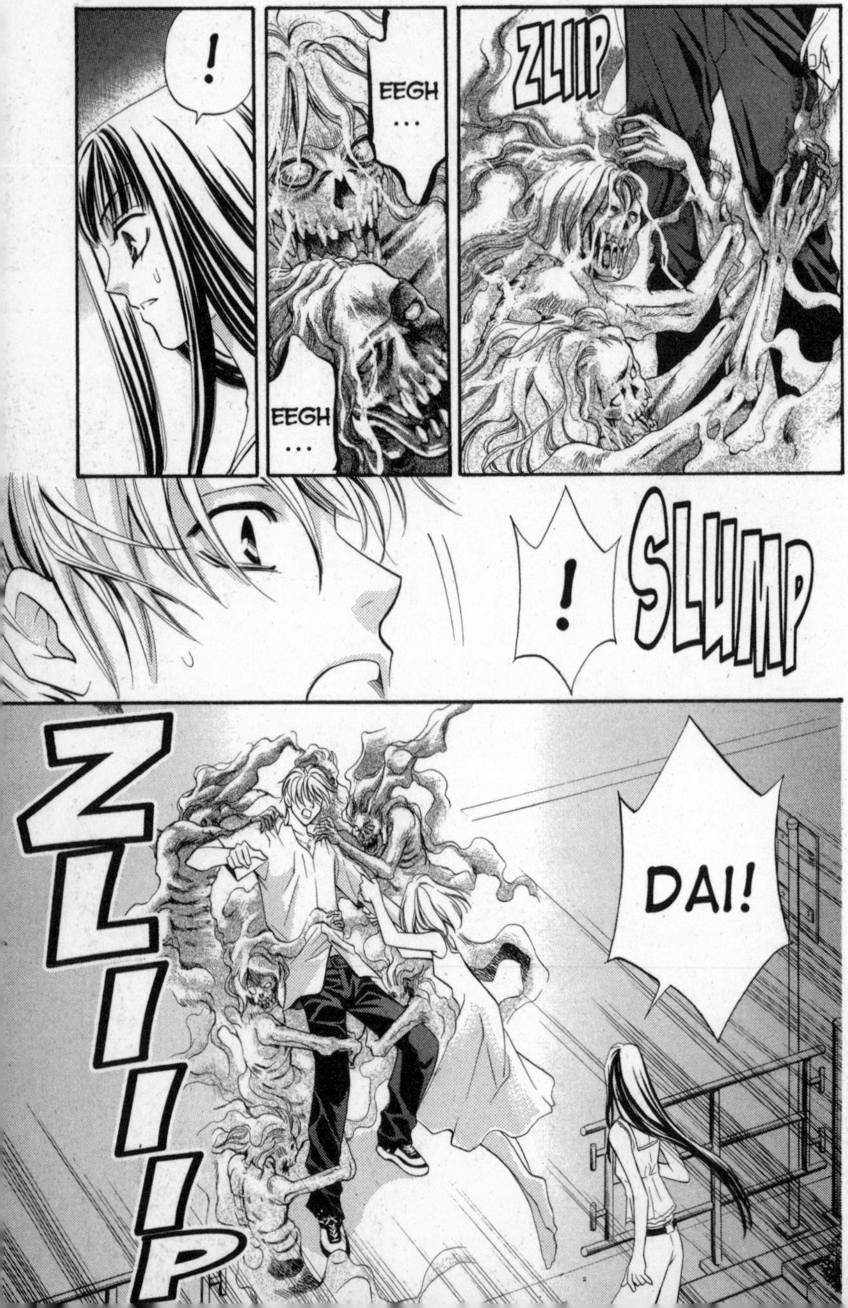
ZLIIP
EEGH …
EEGH …
!
SLUMP
!
DAI!
ZLIIIP

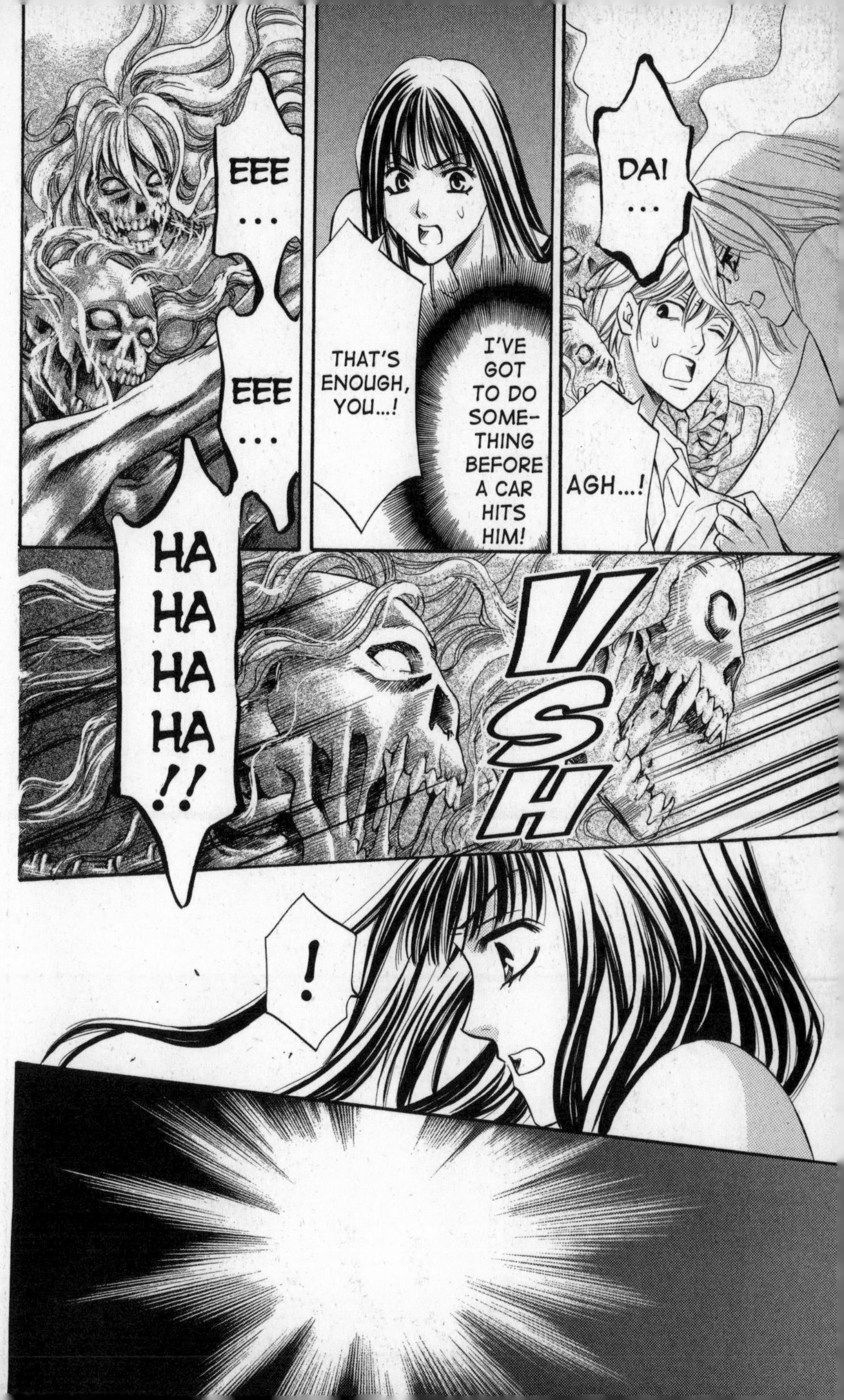
DAI...
AGH...!
THAT'S ENOUGH, YOU...!
I'VE GOT TO DO SOME-THING BEFORE A CAR HITS HIM!
EEE...
EEE...
HA HA HA HA!!
VSH
!

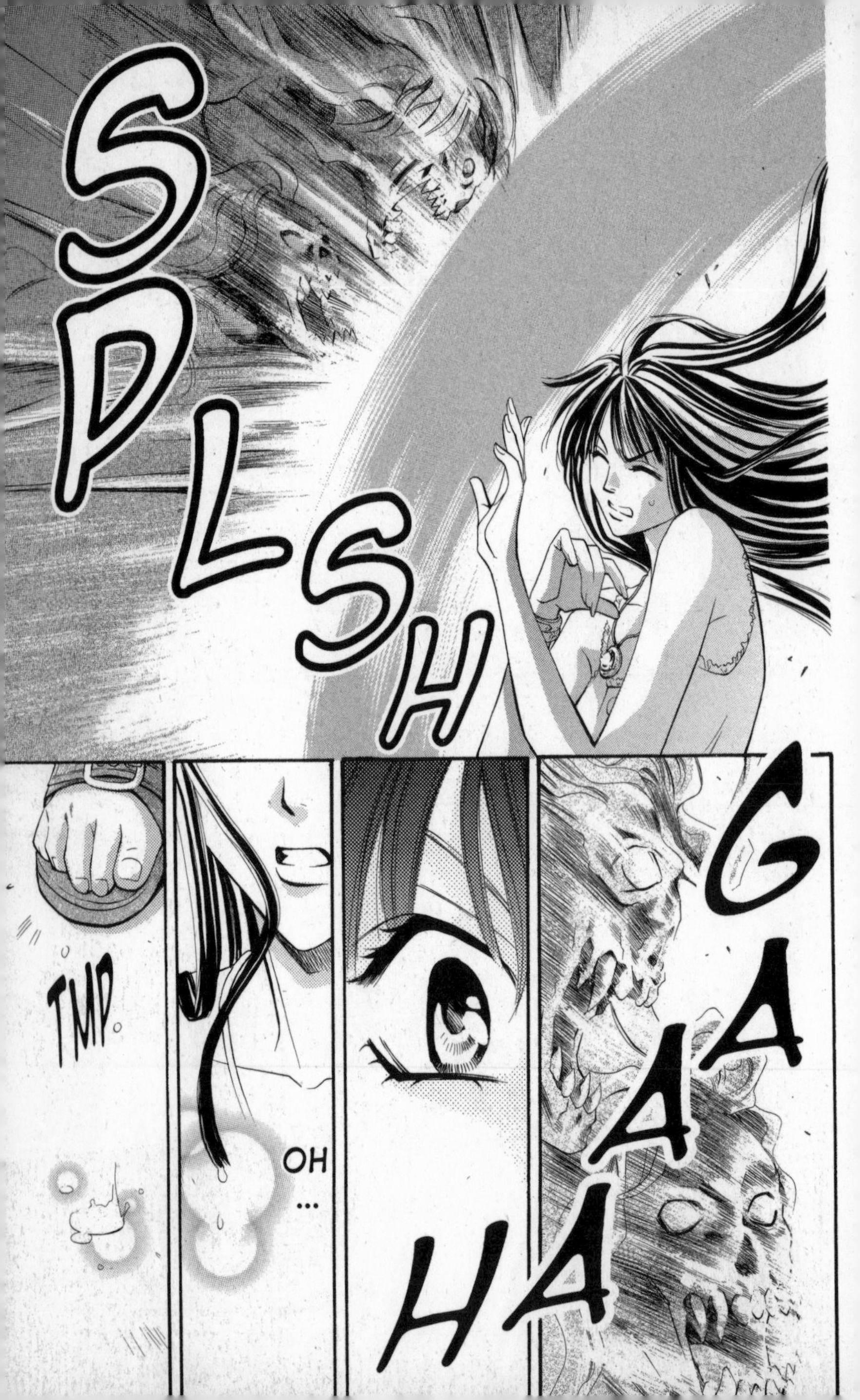

SPLSH
GAAHA
OH ...
TMP

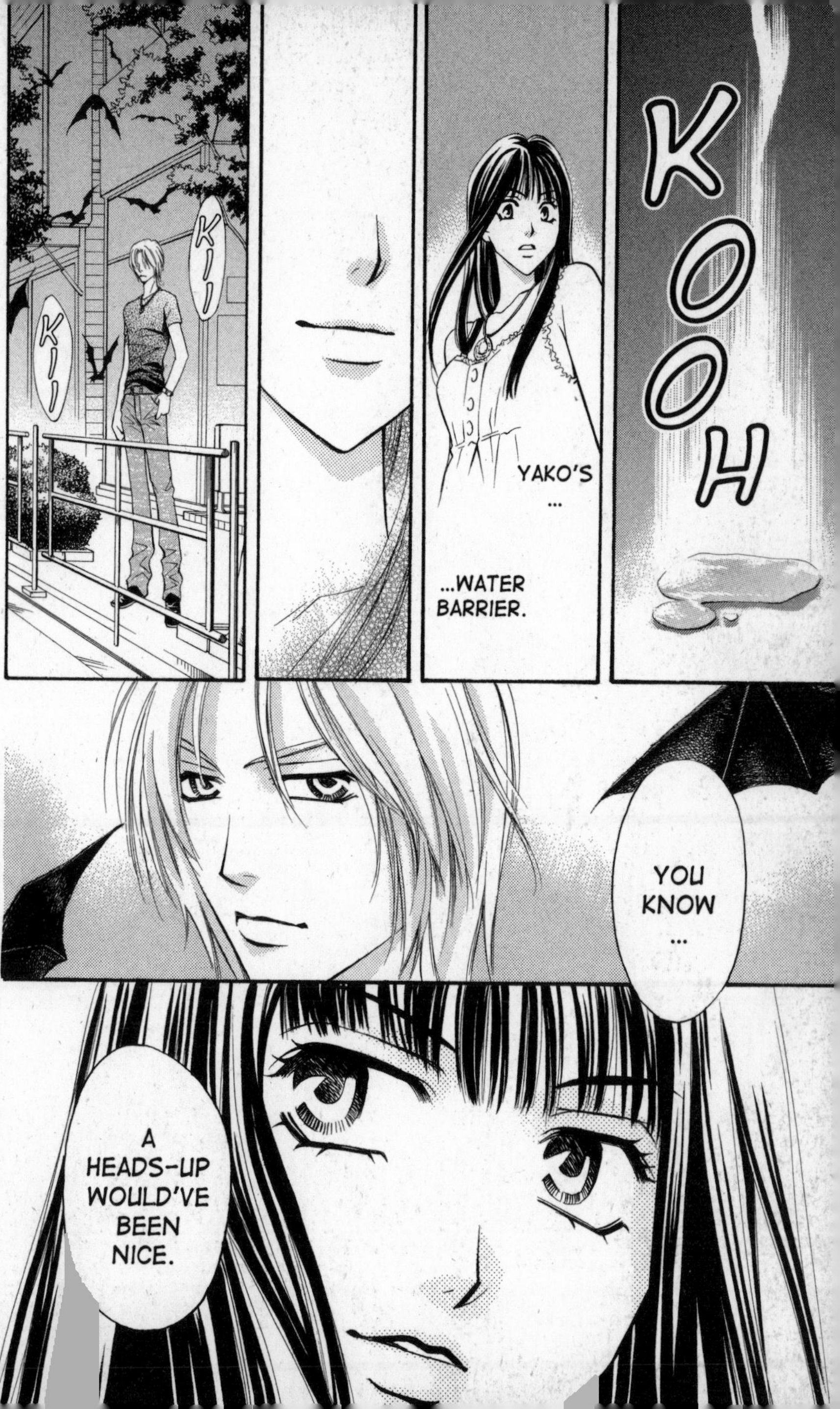
KOOH
YAKO'S ...
...WATER BARRIER.
KIII
KIII
YOU KNOW ...
A HEADS-UP WOULD'VE BEEN NICE.

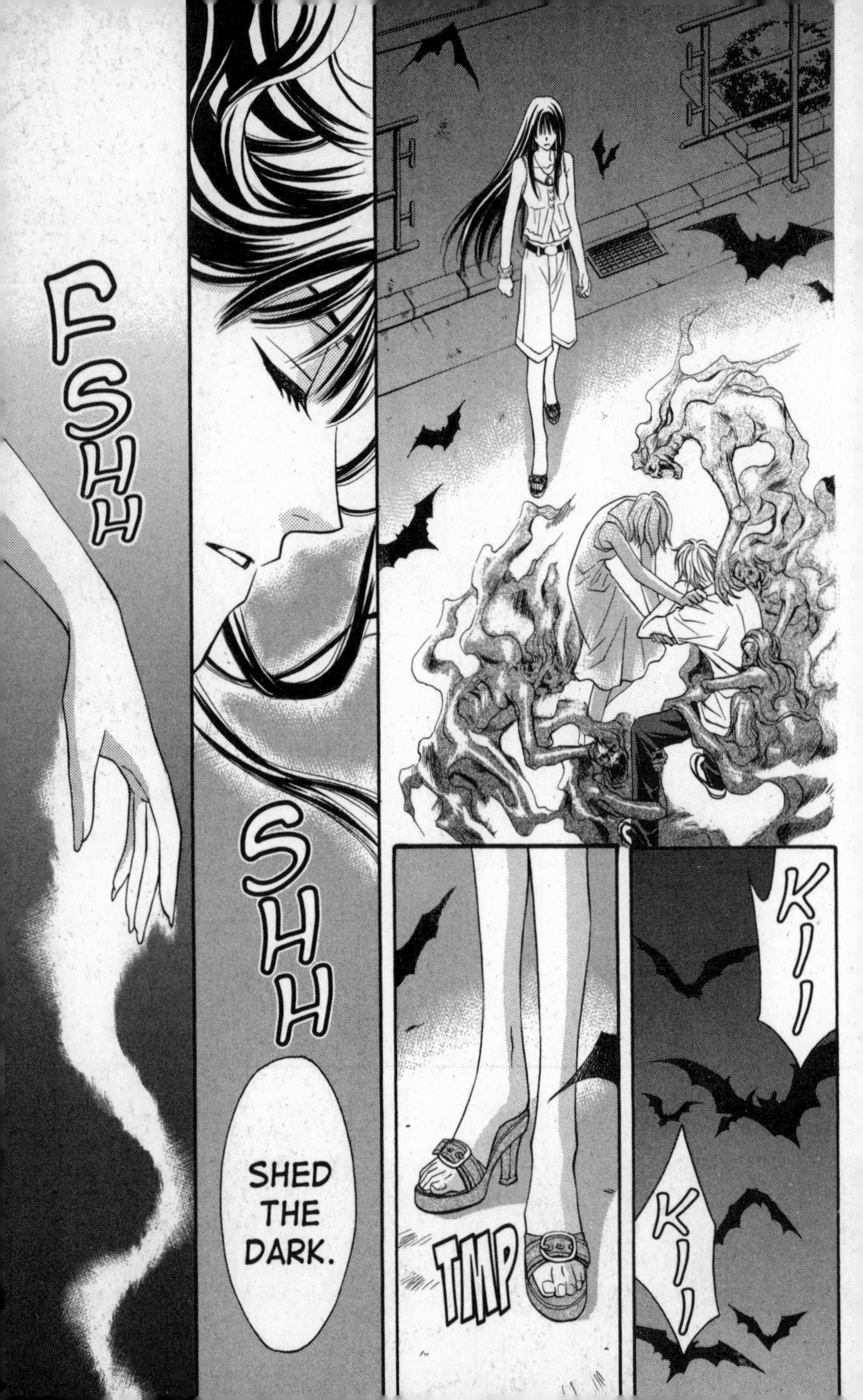
KII
KII
TMP
SHH
SHED THE DARK.
FSHH

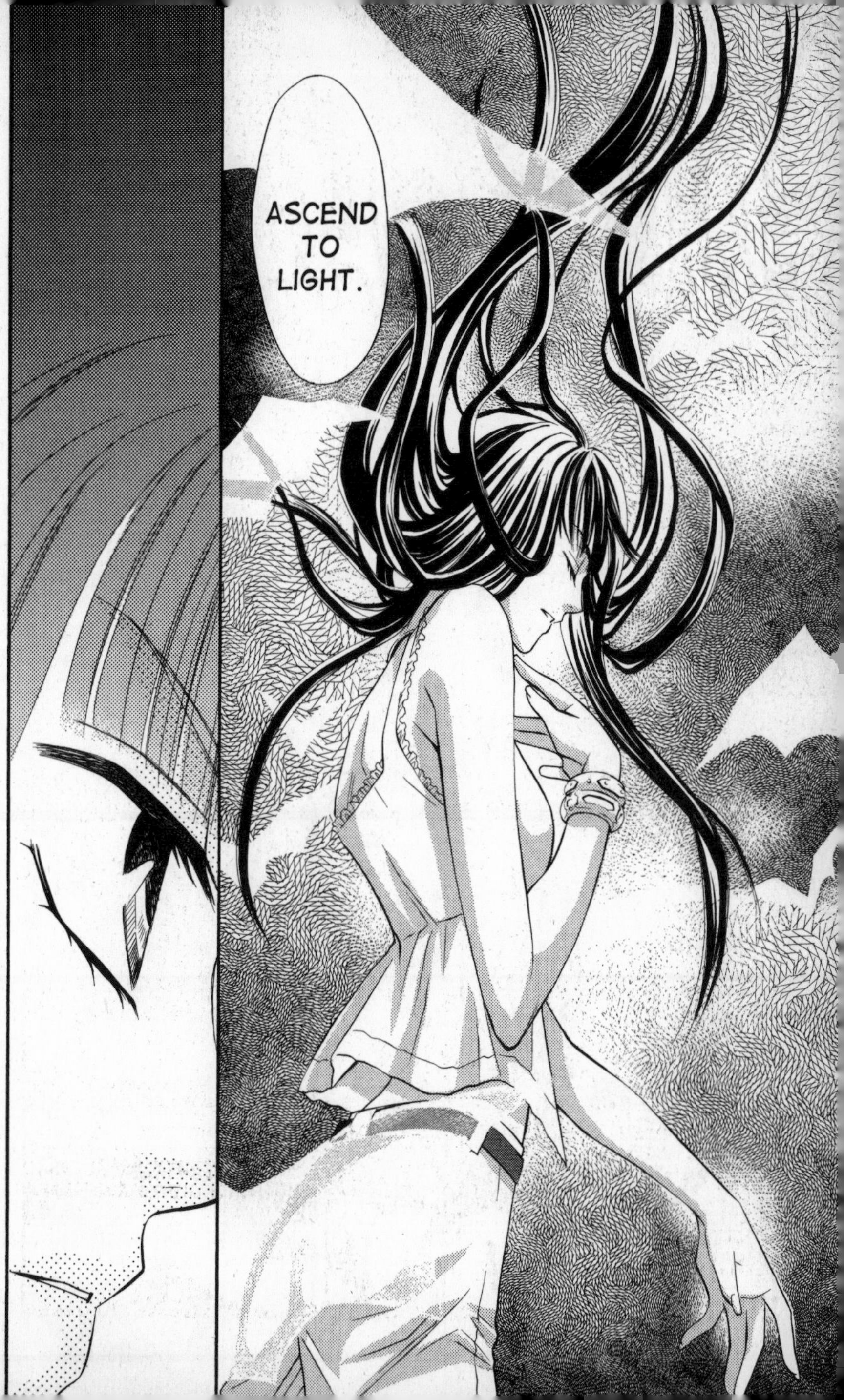
ASCEND TO LIGHT.

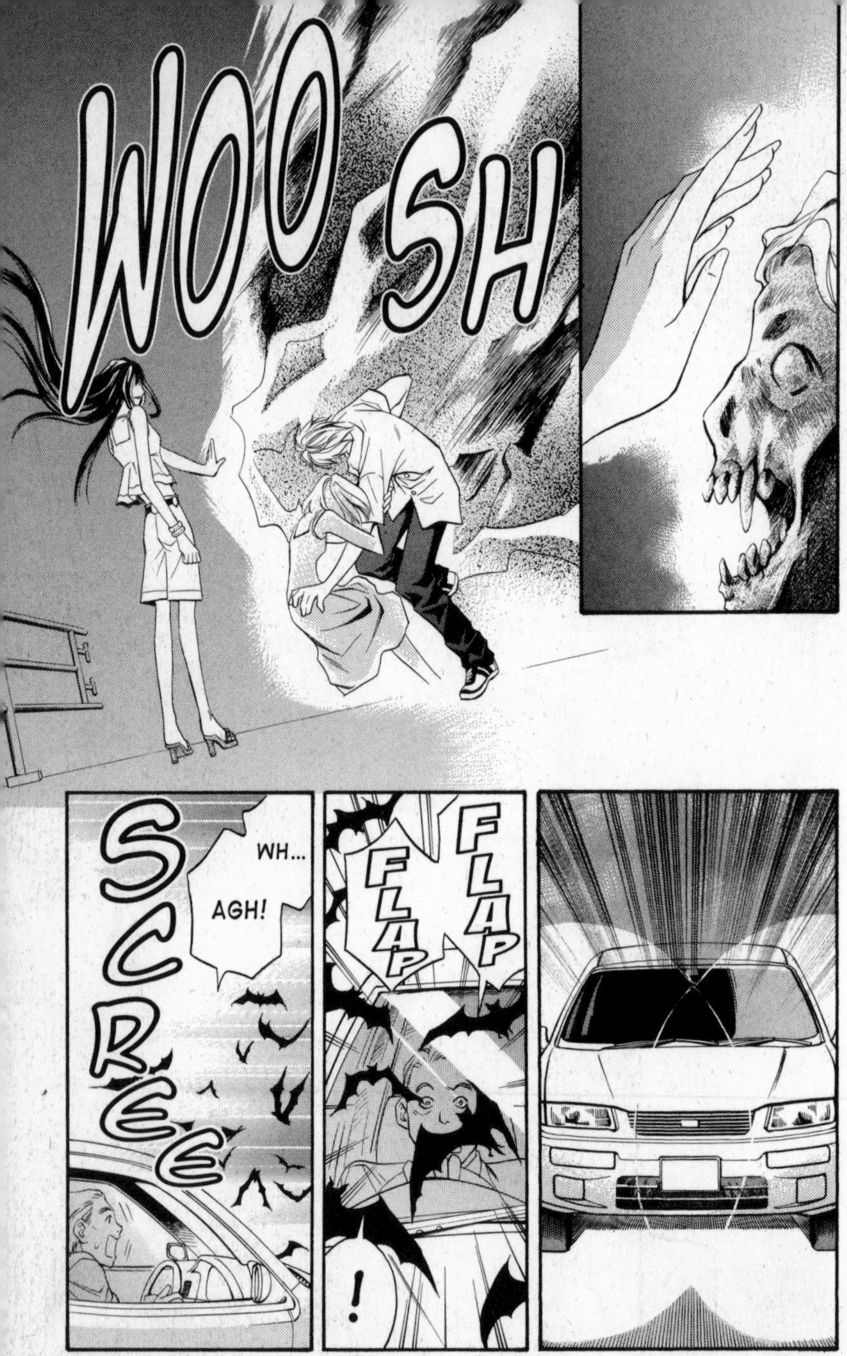
WOOSH
FLAP
FLAP
!
WH...
AGH!
SCREEE

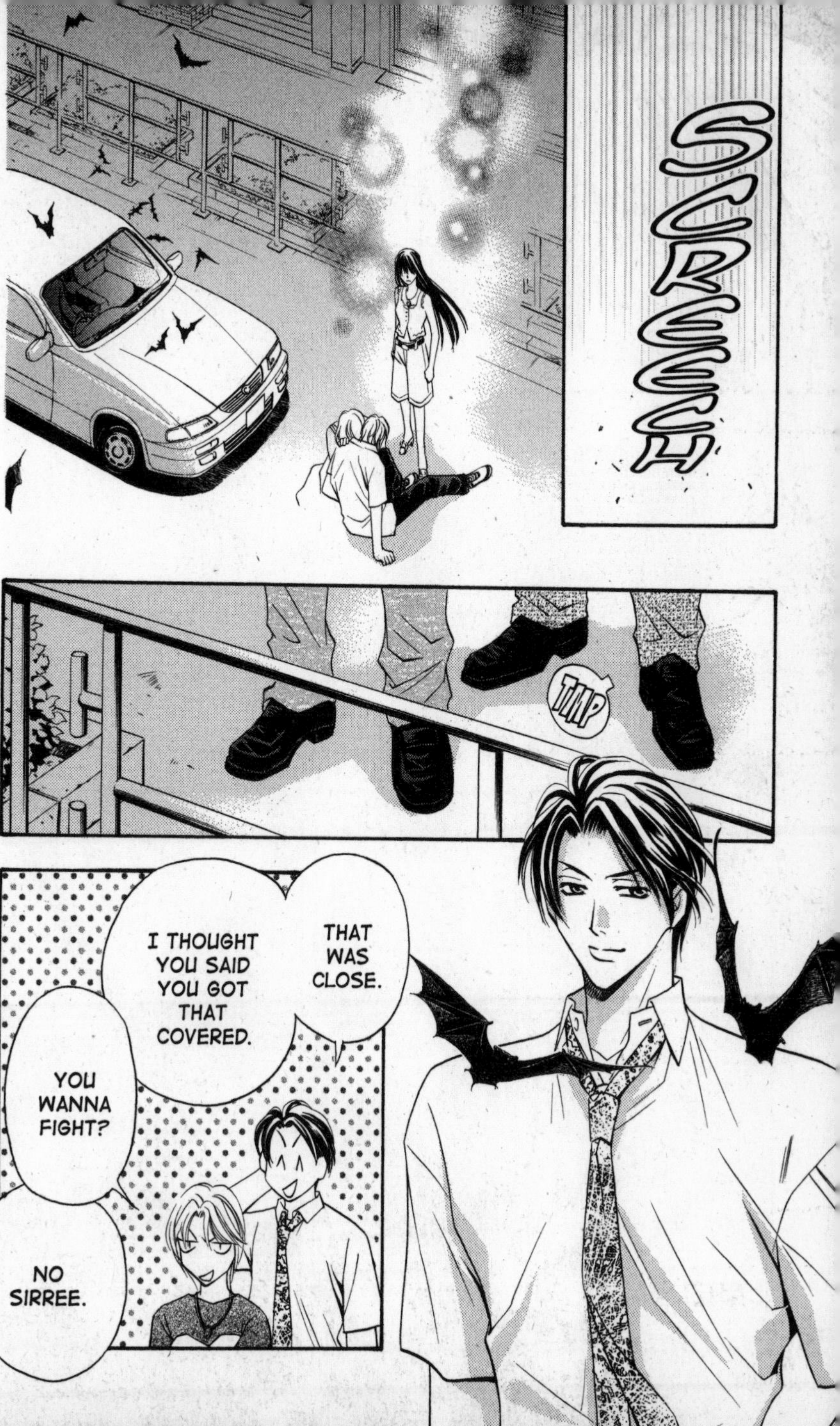
SCREECH
TMP
THAT WAS CLOSE.
I THOUGHT YOU SAID YOU GOT THAT COVERED.
YOU WANNA FIGHT?
NO SIRREE.

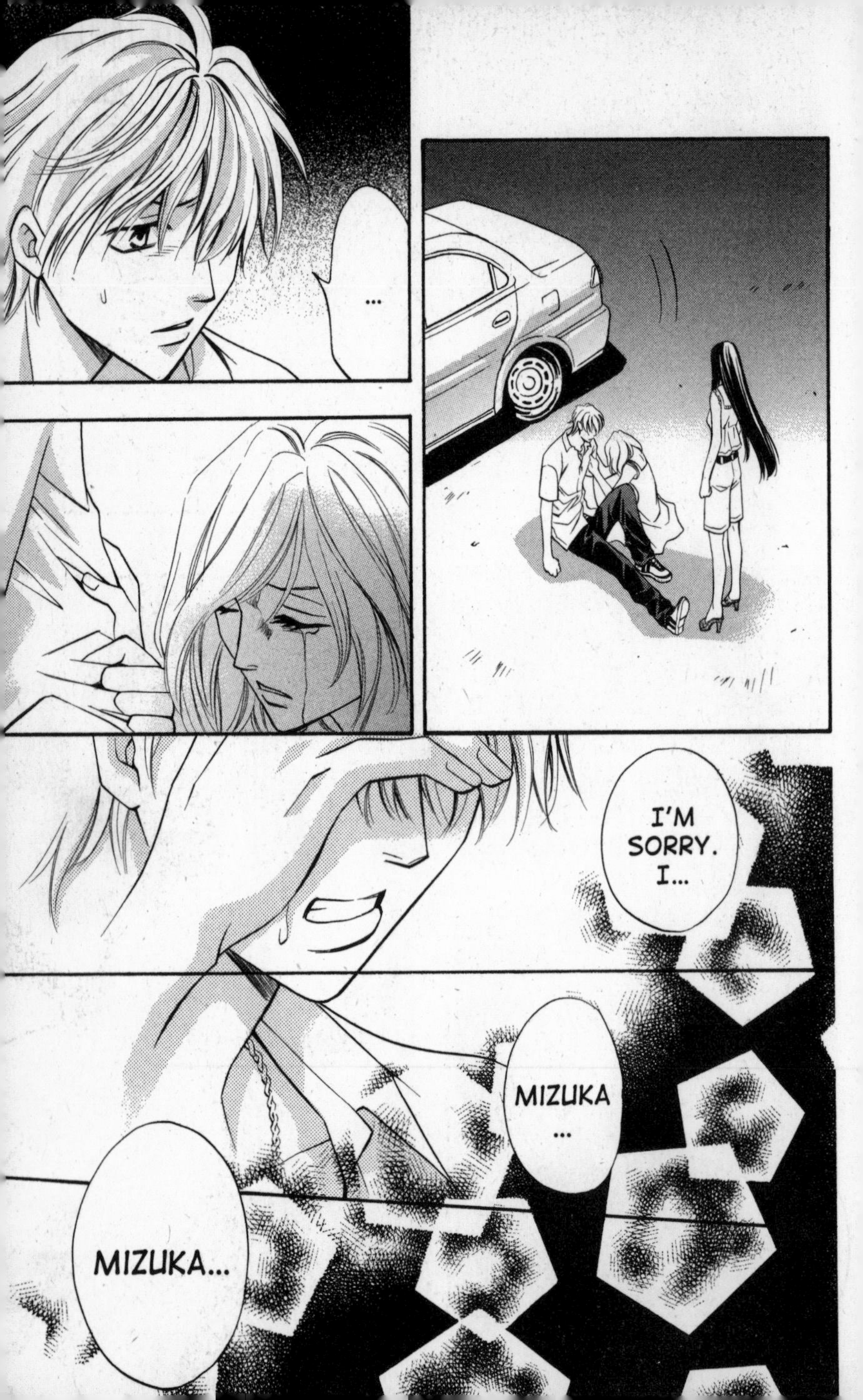
...
I'M SORRY. I...
MIZUKA ...
MIZUKA...

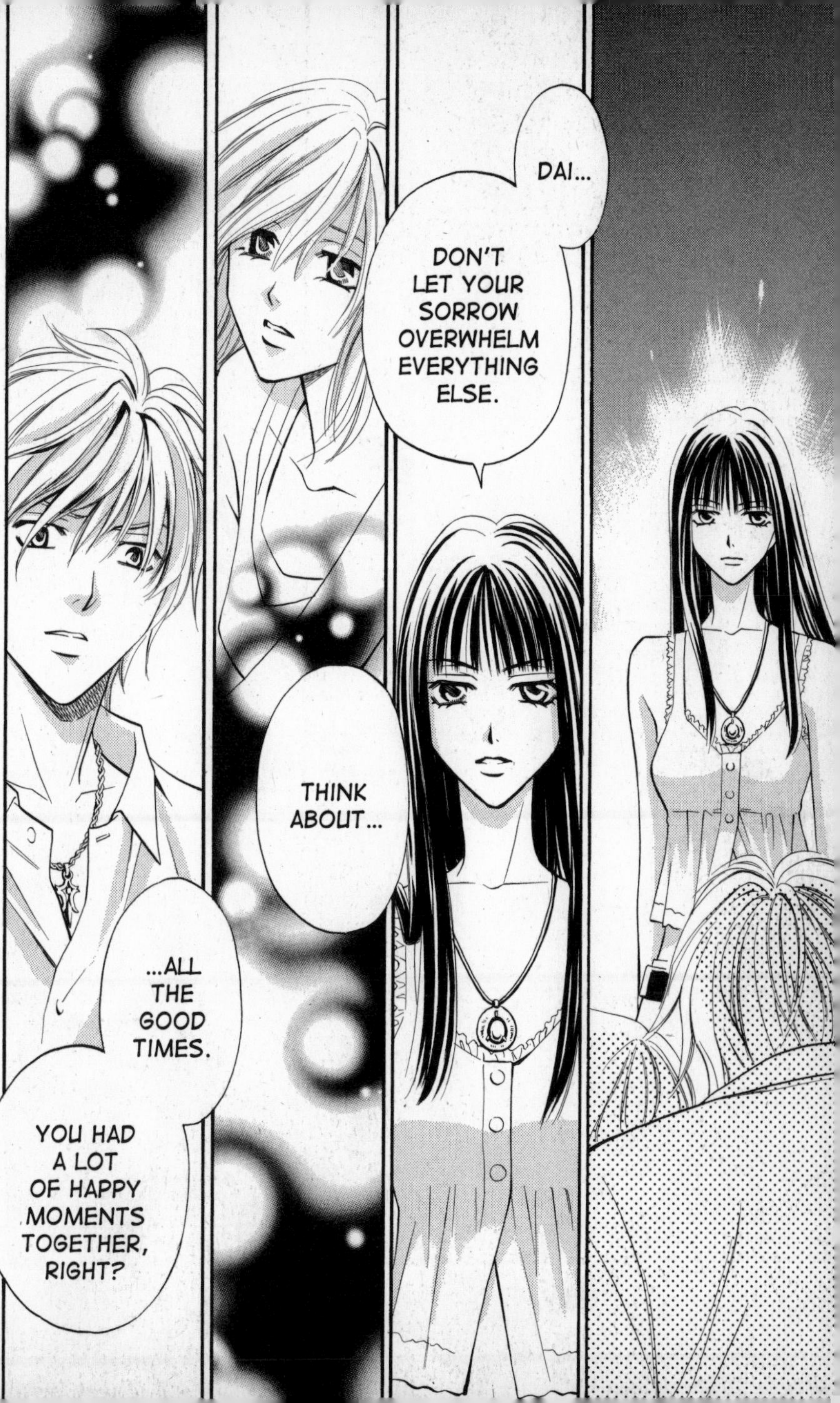
DAI...
DON'T LET YOUR SORROW OVERWHELM EVERYTHING ELSE.
THINK ABOUT...
...ALL THE GOOD TIMES.
YOU HAD A LOT OF HAPPY MOMENTS TOGETHER, RIGHT?

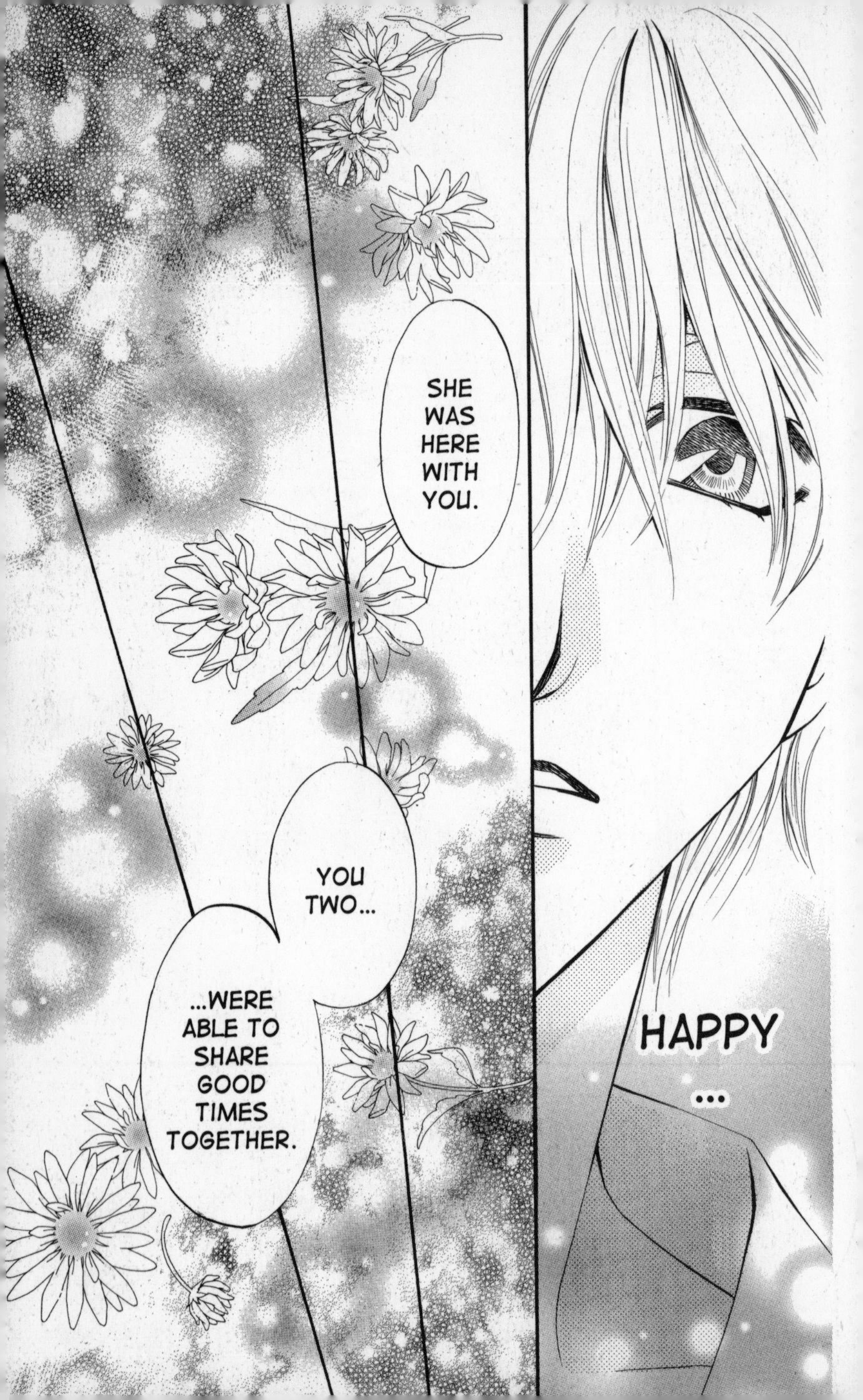
HAPPY ...
SHE WAS HERE WITH YOU.
YOU TWO...
...WERE ABLE TO SHARE GOOD TIMES TOGETHER.

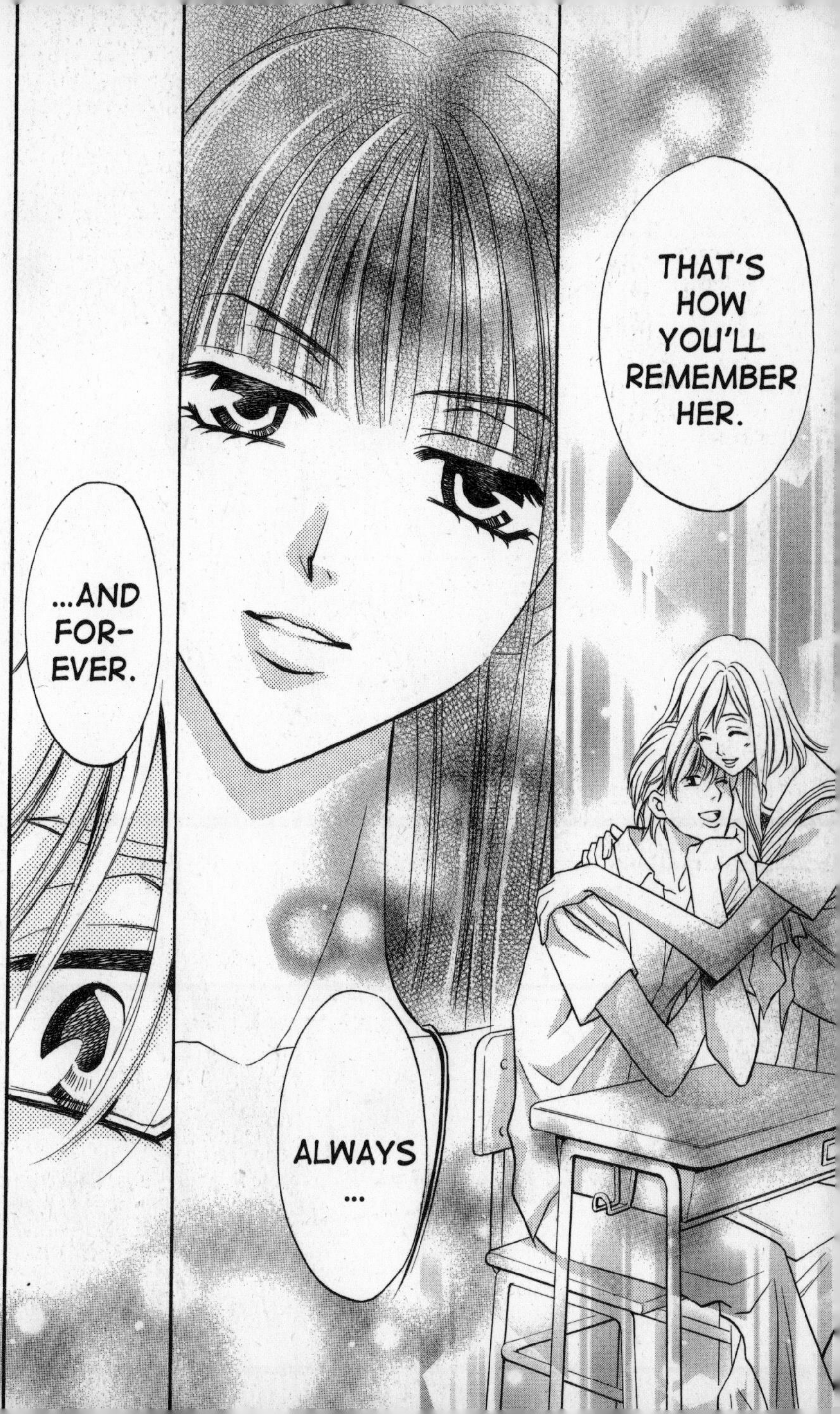
THAT'S HOW YOU'LL REMEMBER HER.
ALWAYS ...
...AND FOR-EVER.

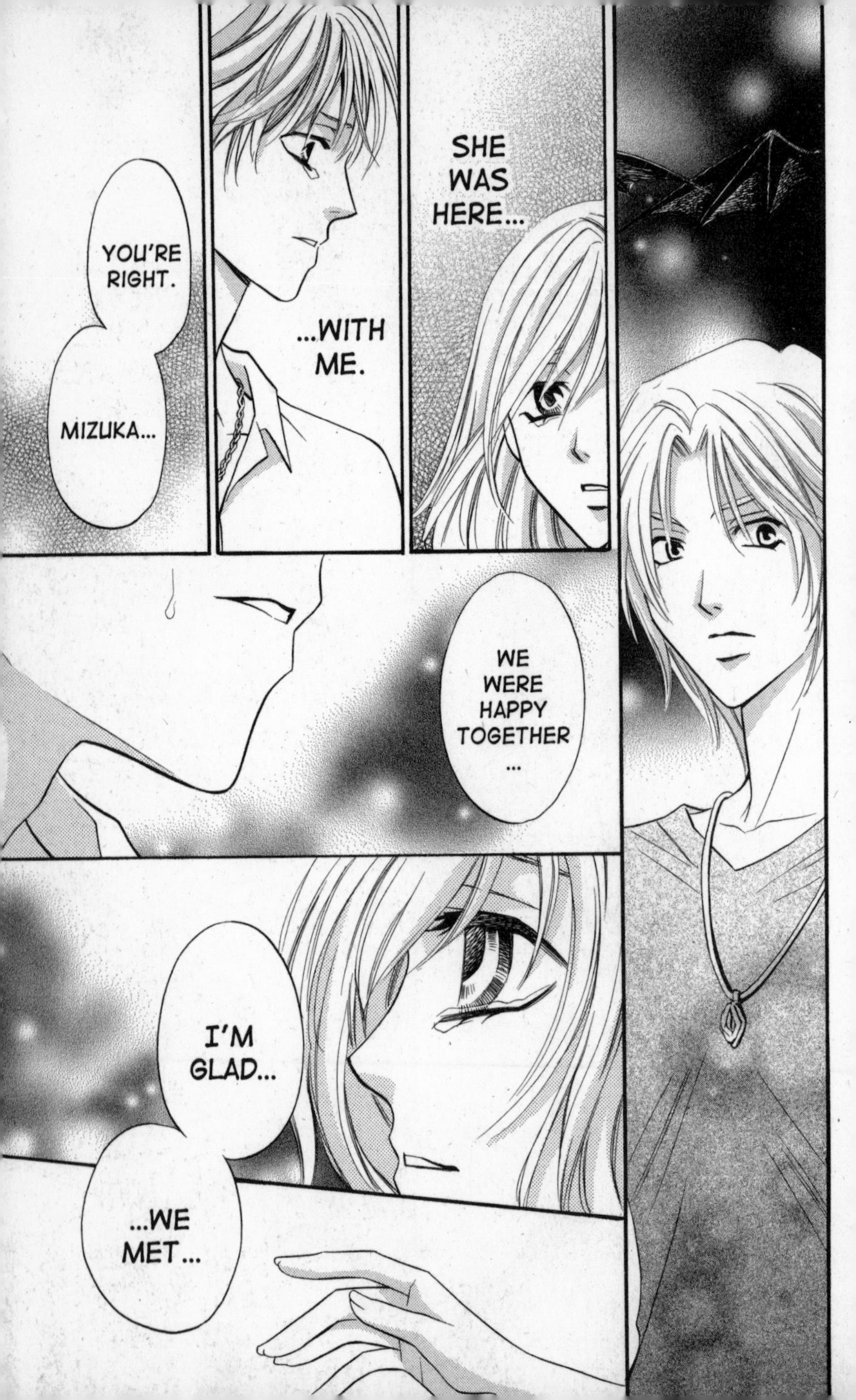
SHE WAS HERE...
...WITH ME.
YOU'RE RIGHT.
MIZUKA...
WE WERE HAPPY TOGETHER ...
I'M GLAD...
...WE MET...

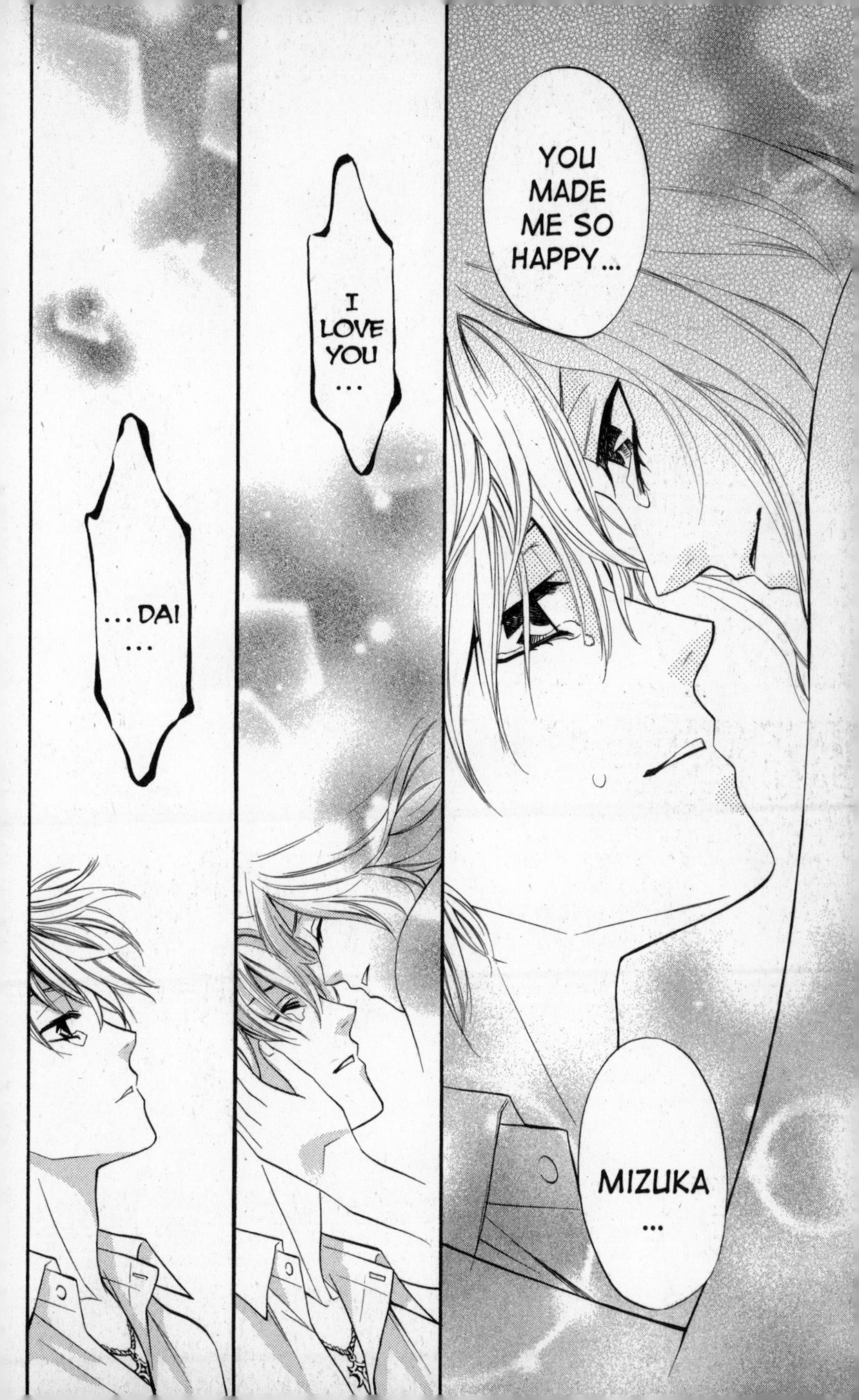
YOU MADE ME SO HAPPY...
MIZUKA ...
I LOVE YOU ...
...DAI ...

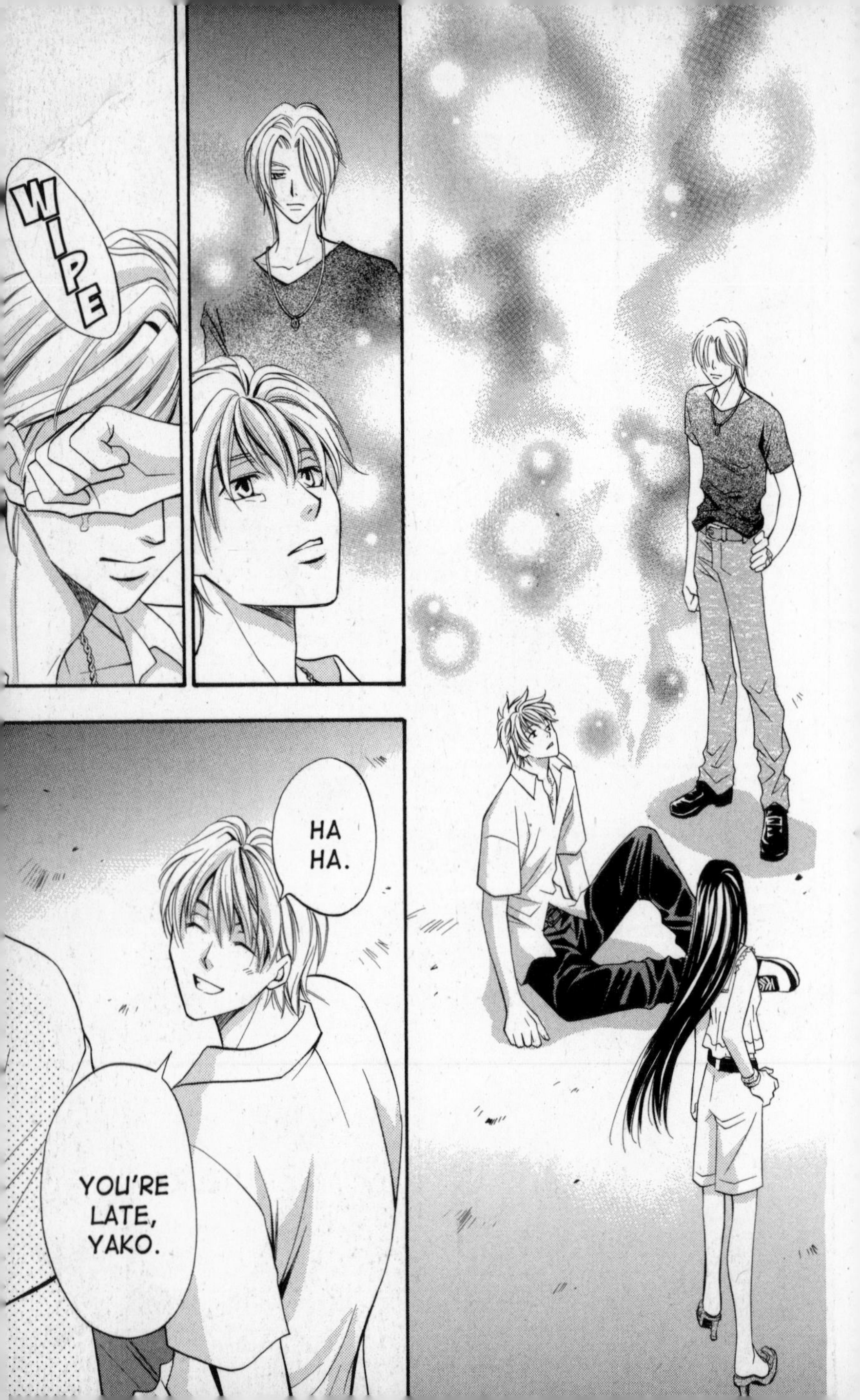
WIPE
HA HA.
YOU'RE LATE, YAKO.

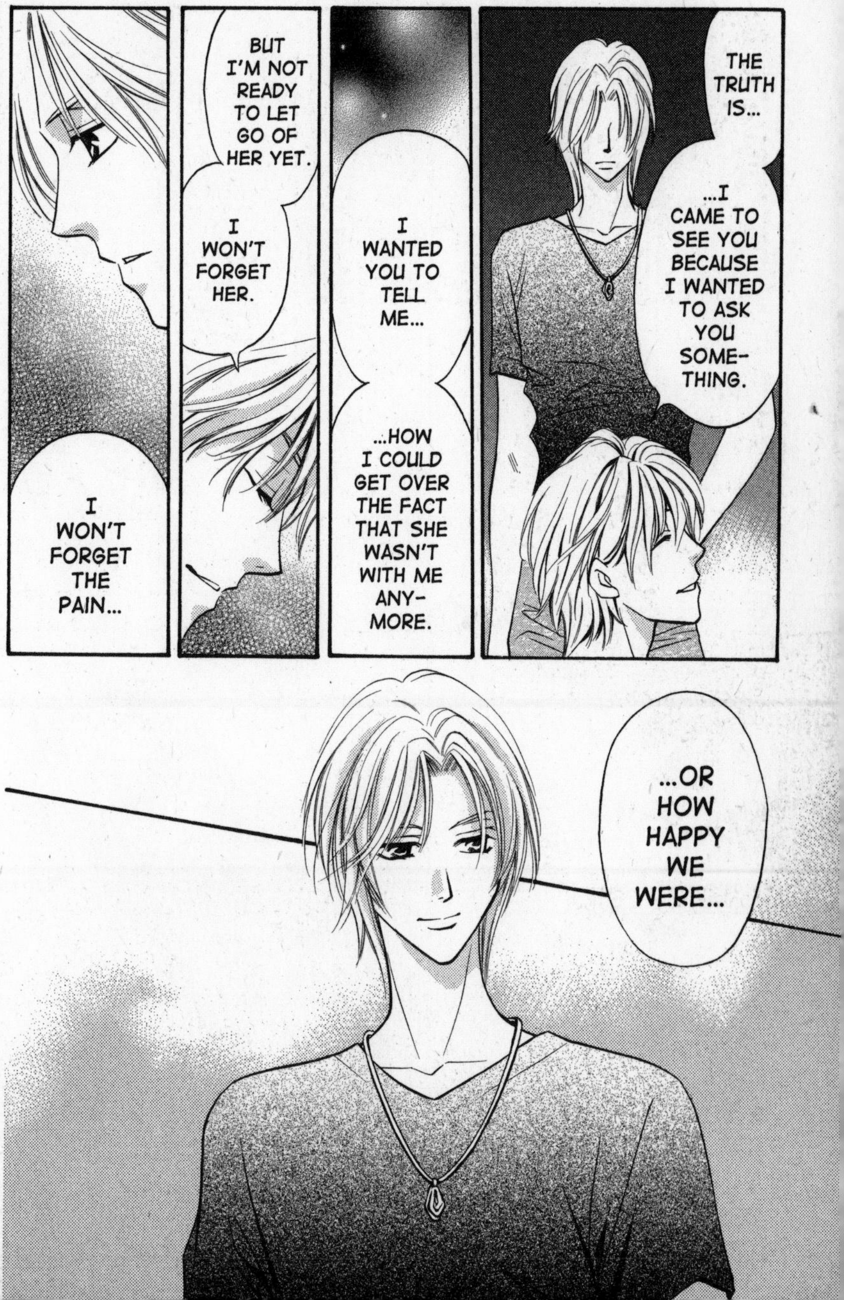
THE TRUTH IS...
...I CAME TO SEE YOU BECAUSE I WANTED TO ASK YOU SOME-THING.
I WANTED YOU TO TELL ME...
...HOW I COULD GET OVER THE FACT THAT SHE WASN'T WITH ME ANY-MORE.
BUT I'M NOT READY TO LET GO OF HER YET.
I WON'T FORGET HER.
I WON'T FORGET THE PAIN...
...OR HOW HAPPY WE WERE...

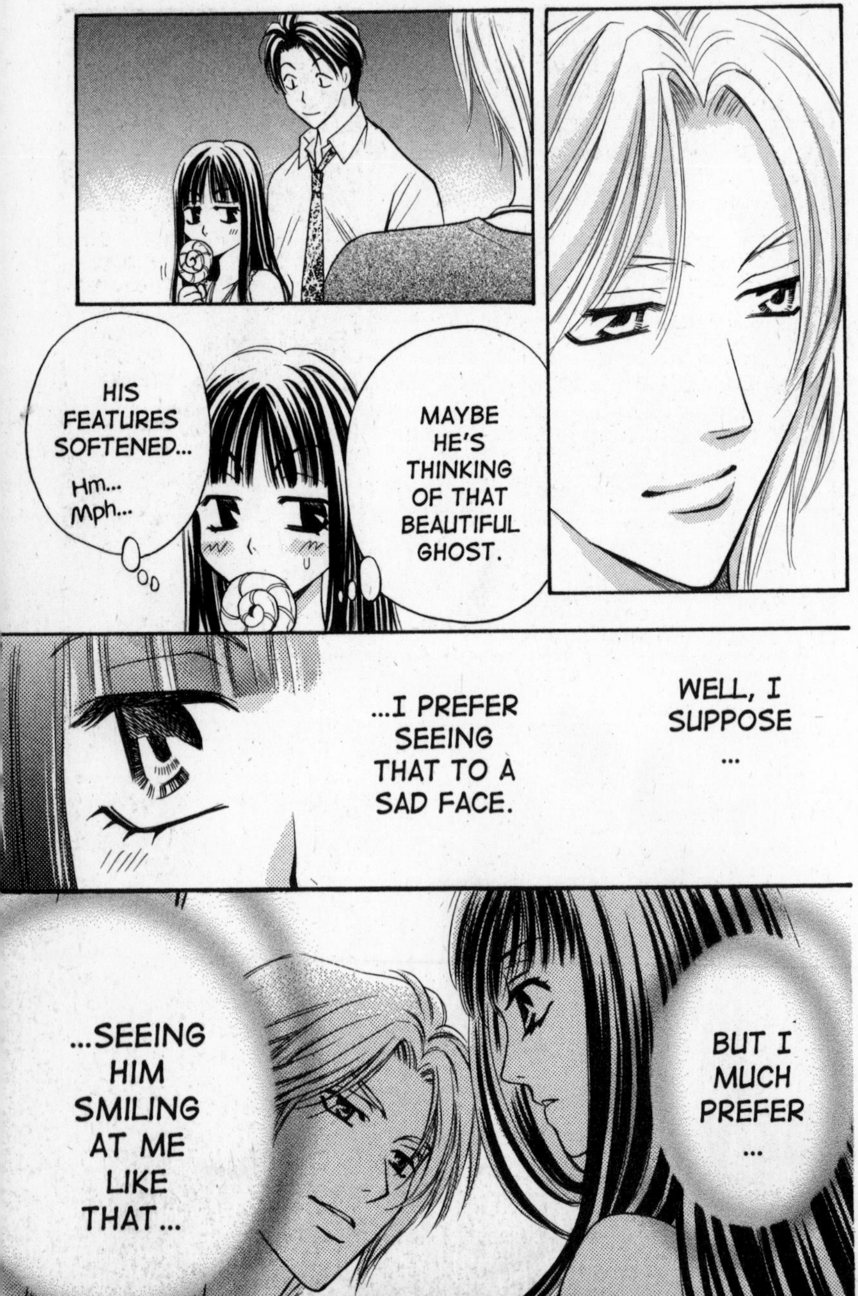
MAYBE HE'S THINKING OF THAT BEAUTIFUL GHOST.
HIS FEATURES SOFTENED...
Hm... Mph...
WELL, I SUPPOSE ...
...I PREFER SEEING THAT TO A SAD FACE.
BUT I MUCH PREFER ...
...SEEING HIM SMILING AT ME LIKE THAT...

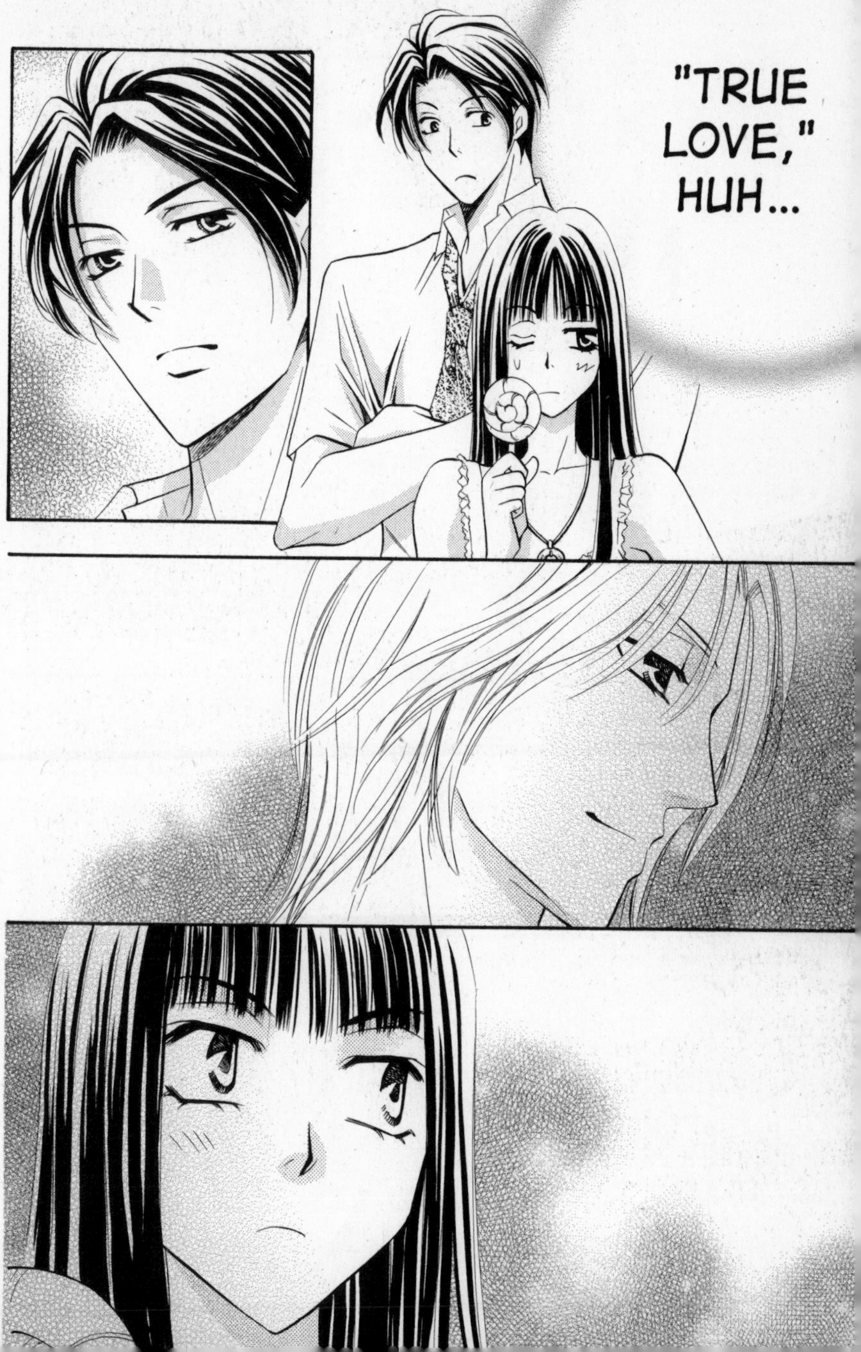
"TRUE LOVE," HUH...

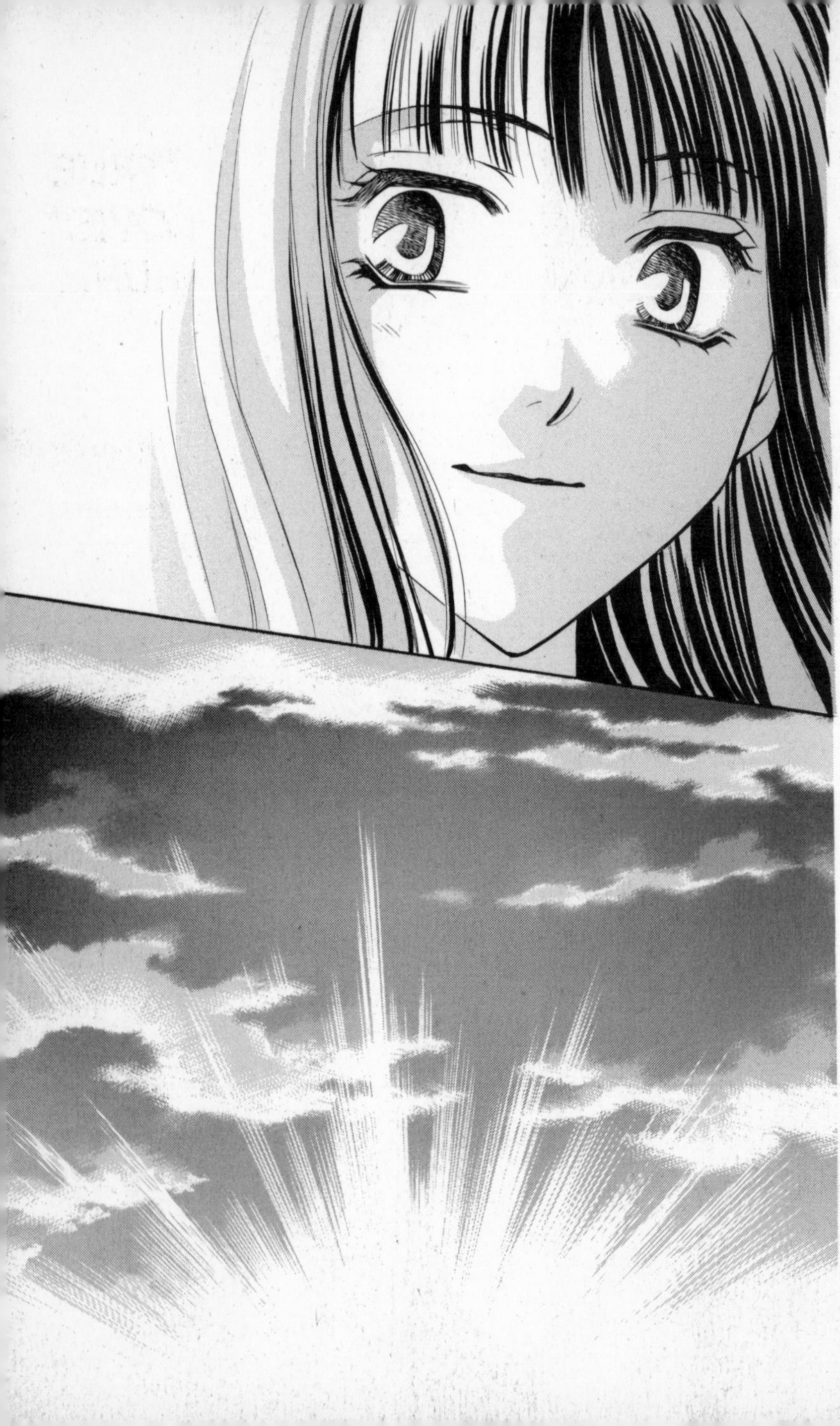

Chapter 11

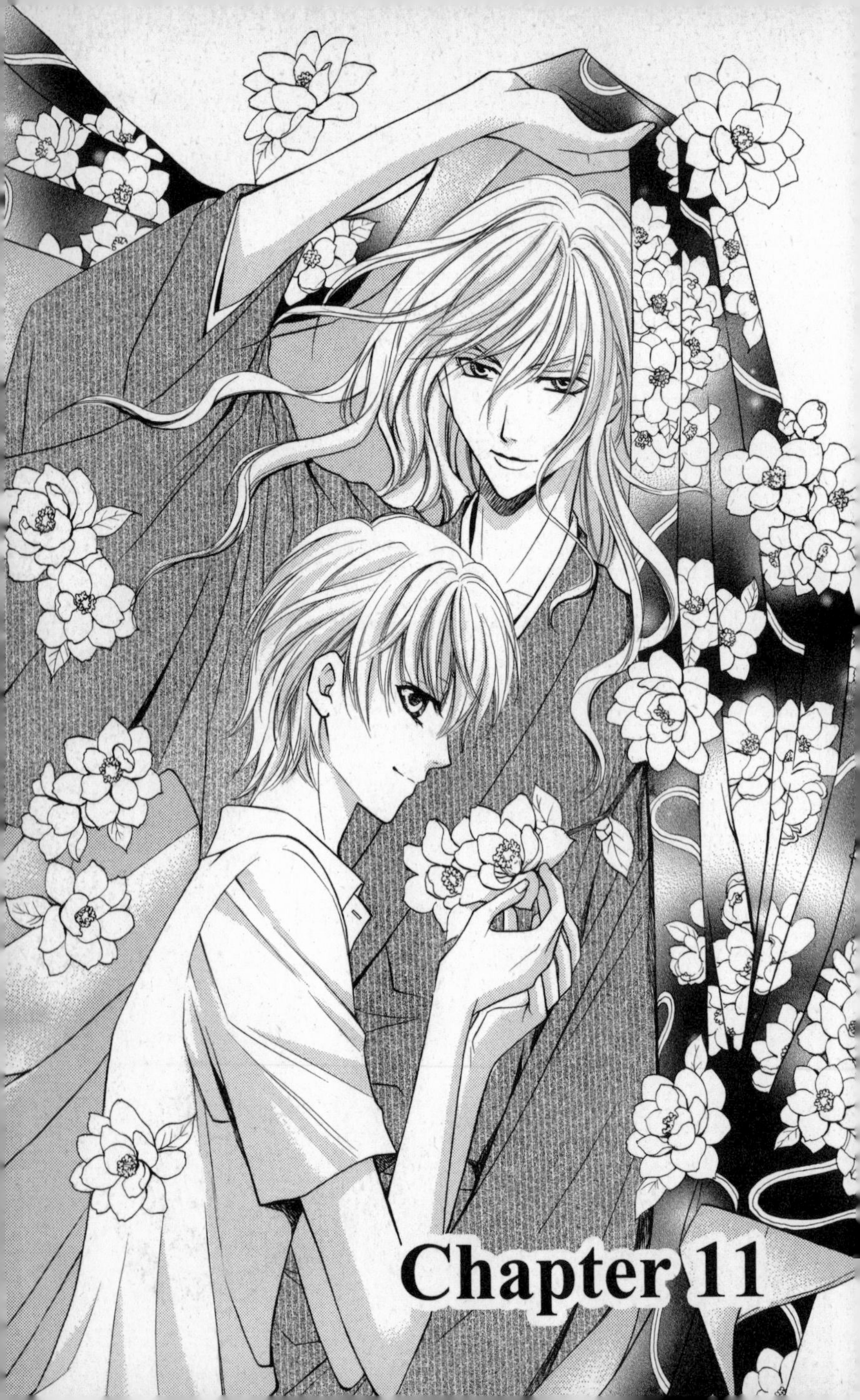

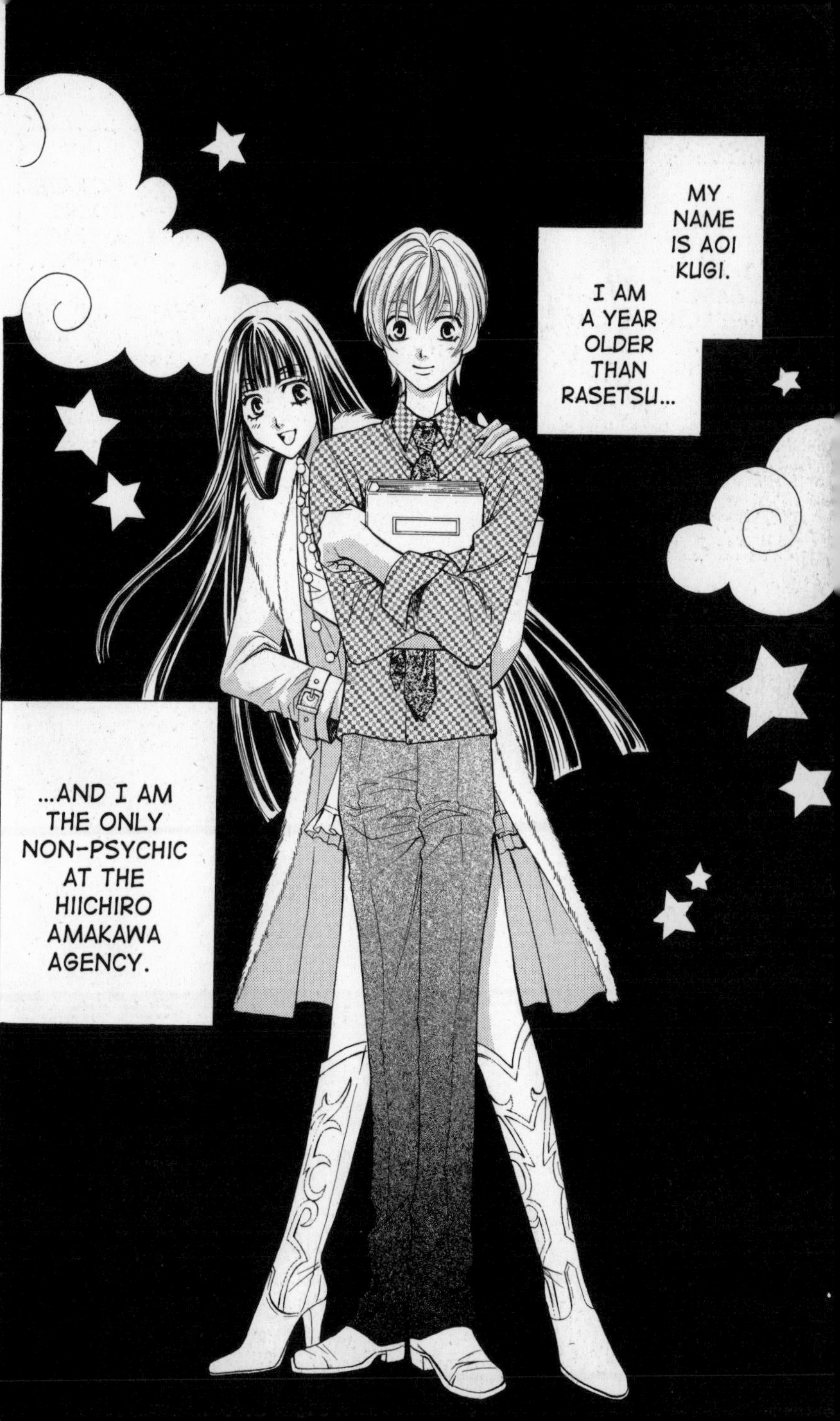
MY NAME IS AOI KUGI.
I AM A YEAR OLDER THAN RASETSU...
...AND I AM THE ONLY NON-PSYCHIC AT THE HIICHIRO AMAKAWA AGENCY.

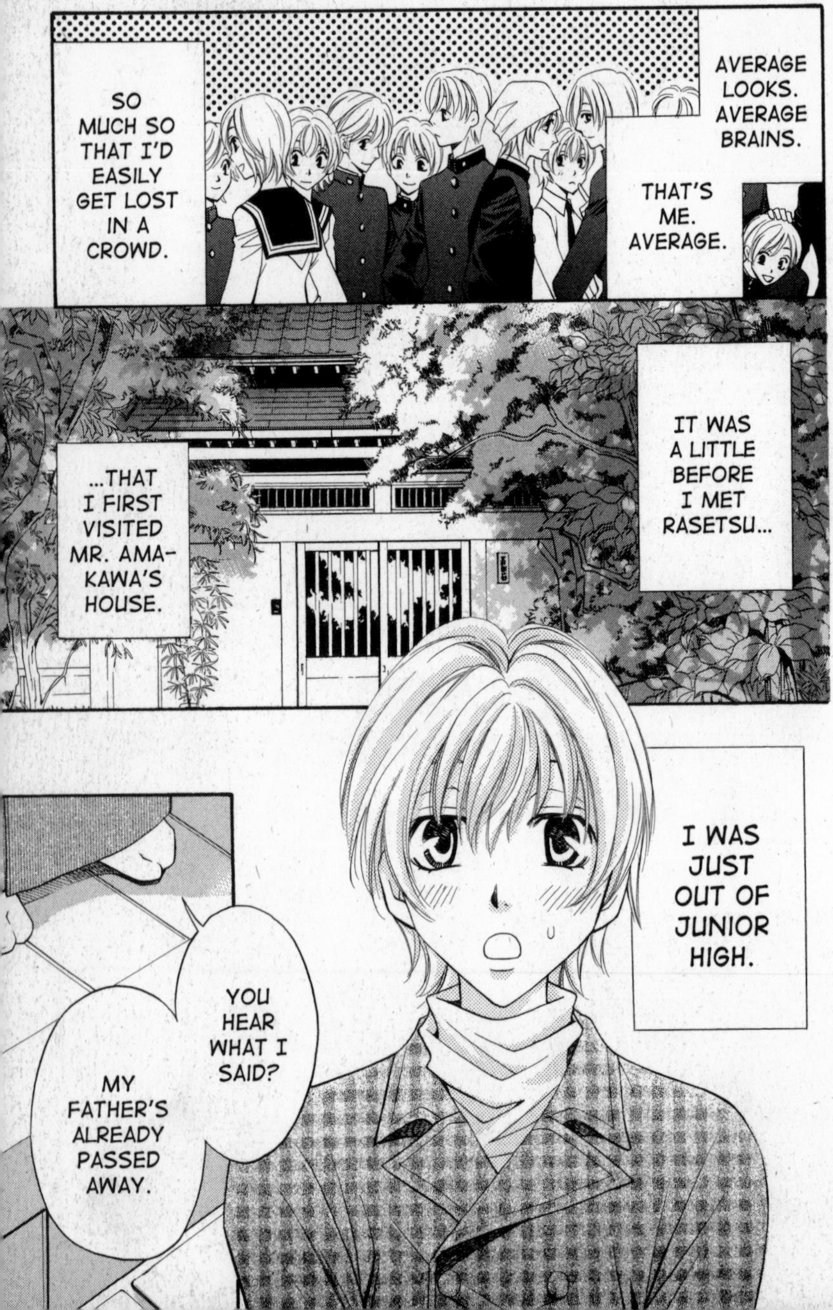
AVERAGE LOOKS. AVERAGE BRAINS.
THAT'S ME. AVERAGE.
SO MUCH SO THAT I'D EASILY GET LOST IN A CROWD.
IT WAS A LITTLE BEFORE I MET RASETSU...
...THAT I FIRST VISITED MR. AMA-KAWA'S HOUSE.
I WAS JUST OUT OF JUNIOR HIGH.
YOU HEAR WHAT I SAID?
MY FATHER'S ALREADY PASSED AWAY.

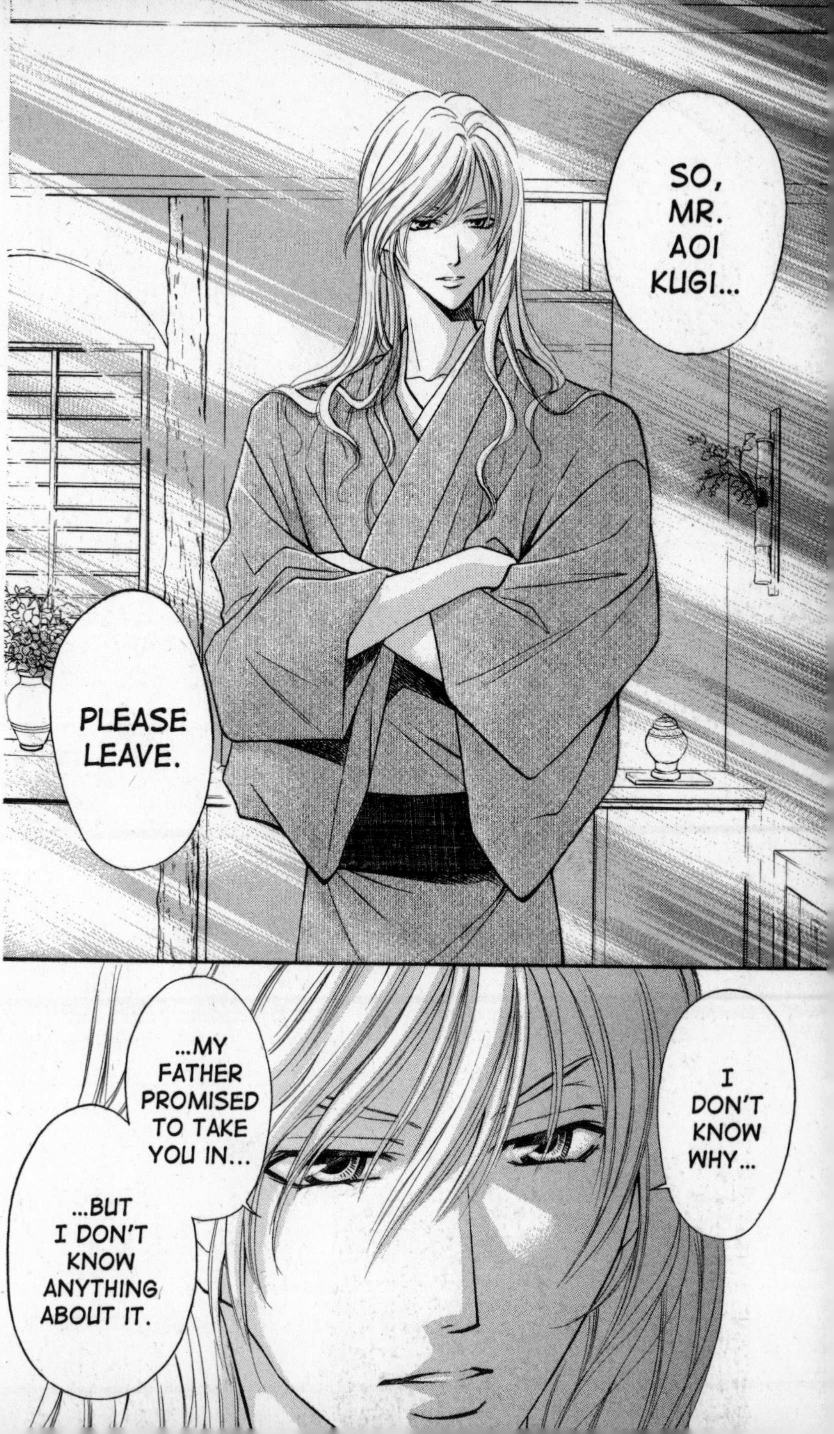
SO, MR. AOI KUGI...
PLEASE LEAVE.
I DON'T KNOW WHY...
...MY FATHER PROMISED TO TAKE YOU IN...
...BUT I DON'T KNOW ANYTHING ABOUT IT.

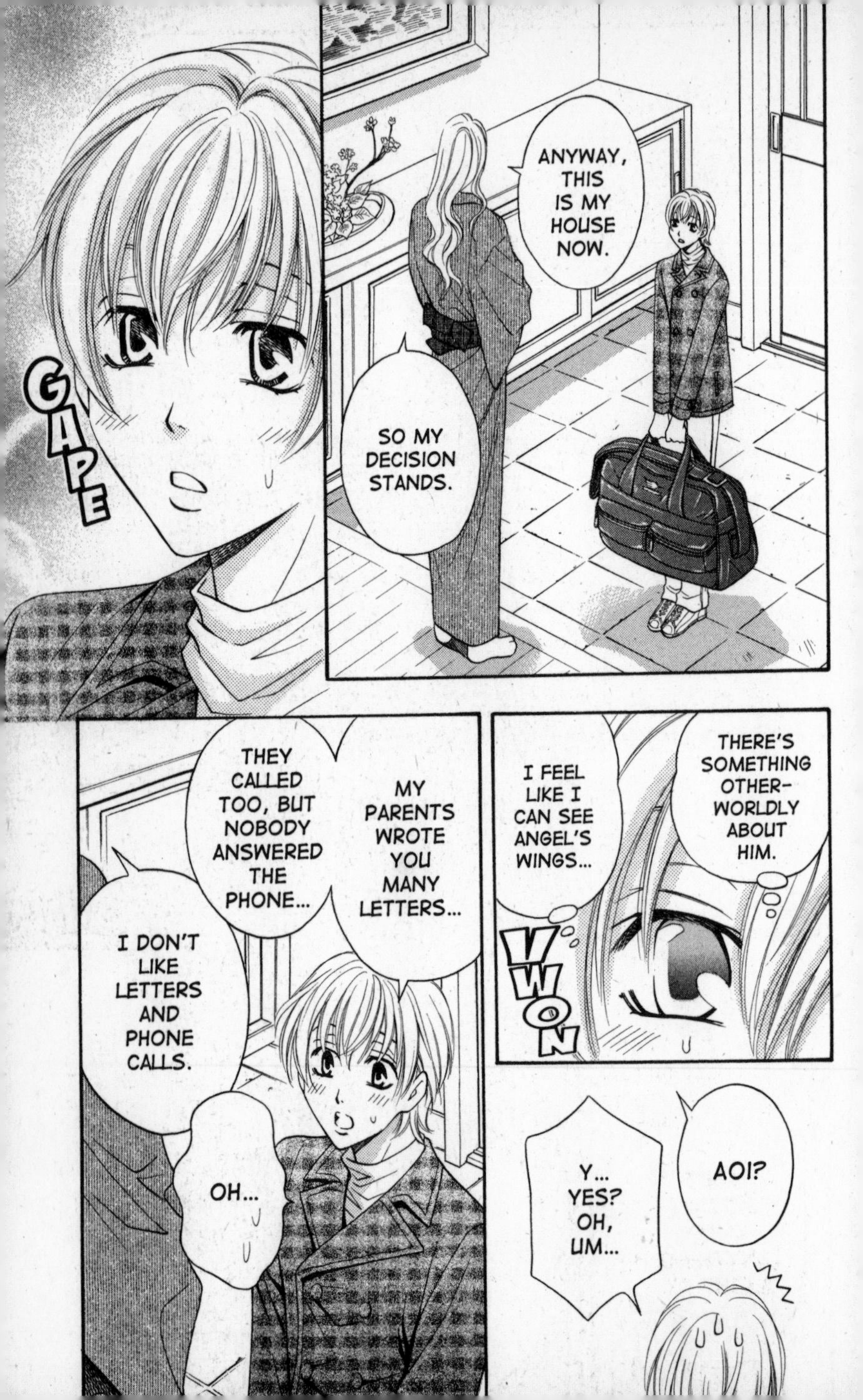
ANYWAY, THIS IS MY HOUSE NOW.
SO MY DECISION STANDS.
GAPE
THERE'S SOMETHING OTHER-WORLDLY ABOUT HIM.
I FEEL LIKE I CAN SEE ANGEL'S WINGS...
VWON
AOI?
Y... YES? OH, UM...
MY PARENTS WROTE YOU MANY LETTERS...
THEY CALLED TOO, BUT NOBODY ANSWERED THE PHONE...
I DON'T LIKE LETTERS AND PHONE CALLS.
OH...

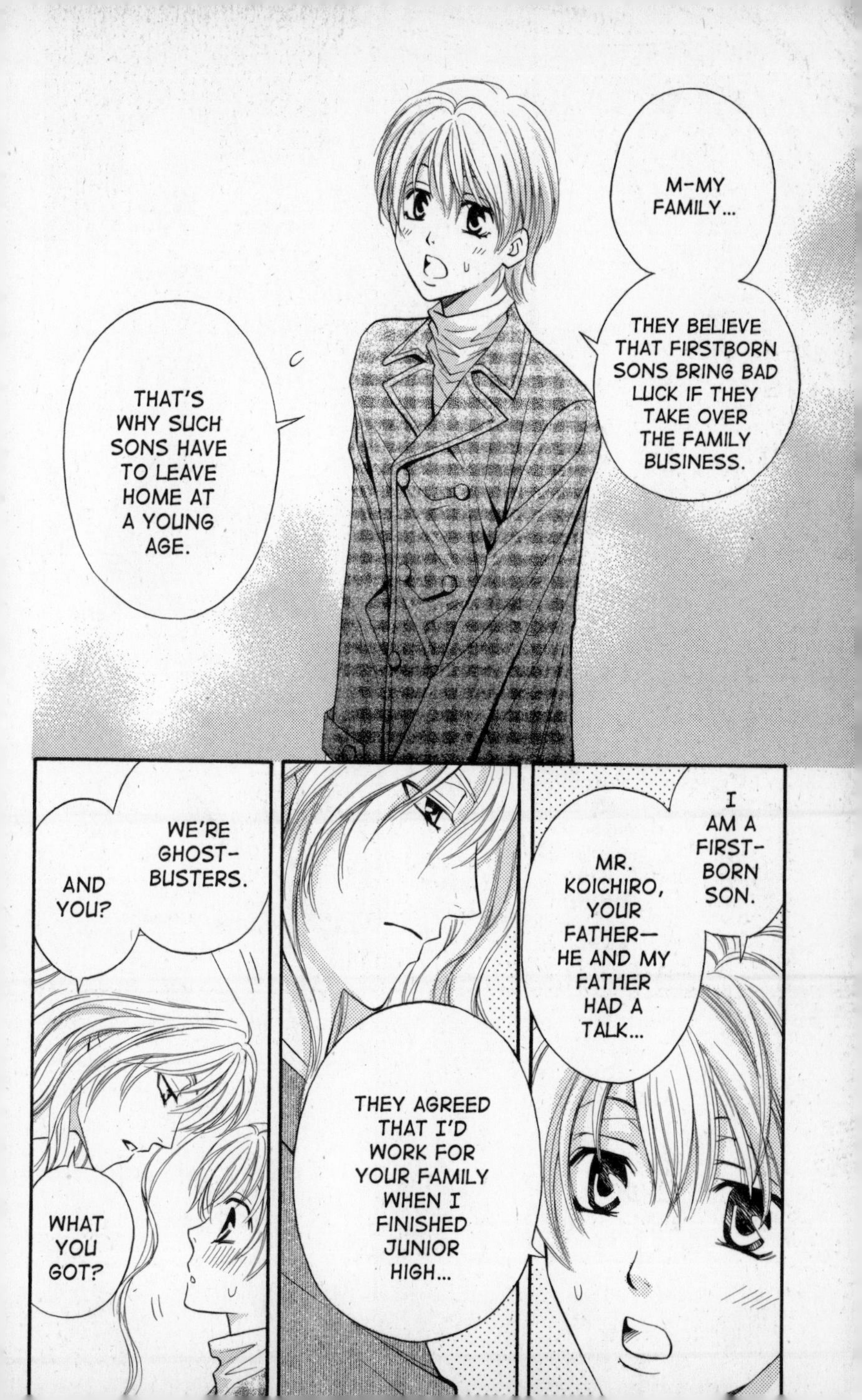
M-MY FAMILY...
THEY BELIEVE THAT FIRSTBORN SONS BRING BAD LUCK IF THEY TAKE OVER THE FAMILY BUSINESS.
THAT'S WHY SUCH SONS HAVE TO LEAVE HOME AT A YOUNG AGE.
I AM A FIRST-BORN SON.
MR. KOICHIRO, YOUR FATHER—HE AND MY FATHER HAD A TALK...
THEY AGREED THAT I'D WORK FOR YOUR FAMILY WHEN I FINISHED JUNIOR HIGH...
WE'RE GHOST-BUSTERS.
AND YOU?
WHAT YOU GOT?

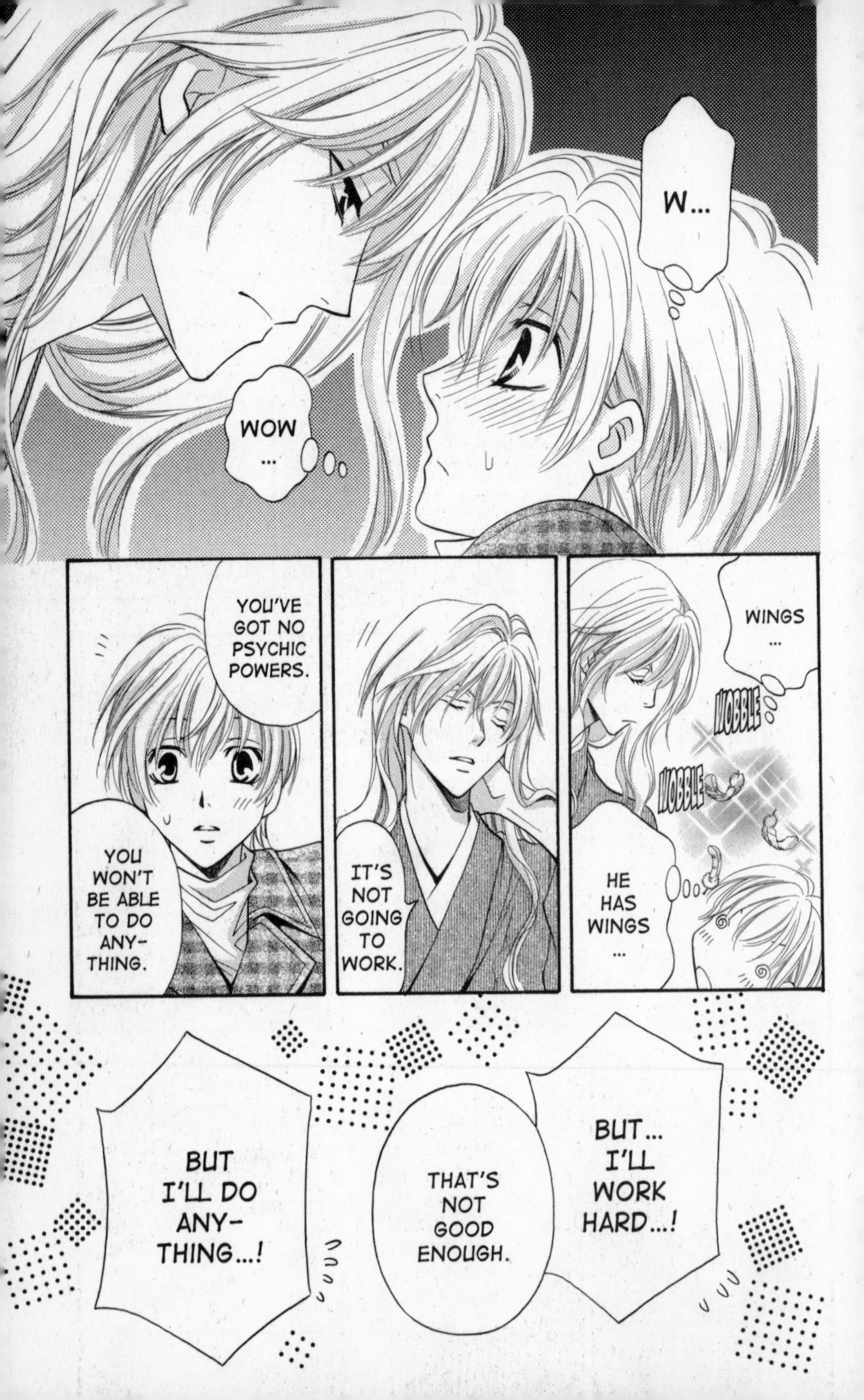
W...
WOW ...
WINGS ...
WOBBLE
WOBBLE
HE HAS WINGS ...
IT'S NOT GOING TO WORK.
YOU'VE GOT NO PSYCHIC POWERS.
YOU WON'T BE ABLE TO DO ANY-THING.
BUT... I'LL WORK HARD...!
THAT'S NOT GOOD ENOUGH.
BUT I'LL DO ANY-THING...!

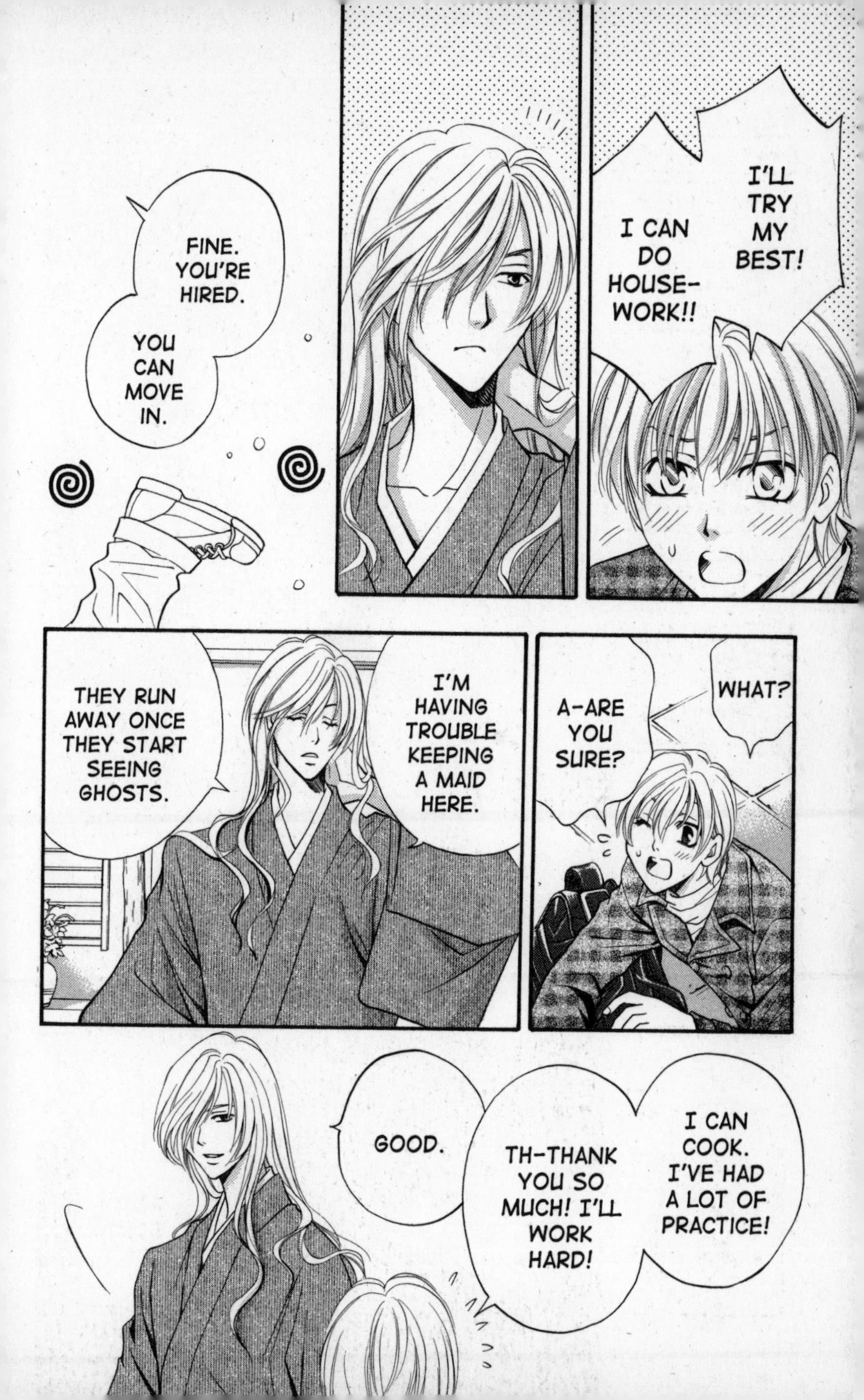
I'LL TRY MY BEST!
I CAN DO HOUSE-WORK!!
FINE. YOU'RE HIRED.
YOU CAN MOVE IN.
WHAT?
A-ARE YOU SURE?
I'M HAVING TROUBLE KEEPING A MAID HERE.
THEY RUN AWAY ONCE THEY START SEEING GHOSTS.
I CAN COOK. I'VE HAD A LOT OF PRACTICE!
TH-THANK YOU SO MUCH! I'LL WORK HARD!
GOOD.

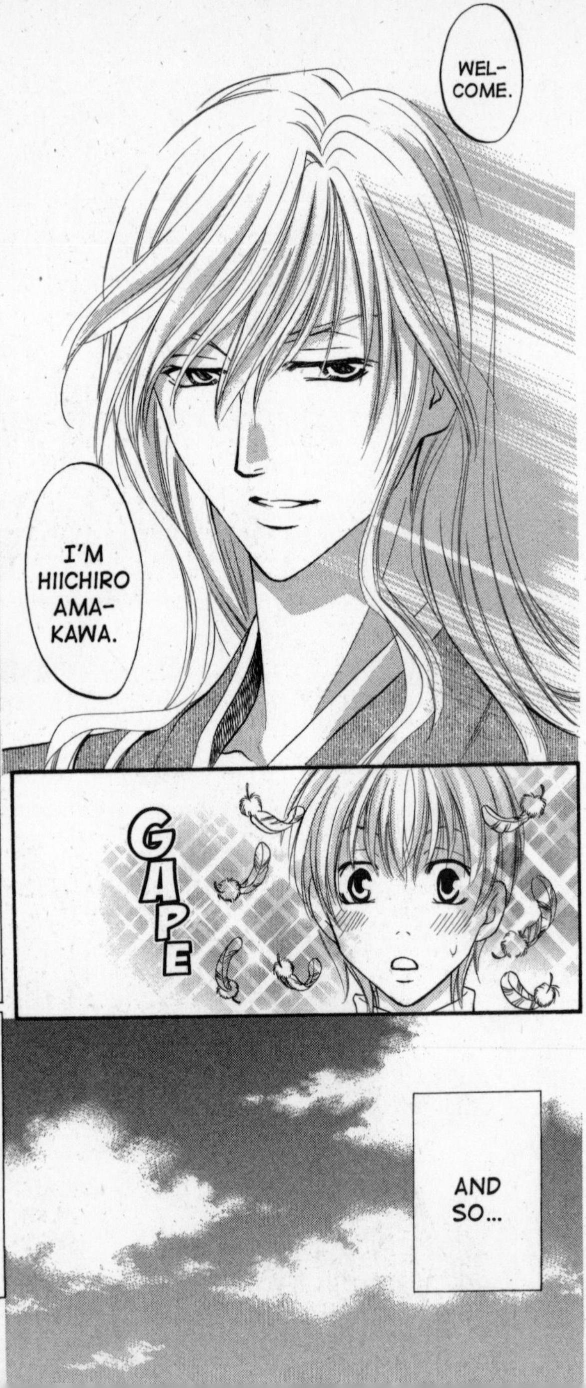
WEL-
COME.
I'M HIICHIRO AMA-KAWA.
GAPE
AND SO...

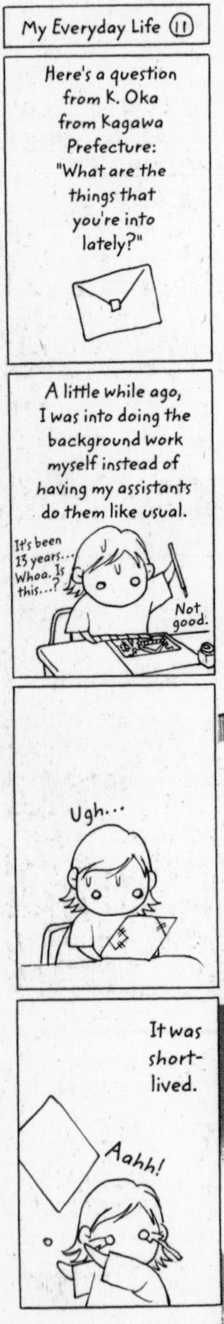
My Everyday Life 11
Here's a question from K. Oka from Kagawa Prefecture: "What are the things that you're into lately?"
A little while ago, I was into doing the background work myself instead of having my assistants do them like usual.
It's been 13 years... Whoa. Is this...?
Not good.
Ugh...
It was short-lived.
Aahh!

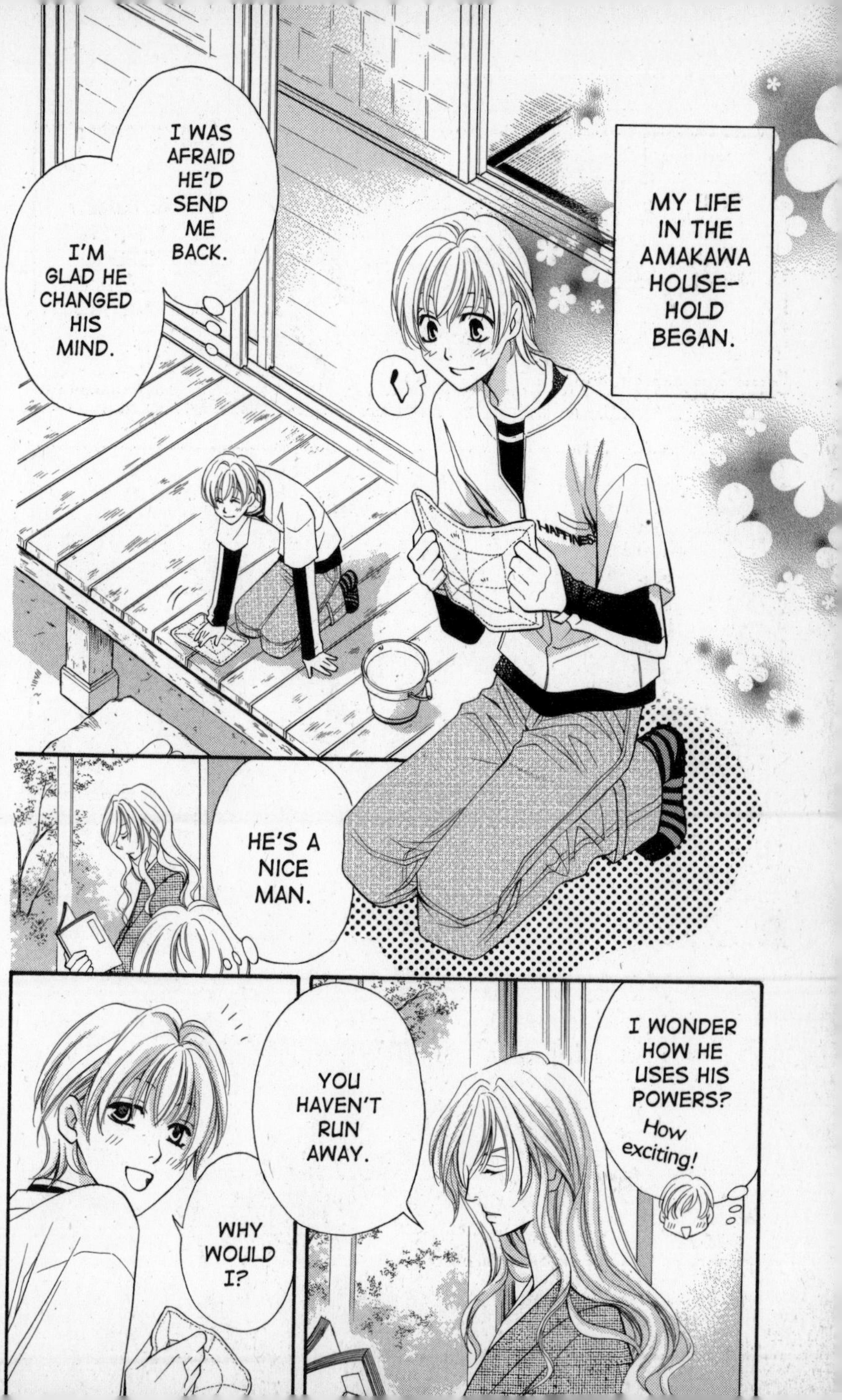
MY LIFE IN THE AMAKAWA HOUSE-HOLD BEGAN.
I WAS AFRAID HE'D SEND ME BACK.
I'M GLAD HE CHANGED HIS MIND.
HE'S A NICE MAN.
I WONDER HOW HE USES HIS POWERS?
How exciting!
YOU HAVEN'T RUN AWAY.
WHY WOULD I?

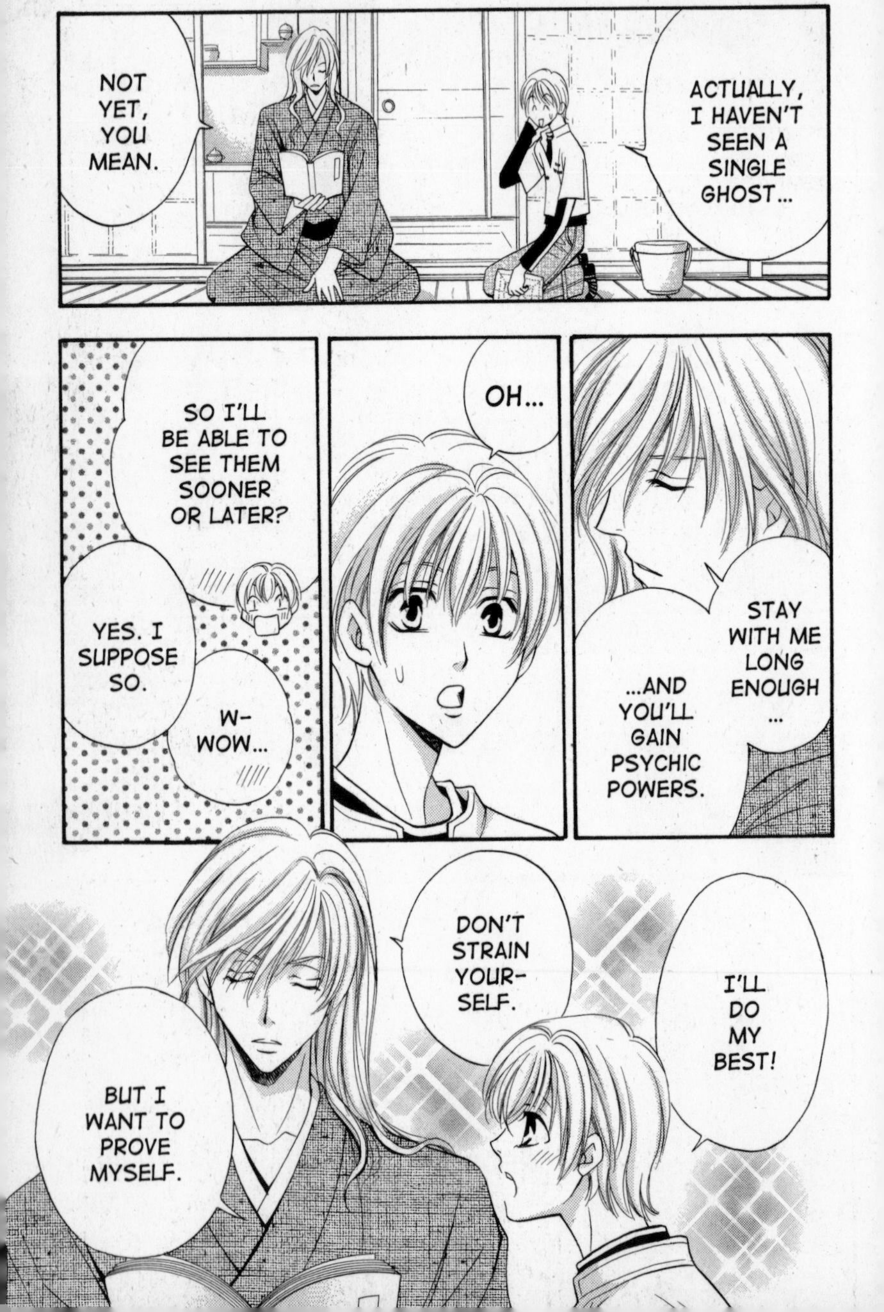
ACTUALLY, I HAVEN'T SEEN A SINGLE GHOST...
NOT YET, YOU MEAN.
STAY WITH ME LONG ENOUGH ...
...AND YOU'LL GAIN PSYCHIC POWERS.
OH...
SO I'LL BE ABLE TO SEE THEM SOONER OR LATER?
YES. I SUPPOSE SO.
W-WOW...
I'LL DO MY BEST!
DON'T STRAIN YOUR-SELF.
BUT I WANT TO PROVE MYSELF.

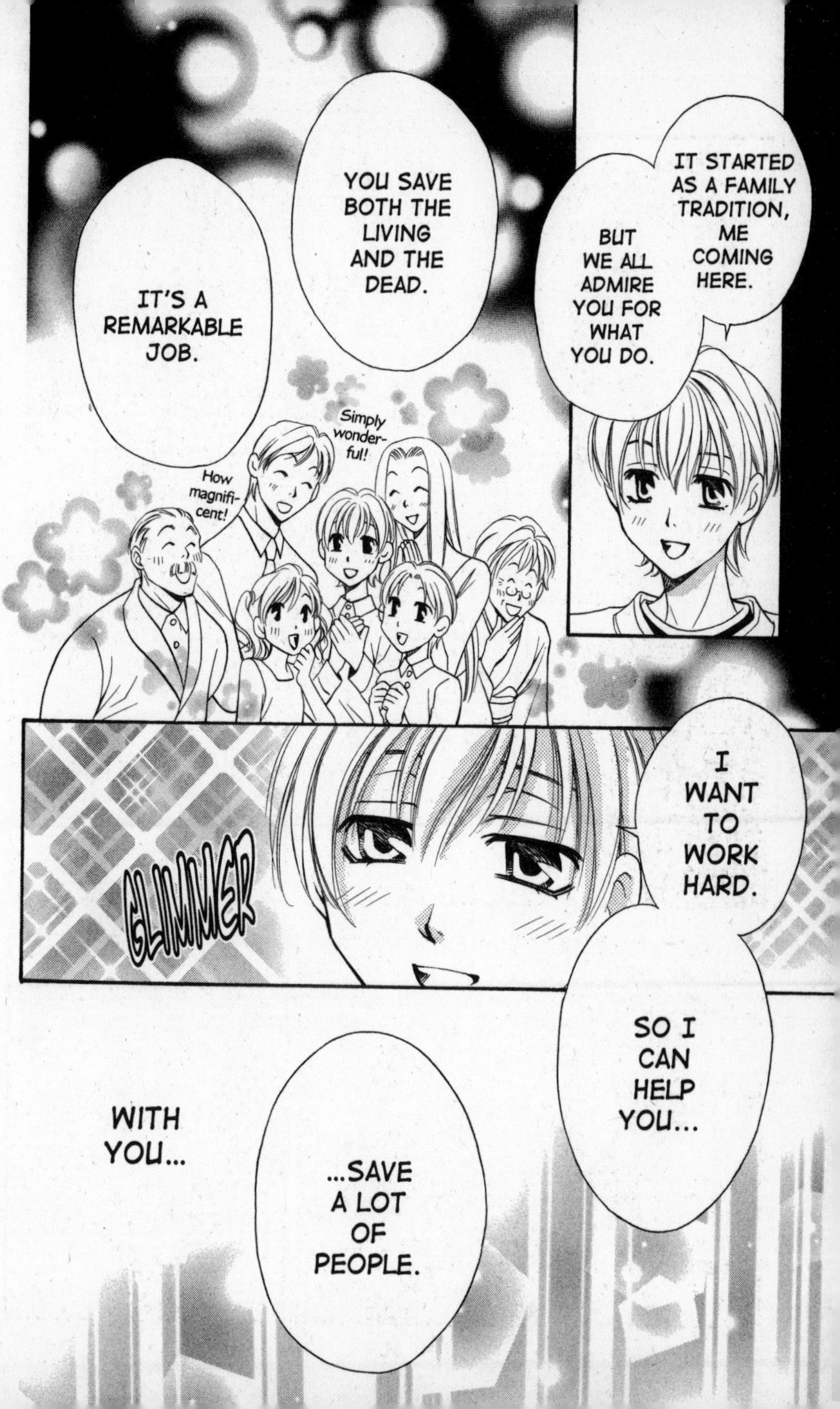
IT STARTED AS A FAMILY TRADITION, ME COMING HERE.
BUT WE ALL ADMIRE YOU FOR WHAT YOU DO.
YOU SAVE BOTH THE LIVING AND THE DEAD.
IT'S A REMARKABLE JOB.
Simply wonder-ful!
How magnifi-cent!
I WANT TO WORK HARD.
GLIMMER
SO I CAN HELP YOU...
...SAVE A LOT OF PEOPLE.
WITH YOU...

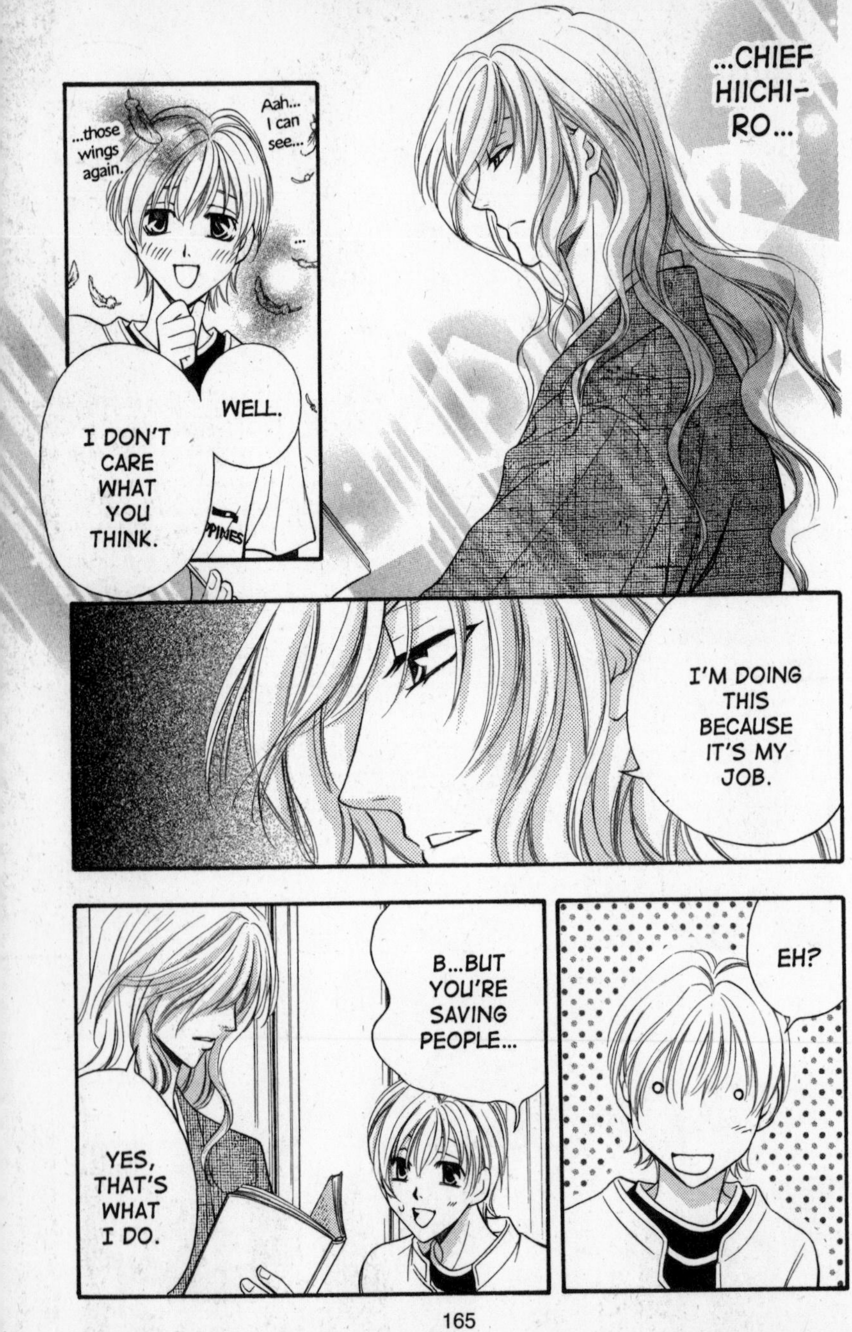
...CHIEF HIICHI-RO...
Aah... I can see...
...those wings again.
...
WELL.
I DON'T CARE WHAT YOU THINK.
I'M DOING THIS BECAUSE IT'S MY JOB.
EH?
B...BUT YOU'RE SAVING PEOPLE...
YES, THAT'S WHAT I DO.

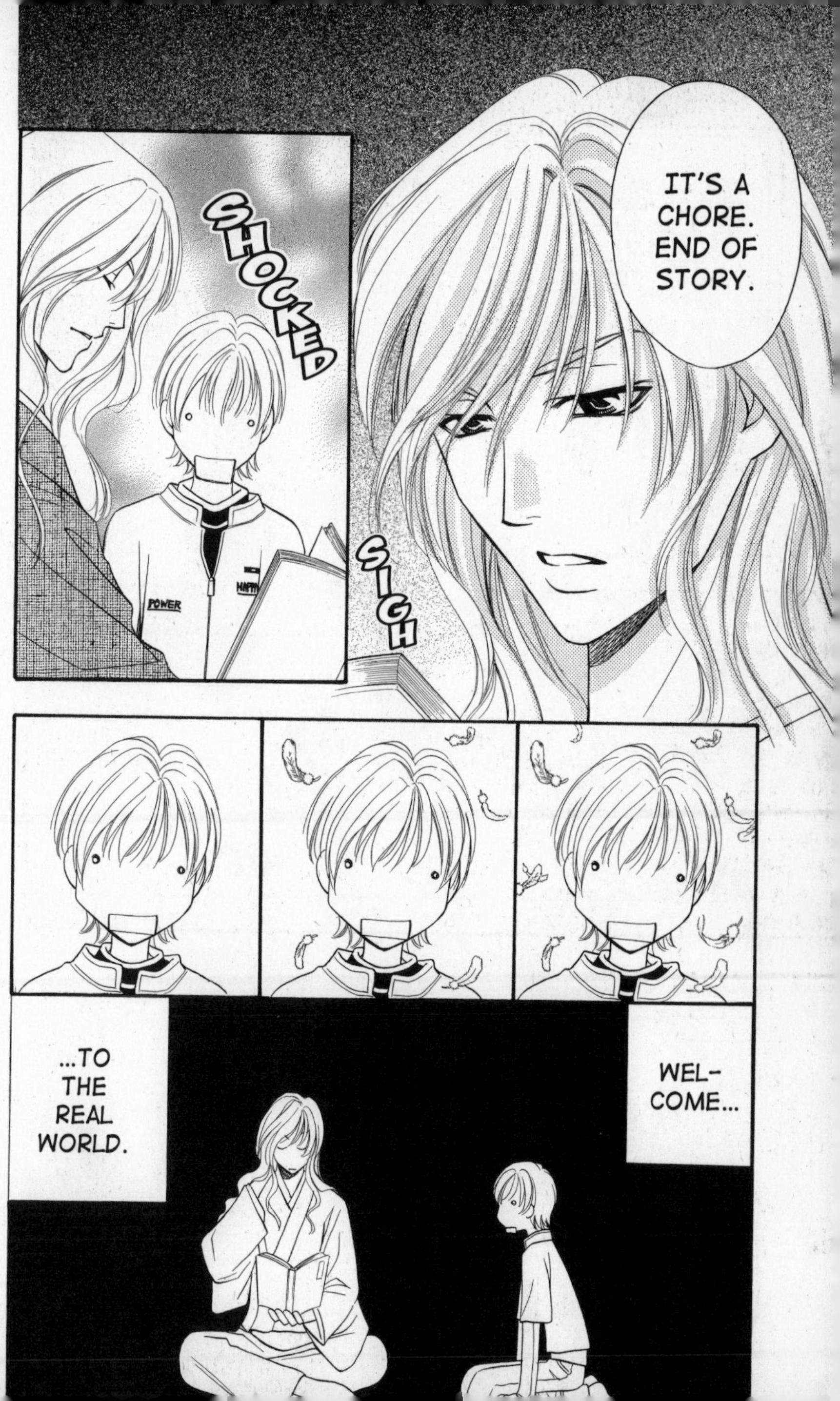
IT'S A CHORE. END OF STORY.
SIGH
SHOCKED
POWER
WEL-COME...
...TO THE REAL WORLD.

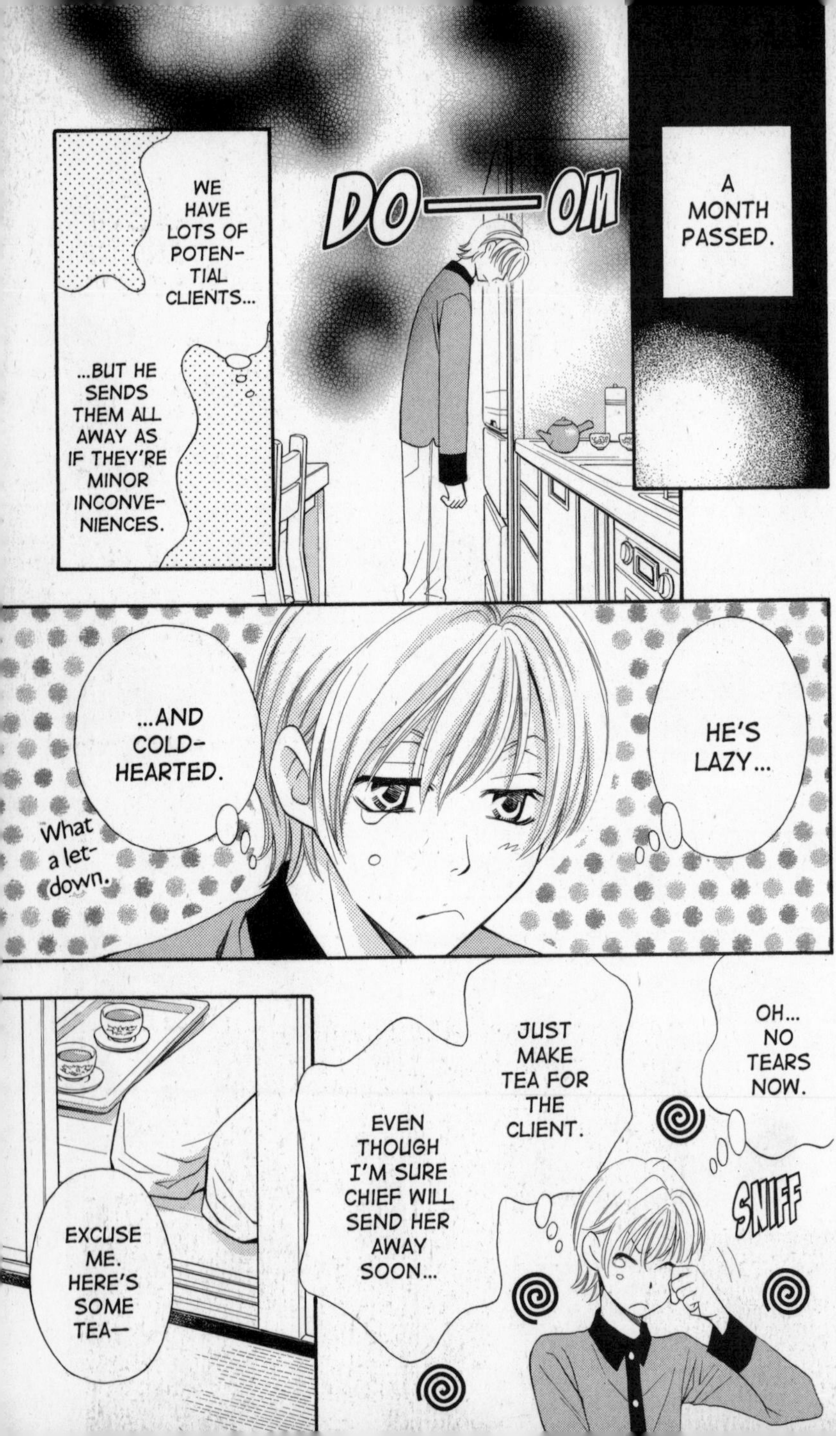
A MONTH PASSED.
DO——OM
WE HAVE LOTS OF POTEN-TIAL CLIENTS...
...BUT HE SENDS THEM ALL AWAY AS IF THEY'RE MINOR INCONVE-NIENCES.
HE'S LAZY...
...AND COLD-HEARTED.
What a let-down.
OH... NO TEARS NOW.
SNIFF
JUST MAKE TEA FOR THE CLIENT.
EVEN THOUGH I'M SURE CHIEF WILL SEND HER AWAY SOON...
EXCUSE ME. HERE'S SOME TEA—

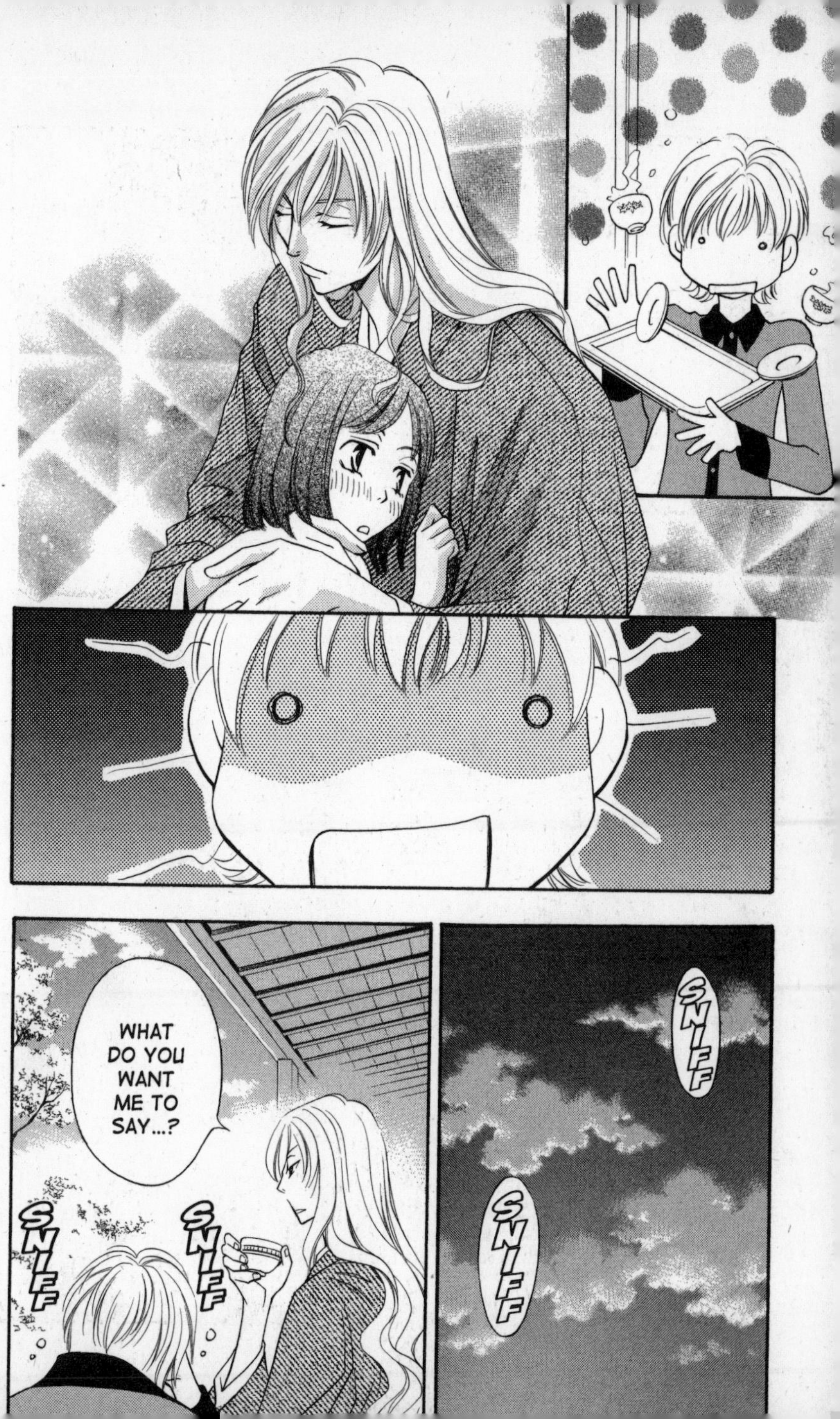
SNIFF
SNIFF
WHAT DO YOU WANT ME TO SAY...?
SNIFF
SNIFF

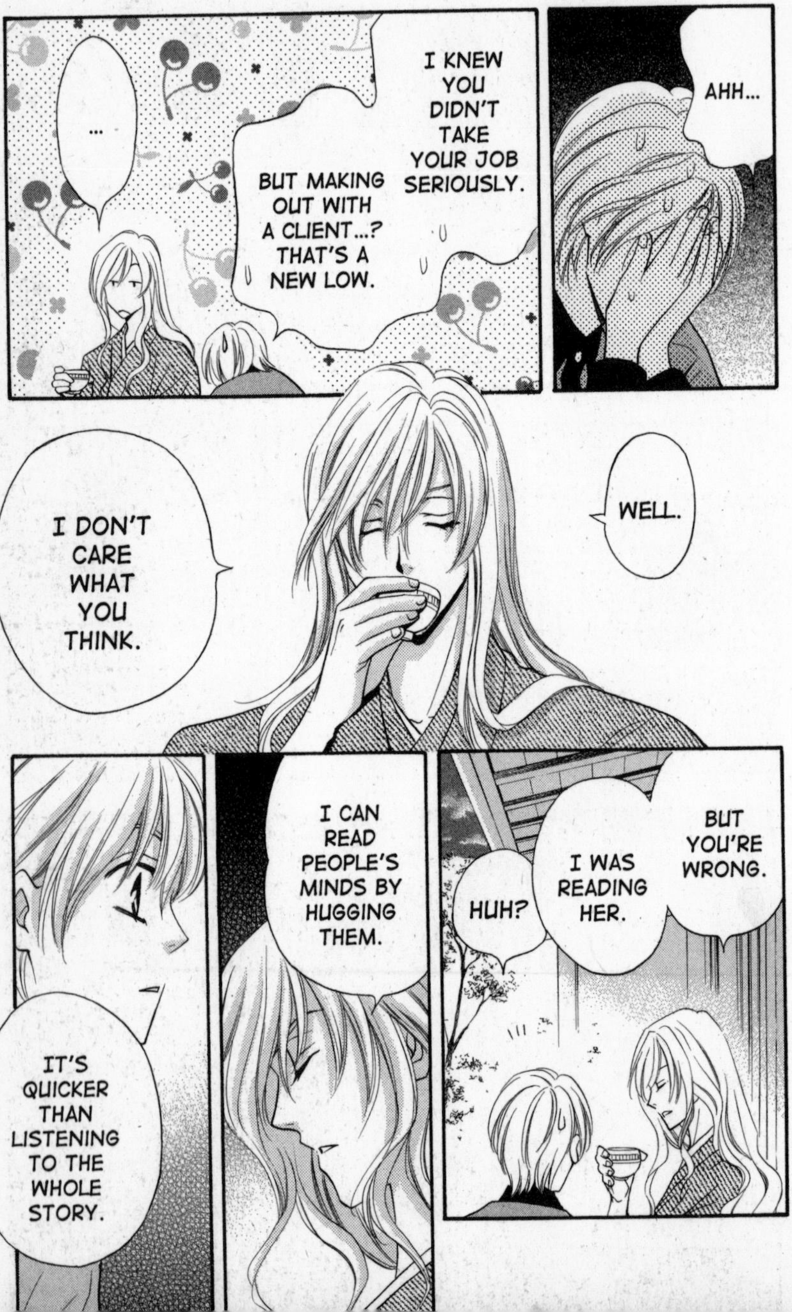
AHH...
I KNEW YOU DIDN'T TAKE YOUR JOB SERIOUSLY.
BUT MAKING OUT WITH A CLIENT...? THAT'S A NEW LOW.
...
WELL.
I DON'T CARE WHAT YOU THINK.
BUT YOU'RE WRONG.
I WAS READING HER.
HUH?
I CAN READ PEOPLE'S MINDS BY HUGGING THEM.
IT'S QUICKER THAN LISTENING TO THE WHOLE STORY.

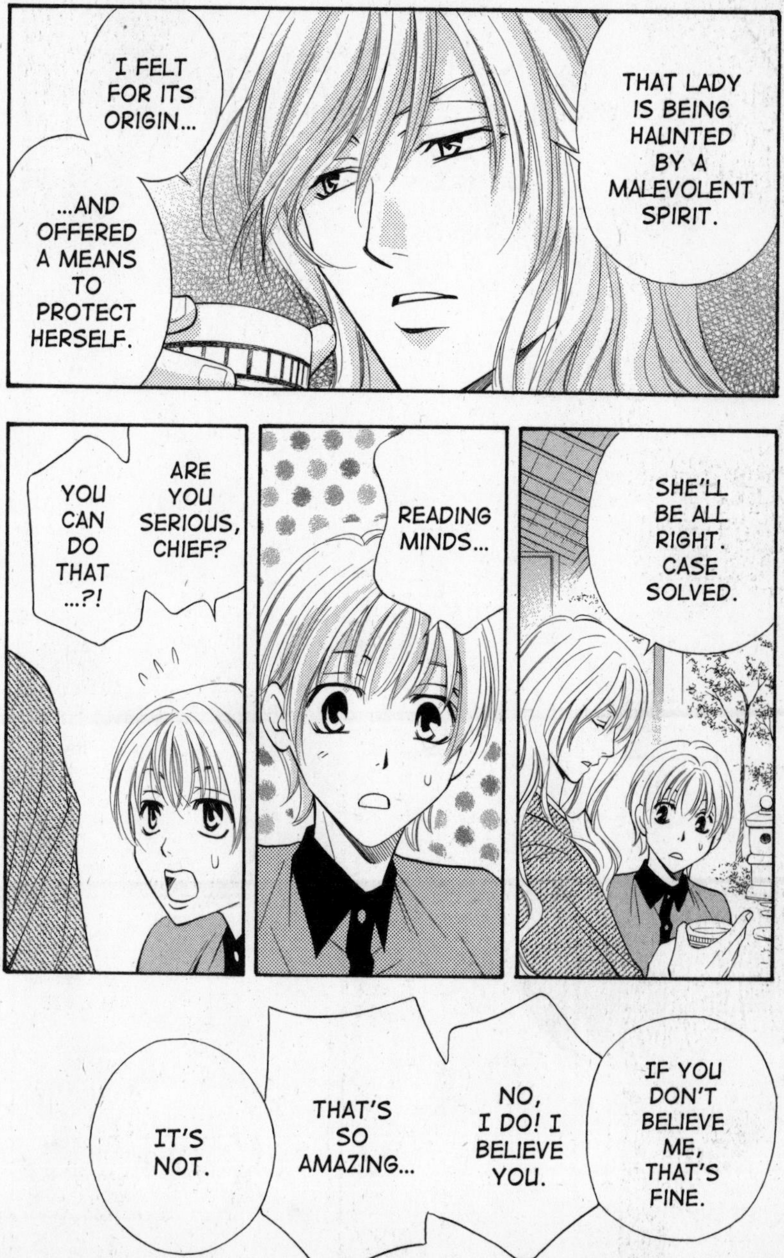
THAT LADY IS BEING HAUNTED BY A MALEVOLENT SPIRIT.
I FELT FOR ITS ORIGIN...
...AND OFFERED A MEANS TO PROTECT HERSELF.
SHE'LL BE ALL RIGHT. CASE SOLVED.
READING MINDS...
ARE YOU SERIOUS, CHIEF?
YOU CAN DO THAT ...?!
IF YOU DON'T BELIEVE ME, THAT'S FINE.
NO, I DO! I BELIEVE YOU.
THAT'S SO AMAZING...
IT'S NOT.

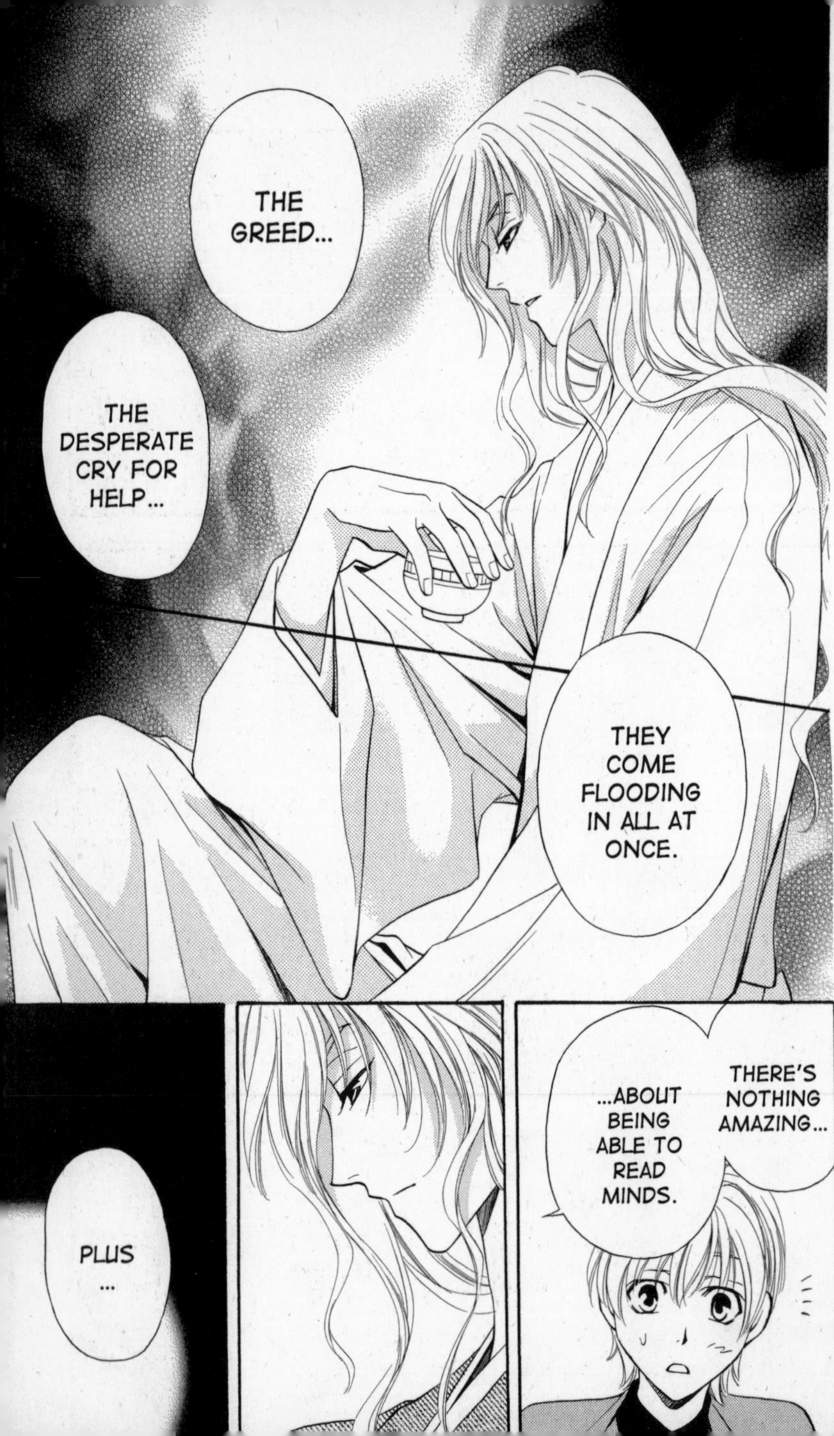
THE GREED...
THE DESPERATE CRY FOR HELP...
THEY COME FLOODING IN ALL AT ONCE.
THERE'S NOTHING AMAZING...
...ABOUT BEING ABLE TO READ MINDS.
PLUS ...

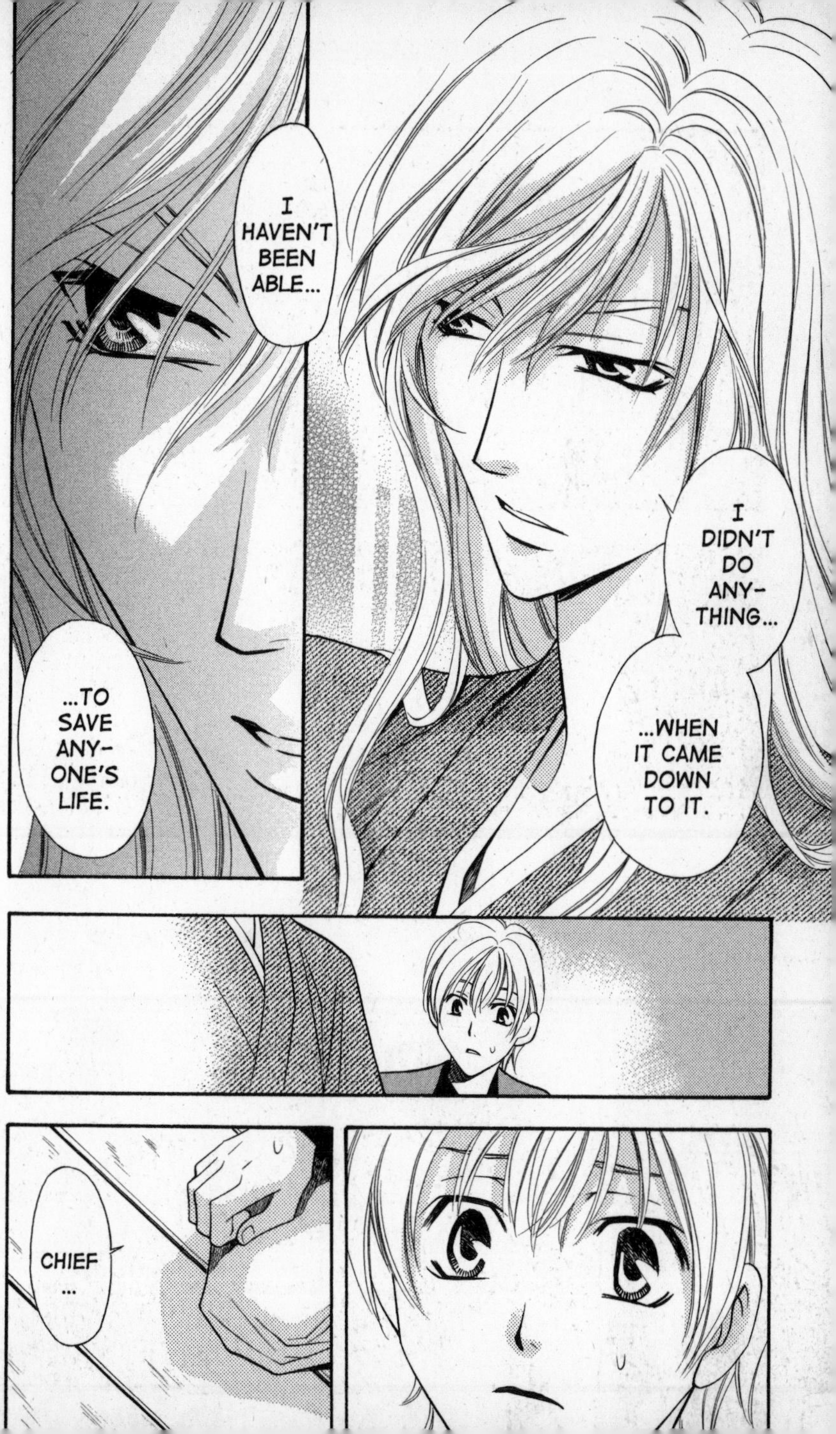
I DIDN'T DO ANY-THING...
...WHEN IT CAME DOWN TO IT.
I HAVEN'T BEEN ABLE...
...TO SAVE ANY-ONE'S LIFE.
CHIEF ...

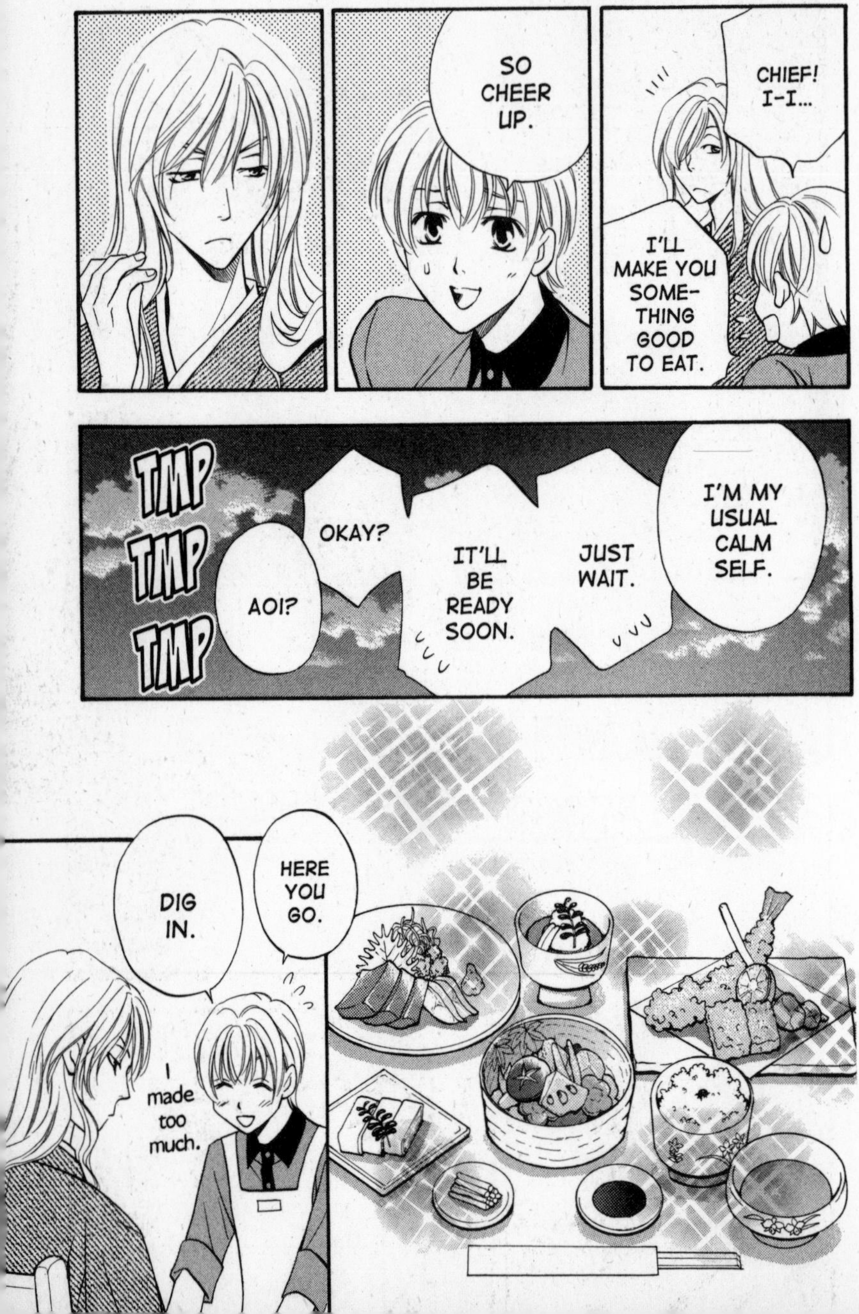
CHIEF! I-I...
I'LL MAKE YOU SOME-THING GOOD TO EAT.
SO CHEER UP.
I'M MY USUAL CALM SELF.
JUST WAIT.
IT'LL BE READY SOON.
OKAY?
AOI?
TMP TMP TMP
HERE YOU GO.
DIG IN.
I made too much.

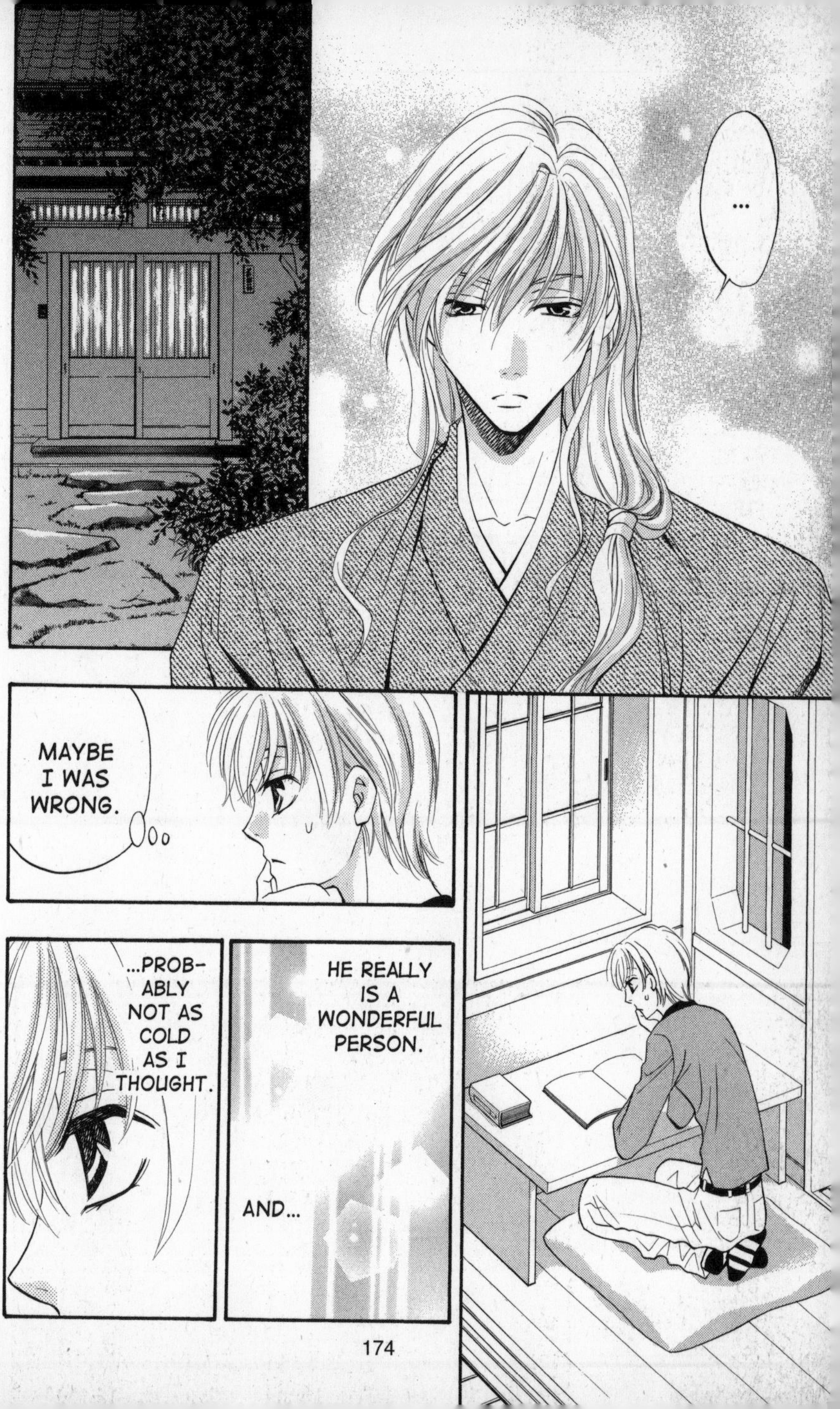
...
MAYBE I WAS WRONG.
HE REALLY IS A WONDERFUL PERSON.
AND...
...PROB-ABLY NOT AS COLD AS I THOUGHT.

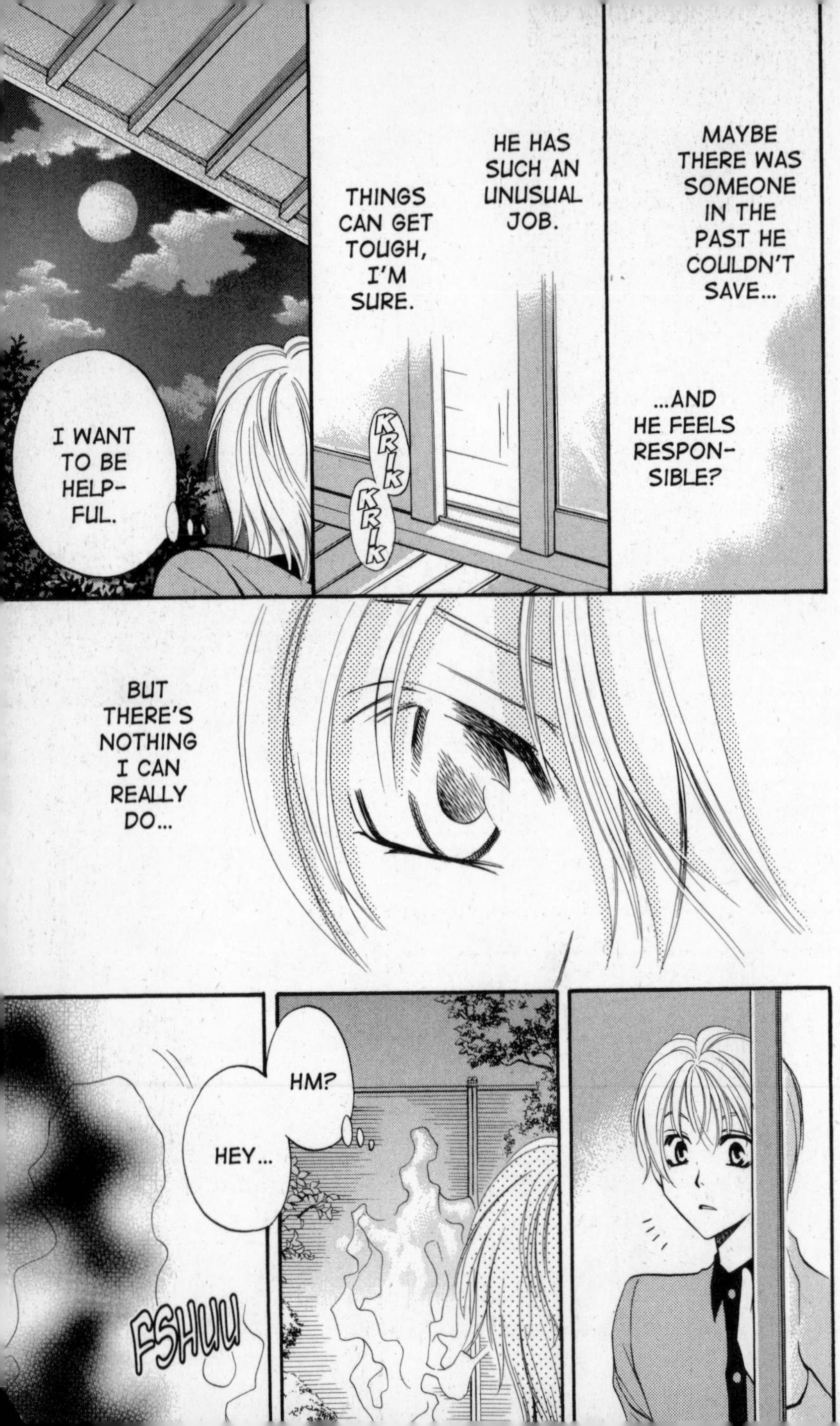
MAYBE THERE WAS SOMEONE IN THE PAST HE COULDN'T SAVE...
...AND HE FEELS RESPON-SIBLE?
HE HAS SUCH AN UNUSUAL JOB.
THINGS CAN GET TOUGH, I'M SURE.
KRIK
KRIK
I WANT TO BE HELP-FUL.
BUT THERE'S NOTHING I CAN REALLY DO...
HM?
HEY...
FSHUU

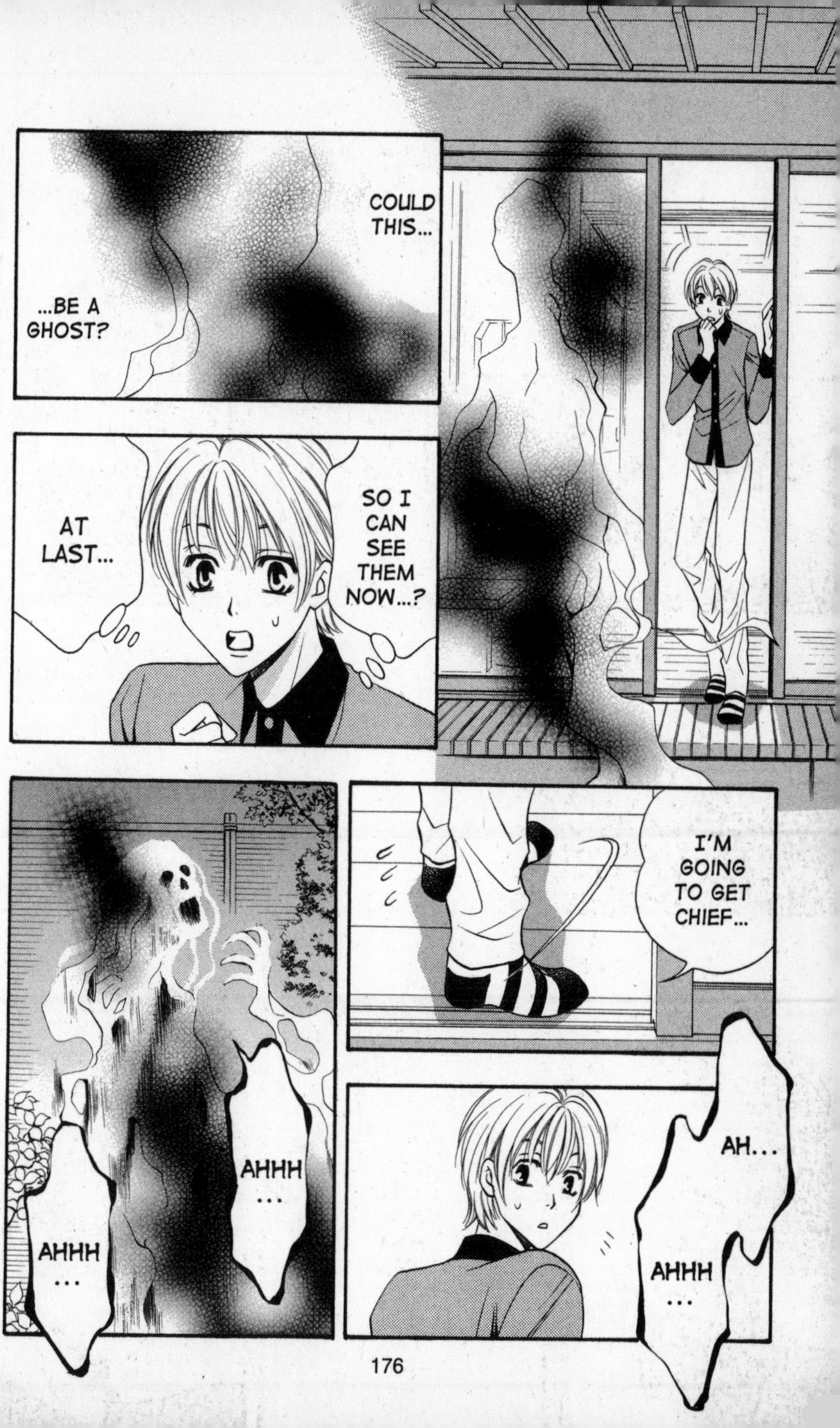
COULD THIS...
...BE A GHOST?
SO I CAN SEE THEM NOW...?
AT LAST...
I'M GOING TO GET CHIEF...
AH...
AHHH...
AHHH...
AHHH...

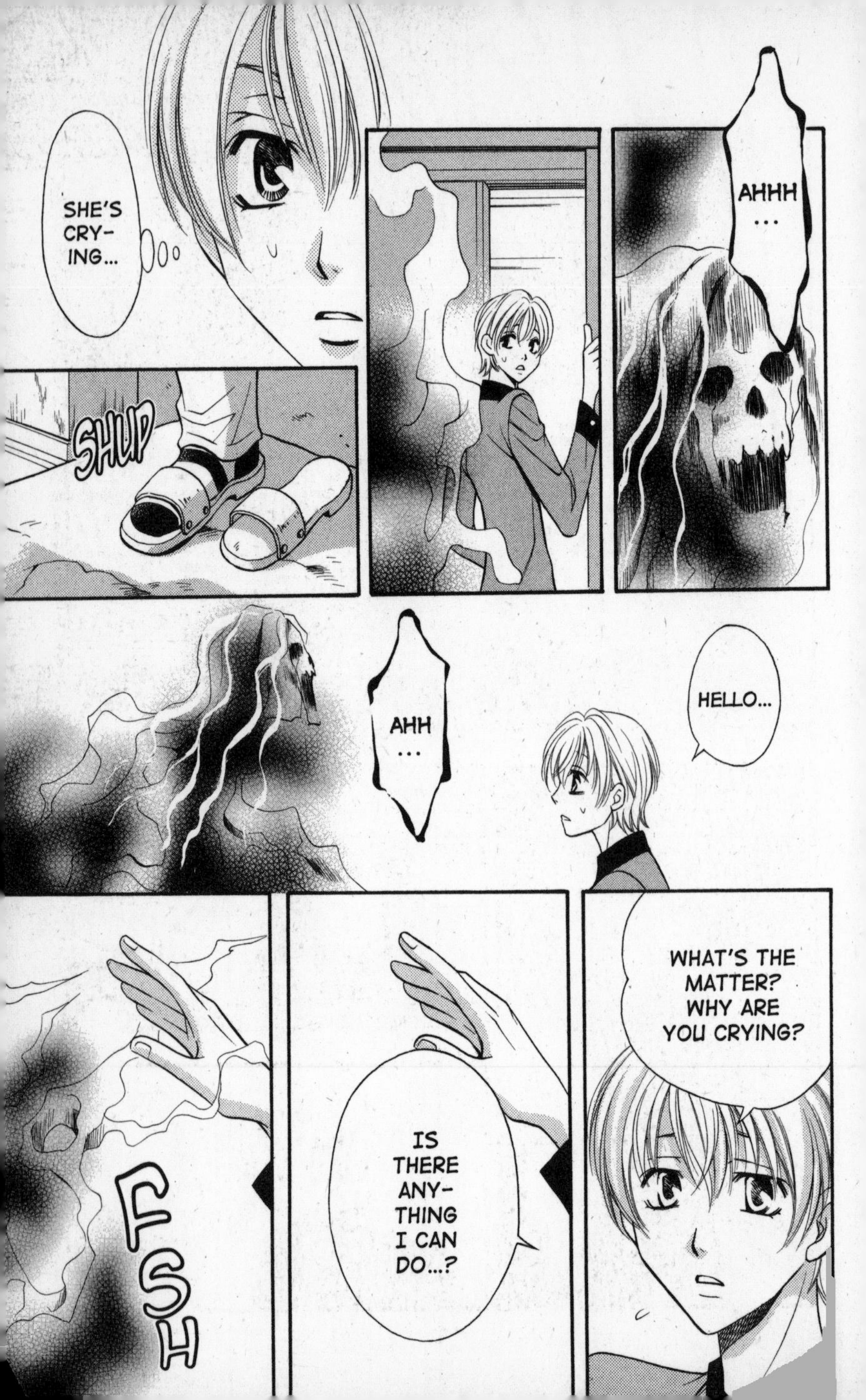
AHHH...
SHE'S CRY- ING...
SHUD
HELLO...
AHH...
WHAT'S THE MATTER? WHY ARE YOU CRYING?
IS THERE ANY- THING I CAN DO...?
FSH

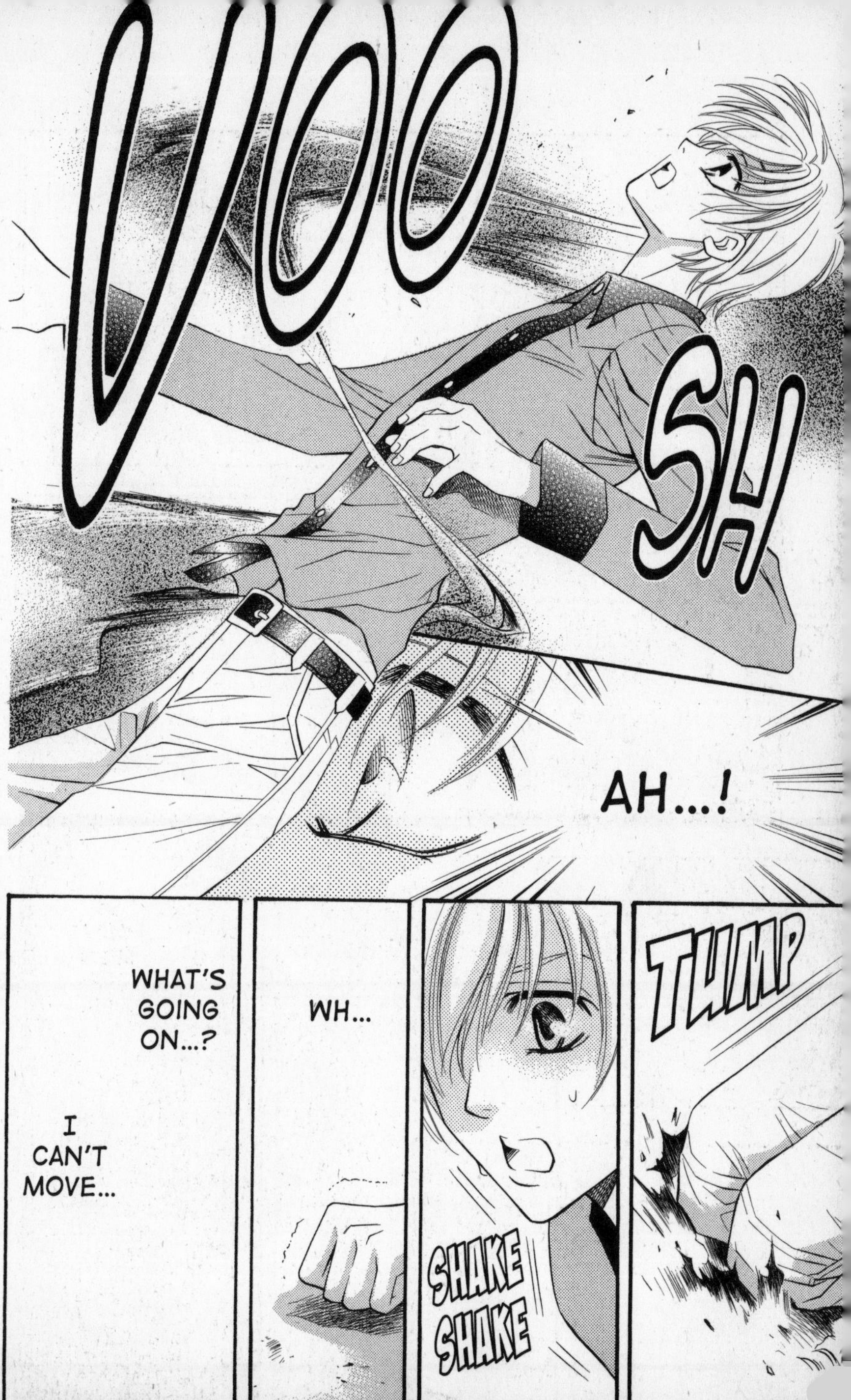
VOOSH
AH...!
TUMP
SHAKE SHAKE
WH...
WHAT'S GOING ON...?
I CAN'T MOVE...

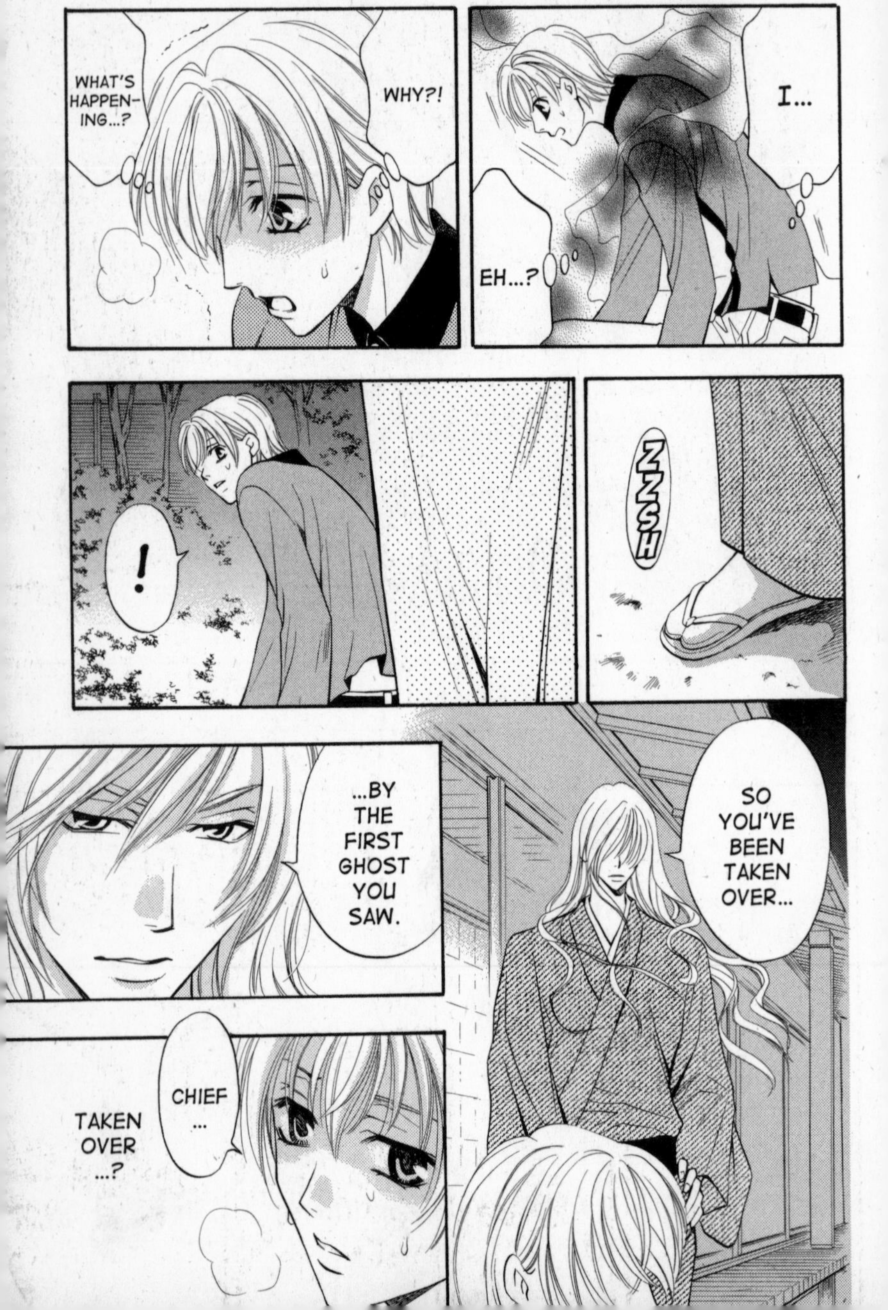
I...
EH...?
WHY?!
WHAT'S HAPPENING...?
ZZSH
!
SO YOU'VE BEEN TAKEN OVER...
...BY THE FIRST GHOST YOU SAW.
CHIEF ...
TAKEN OVER ...?

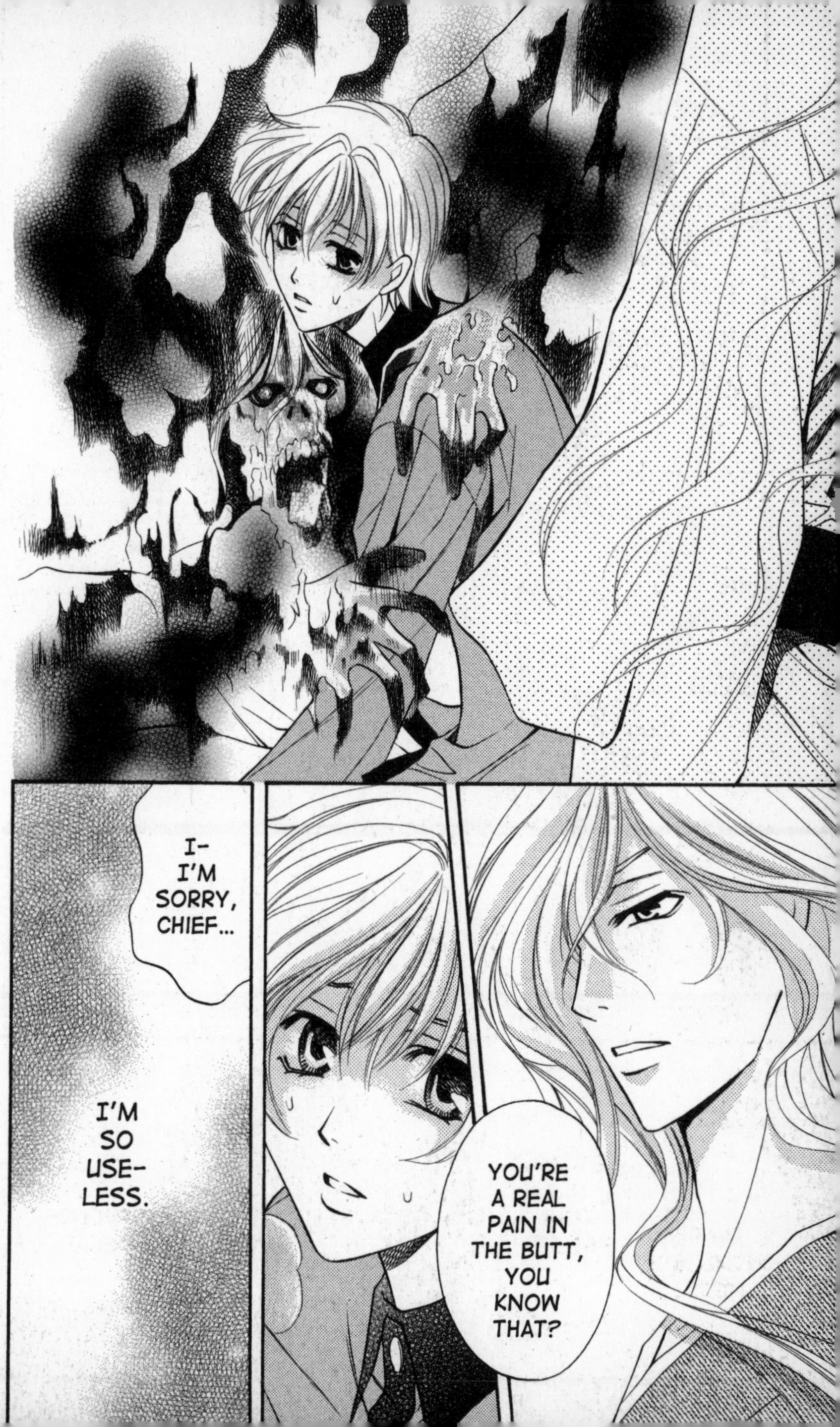
YOU'RE A REAL PAIN IN THE BUTT, YOU KNOW THAT?
I- I'M SORRY, CHIEF...
I'M SO USELESS-LESS.

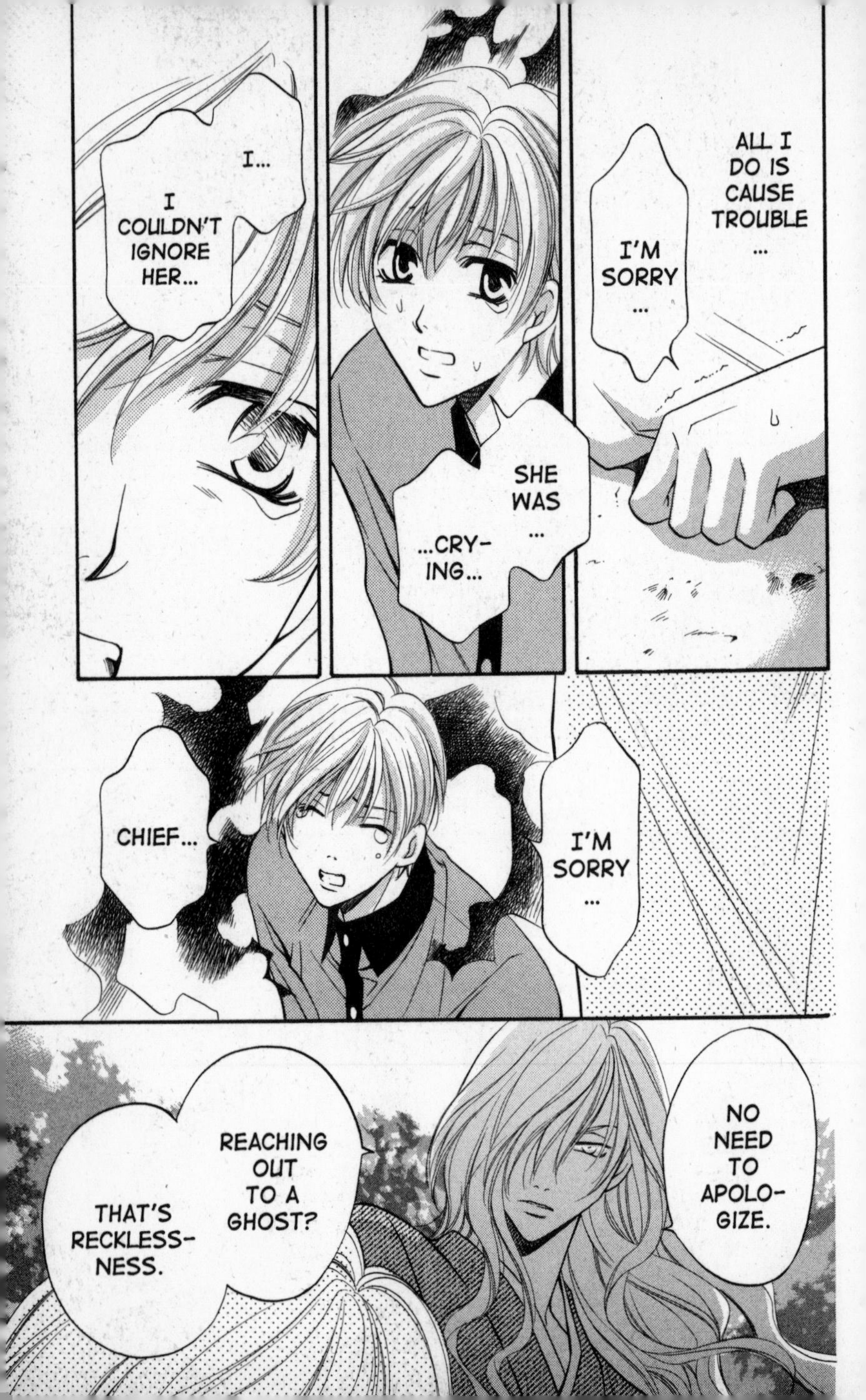
ALL I DO IS CAUSE TROUBLE ...
I'M SORRY ...
SHE WAS ...
...CRY-ING...
I...
I COULDN'T IGNORE HER...
I'M SORRY ...
CHIEF...
NO NEED TO APOLO-GIZE.
REACHING OUT TO A GHOST?
THAT'S RECKLESS-NESS.

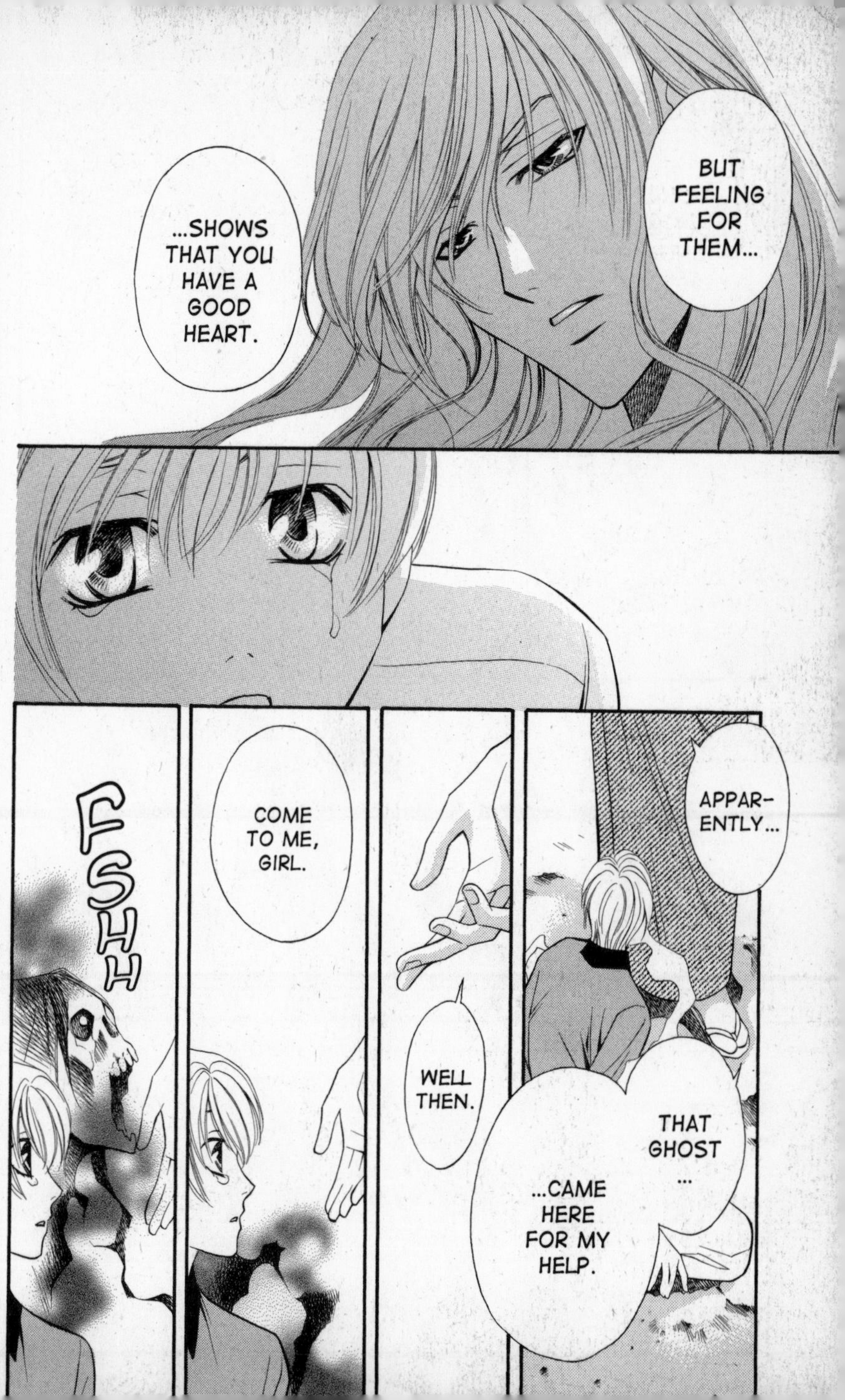
BUT FEELING FOR THEM...
...SHOWS THAT YOU HAVE A GOOD HEART.
APPARENTLY...
THAT GHOST ...
...CAME HERE FOR MY HELP.
WELL THEN.
COME TO ME, GIRL.
FSHH

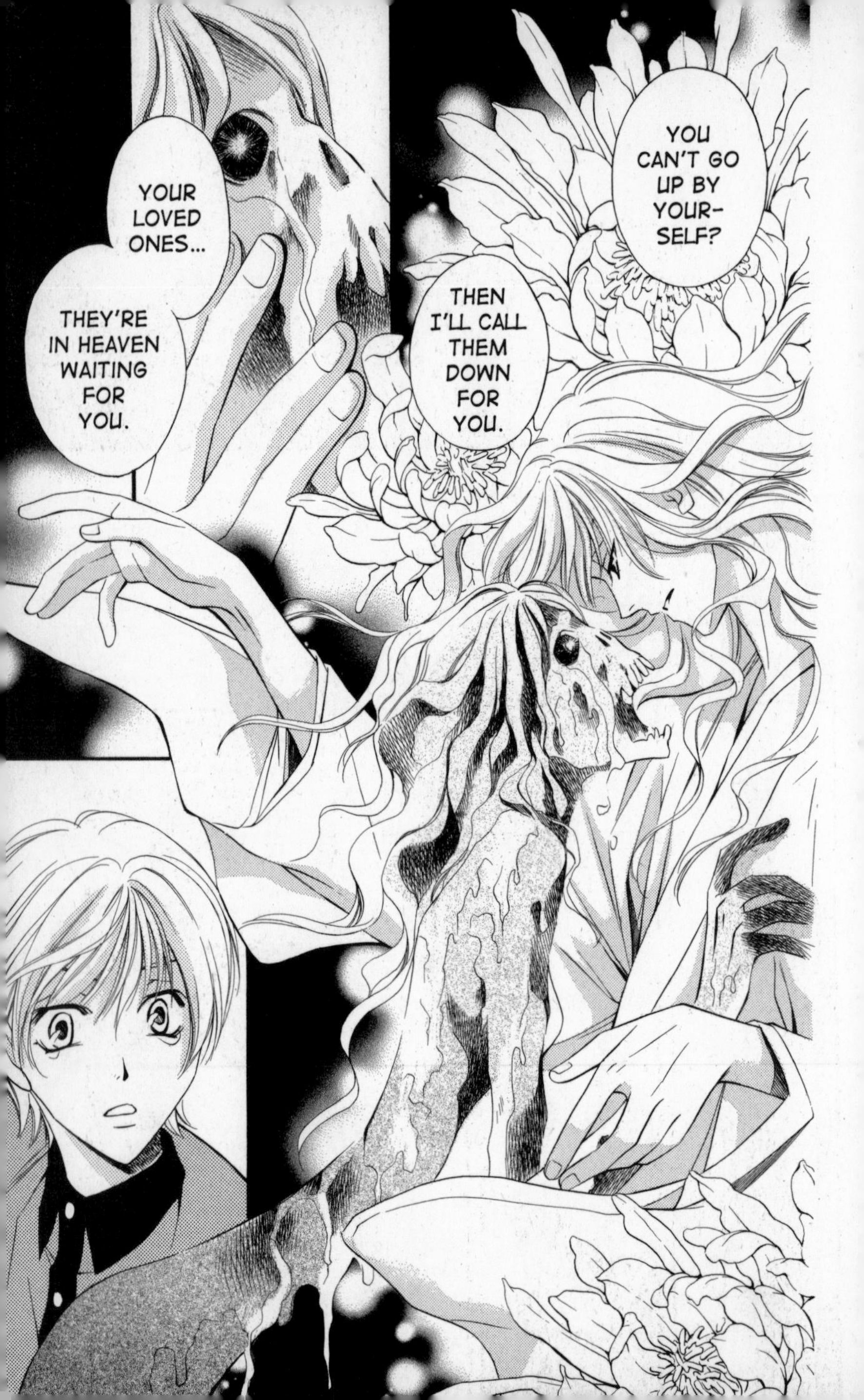
YOU CAN'T GO UP BY YOUR-SELF?
THEN I'LL CALL THEM DOWN FOR YOU.
YOUR LOVED ONES...
THEY'RE IN HEAVEN WAITING FOR YOU.

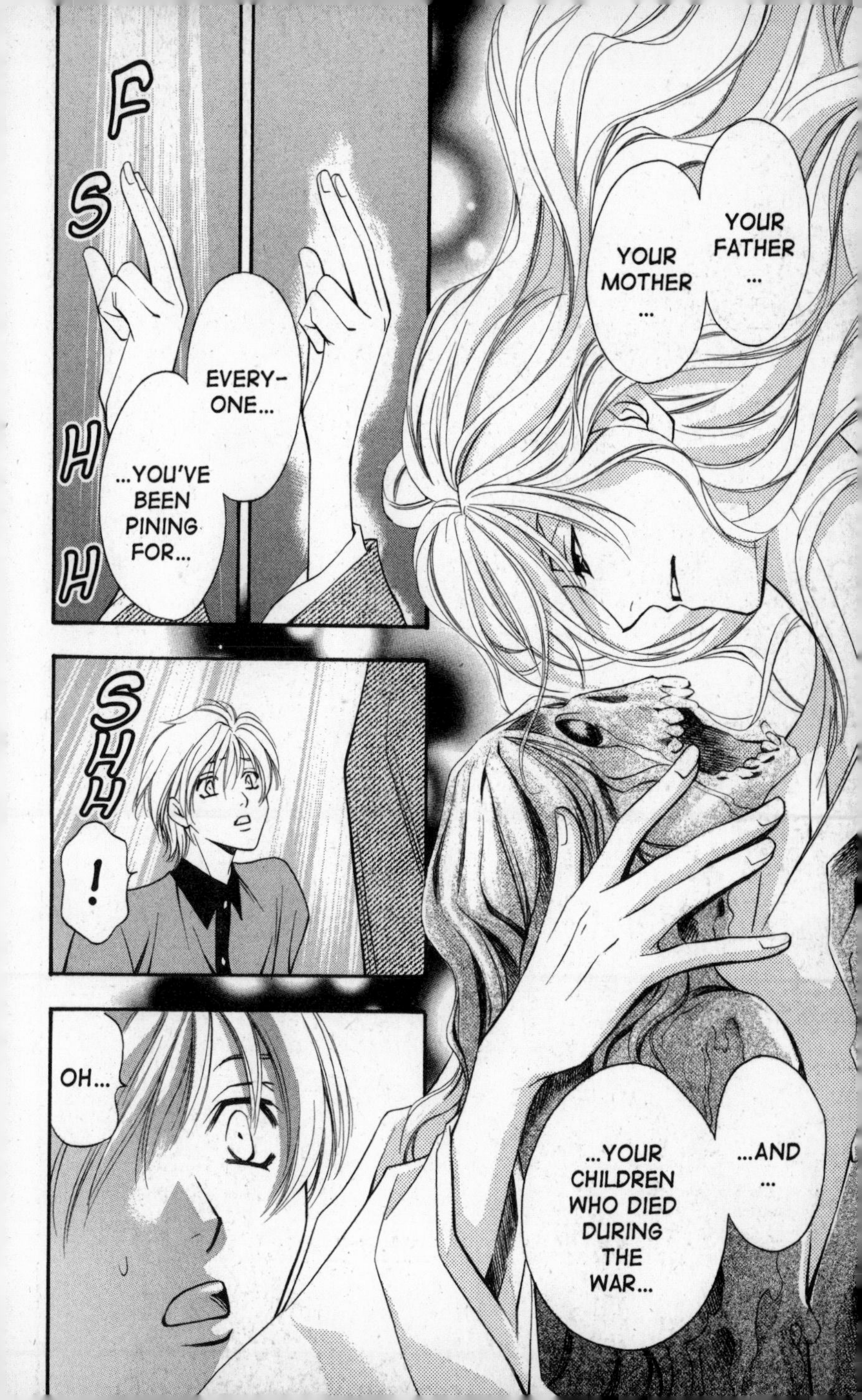
YOUR FATHER...
YOUR MOTHER...
...AND...
...YOUR CHILDREN WHO DIED DURING THE WAR...
FSHH
EVERY-ONE...
...YOU'VE BEEN PINING FOR...
SHHH
!
OH...

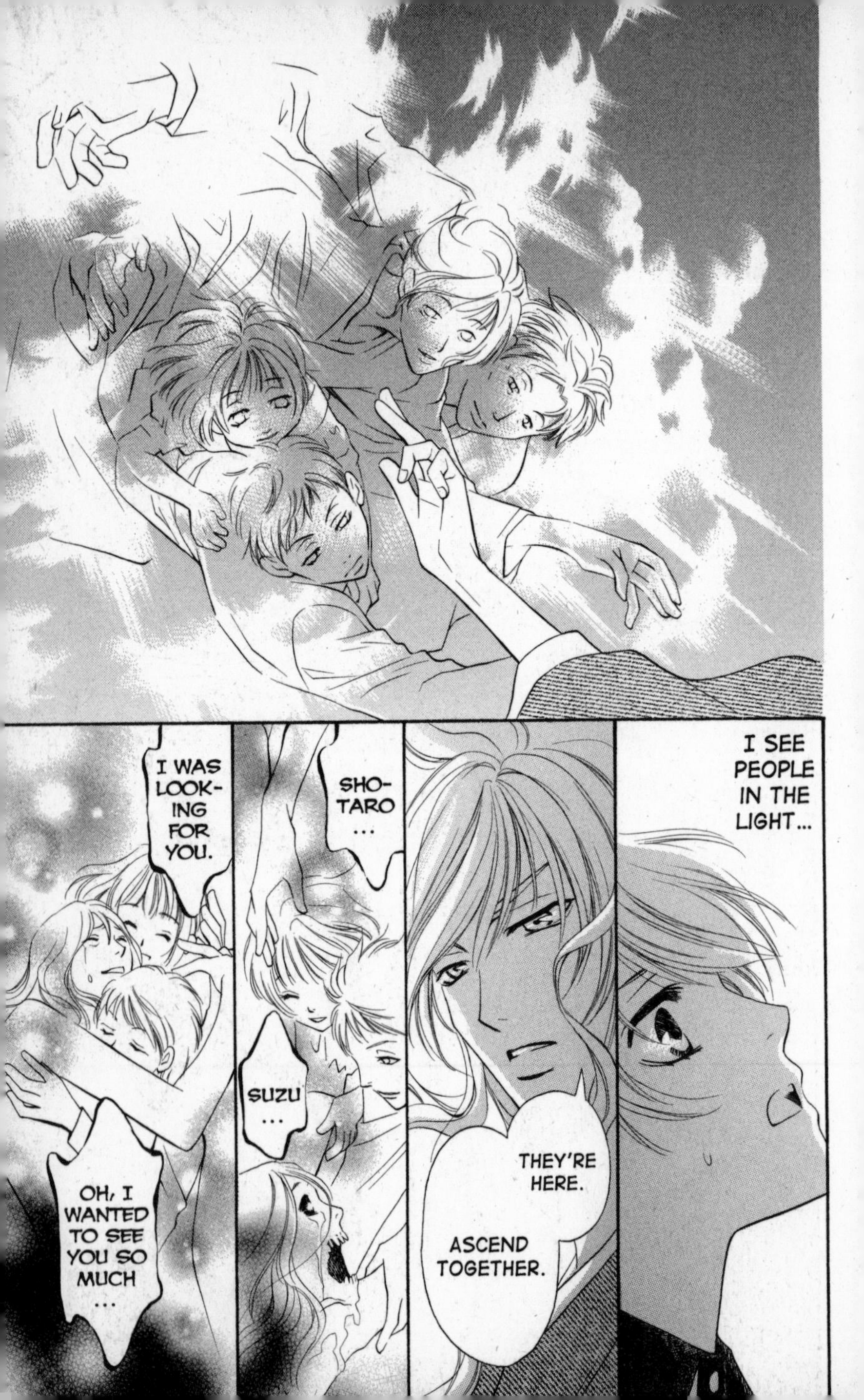

I SEE PEOPLE IN THE LIGHT...
THEY'RE HERE.
ASCEND TOGETHER.
SHO-TARO ...
SUZU ...
I WAS LOOK-ING FOR YOU.
OH, I WANTED TO SEE YOU SO MUCH ...

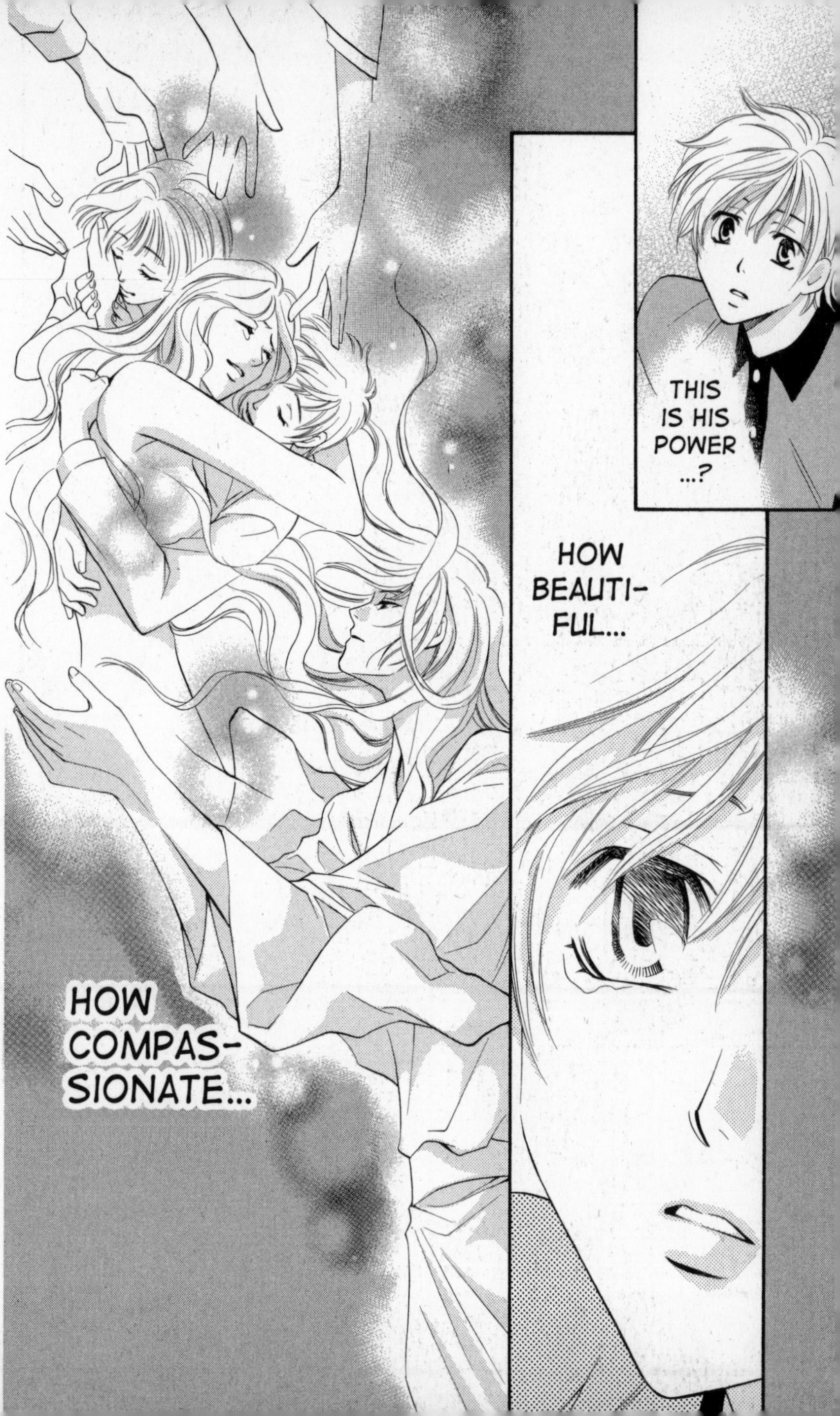
THIS IS HIS POWER ...?
HOW BEAUTI-FUL...
HOW COMPAS-SIONATE...

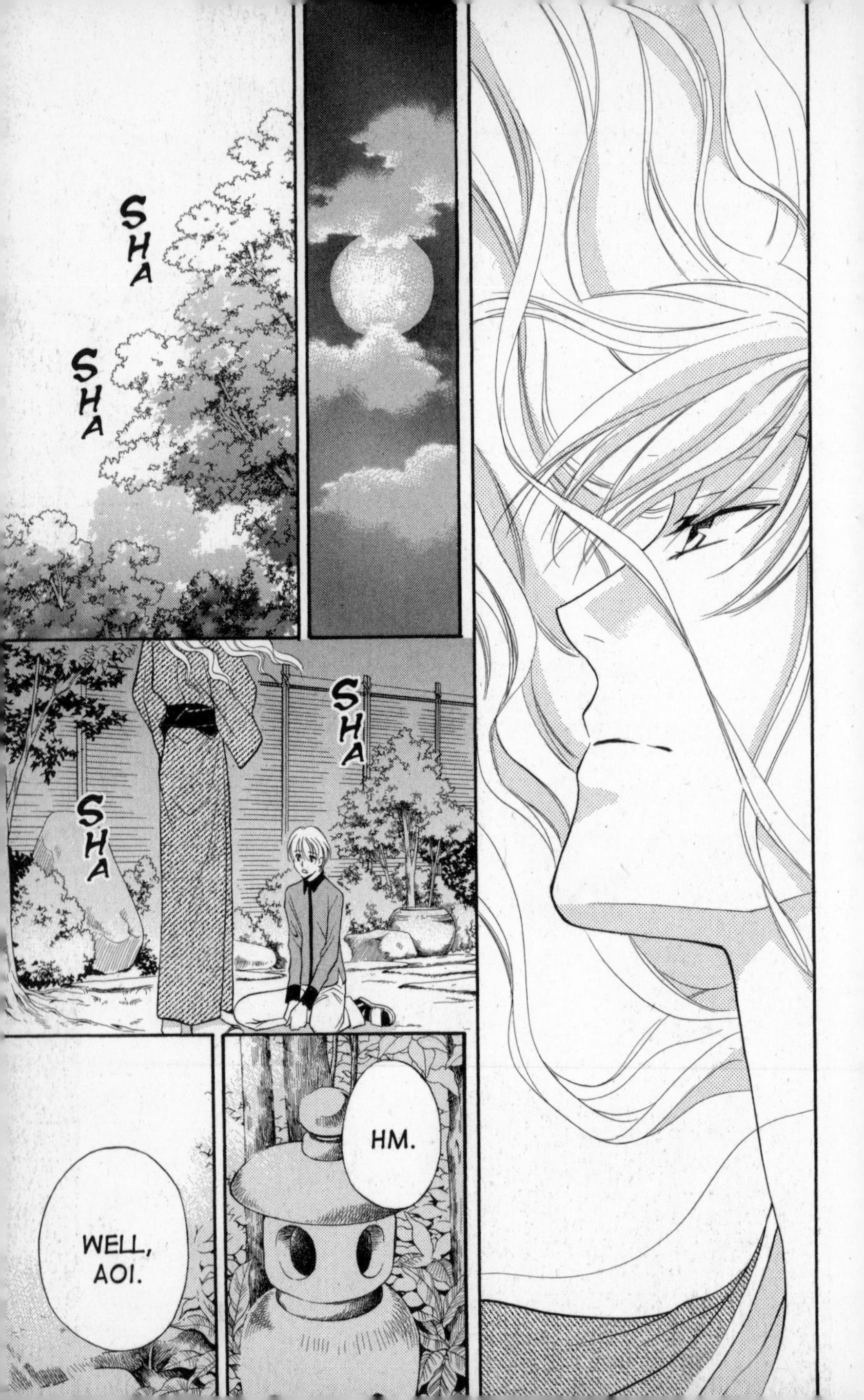
SHA
SHA
SHA
SHA
HM.
WELL, AOI.

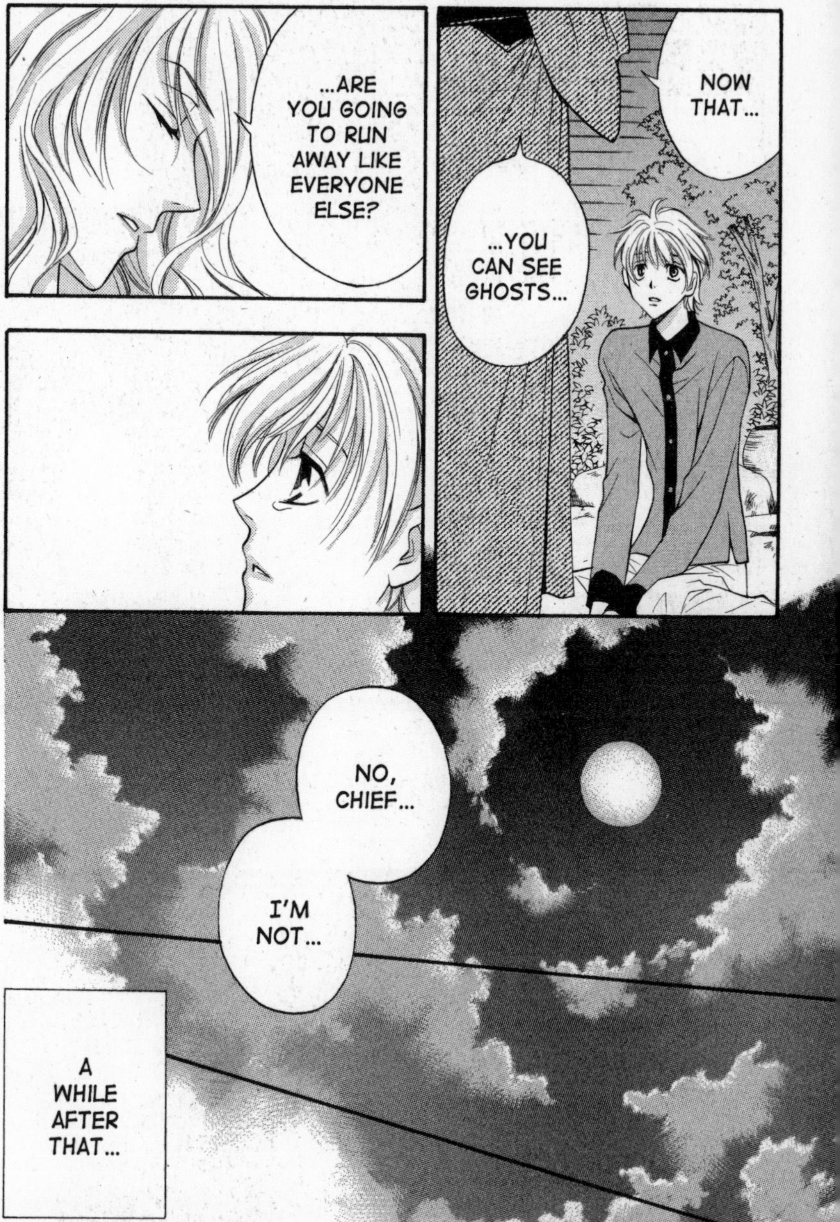
NOW THAT...
...YOU CAN SEE GHOSTS...
...ARE YOU GOING TO RUN AWAY LIKE EVERYONE ELSE?
NO, CHIEF...
I'M NOT...
A WHILE AFTER THAT...

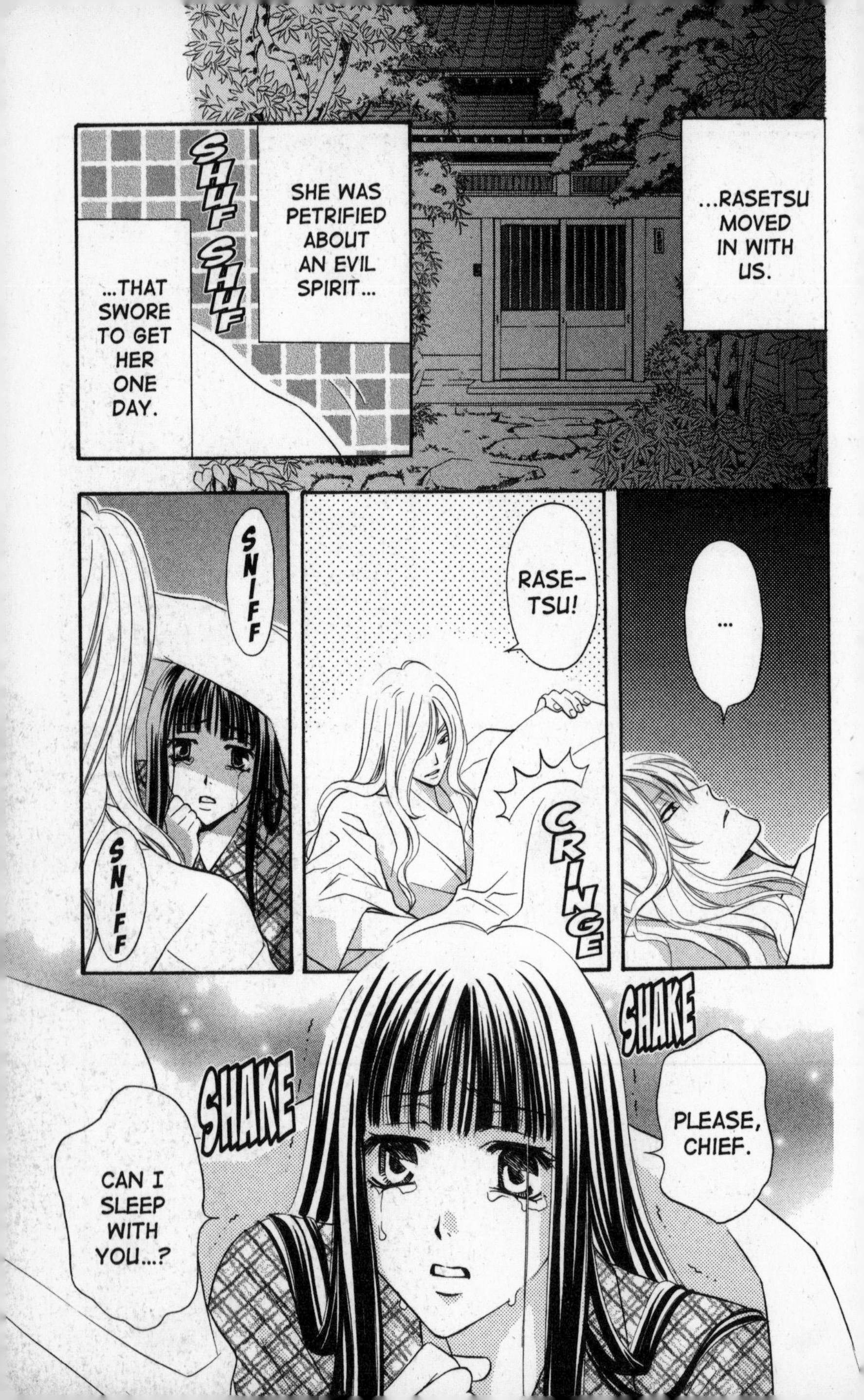
...RASETSU MOVED IN WITH US.
SHE WAS PETRIFIED ABOUT AN EVIL SPIRIT...
SHUF SHUF
...THAT SWORE TO GET HER ONE DAY.
...
RASE-TSU!
CRINGE
SNIFF
SNIFF
SHAKE
PLEASE, CHIEF.
SHAKE
CAN I SLEEP WITH YOU...?

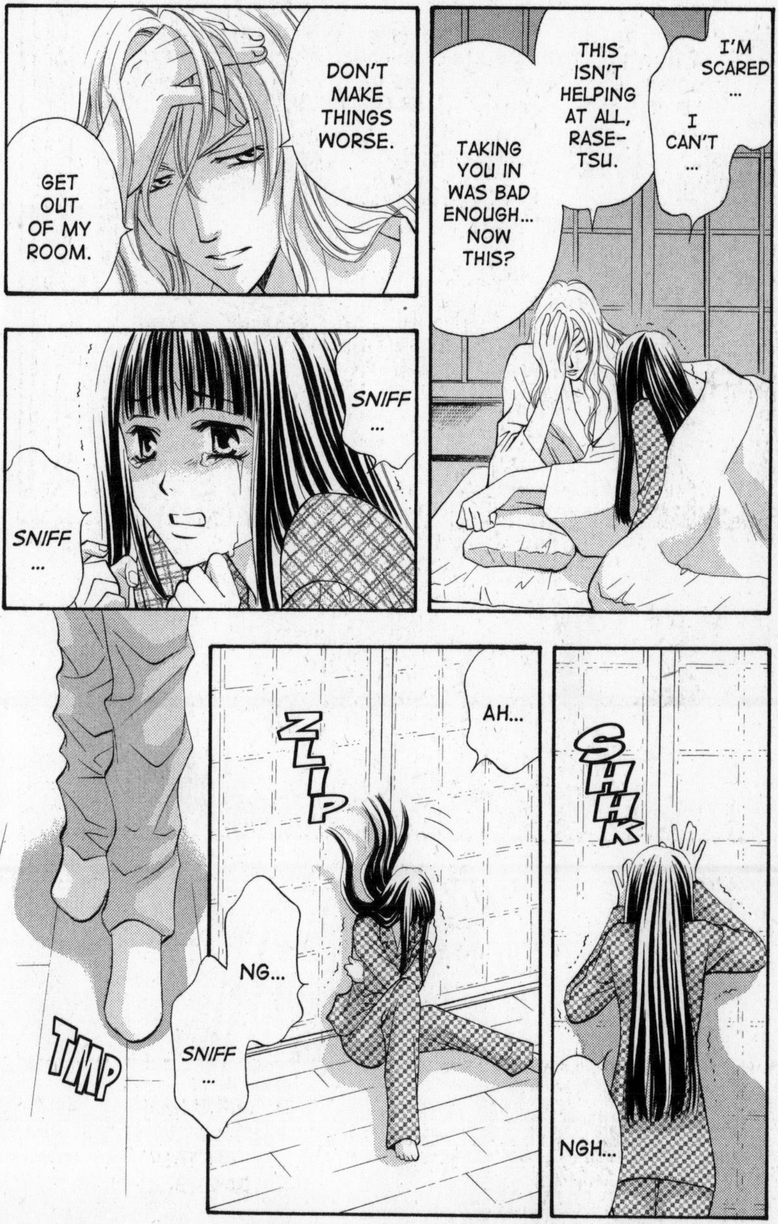
I'M SCARED ... I CAN'T ...
THIS ISN'T HELPING AT ALL, RASE-TSU.
TAKING YOU IN WAS BAD ENOUGH... NOW THIS?
DON'T MAKE THINGS WORSE.
GET OUT OF MY ROOM.
SNIFF ...
SNIFF ...
SHHK
NGH...
AH...
ZLIP
NG...
SNIFF ...
TMP

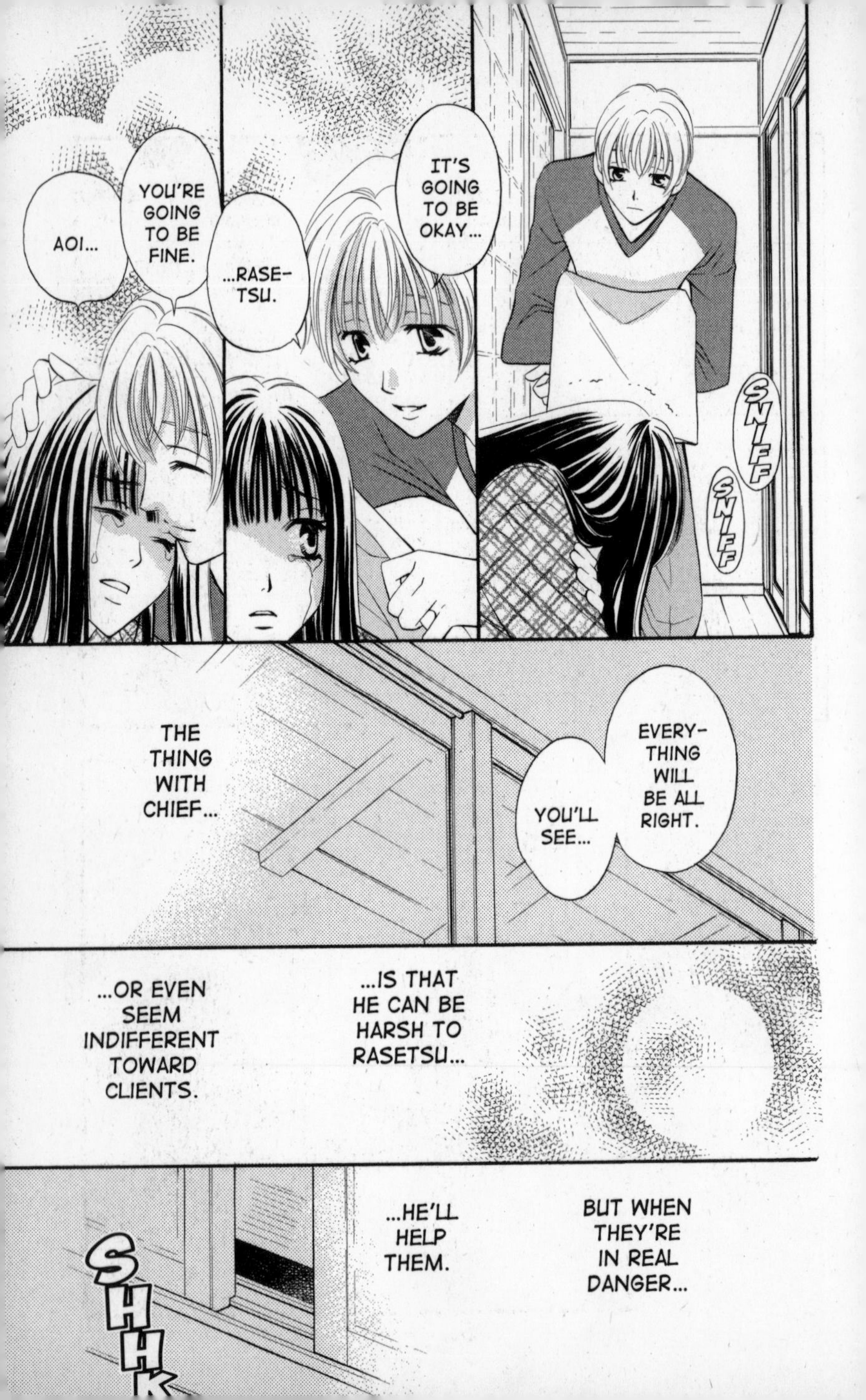
SNIFF
SNIFF
IT'S GOING TO BE OKAY...
...RASE-TSU.
YOU'RE GOING TO BE FINE.
AOI...
EVERY-THING WILL BE ALL RIGHT.
YOU'LL SEE...
THE THING WITH CHIEF...
...IS THAT HE CAN BE HARSH TO RASETSU...
...OR EVEN SEEM INDIFFERENT TOWARD CLIENTS.
BUT WHEN THEY'RE IN REAL DANGER...
...HE'LL HELP THEM.
SHHK

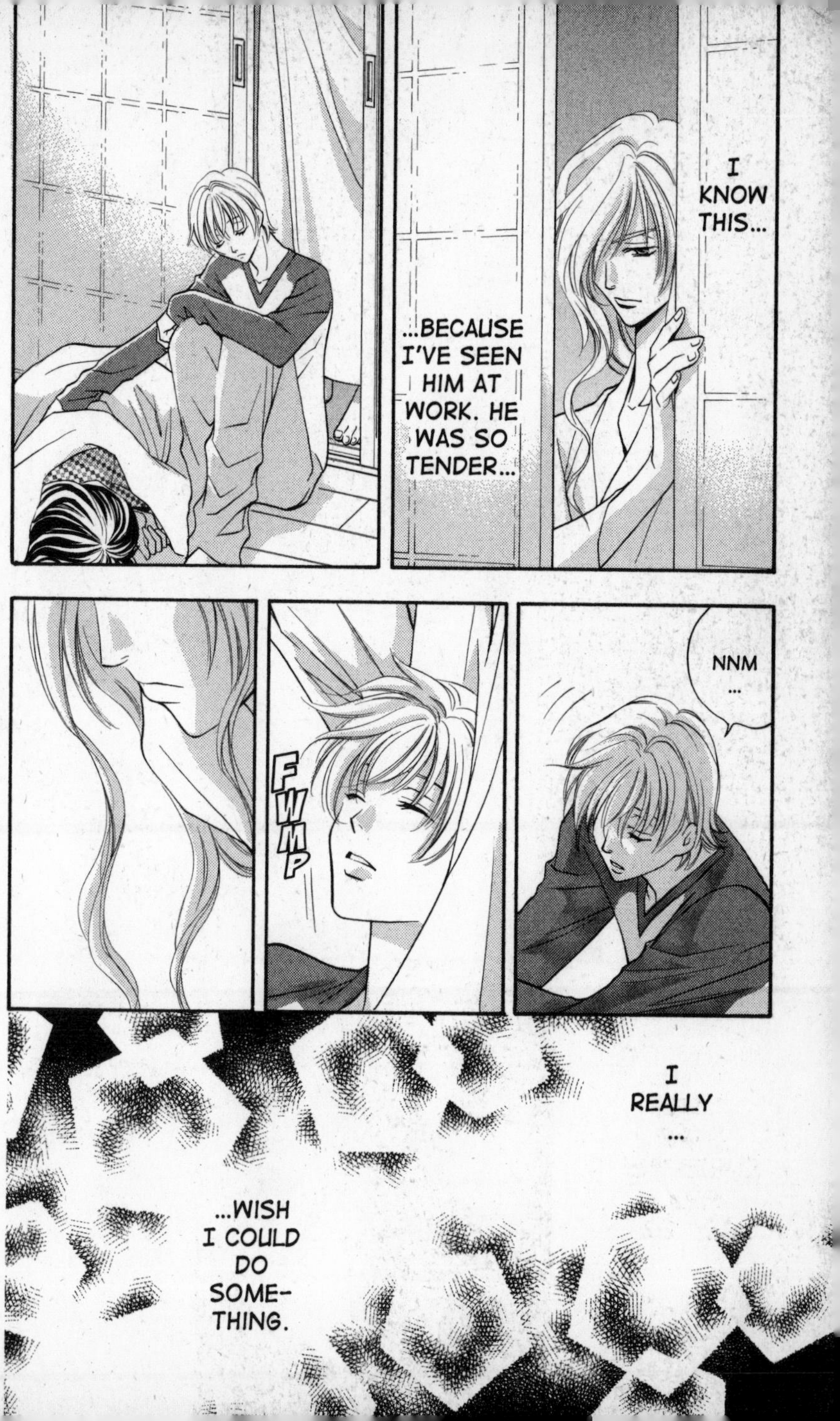
I KNOW THIS...
...BECAUSE I'VE SEEN HIM AT WORK. HE WAS SO TENDER...
NNM ...
FWMP
I REALLY ...
...WISH I COULD DO SOME-THING.

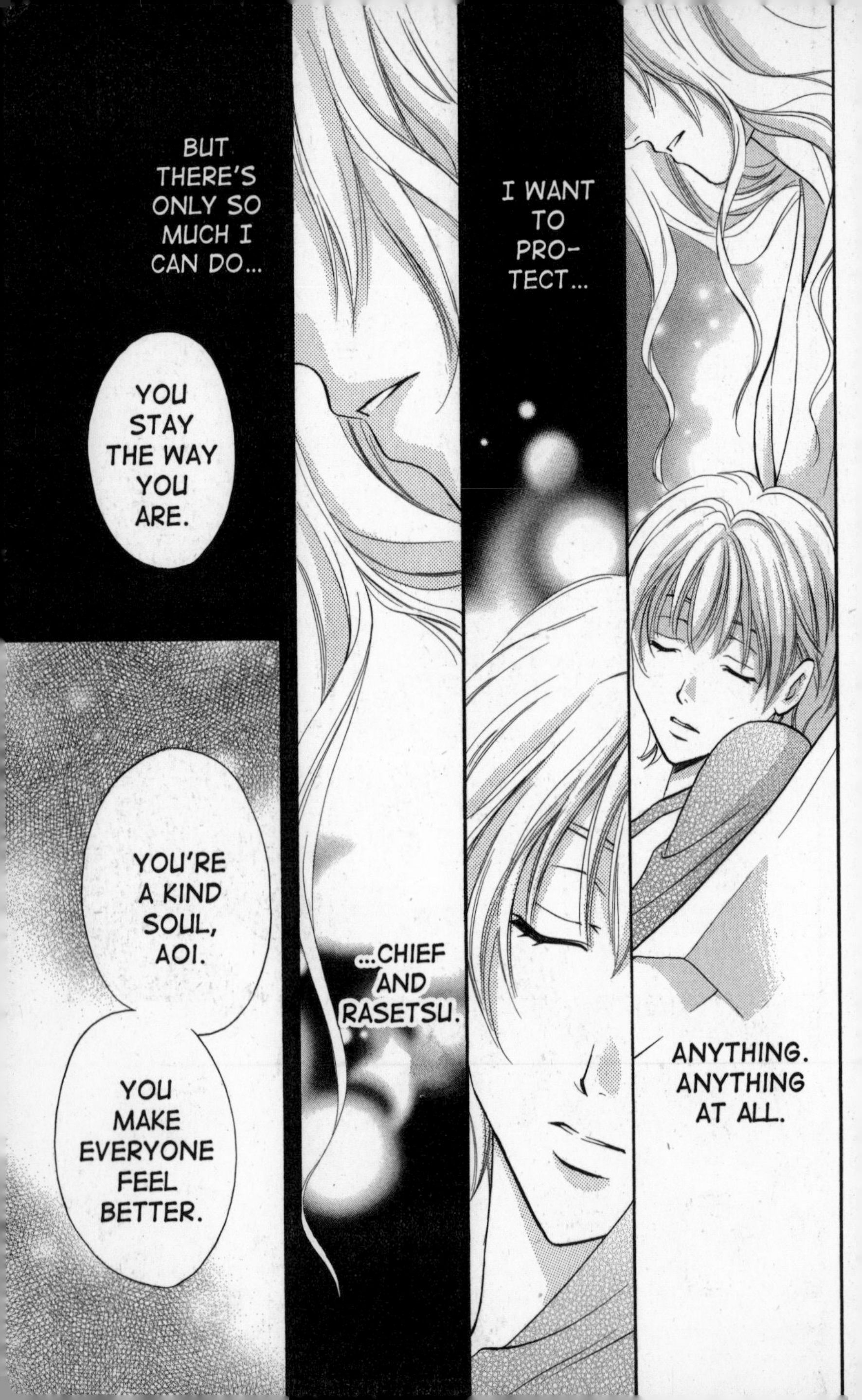

ANYTHING. ANYTHING AT ALL.
I WANT TO PRO-TECT...
...CHIEF AND RASETSU.
BUT THERE'S ONLY SO MUCH I CAN DO...
YOU STAY THE WAY YOU ARE.
YOU'RE A KIND SOUL, AOI.
YOU MAKE EVERYONE FEEL BETTER.

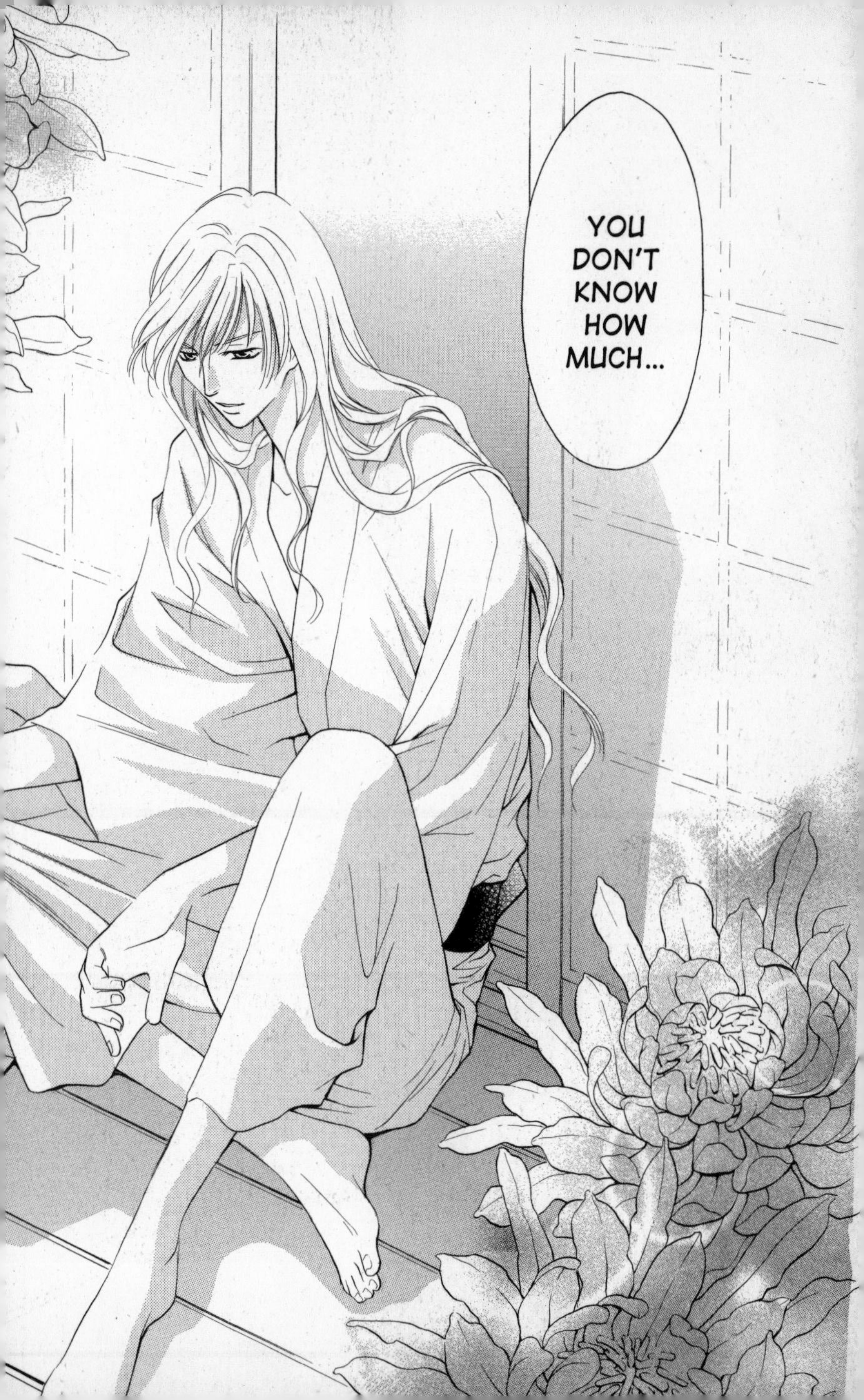
YOU DON'T KNOW HOW MUCH...

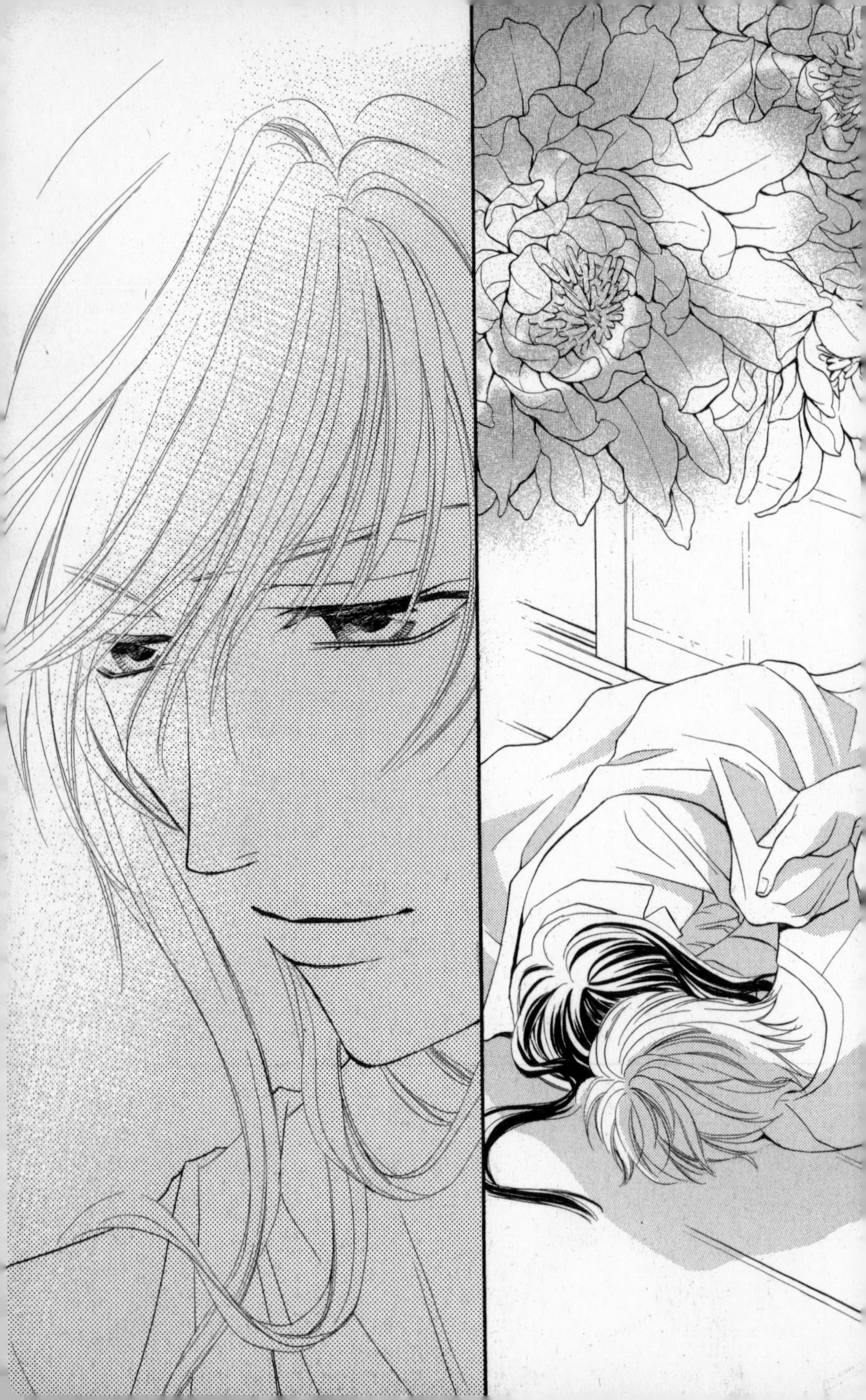

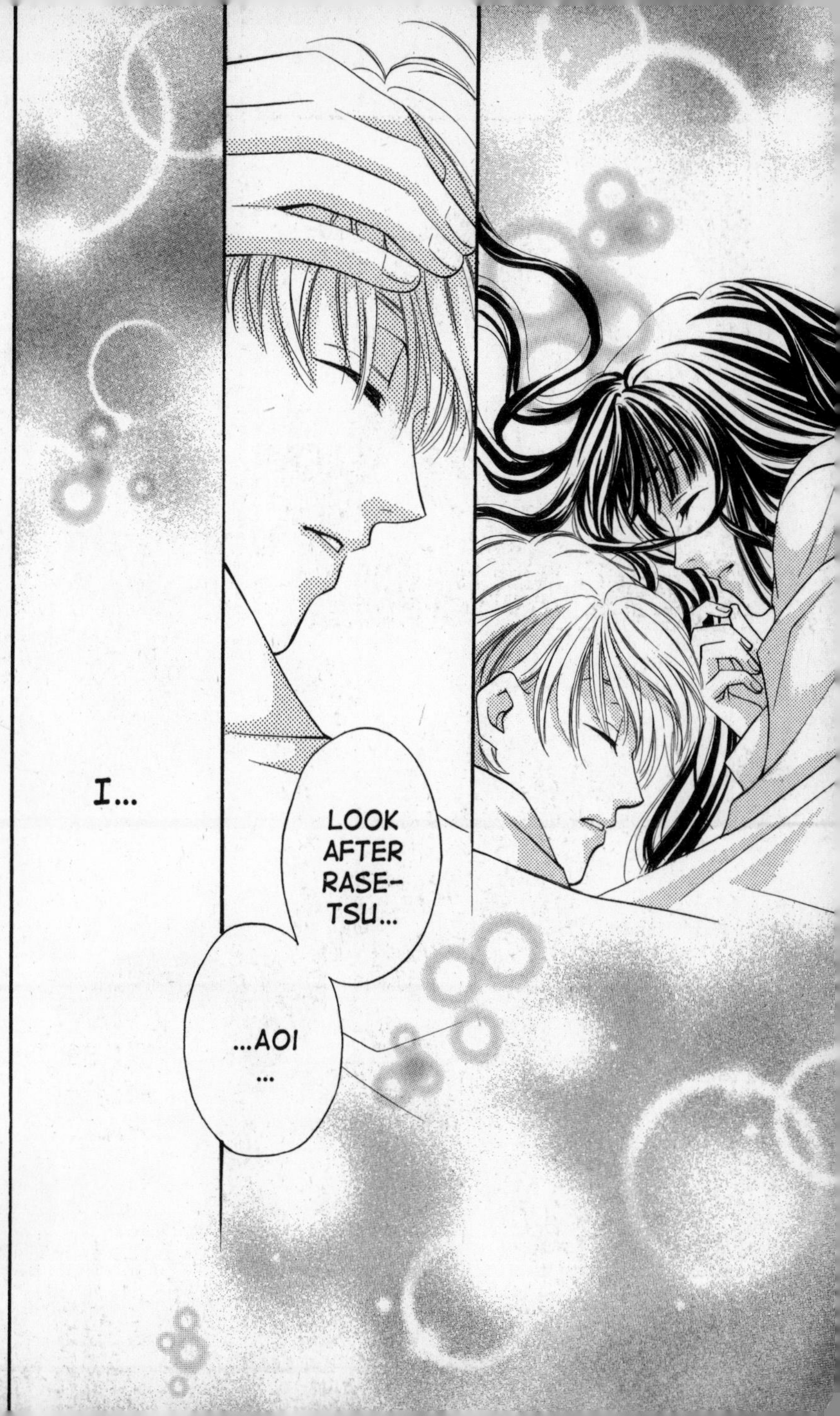
LOOK AFTER RASE-TSU...
...AOI ...
I...

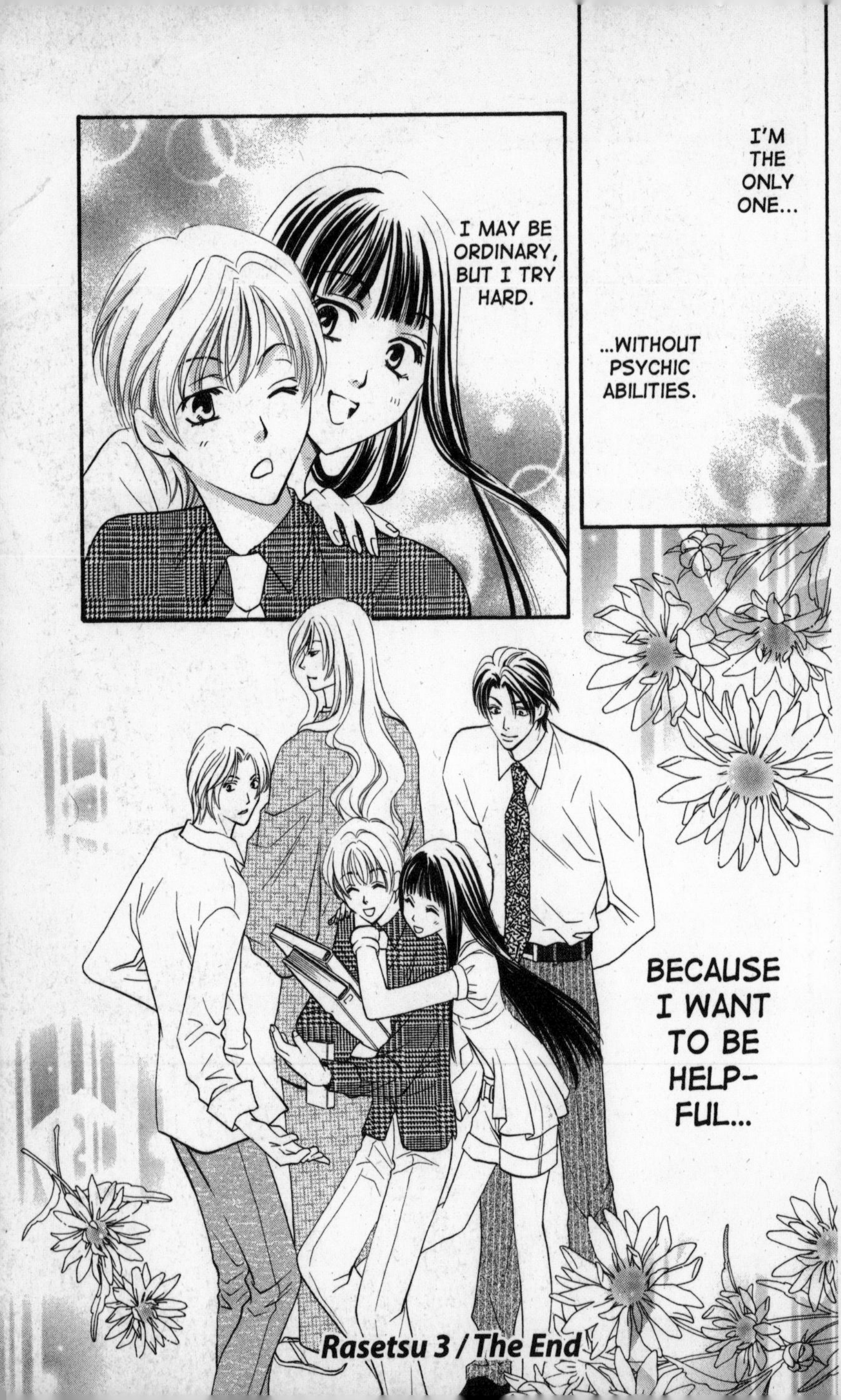
I'M THE ONLY ONE...
...WITHOUT PSYCHIC ABILITIES.
I MAY BE ORDINARY, BUT I TRY HARD.
BECAUSE I WANT TO BE HELP-FUL...
Rasetsu 3 / The End

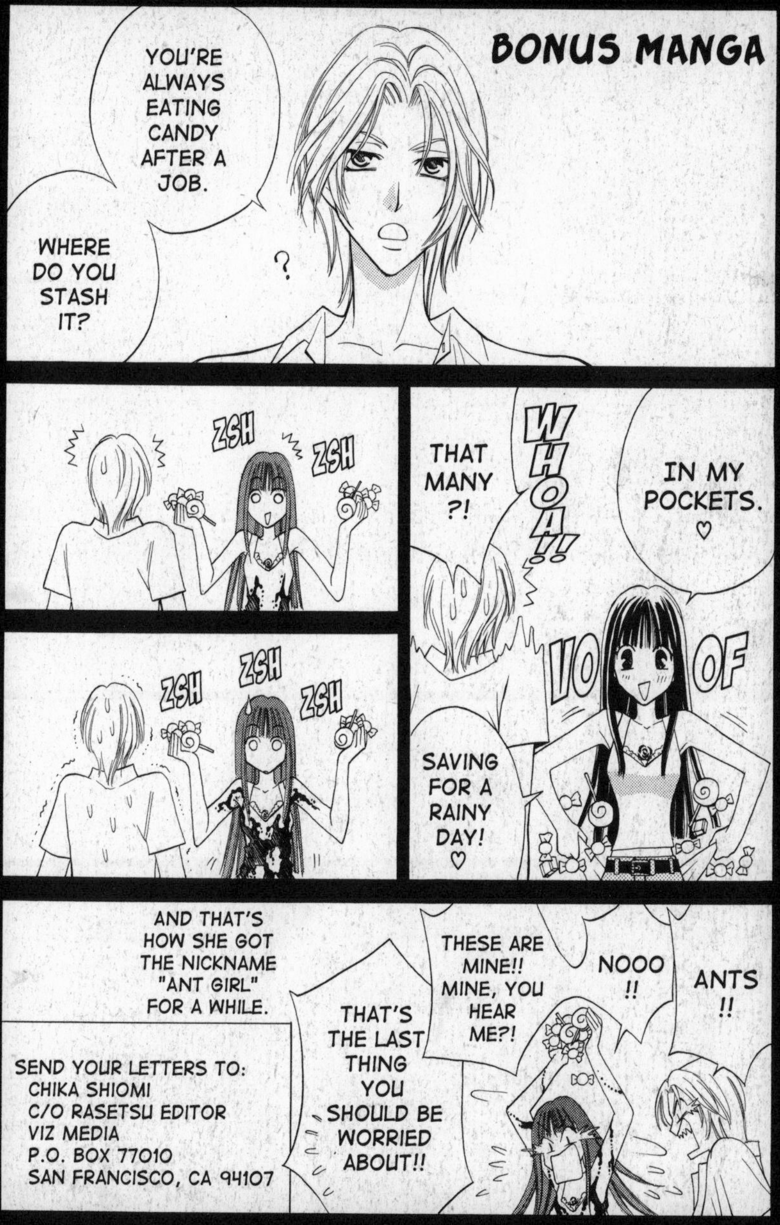
BONUS MANGA
YOU'RE ALWAYS EATING CANDY AFTER A JOB.
WHERE DO YOU STASH IT?
IN MY POCKETS. ♡
WHOA!!
THAT MANY ?!
VOOF
SAVING FOR A RAINY DAY! ♡
ZSH
ZSH
ZSH
ZSH
ZSH
ANTS !!
NOOO !!
THESE ARE MINE!! MINE, YOU HEAR ME?!
THAT'S THE LAST THING YOU SHOULD BE WORRIED ABOUT!!
AND THAT'S HOW SHE GOT THE NICKNAME "ANT GIRL" FOR A WHILE.
SEND YOUR LETTERS TO:
CHIKA SHIOMI
C/O RASETSU EDITOR
VIZ MEDIA
P.O. BOX 77010
SAN FRANCISCO, CA 94107